The New
EDIBLE
WILD PLANTS
OF EASTERN NORTH AMERICA

MAY-APPLE *(Podophyllum peltatum)*

MERRITT LYNDON FERNALD
ALFRED CHARLES KINSEY
STEVE WILLIAM CHADDE

The New Edible Wild Plants of Eastern North America
A Field Guide to Edible (and Poisonous) Flowering Plants, Ferns, Mushrooms and Lichens

Merritt L. Fernald, Alfred C. Kinsey, and Steve W. Chadde

ISBN-13: 978-1500827960
ISBN-10: 1500827967

Grateful acknowledgment is given to the Biota of North America Program (*www.bonap.org*) for permission to use their data to generate the distribution maps.

Author email: steve@chadde.net

VERSION 1.0

Preface to the New Edition

The New Edible Wild Plants of Eastern North America is an updated and revised edition of the book, *Edible Wild Plants of Eastern North America*, first published in 1943 by Merritt Fernald and Alfred Kinsey. This new edition updates the scientific names of plants, provides numerous maps showing each species' distribution in the eastern United States, and adds all new illustrations. Cautions are noted for a number of plants long considered safe to eat but which are now known to be dangerous. Included too is an important section on **Poisonous Plants** (Chapter Two), and an introduction (Chapter Four) to the **Mushrooms** (poisonous and edible), **Seaweeds**, and **Lichens** of the region. The result is a field guide and reference to nearly 1000 plants found in the forests, fields, seashores, wetlands, roadsides and vacant lands across eastern North America.

USING THIS BOOK

To be a safe and successful gatherer of wild food plants, a knowledge of botany will prove to be extremely useful. Once the main features of a plant family are known, identification of unknown plants becomes much easier. Many plants grow only in certain habitats, and knowing these preferences will also aid you in finding edible plants. The distribution maps provided for many species (based on data from the Biota of North America Program or BONAP, see *www.bonap.org*) will help narrow the range of plants for your location. Note that the maps show distribution only for states of the U.S. as county-level data were not available for the Canadian provinces.

With that in mind, the main body of the book treating the edible plants (Chapter Three) is arranged first by major plant group: the **Ferns and Fern Relatives**, the **Conifers**, and the **Seed Plants**. Within each group, plant species are ordered first alphabetically by the scientific name of each plant family (e.g., Asteraceae, the Aster Family), and finally, within each family, alphabetically by the scientific name of each species. The advantage of this arrangement is that closely related species are grouped together, allowing you to quickly view all the edible plants in a particular family of interest.

The Seed Plants are by far the largest group, and include both dicotyledonous plants (or simply 'dicots'), which are our trees and shrubs and most of our plants commonly termed 'wildflowers'; plus the monocotyledons ('monocots'), the grasses (Poaceae) and grass-like plants such as cat-tails, sedges and rushes, and also plants such as the lilies and orchids.

For most species, especially those having high value as a wild food plant, descriptions are provided for the plant's key-characteristics, its typical habitat, its range in eastern North America, season of availability, and uses. Following this are accounts of how the plant was used by native Americans, pioneers, and modern-day foragers, plus, for many plants, basic directions for preparing the plants for eating.

While this book is intended to be a more or less complete guide to plants in eastern North America that have some value as a food, the book is not a complete flora or listing of all the plants in this large region. The **Bibliography** lists more references for identifying plants. Remember to always respect the plants you are gathering by not over-harvesting in any population and by not harvesting plants that may be protected by law, such as most members of the Orchid Family. Always take care to be sure of your identification, especially for plants unfamiliar to you or which require special preparation before eating.

ABOUT THE AUTHORS

Merritt Lyndon Fernald (1873-1950) was a legendary American botanist. In his time he was regarded as the most respected scholar of the taxonomy and phytogeography of the vascular plant flora of eastern North America. Based at Harvard University, he published more than 850 scientific papers and wrote and edited the seventh and eighth editions of *Gray's Manual of Botany*, long the standard flora of the region. As evident in this book, he also had an deep interest in wild food plants, and made many experiments with plants to determine their edibility and how best to prepare them. His access to the Harvard libraries is also evident in this work, with many references to plant use by native Americans and European settlers.

Alfred Charles Kinsey (1894-1956) was an American biologist and professor of entomology and zoology at Indiana University, but perhaps most remembered as the founder, in 1947, of the Institute for Sex Research at Indiana University, now known as the Kinsey Institute for Research in Sex, Gender, and Reproduction. He is best known for writing *Sexual Behavior in the Human Male* (1948) and *Sexual Behavior in the Human Female* (1953), also known as the *Kinsey Reports*. His work with Fernald on edible wild plants took place largely in 1919-1920 when Kinsey was a doctoral student at Harvard's Bussey Institute and Fernald was working at Arnold Arboretum, also at Harvard.

Steve Chadde (born 1955) is a botanist and plant ecologist who developed a passion for the natural world at an early age. His grandparents, German immigrants to the United States, were avid gardeners, and provided him with many memories of picking (and eating!) fruit such as red raspberries, pie-cherries, pears, plums, and currants, and gathering vegetables such as peas, carrots, spinach, lettuce, and radishes, as part of delicious and healthy meals. Later, in addition to his education and professional work as a botanist for the U.S. Forest Service, the Montana Natural Heritage Program, and various consulting firms, he continued to expand on his knowledge of plants in general, and their many uses. He has published numerous books on plants, including his recent state floras for Minnesota (2013), Wisconsin (2013), and for the Upper Peninsula of Michigan (2014). He is pleased to make this landmark work on edible plants once again available to a new generation.

Introduction

Nearly every one has a certain amount of the pagan or gypsy in his nature and occasionally finds satisfaction in living for a time as a primitive man. Among the primitive instincts are the fondness for experimenting with unfamiliar foods and the desire to be independent of the conventional sources of supply. All campers and lovers of out-of-door life delight to discover some new fruit or herb which it is safe to eat, and in actual camping it is often highly important to be able to recognize and secure fresh vegetables for the camp-diet; while in emergency the ready recognition of possible wild foods might save life. In these days, furthermore, when thoughtful people are wondering about the food-supply of the present and future generations, it is not amiss to assemble what is known of the now neglected but readily available vege- table-foods, some of which may yet come to be of real economic importance.

Every one who lives out-of-doors knows a limited number of edible berries, strawberries, raspberries, blackberries, blueberries and a few others; but comparatively few people realize the almost unlimited store of roots, new shoots and young herbage which can safely and acceptably be brought to the table. And even those who do understand in a general way that there are hundreds of possible wild foods about us, are restrained, through a natural and wholesome fear of getting hold of some poisonous plant by mistake, from attempting to use them. As a matter of fact, however, the number of seriously poisonous wild plants which might seem tempting to the searcher for salads and potherbs is very limited. They are all readily recognized by the careful observer, and only the careful observer should ever attempt to use any wild plant for food or to try it on his friends.

In a highly "civilized" community we are so used to the conventional dishes that there are some among us who have a prejudice or squeamishness about eating "weeds." It is natural that those whose daily life leads them far from a sympathetic attitude toward wild nature should balk at an invitation to eat carrion-flower, burdock or pigweed; but, as a matter of fact, these common weeds make wholesome and really delicious food, when properly prepared, and the prejudice against them is chiefly due to the unsavory connotation of their names. Occasionally a common weed, like pokeweed for instance, has, in some sections of the country, become a popular vegetable, so thoroughly familiar as to find ready sale in city markets; although, on account of the prejudice referred to, it is certain that plants advertised as carrion-flower, burdock or pigweed would find no sale whatever. In this connection it may be noted that, although many people are averse to eating pigweed, even the most orthodox Hebrew has no objection to eating pokeweed.

The wild plants are to be considered not merely as possible food for the camper. In many rural communities certain of them, such as the marsh-marigold ("cowslips"), the docks and the dandelion are regularly gathered for greens; and, although eighty years ago Unger, in an exhaustive enumeration of plants used for food, classed the dandelion as "hardly worth mentioning," that common weed has now risen to the dignity of a regular place in the market garden and the city market.

During several years of camping the writers have experimented when possible with the plants of the woods and fields which furnished tolerable or, in many cases, surprisingly attractive food and, in an attempt to amplify their own experiences, they have searched with care the writings of others in various parts of America, Europe and eastern Asia, upon the wild plants which may be used for food, for, although we are geographically far removed from eastern Asia, the similarity and often the identity of plants of eastern North America and of Japan, China and other eastern Asiatic countries is well known. As a result of this study a large mass of data has been accumulated which may be of practical value to others and which, certainly, will be of interest to some who have not been so situated as to have access to many of the sources of information.

The following chapters, therefore, are offered for what they are worth, with the clear understanding that in many cases the information is derived wholly or in part from sources other than the writers' experience, and that many people, with many palates, may find the plants which have proved palatable to others quite unattractive to their own tastes; although new and untried methods of preparation may render them acceptable to any palate. It should be noted that only the flowering plants and ferns are here discussed in great detail. Mushrooms are so dangerous for the novice to experiment with and are already so well treated in many available books that our chapter upon them deals only with a very limited number of easily recognized kinds and, of course, the most deadly "toadstools" which every beginner should be able promptly to recognize.

Every species of plant has a technical Latin name by which it is known to scientists all over the world, whether their mother-tongue be English, Russian or even Chinese, this name having to trained botanists a perfectly definite signification; in other words, the Latin names are the international language of botanists. But, unfortunately, not all colloquial names, such as "cowslip" or "mayflower," have a specific connotation, for these names are very differently appled in different regions; and in many cases plants without very conspicuous flowers or fruits seem never to have received any colloquial name whatsoever. Consequently, although in most cases we have been able to use a well established colloquial name, in some cases we have been forced to use only the Latin name of the plant. In all cases the technical name of the species or at least of the genus (when there are several similar species) which is authorized by the International Rules of Botanical Nomenclature has been entered opposite the colloquial name. When plants are sometimes known in America under different names, the synonyms have been added in parentheses.

The lengthy Chapter Three enumerating the full 1000 ferns and flowering plants of Eastern North America which are useful or which could be used as food is arranged first by group (Ferns and Fern Relatives, Conifers, Seed Plants), then alphabetically by families. This chapter, the longest in the book, contains the detailed matter which will be found more briefly summarized and systematized under appropriate headings in an earlier chapter. Nearly all plants discussed have an accompanying illustration. Known distribution in eastern North America is indicated for most species by a map or in its range-description. The maps, generated from data of the Biota of North America Program (BONAP), illustrate county-level distributions. However, Canadian county distributions were not available and are not shown on the maps. It should again be emphasized that, before attempting to identify unknown but possibly edible plants, every one should thoroughly familiarize himself with the illustrations in the brief chapter on poisonous plants, for in a few cases these are superficially similar to harmless or even edible species.

At the time of preparation of the original manuscript we had not heard of calories; and the designation of vitamins was still in the future. No estimate of the calories or of the vitamin-values of most of these wild plants are available. That many of them have real food-value is evident. When calories first began to be estimated the senior author organized a party of eight botanists, with a corps of guides and packers, to make botanical explorations in the mountains of Gaspe. One member of the party, an enthusiast over calories, took charge of the commissary-department. After three days of living on calories the guides and packers showed evident dissatisfaction; by the end of the fourth day the other scientists in the party joined them and demanded food. We had had the theoretically correct number of calories; we wanted to satisfy our hunger. Luckily, the snow-filled ravines were full of young ostrich-fern and beautifully blanched young cow-parsnip, pushing up under the snow; and on warm slopes the melting snow exposed broad carpets of spring-beauty and alpine cress. With these we supplemented the calories and went happily through the hard trip. Although we are not now able to state the caloric value of most of the wild food-plants nor what vitamins they contain, it is certain that there is abundant nourishment in a plate of sauteed inky mushrooms, with cooked, fresh young cat-tail spikes, salad of dressed, chilled cat-brier sprouts or young milkweed, bread made of wild grains, acorn-flour or seeds of cow-lilies, spread with a butter of beechnut-oil or oil of hickory-nuts, while there is real refreshment in a cup of cassina-tea, served with marmalade of squaw-huckle- berry, topped off by a dessert of pudding made of dried persimmons, with confections of candied wild ginger or root of elecampane, with a cordial, if wished, from any of several wild berries or aromatic herbs. After such an early-summer meal one will not ask about calories or vitamins; he will be perfectly content. Or in mid-summer, if he is lucky enough to find under the leaves of the mixed or hardwood forest a clump of *Lactarius*, rendered firm and solid by an over-growth of *Hypomyces*, he will have a meal as hearty as beef-steak; and if he supplements this with cooked orach-tips, sauteed groundnuts, fresh muffins of Jack-in-the-Pulpit corms, salad of chilled cooked purslane, ice-cream of black raspberry, blackberries or blueberries, tea of sweet gale, inkberry or clover-tops and a cheese (Cheshire cheese) made with the aid (as rennet) of bedstraw or nettle-tips, he will again be quite content. In late autumn he can have the chief entree of giant puffballs, pasture mushrooms, fairy-rings or some other species, hickory-nut bread and butter, a potherb of sow-thistle or a mess of seaside plantain cooked like string-beans, escalloped roots of goat's-beard, jelly or marmalade from any one of two hundred sources, a choice of scores of fruits for dessert, cheese with thistle-flowers or sundew-leaves as rennet, and tea from many mints or from sweet fern, sassafras or strawberry-leaves. Again he will be most content; and every time he will recognize that he has made small draft on the ration-book of coupons.

Gray Herbarium,
Cambridge, Mass.

POKEWEED *(Phytolacca americana)*, the young shoots can be gathered and boiled (in several changes of water) like asparagus; see p. 295.

Contents

CHAPTER ONE

Edible Wild Plants of Eastern North America Classified According to Uses

In this chapter the plants are grouped into different sections according to their uses, special emphasis being given some of the more important species, the unimportant being only listed with page-references to the more detailed discussion in Chapter 3. In the boxes, the more important are **printed in bold**.

1. Purées and Soups

PURÉES

Purées consist largely of boiled green vegetable mashed through a sieve or strainer, sometimes thickened with a little flour or corn-starch mixed with cold water until smooth. A purée is seasoned with salt and pepper to taste, and in the case of more acid plants sugar is necessary. After the purée is thoroughly cooked scalded milk may be added if desired. The following wild plants are used for purées:

Bladder-Campion (young leaves), p. 179	Fireweed (young shoots), p. 146
Cat-brier (young leaves and sprouts), p. 361	Honewort (leaves), p. 102
Cat-tail (young flowering spike), p. 371	**Mountain-Sorrel** (young leaves and stems), p. 316
Docks (leaves), p. 319	**Sorrels** (leaves), p. 321
Elder (pith), p. 78	

Of these the purées made from the **Cat-tail, Cat-brier, Mountain-Sorrel, Docks, Sorrels**, and **Bladder-Campion** can be recommended by the writers; the others they have not tried. The **Mountain-Sorrel, Sorrel** and some of the **Docks** are acid and need a little sugar. Most of the **Docks** are slightly bitter rather than acid, while the **Bladder-Campion** has the flavor of green peas with a slight bitterness. The soup from the young flowering spikes of **Cat-tail**, said to be one of the delicacies of the Pah-Ute Indians, is easy to prepare and, since it proves equally palatable to the white taste, it could be made in early summer by every family throughout the country.

STARCHY OR MUCILAGINOUS SOUPS

These soups are chiefly prepared from starchy substances which, when boiled, form a thickening which adds much nutriment to a soup. The soups of this class can be made from the following plants:

Arbor Vitae (pith of young twigs), p. 69	Prickly-Pear (seeds), p. 172
Burdock (roots), p. 133	**Sassafras** (pith and young shoots or
Chestnuts (meats), p. 232	powdered leaves),p. 250
Cow-Lily (seeds), p. 284	Seaweeds, p. 407
Day-Lilies (buds and flowers), p. 258	**Sunflower** (seeds), p. 141
Hickory-nuts (meats), p. 243	Tobacco-root, p. 378
Lichens, p. 409	Violet (rootstocks), p. 381
Mallow (seeds), p. 267	**Walnuts** (meats), p. 243
Manna-grass (seeds), p. 308	**Wild Rice** (seeds), p. 313

Of these the soups thickened with the seeds of **Wild Rice, Manna-grass** and **Cow-Lily** have somewhat the quality of the familiar barley soups; while most of the others are thickish, viscid soups, in quality suggesting either gumbo- or potato-soup. The gumbo-soups are prepared from the young or dried and powdered leaves or young pith of **Sassafras** (but see **Caution**, p. 251), from the seeds of **Mallows**, or from the young rootstocks of some of the purple **Violets**. The thick soups prepared from powdered nuts and from **Sunflower-seeds** have been in repute among the American Indians and have been highly praised by the Europeans who have tried them.

FRUIT SOUPS

The fruit soups are prepared much like the conventional tomato soups, either as a thin soup carrying the acid of fruit juices, or as a thick soup, in which case flour or cornstarch is added, first mixed with cold water until thoroughly blended and creamy and thoroughly cooked by itself. The cooked thickening is added to the strained extract obtained by boiling the fruits, seasoned to taste, usually a small amount of sugar added and then, if desired, a small amount of scalded milk. Practically any of our juicy or more acid fruits may be used this way, but the sweeter, more highly flavored, or insipid fruits are hardly to be recommended. Among the wild fruits from which a palatable soup can be prepared are:

Blackberries, p. 344	**Elderberries**, p. 78
Cherries, p. 340	**Plums**, p. 340
Dewberries, p. 344	**Raspberries**, p. 344

2. Starchy or Root-Vegetables, Cereals, Nuts and Breadstuffs

A large number of mid plants of eastern America supply farinaceous food or nutritious roots. These may appropriately be grouped according to their uses into 1) those wThich are used like potatoes or parsnips as cooked vegetables; 2) a few used as nuts; 3) a limited number used as cooked cereals or breakfast foods; 4) a long list of possible breadstuffs.

COOKED STARCHY OR ROOT-VEGETABLES

The list of possible cooked vegetables of this class is a long one:

Adder 's-tongue Lily (bulbs), p. 256	**Licorice-root** (roots), p. 223
Alpine Bistort (rootstocks), p. 316	Lilies (bulbs), p. 260
Arrow-Arum (roots and seeds), p. 123	Man-of-the-Earth (roots), p. 186
Arrow-heads (tubers), p. 85	Mud-Plantain (rootstocks), p. 85
Beach-Peas (young peas), p. 226	Nut-Grass (tubers), p. 192-194
Bellflower, *Campanula rapunculoides* (roots), p. 173	Pondweeds (rootstocks and tubers), p. 328
Bellwort (roots), p. 264	**Prairie-Turnip** (roots), p. 227
Bugleweed (tubers), p. 272	Prickly-Pear (stem), p. 172
Bulbous Crowfoot (bulbs), p. 331	Reed (rootstocks), p. 310
Bur-reed (tubers), p. 373	Silverweed (roots), p. 339
Burdock (roots), p. 133	Slippery Elm (inner bark), p. 374
Caraway (roots), p. 101	Spikenard (roots), p. 128
Cat-tail (bases), p. 371	**Spring-beauty** (roots), p. 276
Chestnuts, p. 232	Star-of-Bethlehem (bulbs) ?, p. 262
Chufa (tubers), p. 192	Tobacco-root, p. 378
Cinnamon-vine, p. 196	Tuberous Vetch (tubers), p. 226
Cow-Lily (rootstocks and seeds), p. 284	Water-Chestnuts, p. 370
Cow-Parsnip (roots), p. 106	**Water-Chinquapin** (rootstocks and seeds), p. 282
Day-Lily (thick roots), p. 258	Water-Millet (young rootstocks), p. 315
Dwarf Ginseng (roots), p. 130	Water-Parsnip, *Sium* (roots), p. 110
Erect Day-flower (roots), p. 184	Watershield (rootstocks), p. 171
Evening-Primrose (roots), p. 289	White Water-Lily (rootstocks and seeds), p. 285
False Spikenard (rootstocks), p. 260	Wild Carrot (roots), p. 103
Flowering-Rush (rootstocks), p. 170	Wild Licorice (roots), p. 223
Golden Canna?, p. 175	**Wild Parsnip** (roots), p. 109
Golden-club (roots and seeds), p. 122	**Wild Salsify** (roots), p. 151
Groundnut, *Apios* (roots), p. 219	Woundwort (rootstocks and tubers), p. 272
Harbinger-of-Spring (roots), p. 103	**Yellow Goat's-beard** (roots), p. 151
Hog-Peanut (underground seeds), p. 218	
Honewort (roots), p. 102	
Jerusalem Artichoke (tubers), p. 141	
Lichens, p. 409	

It is obvious that many of these plants are trivial and by the ordinary person will be classed only as emer- gency-foods; but such roots or tubers as those of the **Spring-beauty, Groundnut, Evening-Primrose, Caraway, Bugleweed** and **Jerusalem Artichoke** are so abundant where they occur as already to have many users. The root of **Licorice-root**, *Hedysarum alpinum* or *H. boreale*, is very large, and it might become of some importance in the regions of Labrador, Newfoundland, Canada and Maine where it abounds.

Certain plants which supply abundant starchy material or inulin and which are eaten by the Indians are so unpalatable to the European taste that, until some method of preparation is found by which their undesirable qualities may be removed, they are likely to be ignored. This group includes the **Arrow-Arum, Golden-club** and **Prickly-Pear**.

Among the edible seeds the **Chestnut, Cow-Lily**, and **Beach-Pea** are most important and, where abundant, the **Hog-Peanut**, although the latter is rarely found in sufficient quantity to supply a large company.

NUTS AND LARGE SEEDS

The wild nuts are mostly well known, although two or three species which supply nuts or nut-like roots are less familiar. The nuts and edible large seeds of eastern America include:

Alpine Bistort (roots), p. 316	**Hickory-nuts**, p. 243
Bastard Toadflax (fruits), p. 353	Hornbeam-nuts, p. 157
Beechnuts, p. 233	Kentucky Coffee-tree (seeds), p. 223
Bladder-nut (seeds), p. 367	Peanut (seed), p. 221
Butternuts, p. 243, 244	**Pecans**, pp. 243–244
Chestnuts, p. 232	**Pickerel-weed-seeds**, p. 323
Chinquapins, p. 232	Pine-seeds, p. 73
Cow-Lily (seeds), p. 284	Sweet Acorns, p. 236
Dwarf Ginseng (roots), p. 130	**Walnuts**, p. 243
Hazelnuts, p. 159	Water-Chinquapin (seeds), p. 282
Hemp, p. 174	

Except that they have uses which are often unfamiliar, the more important nuts, as already said, are well known and consequently need little discussion. The detailed notes under **Walnuts, Hickory-nuts, Beechnuts** and **Chestnuts** indicate how universal has been their use as cooked vegetables and as sources of soups, oils and, especially, breadstuffs. Some, like the **Pine-seeds** or the nuts of **Bastard Toadflax** and the roots of **Dwarf Ginseng**, occur in such limited quantities or are so difficult to procure that they are likely to be used only as occasional relishes or nibbles; and the nuts of the **Hornbeams** are so small as to be tempting only in time of great need; but in late summer and autumn Pickerel-weed supplies an abundance of palatable and nutritious nutty seeds, enough to supply every tramper in the eastern states.

The use of nuts at the present time is not so general as it should be but the following extract from old Dr. Culpepper indicates that in the 18th century, also, nuts were not generally appreciated.

"And if this be true, as it is, then why should the Vulgar so familiary affirm, That eating Nuts causeth shortness of Breath, than which nothing is falser ? For, how can that which strengthens the Lungs, cause shortness of Breath ? I confess the Opinion is far elder than I am; I knew Tradition was a Friend to Errors before, but never that he was the Father of Slanders: or are Mens Tongues so given to slandering one another, that they must slander Nuts too, to keep their Tongues in use? And thus I have made an Apology for Nuts, which cannot speak for themselves."

BREAKFAST CEREALS

Only a few species of our wild plants furnish seeds of such quality or in sufficient quantity to supply breakfast foods. In fact, only the following have been specially recommended.

Arrow-grass, p. 247	Reed, p. 310
Cane, p. 303	Water-Chinquapin, p. 282
Cow-Lily, p. 284	**Wild Rice**, p. 313

Of these, **Arrow-grass**, on account of the peculiar, oily flavor of its seeds is not likely to be palatable to the European taste. Some of the larger-seeded grasses besides **Wild Rice** would doubtless supply a breakfast food, if they could be secured in sufficient quantity.

BREADSTUFFS

An amazing number of plants have been drawn upon by primitive peoples to supply breadstuffs, and a surprising diversity in the part of the plant used is exhibited in the list of possible breadstuffs in eastern America. The important requirement seems to be merely a large amount of nutritive material more or less farinaceous, flavor being secondary. The breads made by primitive races were often quite unpalatable to the whites and even the breads made in northern Europe in times of famine are more nutritious than attractive. Many of the breadstuffs, however, are not merely nutritious and wholesome, but, when properly prepared, are often delicious and supply breads, muffins and cakes which rival those made from the cultivated cereals. The wild breadstuffs of eastern America are listed on the following page.

As already said, many of these breadstuffs are to .be considered as emergency-foods and only as last resorts in time of famine were they depended upon by primitive peoples or those remote from abundant crops; for instance, the rootstocks of **Buckbean** which have furnished a missen (famine)-bread in Scandinavia, described as nutritious but bitter and disagreeable. Similarly, many members of the Arum family, although containing abundant starchy material, also have such a fiercely puckering, peppery principle that their roots may be used only after prolonged drying and even then there will often be left some of the peppery quality.

Some of the other plants supply breadstuff of considerable importance. For instance, the juicy inner bark of the **Scotch Pine**, stripped off in early summer and dried, has long been recognized in Scotland and in Scandinavia as a source of nutritive flour in times of scarcity of wheat; and the sappy inner bark of our **Sugar-Maple** was similarly used by our American Indians and it certainly suggests the possibility of furnishing a palatable breadstuff. In this connection it is well to remember the statement, attributed to the late Dr. Harvey Wiley, that "Sawdust is fine board."

Bread and cake made from flour prepared from nuts is so familiar in these days of vegetarian recipes as to need no special introduction, but it is noteworthy that the American Indians were much more alive to the desirability and the highly nutritive qualities of these breads than are the whites. The use of acorns as a source of bread was so general among the Indians, particularly of the Southwest, where acorn-bread is described by army surgeons as extremely wholesome and fattening, that it is surprising that few efforts have been made by the whites to use the abundant crop of acorns that annually goes to waste. The acorns of the **White Oaks** are sweet and only slightly bitter and, when properly prepared by leaching out the tannin, furnish a flour from which the most delicious cake and bread may be prepared.

Only a few of the smaller seeds occur in sufficient quantity for practical use in bread-making, but from such common weeds of cultivated fields and barnyards as the **Pigweeds** and **Amaranths** a remarkable quantity of seeds can be readily rattled out. Bread prepared from the ground seeds of these plants is thoroughly palatable and apparently wholesome, although with as characteristic a flavor as that of barley and some other cereals to which the American taste was forced during the last war to accustom itself. The Indians even prepared breads from some of the stone-fruits and dried berries, grinding such fruits as dried persimmons, stones and all!

The ubiquitous **Elder** is the source of delicious rolls and muffins. The fluffy cream-white corollas and buds shaken or pulled off the broad clusters and used on the 50-50 principle with white flour yield muffins which are marvelously light and of delicate flavor. This "flour" can be stored for winter use by rattling off the corollas and drying them rapidly; then storing in tight receptacles.

3. Cooked Green Vegetables

The wild plants which can be used as cooked green vegetables are about as numerous as the starchy vegetables or those with inulin. They group rather naturally into (1) those used as potherbs or greens; (2) some served like asparagus, in lengths; and (3) a few prepared like string beans, stewed celery, or other conventional vegetables.

POTHERBS OR "GREENS"

The potherbs or "greens" are more familiar to the layman than any other of our green vegetables; and almost every one is accustomed to the use of one or another of our wild greens, such as **Dandelion, Dock, Mustard,** or **Marsh-**

Marigold. The prejudice against this group of plants is likely to be much less with those not particularly familiar with wild plants than that against the making of bread from acorns or from the seeds of various wild herbs.

In preparing greens, great pains must be taken to include only the young and tender foliage, since a single tough or old leaf will injure the quality of the entire dish. Particular pains should also be taken in the identification of the species, since, at the stage when most plants are available for greens, flowers and fruits are rarely found and the dangers of confusion are much greater than at other seasons.

In cooking greens certain general principles should be followed. Our wild potherbs fall into two groups; the first with mild flavor and harmless juices, the second with strong or bitter principles or poisonous properties which are withdrawn in boiling. The species with mild and entirely wholesome foliage should, after being picked over, and thoroughly washed and drained, be put into as little boiling water as will cook them and then allowed to simmer in their own juices, to which a pinch of soda (in case only of plants with very tough or stringy fibers), and salt according to judgment, has been added. Occasionally, if the leaves are of dry texture, the addition of a bit of salt-pork (unless one objects to it) while cooking may be desirable. The coarser-leaved greens, after cooking and draining, should be finely chopped and seasoned with a little pepper and additional salt if needed, with as liberal an addition of butter, oil or cream, as may be desired or available. The thoroughly chopped, creamy mass should then be heated and allowed to dry out to the required consistency.

Attractive modifications are the mixing of some of the greens with buttered crumbs and, after the addition of a beaten egg (or eggs) and some milk, baking the dish until the top is delicately browned. The addition of slices of hard-boiled eggs also makes the greens more attractive. Most greens when thoroughly cooked, chopped and seasoned, make delicious salads after they have been chilled, the only addition being the usual dressings of conventional salads.

The following species (see chart next page) are sufficiently mild to be cooked in their own juices, although by throwing off the first water the herby and often slightly disagreeable flavor may be removed.

The second series of potherbs consists of species with such strong flavor or such bitter or slightly poisonous properties when green that it is necessary to cook them in two or more waters, sometimes with a pinch of soda, the strong qualities of the plant being extracted by the water and thrown off with it. It is perhaps a bit shocking to persons who are not familiar with the fact, that many of our staple foods come from plants which, in their fresh state, are notoriously poisonous. For instance tapioca, cassava, and arrowroot-flour are prepared from the tuberous roots of species of Manihot, the fresh juice of which is highly poisonous. In cooking the strong-tasting or somewhat doubtful potherbs it is wisest to throw off at least two of the waters, and experience will sometimes show the desirability of using even more waters before the final

POTHERBS OR "GREENS," MILD
Alpine Cress, p. 161
Amaranth, p. 90
Aneilema, p. 184
Angelica-tree, p. 129
Beech (young leaves), p. 233
Brooklime, p. 297
Canary-grass, p. 310
Centella?, p. 102
Chickweed, p. 181
Cleavers, p. 348
Clover, p. 230
Common Plantain, p. 297
Corn-Lily (cucumber-flavor), p. 256
Cosmos, p. 138
Day-flower, p. 184
Dicliptera, p. 77
Docks (watery), p. 319
Eclipta, p. 139
Fireweed (*Epilobium*), p. 288
Fireweed (*Senecio hieraciifolius*), p. 146
Galinsoga, p. 139
Goat's-beard, p. 151
Hedge-Mustard, p. 169
Henbit, p. 271
Honewort, p. 102
Hop, p. 174
Horseradish (strong, pungent flavor), p. 162
Hyacinth-Bean, p. 224
Japanese Knotweed (acid), p. 318
Live-forever, p. 189
Mallow, p. 267
Matrimony-vine, p. 364
Mountain-Sorrel (acid and watery), p. 316

Mouse-ear Chickweed, p. 178
Mustard, p. 169
Nettles, p. 36
Orach, p. 90
Pickerel-weed, p. 323
Pigweed, p. 90
Pimpernel, p. 327
Purslane (mucilaginous), p. 325
Reed (young shoots), p. 310
Richweed?, p. 376
River-beauty, p. 288
Roseroot, p. 189
Sachaline (acid), p. 319
Salsify, p. 151
Scurvy-Grass (horseradish-flavor), p. 167
Sea-Purslane, p. 178
Sea-Rocket (strong turnip-odor), p. 163
Seaside Plantain, p. 297
Shepherd's-purse, p. 164
Sorrel (acid), p. 321
Spiderwort, p. 185
Spring-beauty, p. 276
Strawberry-Blite, p. 94
Summer-Cypress, p. 91
Sweet Coltsfoot, p. 146
Sweet Pepperbush, p. 183
Wake-Robin, p. 264
Water-Chinquapin, p. 282
Water-Hyacinth, p. 323
Waterleaf, p. 160
Water-Pennywort?, p. 107
Wild Lettuce, p. 143
Wild Senna, p. 229

seasoning, chopping and simmering. To some people the bitter of the **Dandelion** or the **Marsh-Marigold** is agreeable, but to most of us these and other strong greens are more palatable after two or three waters have been thrown off. In the final cooking these stronger-flavored greens are treated exactly as the milder ones described above.

The following chart (next page) are the chief species in our flora belonging to this class.

POTHERBS OR "GREENS," STRONGER	Hydrolea, p. 242
Balloon-vine, p. 357	Large-leaved Aster, p. 139
Black-berried Nightshade, p. 364	**Marsh-Marigold** (bitter), p. 329
Bladder-Campion, p. 179	**Milkweed** (bitter), p. 112
Burdock (bitter), p. 133	Nipplewort (bitter), p. 145
Caraway, p. 101	**Pokeweed**, p. 295
Chicory (bitter), p. 135	**Scotch Lovage** (celery-like), p. 108
Clover, p. 230	Sea-Blite, p. 95
Comfrey, p. 160	Skunk-Cabbage, p. 125
Cursed Crowfoot, p. 331	Sow-Thistle (bitter), p. 149
Dandelion (bitter), p. 150	Storksbill, p. 238
Dog-tooth Violet, p. 256	**Wild Onion**, p. 253
Fennel (aromatic), p. 104	**Winter-Cress** (bitter), p. 162
Honewort, p. 102	

SERVED LIKE ASPARAGUS

The wild plants which are cooked like asparagus are, naturally, available only in the early part of the season, while the new shoots are very tender. Only the young and tender tips should be used; these should be gathered and carefully kept from wilting before use, the hairy or scaly portions rubbed off and the shoots thoroughly washed and drained. They are then cooked either immersed in or steamed over boiling water; in either case salt should be added, the cooked sprouts when thoroughly tender drained, seasoned with pepper and more salt if needed, and dressed with butter, oil, or a sauce.

Several of our wild plants, such as the **Pasture-Brake**, **Ostrich-Fern**, **Carrion-flower**, **Cat-brier**, **Pokeweed** and **Milkweed**, are rather extensively used by those who know them and in many regions may be gathered in large quantities. Many of the remaining species in the following list are included on the recommendation of others, some of the plants being extremely local, although a few are sufficiently abundant for any one so inclined to test their quality.

As in the case of the potherbs, these sprouts which may be cooked like asparagus are difficult to describe so that the novice may recognize them, for they are in condition for use long before the flowers or fruits are developed. Furthermore, many poisonous species produce vigorous and tempting sprouts which might by the less observant be very easily mistaken for the new shoots of edible species. Consequently it is necessary to urge that the greatest care be taken in the use of this class of plants and, as in the case of mushrooms, the general rule should be: when in doubt let them alone; although many plants, such as the ferns, **Wild Onions**, **Cat-brier**, **Hop**, and **Milkweed** are so distinct in appearance that there is practically no danger of confusing them with poisonous species.

The following have been used like asparagus.

Bellwort, p. 264	**Ostrich-Fern**, p. 65
Cane, p. 303	**Pasture-Brake**, p. 61
Carrion-flower, p. 360	**Plumeless Thistle**, p. 135
Cat-brier, p. 361	**Pokeweed**, p. 295
Cat-tail, p. 371	Reed, p. 310
Elder, p. 78	**River-beauty**, p. 288
False Spikenard, p. 260	Solomon's-seal, p. 263
Fireweed, p. 146	Spikenard, p. 128
Hop, p. 174	Water-Chinquapin, p. 282
Indian Pipe, p. 211	**Wild Onion**, p. 253
Japanese Knotweed, p. 318	**Yellow Goat's-beard**, p. 151
Milkweed, p. 112	

OTHER GREEN OR STARCHY VEGETABLES

Besides the large group of potherbs and substitutes for asparagus there are a certain number of wild plants which make palatable vegetables as substitutes for string beans, stewed celery, and other vegetables of the market. Some of these are commonly used in country districts; for instance, the **Pasture-Brake**, its young stems cut into short pieces and served like string beans; or the **Seaside Plantain** similarly treated. Others, like **Burdock** and **Cow-Parsnip**, are less generally known as excellent vegetables when properly prepared. In fact, the tender young stems of Burdock, when carefully peeled, cut into small cubes and deprived, by cooking in two or more waters, of their bitter or rank properties, furnish a vegetable as delicious as salsify—one long advocated by European writers, while in Asia a garden form of the Burdock has long been cultivated for food.

This somewhat miscellaneous group of wild vegetables contains the following limited number of species (next page), the details of uses of which will be found in the systematic section of the book:

4. Salads

The wild salad plants fall naturally into different groups according to the part used or its preparation. Several are used in the raw state much as lettuce, water-cress, or cucumbers; others are more desirable when cooked and served cold with salad-dressing. A few belong perhaps as much in our group of nibbles and relishes as to the group of fresh salads, but because of their delicacy or fresh attractiveness are here included.

Some of the best salad-plants, **Water-Cress** for instance, luxuriate in slow-moving or standing water, the source and the purity of which is questionable. It is, therefore, advisable to disinfect all aquatic salads before eating. The addition to the water in which they are washed of a tablet of " chlorazene," a well known disinfectant, is advisable. One tablet in two quarts of water purifies the latter and, as emphasized, should be used in washing all salads from doubtful sources—including **Water-Cress** from the market.

For the most part these salads are best when dressed with oil, vinegar, salt and pepper, with the addition, if one wishes, of a bit of **Wild Onion** or **Wild Chives**. Many of the species are best when used as ingredients in mixed salads—such plants as **Sweet Flag**, **Sorrel**, **Peppergrass, Shepherd's-purse**, **Sea-Rocket, Scurvy-Grass**, **Water-Cress**, **Winter-Cress, Spring-Cress**, **Wood-Sorrel**, **Caraway** and **Brooklime**. Others, like **Corn-Lily, Purslane**, **Live-forever**, **Roseroot, and Seaside Plantain**, are sufficiently mild and succulent to be used by themselves like lettuce; and a few species are bitter or strong and are best when they have grown through litter or have been allowed otherwise to blanch—such plants as **Scotch Lovage**, **Chicory** and **Dandelion**.

In a few cases, for example **Cat-brier** sprouts and **Beach-Pea** sprouts, the shoots need to be cooked. A few are merely crisp roots which, dressed like cucumbers, make a palatable substitute for them—such as the white roots of the **Indian Cucumber**. Besides the plants enumerated in the list below practically any of the potherbs, as already stated, may be served cold with salad dressing, most of them making a highly satisfactory salad. The following wild plants supply salads.

5. Nibbles and Relishes

Here belong a few plants which supply pleasant radishlike roots, or seeds or sprouts which are eaten raw chiefly by children or as minor relishes, though rarely brought to the table. The list is so miscellaneous in character that it is not readily classified, but the reason for here entering these minor food-plants will be apparent from the comment appended to each name.

Alder (buds and bark), p. 156

Alpine Bistort (rootstock and bulblets nut-like), p. 316

Bamboo-vine (young shoots), p. 361

Barberry (young leaves acid), p. 154

Bastard Toadflax (nut-like fruits), p. 353

Black Haw (sweet stone-fruit), p. 81

Blackberry (young sprouts peeled), p. 344

Blueberry (flowers mildly acid), p. 214

Bryony-leaved Jacob's-ladder (berries), p. 360

Buckhorn (young fronds), p. 68

Bugleweed (crisp tubers), p. 272

Bunchberries (insipid stone-fruit), p. 187

Cat-brier (young leaves), p. 361

Checkerberry (young leaves and berries), p. 208

Chufa (tubers), p. 192

Clover (flowers with abundant honey at base), p. 230

Deergrass (acid leaves and nutty tubers), p. 270

Eel-Grass (rootstock), p. 383

Fennel (young tips), p. 104

Ground-Hemlock (berries), p. 76

Ground-Juniper (berries), p. 69

Hackberry (thin pulp of berries), p. 374

Hobblebush (sweet stone-fruit), p. 81

Honey-Locust (sweet, pulpy lining of pod), p. 222

Mallow (young seeds, called "Cheeses"), p. 267

Mints (young shoots), p. 271

Partridge-berry (insipid, seedy berries), p. 350

Pasture-Brake (young stems), p. 61

Peanut, p. 221

Raspberry (young sprouts peeled), p. 344

Sand-reed (tender bases of joints), p. 301

Seaweeds, p. 407

Sorrel (leaves acid), p. 321

Sweet Fern (young nutlets), p. 279

Trailing Arbutus (flowers pleasantly acid), p. 206

Water-Parsnip (nutty roots), p. 110

Wild Ginger (rootstock gingery), p. 132

Wild Raisin (sweet stone-fruit), p. 81

Wild Rose (petals), p. 344

Woundwort (crisp finger-like rootstocks), p. 272

6. Pickles

A rather large number of wild plants are used in various communities as pickles, ordinarily soaked in alum-water, then in salted water, and finally preserved in boiling, spiced vinegar; though a few plants are of such mild flavor and delicate texture that they can be put at once into weak vinegar without the use of the alum-water. Such pickles as those made from **Walnuts** and **Butternuts** have long been popular and their preparation is usually described in the better cook-books. Others, like the **Wild Onion**, are prepared exactly as if they were small, cultivated onions, and to this class of roots and tubers belong several wild plants that are less generally used.

The wild roots and tubers which furnish good pickles are:

Bugleweed, p. 272	**Jerusalem Artichoke**, p. 141
Cat-tail, p. 371	**Live-forever**, p. 189
False Spikenard, p. 260	Solomon's-seal, p. 263
Indian Cucumber, p. 262	**Wild Onion**, p. 253

In a few cases the leafy young plants or the young branches are used entire. These are all succulent or fleshy plants, the best-known of which is the salty "**Samphire**" of the salt marshes. The latter, with a few other species similarly used, makes the following list.

Pokeweed, p. 295	Sea-Milkwort, p. 327
Purslane, p. 325	Sea-Purslane, p. 178
"Samphire," p. 94	

A number of flower-buds or young fruits are pickled like capers and used like them, and presumably many more might be added to the list. The following have been definitely tried or recommended.

Ash (fruits), p. 287	Elder (buds), p. 78
Barberries (green), p. 154	**Marsh-Marigold** (buds), p. 329
Broom (buds and young pods), p. 222	Red-bud (buds and flowers), p. 221

The remaining species are so differently prepared and used that they are merely enumerated, with a note as to the part which is pickled.

Cat-tail (tender young shoots), p. 371	Reed (tender young shoots), p. 310
Kentucky Coffee-tree (pods like tamarinds), p. 223	Unicorn-plant (young pods), p. 269
	Walnuts and Butternuts (young), p. 243

7. Condiments and Seasoning

It is naturally difficult to draw a sharp line between condiments, nibbles and pickles. As here classified, however, the condiments are the plants generally used in seasoning or flavoring, or which, like **Horseradish**, stand somewhat intermediate between the seasonings, relishes and pickles.

Onion-flavor is, of course, readily found wherever species of **Wild Onion** occur. Pepper finds a tolerable substitute in the **Smartweeds** and in a milder form in the seeds of **Peppergrass**. Salt is not so easily obtained, although the Indians claimed that the hollow basal portions of the stems of **Cow-Parsnip** furnish a substitute, and some of the fleshy salt-marsh plants like "**Samphire**" are highly charged with salt and can be added, either green or cooked, to season other plants.

Sweet herbs and savory seeds quite as good as the imported bay and other conventional condiments of the grocer are supplied by **Sweet Gale, Wax-Myrtles, Wild Ginger, Sassafras, Red-Bay, Spice-bush, Sweet Cicely, Caraway,** and **Tansy**. Checkerberry-flavor is found not only in the **Checkerberry** plant but in the **Moxie-vine**, and abundantly in the twigs and buds of the **Sweet Birch** and somewhat less so in the **Yellow Birch**. Pleasant acid is readily secured from the **Sorrels, Mountain-Sorrel,** and **Wood-Sorrel**; good substitutes for Horseradish are found in the roots of **Crinkle-root** and **Spring-Cress**; while the wild species of Mints, the **Mugwort** and **Wormwood**, are as good as those ordinarily used in the kitchen.

More concisely stated this list of condiments is as follows:

CONDIMENTS AND SEASONINGS	Pepper grass (mildly peppery), p. 167
Bayberry (savory), p 154.	Poppy (seeds), p. 293
Bee-balm, p. 271	Red-Bay, p. 249
Caraway, p. 101	"Samphire" (salt), p. 94
Checkerberry, p. 208	**Sassafras** (savory), p. 250
Costmary, p. 149	Shepherd's-purse (seeds), p 164.
Cow-Parsnip (salt?), p. 106	Smartweed (peppery), p. 318
Crinkle-root (like Horseradish), p. 166	**Sorrels** (acid), p. 321
Fennel (aromatic), p. 104	Spice-bush (savory), p. 249
Garlic-Mustard, p. 161	Spring-Cress (like Horseradish), p. 164
Hackberry (sweetish), p. 374	Sweet Birch (checkerberry-flavor), p. 157
Horehound, p. 271	**Sweet Cicely** (anise-oil), p. 109
Horseradish (mildly peppery), p. 162	**Sweet Gale** (savory), p. 281
Mints, p. 271	Tansy, p. 150
Mountain-Mint, p. 271	Water-Parsnip, p. 110
Mountain-Sorrel (acid), p. 316	**Wax-Myrtle** (savory), p. 279
Moxie-plum (checkerberry-flavor), p. 207	Wild Chives, p. 253
	Wild Garlic, p. 253
Mugwort, p. 134	**Wild Ginger**, p. 132
Mustard, p. 169	**Wild Onion**, p. 253
Muster John-Henry (savory), p. 149	Wood-Sorrel (acid), p. 292
Penny-Cress (peppery), p. 169	Wormwood, p. 134
Pennyroyal, p. 271	Yellow Birch (checkerberry-flavor), p. 157

8. Drinks

TEA

Singularly enough there are as many substitutes for tea and some other conventional drinks as for spinach or flour. In fact almost any plant with harmless properties or only mildly medicinal tendencies seems to have been used by some one in the preparation of tea. The familiar herb-teas of a few generations ago, while still sometimes used as "spring medicine" or as cures for catarrh (or for anything else), are no longer popular; but a few of them have outgrown their medicinal uses and are now recommended as camp-teas. Thus the teas prepared from **Sweet Gale** or from **Sweet Goldenrod** have their enthusiastic advocates. Some sing the praises of **Sassafras-tea**, others of **Clover-tea** or **Basswood-tea**; while the numerous names like **New Jersey Tea**, **Oswego Tea** and **Labrador Tea** hark back to early uses of these plants.

The following list includes the principal wild plants (excluding the mints and other strong-flavored plants, which to some are too suggestive of medicine to form an entirely pleasant beverage, but to others are attractive and well known) which have been recommended as substitutes for tea. The approved method of curing the leaves in Revolutionary days will be found under the discussion of **New Jersey Tea** (p. 333) or of **Cassina** (p. 115).

TEA	Mints, p. 271
Arbor Vitae (twigs, chips), p. 69	**Moxie-plum** (whole plant), p. 207
Basswood (flowers), p. 267	**New Jersey Tea** (leaves), p. 333
Black Alder (leaves), p. 115	Persimmon (leaves), p. 198
Blackberry (leaves), p. 344	Raspberry (leaves), p. 344
Bog-Rosemary (leaves), p. 202	**Sassafras** (bark of roots), p. 250
Cassina (leaves), p. 115	Shrubby Cinquefoil (leaves), p. 337
Checkerberry (leaves), p. 208	Slippery Elm (inner bark), p. 374
Clover (heads), p. 230	Speedwell (leaves) p. 298
Elder (flowers), p. 78	Spice-bush (leaves and twigs), p. 249
Fireweed (leaves), p. 146	**Strawberry** (leaves), p. 337
Ginseng (leaves), p. 130	Sweet Birch (leaves, bark, twigs), p. 157
Hemlock (young tips), p. 75	**Sweet Fern** (leaves), p. 279
Holly (leaves), p. 115	**Sweet Gale** (leaves), p. 281
Inkberry (leaves), p. 116	Sweet Goldenrod (young leaves and
Labrador Tea (leaves), p. 212	flowers), 147
Lapland Rosebay (leaves), p. 213	Sweet Vernal-grass, p. 302
Leather-leaf (leaves), p. 204	Witch-Hazel (leaves), p. 241
Mexican Tea (leaves), p. 94	

COFFEE

The number of substitutes for coffee is decidedly less than for tea. One or two, like **Chicory-** and **Dandelion-roots**, are already market-substitutes, in some countries extensively raised for this purpose, and by many people preferred to coffee itself or used mixed with coffee. The bristly, nut-like seeds of **Cleavers or Goose-grass**, *Galium*, have long been recommended as a most satisfactory substitute for coffee and, belonging to the same natural group with coffee, these seeds when parched and properly prepared may well sustain their reputation.

In colonial days the seeds of the **Kentucky Coffee-tree** acquired considerable fame, although it is noteworthy that all travellers agree that, when imported coffee could be secured it was always preferred. Various other large seeds and nuts, when parched, have had temporary popularity, and it is probable that many species could be added to the brief list here appended.

COFFEE SUBSTITUTES	Dandelion (root), p. 150
Arrow-grass (seeds), p. 247	Ground-Juniper (berries), p. 69
Asparagus (seeds), p. 254	Kentucky Coffee-tree (seeds), p. 223
Beechnuts, p. 233	Peanuts, p. 221
Broom (seeds), p. 222	Persimmons (seeds), p. 198
Chestnuts, p. 232	Sunflower (seeds), p. 141
Chicory (root), p. 135	Wild Coffee (berries), p. 176
Chufa (tubers), p. 192	Wild Senna (seeds), p. 229
Cleavers (seeds), p. 348	

CHOCOLATE

There are only three genera of plants in our flora which have achieved any fame as substitutes for chocolate. The most important of these is the **Basswood or Linden**, the young fruit of which when mashed has a chocolate-odor or flavor; in fact so promising was the Linden-fruit as a source of cocoa that, at various times in European history, extended experiments were made with the hope of producing a marketable product. Although the European experimenters eventually abandoned the problem, they suggested that in North America, where there are different species of Linden, the experiments might prove successful. Early explorers in Carolina stated that, from the **Dwarf Chestnut or Chinquapin** was prepared a " Chocolate, not much inferiour to that made from Cacoa"; while some enthusiasts, among whom the present writers are not yet to be counted, claim that a delicious chocolate-drink may be prepared from the root of the **Purple Avens**.

The three chocolate-substitutes are, then:

CHOCOLATE SUBSTITUTES	Linden (young nuts), p. 267
Chinquapin (nuts), p. 232	Purple Avens (root), p. 338

COLD DRINKS

In this group are included the various home-brewed drinks such as birch-beer, and the simple summer drinks prepared from acid fruits and used like lemonade. We have not entered the very extensive field of distilled liquors, and there are some people who might object to indication of the ingredients of birch-beer, root-beer and other mildly alcoholic beverages, but no one can object to pink lemonade prepared by bruising **Sumach-berries** in water or from the juice of **Prickly-Pears** or **Barberries**. The number of these refreshing cold drinks is larger than we should have imagined; they may be prepared from the following:

9. Rennets

Warm milk can be coagulated or turned to a curd by pouring it into fruit syrups just as it is frequently curdled in the kitchen by the use of rennet. Besides these fruit-acids there are several wild plants which have become especially noteworthy as substitutes for rennet, and which have won considerable recognition in the literature of folk-botany. A strong decoction of **Nettles** has been used in some of the Scotch islands, Lightfoot saying of it: "A common spoonfull of this liquor will coagulate a large bowl of milk very readily and agreeably, which we saw and experienced." **Sorrel** has a similar use, but the most interesting plants with this property are the insectivorous **Sundews** and **Butterworts**.

This brief list, then, excluding the acid fruits, is:

10. Syrups and Sugars, Confections

SYRUPS AND SUGARS

The heading Syrups and Sugars inevitably suggests **Maple** which is, of course, our most important native source of sugar; but the sap of many other trees contains appreciable sugar and some species, like the **Walnuts, Hickories, Birches, Plane-tree, Basswood** and **Ash**, have supplied syrups and sugars which by those who have used them are stated to be of good quality, although often more scanty than the product from the **Sugar-Maple** and the **Ash-leaved Maple**. Other sources are less important, but it is stated that the meat of the European Chestnut contains 14 per cent of sugar. Decidedly picturesque but of little practical value is the extraction of sugar, reported by various travellers, from the dew-drops gathered from the flowers of **Milkweed**! And decidedly difficult, because of the labor of securing the roots, is the conventional Indian method of extracting sugar from the rootstocks of the tall **Bulrushes** or **Tules**.

It is probable that other sources of sugar may be discovered among our wild plants, but the following include the principal ones which have been recommended.

SYRUPS AND SUGARS	Honey-Locust (pulpy lining of pod),
Basswood (sap), p. 267	p. 222
Birches (sap), p. 156	**Maples** (sap), p. 354
Bulrush or Tule (rootstock), p. 194	Milkweed (dew on flowers), p. 112
Chestnut (fruit), p. 232	Plane-tree (sap), p. 299
Hickories (sap), p. 244	Walnuts (sap), p. 243

CONFECTIONS

Such confections as candied Chestnuts (marrons glaces), Marshmallows, candied Sweet Flag-root and candied Angelica-shoots are familiar and have found their place at the confectioners, while candied Rose-petals and Violets are dainties appreciated chiefly for their color and delicate flavor; but confections prepared from **Burdock, White Pine** or **Reeds** are certainly less familiar. Nevertheless, in the early days of New England the stripped young shoots of the White Pine were candied; by the Indians of western America a taffy-like confection is prepared from the young shoots of the Reed; while by some European authors the pith of the young stems of Burdock is recommended to make a confection. In early days the root of **Elecampane** was similarly used; and on northern seacoasts the root and shoots of **Scotch Lovage** are considered worthy rivals of Angelica.

Confections may be prepared from these wild plants (chart, next page).

CONFECTIONS	Rose (petals), p. 344
Angelica (root and new shoots), p. 99	**Scotch Lovage** (root and new shoots),
Burdock (young pith), p. 133	p. 108
Chestnuts, p. 232	Soapberry, p. 200
Coltsfoot, p. 152	**Sweet Flag** (root), p. 118
Elecampane (root), p. 143	Violets, p. 381
Horehound, p. 271	Water-Chestnuts, p. 370
Marsh-Mallow (juice), p. 267	White Pine (young tips), p. 73
Reed (new shoots), p. 310	**Wild Ginger** (rootstock), p. 132

11. *Fresh or Preserved Fruits, Jellies, Marmalades*

FRUITS, FRESH OR COOKED

Although some people have the false notion that any fruit is edible, the number of really poisonous ones is limited and the number of wild fruits which are edible or at least eatable is surprisingly large. The majority of our best wild fruits are, naturally enough, known to every one who is familiar with the fields and woods: the **Red or Black Mulberry**, **Pawpaw**, **May-Apple**, **Barberry**, **Gooseberries**, **Currants**, **Strawberries**, **Raspberries**, **Blackberries**, **Dewberries**, **Grapes**, **Huckleberries**, **Blueberries**, **Persimmon**, etc. These need no special comment, but there are many others less familiar and looked upon with suspicion by the uninitiated; e.g. the **Service-berries or Shad-berries** or, as they are often called, **Sugar-Pears**, are by a large proportion of people considered poisonous but they are not only harmless but make a most delicious pie, comparable only with sweet cherry-pie. Again, the **Dangleberry** and the **Squaw-Huckleberry** are commonly ignored, under the impression that they are inedible, but the Dangleberry, when well developed, is one of the juiciest and most delicious of the genus, while the Squaw-Huckleberry when properly cooked and sweetened makes a sauce as delicious as good old-fashioned goose-berry-sauce.

A few berries which in small quantity are edible are, if eaten to excess, cathartic or otherwise medicinal; e.g., the **False Solomon's-seal** and **Twisted-stalk**; while some others, though trivial as fruits, afford to those who are still young in spirit a pleasant nibble, for example the deliciously sweet pulp of the red berries of **Ground-Hemlock**, or the date-like film over the large stones of some species of **Viburnum**. Several of these minor fruits, like the berries of **Ground-Hemlock**, **Hackberry**, **Hobblebush** and **Wild Raisin**, have such large stones and such extremely limited pulp that few people would attempt to cook them. Their chief value is as masticatories. Others, however, like the **Crowberry**, **Alpine Bearberry**, **Squaw-Huckleberry**, **Black-berried Nightshade** and **Squashberry**, although eatable in the raw condition, are much better when properly cooked.

The edible wild fruits of our region are:

WILD FRUITS	
Akebia, p. 248	Ground-Plum, p. 221
Alpine Bearberries, p. 203	Hackberry, p. 374
Barberry, p. 154	**Haws**, p. 336
Bearberries, p. 202	**High-bush Cranberry**, p. 82
Beauty-berry, p. 271	Hobblebush, p. 81
Black Haw, p. 81	Husk-Tomato, p. 364
Black Huckleberry, p. 209	**May-Apple**, p. 263
Black-berried Nightshade, p. 364	Maypops, p. 294
Blackberries, p. 344	**Mountain-Cranberry**, p. 216
Blueberries, p. 214	**Moxie-plum**, p. 207
Bog-Cranberries, p. 215	**Pawpaw**, p. 98
Buffalo-Berry, p. 200	**Persimmon**, p. 198
Bunchberries, p. 187	**Plums**, p. 340
Checkerberry, p. 208	Prickly-Pear, p. 172
Cherries, pp. 340-342	**Raspberries**, p. 344
Cloudberry, p. 344	**Red or Black Mulberry**, p. 277
Crowberries, p. 205	**Service-berries**, p. 334
Currants, p. 239	Silver-bell, p. 368
Dangleberry, p. 210	Silverberry, p. 200
Dewberries, p. 344	**Squashberry**, p. 80
Dwarf Huckleberry, p. 210	**Squaw-Huckleberry**, p. 216
Elderberries, p. 78	**Strawberries**, p. 337
False Spikenard, p. 260	Strawberry-Blite, p. 94
Fig, p. 277	Twisted-stalk, p. 263
Gooseberries, p. 239	Two-leaved Solomon's-seal, p. 260
Grapes, p. 382	**Waterberry**, p. 176
Ground-Hemlock, p. 76	White Mulberry, p. 277
Ground-Juniper, p. 69	Wild Raisin, p. 81

JELLIES AND MARMALADES

The making of jelly and marmalade from the conventional fruits is too well known to need special discussion here, but several of the wild fruits, furnishing the best of jellies and marmalades and now going almost wholly to waste, should be better known and more widely used; for example, such fruits as the Haws, which often yield a surprising quantity of syrup; the **Rum-Cherry**, famous in old New England as the source of cherry bounce, but also the source of a rich jelly as delicious as that from guava; the despised **Choke-Cherry**, now commonly used only as the source of practical jokes but yielding a clear, acid jelly; and the **Squaw-Huckleberry**, described in our manuals of botany as having a mawkish and inedible fruit, but really furnishing a rich palate-tickling marmalade comparable with the best gooseberry-sauce. Besides the wild fruits there are other and rather surprising sources of jelly in our flora. It is stated, for instance, that the Indians extracted a jelly from the roots of the **Cat-tail**; and one of the most famous jellies of the southern Indians was prepared from the roots of the common **Cat-brier**.

In preparing jelly from the wild fruits it will be found necessary in many cases, the **Cherries** for example, to add a fair proportion of tart apples, for many of the wild fruits contain little or no pectin, which is required to make the syrup "jell." Wherever in the detailed discussion of each species the addition of apple or the market "certo" seems important to jelly-making, the fact is specially noted.

Fruits to be used for jelly should be gathered, whenever possible, before they are thoroughly ripe. The juices are then thicker and more inclined to "jell," whereas the overripe fruit is apt to be infected with germs of mold and decay. After being picked over, washed and drained, the fruit is boiled in as little water as possible—enough to keep it from burning. When thoroughly cooked the fruit is mashed with a pestle or heavy spoon in order to free the juices, then drained through a closely woven cloth (or two layers of fine cheesecloth or other convenient "jelly-bag"). This juice, to which has been added apple-juice if needed, is then boiled vigorously for twenty minutes or half-an-hour in order to drive off excess water, then measured and in most cases boiled vigorously for five minutes with an equal quantity of granulated sugar. The ideal jelly will "jell" or become "stringy" when dripped from a spoon during the first five minutes of boiling; if it does not "jell" within at most fifteen minutes it will be necessary to add more sugar and boil again. The latter procedure is an unfortunate one, since jelly which has been too long boiled with sugar is apt to become gummy and to have a stinging taste. As soon as the syrup has jelled it should be removed from the fire, skimmed and poured, by means of a small sterilized pitcher or dipper, into glasses, allowed to cool and then to stiffen, which ordinarily requires two or three days.

Marmalades are prepared like jellies except that the pulp as well as the juice is retained, the whole being pressed through a sieve.

The wild plants listed on the next page are possible sources of jellies or marmalades.

DRYING OF FRUITS

Although we read of the drying of berries and other fruits by the American Indians, concrete directions are generally lacking. Very practical processes are described by the late Dr. George W. Carver, the Tuskegee scientist who accomplished so much in improving economic and agricultural conditions in Alabama. From his *Nature's Garden for Victory and Peace* we freely quote: "The shortage of tin cans, glass containers, the high price of sugar as well as the containers, make it emphatic that we have some other method within the reach of the humblest citizen.

"Drying is without doubt the simplest and best method of preserving a number of fruits and vegetables. And it is a source of much regret that such a few know how to appreciate the delicious taste of home-dried fruits and vegetables.

FRUITS

"Begin drying just as soon as the seed matures, or as soon as the fruit is two-thirds ripe, and continue as long as you can handle it without mashing the pulp.

"Caution: In drying either fruits or vegetables in the sun, screen wire or mosquito netting should be stretched over a suitable frame to keep off the flies and other insects; and everything, of course, must be scrupulously clean if a superior flavored, the most attractive appearing and the most appetizing, healthy and wholesome product is desired.

STRAWBERRY LEATHER (Delicious)

"Take thoroughly ripe strawberries, mash to a pulp, spread on platters, and dry in the sun or oven; when dry, dust with powdered sugar, and roll up like a jelly cake into suitable sized pieces and pack away in jars. This may be eaten as a confection or soaked in water and used for pies, short cake, sauce, tarts, etc. The powdered sugar is a matter of taste and may be left out if desired.

DRIED STRAWBERRIES

"Put the berries in a moderate oven, heat through thoroughly, but not enough to become soft and juicy, spread out in the sun or finish in the oven."

Then follow specific directions for Blackberries and Dewberries, treated like strawberries, or first mashed through a sieve to remove the hard stones; for Plums, covered with boiling water and left standing for twenty minutes; "drain and spread in the sun to dry. Stir occasionally; when dry examine them frequently and at first appearance of worms put in the oven and heat for a few minutes." Peaches, figs, pears, apples and various vegetables are similarly dried, and the **Muscadine Grape** is given a special treatment which will be quoted under that delectable fruit (see p. 382).

12. Oils and Butter

The sources of oil and butter in our wild flora are very limited, the Indians having depended almost exclusively upon the rich oils from the **Walnuts**, **Hickory-nuts** and **Sunflower-seeds**, the oil from the nuts of the **Shagbark-Hickory** having been one of the most prized staples of the Indian household. At the present time these nut-oils are rarely seen, but Sunflower-oil has become very familiar to the white man. In France and some other countries of Europe the preparation of oil from **Beechnuts** has been an important industry and a century and a half ago it was estimated that the forests of Compiègne alone in a single season furnished sufficient oil to supply all the needs of that district for half a century. This oil, properly clarified, is said to be as delicate as olive oil and to be substituted extensively for it. The amateur preparation of table-oils is a somewhat exacting task and only the enthusiast is likely to undertake it. A somewhat detailed account of the method will be found in the discussion of the Beech (see p. 233).

The chief wild sources of table-oil and butter are as follows:

Beechnuts, p. 233	Sunflower-seeds, p. 141
Hickory-nuts, p. 243	Walnuts, p. 243
Peanuts, p. 221	

13. Masticatories and Chewing Gums

MASTICATORIES

Under this heading are included a few plants the chewing of which usually relieves thirst. It is of course needless here to mention such thirst-quenchers as juicy fruits. A few of the masticatories, like the juicy cambium of the White Pine, which is familiar to real northeastern country boys under the name of "slivers," or the mucilaginous inner bark of the **Slippery Elm** (too strongly suggestive of medicine to be very popular), supply considerable nourishment as well as stimulating salivation. Others, like the buds of **Alder** or **Basswood**, stimulate the salivary glands without overloading the stomach with food; while such leaves as those of **Sorrel**, young **Barberry**, **Wood-Sorrel**, **Deergrass** and **Sorrel-tree** are pleasantly acid, and several of them have long been recognized by trampers as comforting nibbles during a long, hot tramp. In the Southwest the new shoots of the **Bulrush** or **Tule** have a considerable reputation as a masticatory, but in regions of abundant springs and fresh water the labor of securing the Tule-rootstock is too great for the amount of relief obtained in chewing it.

Our more important masticatories are:

Alder (buds), p. 156	Slippery Elm (inner bark), p. 374
Barberry (young leaves and berries), p. 154	Sorrel-tree (leaves), p. 212
Basswood (inner bark and buds), p. 267	**Sorrels** (leaves), p. 321
Black Haw (berries), p. 81	**Sour Gum** (berries), p. 188
Deergrass (leaves), p. 270	**Sweet-leaf**, p. 369
Ground-Hemlock (berries), p. 76	Tule (new shoots), p. 194
Ground-Juniper (berries), p. 69	**Wild Cherries**, p. 340
Hackberries, p. 374	**Wild Grapes**, p. 382
Hobblebush (berries), p. 81	Wild Olive or Silver-bell (acid drupes), p. 368
Pasture-Brake (young croziers), p. 61	Wild Raisin (berries), p. 81
Pines (sappy inner bark), p. 73	**Wood-Sorrel** (leaves), p. 292

CHEWING GUM

Unfortunately the modern American is too apt to feel lost without his chewing gum, and, although the gum of **Red Spruce** is the standard among our native gums, there are other wild gums available in regions where the Spruce is not found. On account of its fragrance, the sweet gum from *Liquidambar* is chewed in the Southern states; and the gum of **Bird-Cherry** trees is sought by children and occasionally by those who have overlooked the fact that they are no longer children. The Omaha Indians chew the resinous gum of the **Rosin-weed**; while a chewing gum is prepared by the Indians and by young boys from the juice of the **Milkweeds**.

This small group of plants indispensable to the comfort of many Yankees is:

Bird-Cherry, p. 340	**Spruce**, p. 72
Milkweed, p. 112	**Sweet Gum**, p. 89
Rosin-weed, p. 147	

14. *Emergency-Foods*

Most of the plants already discussed naturally serve as the best sort of emergency-foods; but under this heading are here included a few plants or plant-products which, although not ordinarily sought when better food is available, would temporarily support life. Among the roots which it is possible to eat and which furnish considerable nutrition are those of the **Wild Sarsaparilla**, the **Spikenard** and the **Ginseng**, all slightly aromatic and with mucilaginous juices, but woody in texture. The thickened tuber-like roots or bulbs of our **Orchids** are full of nutrition but most of them are rare and only under pressure of extreme hunger would it be justifiable to attempt eating them. The roots of the common **Locust-tree** which, however, rarely occurs in regions remote from civilization, are sweet and suggestive of licorice but, although sometimes eaten, are to be avoided as being unwholesome. The sapwood or cambium of many trees has been resorted to in emergency, for, although tough and somewhat difficult to secure, this sappy inner bark is full of nutrition. Similarly, the young twigs of many trees, especially the **Pines**, **Spruce**, **Fir** and **Hemlock**, and the pith of the **Cedars**, are nutritious but of strong flavor. One of the most available emergency foods of the North, though one disagreeable to eat, is the pitchy balsam found in the blisters on the bark of **Balsam-Fir**. This is reported to have saved lives in the woods but only under the most extreme pressure of hunger would one be tempted to eat it.

These emergency-foods which, as above stated, are available, though unattractive, are listed below.

EMERGENCY-FOODS	
Alders (inner bark, buds), p. 156	Lichens, p. 409
Basswood (inner bark, young twigs), p. 267	Locust (inner bark), p. 229
Bittersweet (inner bark, young twigs), p. 182	Maple (inner bark), p. 354
Cedars (young twigs), p. 69	Orchids (thick roots), p. 291
Cursed Crowfoot (leaves), p. 331	Pines (inner bark and young twigs), p. 73
Fir (inner bark, young twigs and balsam), p. 71	Poplars (inner bark), p. 352
Ginseng (root), p. 130	Sand-reed (rootstocks), p. 301
Hackmatack or Larch (young shoots), p. 71	Silverweed (roots), p. 339
Hemlock (inner bark and young twigs), p. 75	Slippery Elm (inner bark), p. 374
Ironwood (small nuts), p. 157	Spikenard (root), p. 128
	Spruces (inner bark and young twigs), p. 72
	Vetch (seeds), p. 230
	Wild Sarsaparilla (root), p. 128
	Willows (inner bark), p. 352

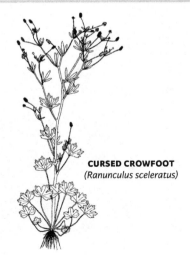

CURSED CROWFOOT
(Ranunculus sceleratus)

OSTRICH-FERN *(Matteucchia struthiopteris)*, young croziers ("fiddleheads") ready for harvest.

CHAPTER TWO

Poisonous Flowering Plants

Under poisonous plants we here include only such species as might be mistaken for edible ones or which are actively poisonous if eaten, i.e. plants with fleshy roots or bulbs which might prove tempting or with attractive berries or with tender shoots which might lead the over-bold to try them as food. Many plants poisonous to eat but tough and uninviting, like **Poison-Ivy** and **Poison Sumach**, are naturally omitted. In the wild flora of eastern America there are, however, several species which are sufficiently poisonous, when eaten by mistake, to cause serious inconvenience or in a few cases violent illness or even death. These are enumerated below, a brief description given of each and, for most species, an illustration given. In some plants, like **Marsh-Marigold**, the raw plant is poisonous but the cooked one quite wholesome and much used; in some others the green fruit is at least unwholesome while the ripe fruit is regularly eaten. These cases are specially noted under each species in Chapter 3 and the poisonous **Mushrooms** are discussed in Chapter 4.

The old saying that one man's poison is another man's food finds exemplification in the wild plants. Many plants eaten by the American Indians are often at least unpalatable to the white man's taste. As one reads of the plants sometimes eaten by the natives of Java, for instance, or in other regions where habit or racial differences may have established immunity, he is impressed with the soundness of the advice given nearly two and a half centuries ago by John Evelyn:

"How cautious then ought our Sallet-Gatherers to be, in reading ancient Authors; lest they happen to be imposed on, where they treat of Plants that are familiarly eaten in other Countries, and among other Nations and People of more robust and strong Constitutions; besides the hazard of being mistaken in the Names of divers Simples, not as yet fully agreed upon among the Learned in Botany."

When we read of oriental people cooking and eating the plant of **Castor-bean** or even eating the cooked seed, three of which raw, the source of castor-oil, would kill an ordinary occidental, it is evident that racial differences may extend beyond color, speech and methods of thought. Some plants entered, because eaten by some peoples, in Chapter 3 may seem to the experimenter to belong in Chapter 2.

1. POISONOUS BULBS AND ROOTS

In regard to tunicated bulbs, those consisting of broadened and fleshy leaf-like coats, as in the onion, no one not absolutely certain of his diagnosis should ever attempt to eat any which lack the familiar odor of onions (onion-oil). Some bulbs which superficially resemble onions are among the deadliest of poisons, **Fly-poison** (*Amianthium*), **Death-Camass** (*Anticlea*), **Atamasco Lily** (*Zephyranthes*) etc., while the bulbs of **Narcissus, Tulip** and other cultivated ornamentals are open to suspicion. *Allium* (**Onion, Leek** and **Garlic**) has the flowers or top-bulblets in an umbel (all arising like rays of an umbrella), the others (except **Narcissus**) do not. In the following descriptions, plants are arranged alphabetically by their scientific name.

Atamasco Lily (bulb), p. 57	Fly-poison (bulb), p. 33
Bloodroot (rootstock), p. 54	May-Apple (rootstock), pp. 52, 263
Blue Flag (rootstock), p. 46	Pokeweed (root), pp. 52, 295
Butterfly-weed (root), pp. 36, 113	Red-root (rootstock), p. 47
Cowbane (fleshy roots), p.	Star-of-Bethlehem (bulb), pp. 50, 262
Death-Camass (bulb), p. 33	Water-Hemlock (roots), pp. 39, 109, 168

2. POISONOUS NEW SHOOTS AND YOUNG FOLIAGE RESEMBLING EDIBLE PLANTS

This series contains the following some of which have been suggested as food and others sufficiently succulent or fragrant as to be tempting.

Castor-bean, p. 53	Jimson-weed, Thorn-Apple, p. 43
Celandine, p. 38	Marsh-Marigold, pp. 36, 329
Cherry and Plum leaves, p. 52	Mexican Tea, pp. 44, 94
Devil's-bit, p. 38	Milkweeds, p.
Dogbanes, p. 34	Nightshades, p. 54
Fool's Parsley, p. 32	Pimpernel, p. 48, 327
Hemp, pp. 37, 174	Poison Hemlock, pp. 41, 99
Horsetail, pp. 44, 64	Velvet-grass, pp. 45, 301
Indian Poke, p. 57, 126	Wild Indigo, p. 36
Jewel-weed, p. 46	Yellow Jessamine, p. 37

3. POISONOUS DRY FRUITS OR SEEDS RESEMBLING EDIBLE SEEDS

Apple-of-Peru, p. 50	Hoary Pea, pp. 56, 230
Arrow-grass, p. 57, 247	Jimson-weed, p. 43
Buckeyes, Horse-Chestnut, pp. 32, 357	Locust, pp. 54, 229
Burning-bush, Strawberry-bush, p. 44	Lupines, p. 48, 227
Castor-bean, p. 53	Rattle-box, p. 42
Henbane , p. 45	Vetches, pp. 30, 230

4. POISONOUS BERRIES

Baneberry, p. 31	Melonette, pp. 49, 191
Beauty-berry, pp. 36, 271	Mezereum, p. 42
Bittersweet, p. 54	Mistletoe, p. 51
Black-berried Nightshade, pp. 56, 364	Moonseed, p. 49
Buckthorn, p. 68	Pride-of-India, China-tree, p. 48
English Ivy, p. 45	Privet, p. 47
Ground-Hemlock (stones), pp. 56, 76	

DESCRIPTIONS

Baneberry, Snakeberry, Necklace-berry
Actaea rubra (Ait.) Willd.
Actaea pachypoda Ell.

Family Apiaceae (Parsley Family)
Synonym *Actaea alba* (for *A. pachypoda*)
Key-characters herbs with slender, erect stems; bearing compound leaves divided on the plan of 3 into numerous oval, sharply toothed leaflets; berries cherry-red or ivory-white, short-ellipsoid, inch long, borne horizontally in elongate, loose clusters, in summer.
Habitat and Range rich woods and thickets, Newfoundland to British Columbia, south throughout the northern states and in upland woods southward.
Poisonous Part berry.

The **Baneberry** has such beautiful fruit that it should be known that the berries are somewhat poisonous. A few of them eaten by an experimenter caused dizziness and other symptoms which indicate their toxic power.

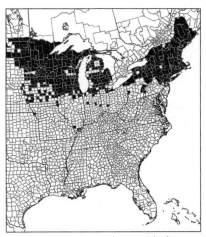

RED BANEBERRY *(Actaea rubra)*

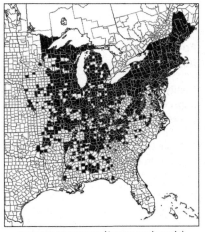

WHITE BANEBERRY *(Actaea pachypoda)*

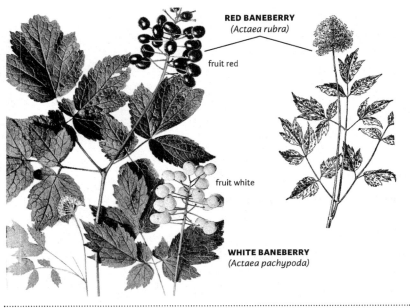

RED BANEBERRY
(*Actaea rubra*)

fruit red

fruit white

WHITE BANEBERRY
(*Actaea pachypoda*)

Horse-Chestnut, Buckeye
Aesculus (various species)

Family Sapindaceae (Soapberry Family)
Poisonous Part nuts (seeds).

Although some authors advocate the use of **Horse-Chestnuts** after thorough leaching (see p. 357), the nuts should be used with great caution, for the fresh seeds are notoriously poisonous, causing vertigo and coma. Children, who are so fond of collecting Horse-Chestnuts in the autumn, should be clearly instructed never to bite into them.

Fool's Parsley
Aethusa cynapium L.

Family Apiaceae (Parsley Family)
Key-characters slender plant strongly resembling parsley; the leaves beautifully dissected and fern-like; the secondary clusters of the umbels bearing slender, spreading or reflexed leafy bracts.
Habitat and Range waste grounds about towns, locally abundant in eastern Canada and the United States.
Poisonous Part all.

Fool's Parsley so strongly simulates carrots and the finer-leaved strains of parsley that it is very difficult to define differences which would be appreciated by the novice. Consequently, the strict rule must be adhered to: never pick to use as parsley the foliage of any wild plant.

Fly-poison
Amianthium muscaetoxicum (Walt.) Gray

Family Liliaceae (or Melanthiaceae, Lily Family)
Synonym *Chrosperma muscaetoxicum*
Key-characters bulb coated as in the onion, without its odor; leaves basal, broadly linear; flowers in an elongating raceme, the flowers on expanding white, with no glands at base of the segments, then turning green or slightly purplish, enlarging and persisting.
Habitat and Range acid peaty or sandy low woods, thickets and bogs, Florida to southern Missouri and Oklahoma, north along the mountains to West Virginia and Pennsylvania and on the coastal plain to Long Island.
Poisonous Part bulb.

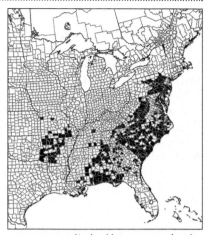

FLY-POISON *(Amianthium muscaetoxicum)*

Fly-poison, as its name implies, is deadly to flies, and is known to poison cattle. Recently, a well known botanist, after gathering the bulbs for drug-studies and most scrupulously washing his hands before touching his mouth, has spent some weeks prostrated and in the hospital. The toxic alkaloid in bulb and foliage is not one to treat lightly.

Death-Camass, White Camass, Poisonous Camass
Anticlea elegans (Pursh) Rydb.

Family Liliaceae (or Melanthiaceae, Lily Family)
Synonym *Zigadenus elegans*
Key-characters bulbous plants with narrow grass-like leaves clustered at base, the racemes or panicles with white, yellowish, greenish or bronze flowers with 6 segments, each segment with a shining spot (gland) at. base, the elongate capsule with 3 beaks.

bulb

FLY-POISON *(Amianthium muscaetoxicum)*

Habitat and Range one species or another across the continent from the lower St. Lawrence in Quebec to Alaska, south to our southernmost states. In gravels, rock-

crevices, meadow, prairie or sandy and peaty pinelands.
Poisonous Part bulb.

The related genus *Zigadenus*, which from Virginia southward also has a tall species (*Zigadenus glaberimus* Michx.) with stout rootstock instead of a bulb, but marked by the pale perianth with 6 glands at base, must be most scrupulously avoided by the seeker for edible bulbs. Its violently poisonous alkaloid, zygadenine, is responsible for the deaths of many grazing animals, statistics showing that in some droves which have been allowed to eat the plant more than half have died from the poison. The bulbs are attractive and look "good." In eastern Quebec, where one species abounds, it is reported to be "a powerful medicine for the guts."

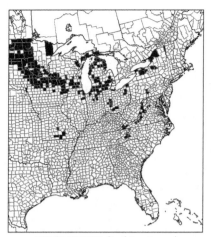

DEATH-CAMASS (*Anticlea elegans*)

Dogbanes, Indian-Hemp
Apocynum androsaemifolium L.
Apocynum cannabinum L.

Family Apocynaceae (Dogbane Family)
Key-characters herbs with cylindric stems having a milky juice similar to that of Milkweed; and opposite, oblong to ovate, nearly sessile leaves; stem soon forking and bearing ita bell-shaped flowers in loose, spreading clusters.
Habitat thickets, borders of woods and banks of streams.
Range throughout temperate America.
Poisonous Part all.

On account of their milky juice and opposite leaves the young sprouts of the **Dogbanes** might be confused with

DEATH-CAMASS (*Anticlea elegans*), flowers

the sprouts of the Milkweeds; but the young stems are usually tougher, entirely smooth, and quickly forking. The plants are emetic and cathartic and are sometimes held responsible for the poisoning of young cattle and sheep, even when dry. The name "Dogbane" was early transferred from a related Old

World genus. They are both related to the cultivated **Oleander**, well known to be poisonous if eaten.

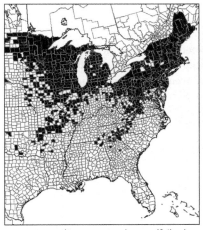
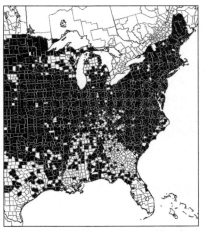

DOGBANE *(Apocynum androsaemifolium)* **INDIAN-HEMP** *(Apocynum cannabinum)*

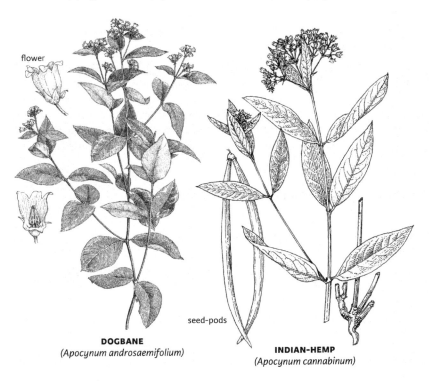

flower

seed-pods

DOGBANE
(Apocynum androsaemifolium)

INDIAN-HEMP
(Apocynum cannabinum)

Milkweeds
Asclepias

Family Apocynaceae (Dogbane Family)
Poisonous Part all (if eaten raw).

See p. 112. Although several of the **Milkweeds** supply wholesome and delicious cooked sprouts, buds and flowers, it should be kept constantly in mind that the raw plants are somewhat poisonous, even the common and much cooked *Asclepias syriaca* L. in the raw condition known to poison livestock.

Butterfly-weed
Asclepias tuberosa L.

Family Apocynaceae (Dogbane Family)
Poisonous Part root.

See p. 113.

Wild Indigo
Baptisia, several species

Family Fabaceae (Pea Family)
Poisonous Part all.

The **Wild Indigos**, *Baptisia tinctoria* (L.) R. Br., *B. alba* (L.) Vent., *B. australis* (L.) R. Br., etc., would never be tempting except before the sprouting stem has become tough and has branched. In the very young condition the shoots are thick and by some might be mistaken for asparagus. They are quickly told by having 3 leaflets which, not fully developed, will be found along the shoot. They grow chiefly in dry woods and clearings. They are reputed to poison browsing cattle.

Beauty-berry or French Mulberry
Callicarpa americana L.

Family Menthaceae (Mint Family)
Poisonous Part berry.

See p. 271. The pinkish, pungent-flavored berries are in the doubtful class.

Marsh-Marigold
Caltha palustris L.

Family Ranunculaceae (Buttercup Family)
Poisonous Part uncooked stems, leaves, flowers.

See p. 329. The boiled young plant is a wholesome and much appreciated potherb. The uncooked stems, leaves and flowers should not be eaten. They contain the deadly glucoside, helleborin, which is given off to the water in boiling.

Hemp
Cannabis sativa L.

Family Cannabaceae (Hemp Family)

The tall annual weed of rubbish-heaps, railroad-yards, etc., **Hemp**, should be known to all, for it is the source of the narcotic drug marijuana. The plant contains a number of potent alkaloids. Its most legitimate use is as a source of strong fiber. After the fiber is removed the waste is used in packing bottled goods. Consequently, waste, carrying seeds, is swept into backyards and waste lots, or from freight-cars to the freight-yards. See p. 174.

Yellow Jessamine
Gelsemium sempervirens (L.) Ait. f.

Family Gelsemiaceae (Trumpet-Flower Family)
Poisonous Part all.

Yellow Jessamine, climbing high in the trees, is in earliest spring one of the glories of the southeastern states, northward into Virginia, its superb funnel-shaped yellow flowers scenting the air with their delicious fragrance. They are so full of aroma that it is a temptation to let them wander to the mouth; but the distinguished botanist of North Carolina, Moses Ashley Curtis, recorded the deaths of children from sucking the corollas.

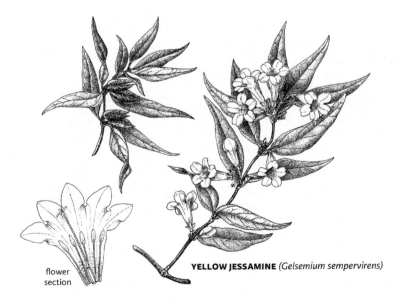

flower
section

YELLOW JESSAMINE *(Gelsemium sempervirens)*

Devil's-bit
Chamaelirium luteum (L.) Gray

Family Heloniadaceae (Swamp-Pink Family)
Poisonous Part all.

Devil's-bit (because its short rootstock looks as if bitten off at one end—by the Devil) is tender in the young condition and might be taken to be edible. Its stem arises from a short rootstock, is up to 2 feet high, with several flat and appressed, narrow, parallel-veined leaves, the lowest ones spatula-shaped and petioled; the inflorescence is a slender spike-like cluster of small yellow or greenish flowers with 6 segments, the male and female flowers on different plants. Growing in meadows and rich woods from Florida to Arkansas, north to western Massachusetts, New York and southern Ontario. If eaten it causes vomiting, itself not a recommendation; and it is closely related to many very poisonous genera.

DEVIL'S-BIT *(Chamaelirium luteum)*

Celandine or Swallow-wort
Chelidonium majus L.

Family Papaveraceae (Poppy Family)
Key-characters plant with a rosette of leaves developing in earliest spring or often over winter; the leaves somewhat resembling those of Winter-Cress but very pale in color, with midrib hairy beneath, and with a bright orange-colored milky juice; flowers yellow, like tiny poppies, followed by slender, elongate pods somewhat resembling those of a mustard.
Habitat about old houses, cellar-holes, wood-roads, and other half-wild or neglected spots near towns.
Range throughout the eastern states.
Poisonous Part all.

Celandine is not likely to be eaten by one who first tastes it, for it has a

CELANDINE *(Chelidonium majus)*

strong, bitter, yellow juice; but in its vigorous early growth it so strongly resembles **Winter-Cress**, which often grows with it, that care should be taken by the beginner sharply to distinguish between the two.

It is a member of the Poppy Family, in which toxic or narcotic properties are frequently present, and has long been viewed with suspicion. However, when young and inexperienced domestic rabbits, who instinctively turn away from leaves of *Nicotiana*, which many humans more and more consume, get into a patch of Celandine, they devour all within reach. Taking this hint, the senior author has eaten young Celandine-leaves, dressed with oil and vinegar, with some enjoyment; nor has he acquired a habit from so doing. Perhaps *Chelidonium* has been slandered. In many families which supply our most prized vegetables, the Apiaceae, Solanaceae and Fabaceae, for instance, harmless and toxic genera both occur. Celandine should be checked.

Bulb-bearing Water-Hemlock
Cicuta bulbifera L.

Family Apiaceae (Parsley Family)
Key-characters plant somewhat re-sembling carrot or caraway, but with the stem taller; the lower leaves with 3 primary forkings and with numerous, very elongate and slender leaflets; the upper branches and the leaf-axils bearing numerous small bulblets; root similar to that of the last species but smaller.
Habitat and Range Shallow water and swamps, throughout north-central and northeastern America.
Poisonous Part fleshy roots.

The root is presumably as poisonous as that of the larger **Water-Hemlock**.

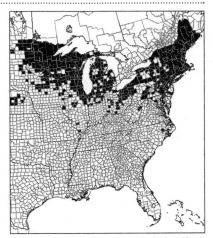

BULB-BEARING WATER-HEMLOCK *(C. bulbifera)*

Water-Hemlock or Beaver-poison
Cicuta maculata L.

Family Apiaceae (Parsley Family)
Key-characters plant somewhat resembling the carrot plant, but with much coarser leaves and thicker and taller stem (commonly several feet high); the lower leaves with the leaf-stalk 3-forked and bearing lance-shaped to egg-shaped, toothed leaflets 1-4 inches long; stem smooth, round and hollow, 2-8 ft. high, with alternate leaves having a broadly winged base; flowers in flat-topped umbrella-like clusters, white; the dry fruits plump, grooved on the surfaces, scarcely 1/8 inch long; root, when well filled from autumn to spring, consisting of a bunch of tuber-like branches 1 to 4 inches long, fleshy and with the odor of parsnips.

Habitat meadows, swales and shallow water.
Range throughout temperate eastern America; related species westward and southward.
Poisonous Part fleshy roots.

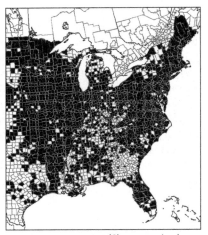

WATER-HEMLOCK *(Cicuta maculata)*

The **Water-Hemlock** is one of the most dangerous of our wild plants because from autumn to spring its roots, resembling dahlia-roots and smelling like parsnips, are by the untrained often mistaken for small, wild parsnips. Many cases of fatal poisoning of children and ignorant laborers who have indulged in these little "parsnips" are recorded. The roots are frequently thrown out of the ground by the action of frost or of water, and everyone who has children or who attempts to eat any wild roots should be thoroughly acquainted with the plant.

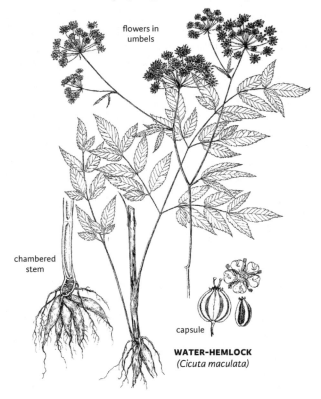

flowers in umbels

chambered stem

capsule

WATER-HEMLOCK
(Cicuta maculata)

Poison Hemlock
Conium maculatum L.

Family Apiaceae (Parsley Family)
Key-characters foliage finely dissected and fern-like, strongly suggesting carrot- or parsley-leaves; the stem coarse and cylindric, heavily spotted with large and small purple, sticky blotches; flowers white, in flat- topped umbrella-like clusters.
Habitat waste lands, dumping grounds, old lime-quarries, and roadsides about towns.
Range locally abundant about ports and occasionally inland throughout the eastern and central states.
Poisonous Part all.

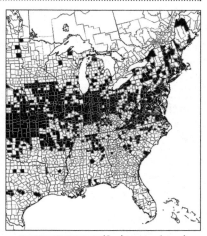

POISON HEMLOCK *(Conium maculatum)*

On account of the strong resemblance of its foliage to parsley and its odor suggestive of the cultivated members of the parsley family, **Poison Hemlock** should be known to every person who attempts to gather wild plants for food.

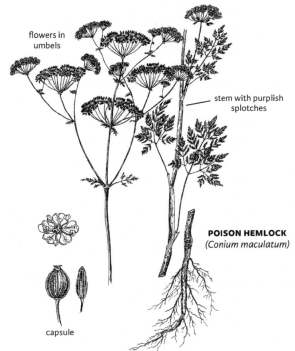

flowers in umbels

stem with purplish splotches

POISON HEMLOCK
(Conium maculatum)

capsule

And never should the novice attempt to gather to eat any foliage of a wild plant which he supposes to be parsley nor seeds which he supposes to be anise or caraway! Since classical times Poison Hemlock has been famous as one of the deadliest of plants, being the basis of various suicidal cups recorded in literature. While the roots of the **Water-Hemlock** (*Cicuta*) produce violent convulsions, the Poison-Hemlock (either leaves or seeds) produces a paralysis which eventually results in death, although the mind is said to remain clear until the end. The toxic principle is the alkaloid, coniine.

Rattle-box
Crotalaria, ca. six species

Family Fabaceae (Pea Family)
Key-characters herbs with yellow pea-like flowers and simple, narrow to rounded, sessile leaves alternate on the stem, these often accompanied by inversely arrow-shaped stipules along the stem; pods like small pea-pods, inflated, the peas soon loosening and rattling when the plant is shaken.
Habitat and Range native species from Tropical America north to southern New England, New York, Ohio, Michigan, Wisconsin, Minnesota, etc.; cultivated species (for soil-renovation and forage) south ward.
Poisonous Part seeds.

The small pea-like seeds of **Rattle-box** have been recommended as substitutes for coffee, but caution should be exercised in using them. Muenscher states that recent experiments have demonstrated that the ground seeds are poisonous to pigs, whole seed to poultry, and the herbage to cattle. Roasting, of course, may dispose of the toxic alkaloid.

Mezereum, Daphne
Daphne mezereum L.

Family Thymelaeaceae (Mezereum Family)
Poisonous Part berry.

This old-fashioned garden shrub often escapes from cultivation to rocky banks, particularly to abandoned lime-quarries and similar places, and on account of its handsome red berries, borne in dense masses along the branches, is apt to prove tempting. The berries of various members of the genus *Daphne*, however, are highly poisonous and Linnaeus records a case in which a girl died after eating only twelve berries. The fragrance of the flowers is said sometimes to produce headache.

MEZEREUM (*Daphne mezereum*)

Jimson-weed, Thorn-Apple, Stramonium
Datura stramonium L. and other species

Family Solanaceae (Nightshade Family)
Key-characters coarse, loosely branched, annual herbs, commonly 2 to 4 feet high; with very coarsely toothed large leaves (often 4-6 inches long); flowers petunia- or nicotiana-like, white or violet, borne in the leaf-axils or forks of the stems; fruit an egg-shaped, usually soft-prickly capsule 1-1/2 to 3 inches long, with a conspicuous, reflexed papery disc at base, cracking into 4 valves; seeds lentil-like.
Habitat waste lands, vacant lots, railroad-yards, roadsides, and occasionally in cultivated fields, about towns.
Range throughout temperate and tropical regions, often too abundant.
Poisonous Part all, especially seeds.

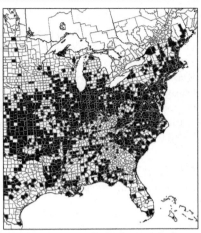

JIMSON-WEED *(Datura stramonium)*

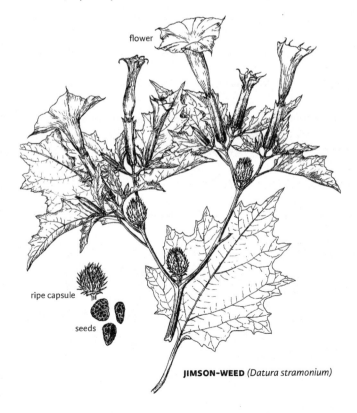

flower

ripe capsule

seeds

JIMSON-WEED *(Datura stramonium)*

Jimson-weed, which is one of the most dangerous weeds of vacant lots and rubbish-heaps about towns, should be known to every parent, since its fruits are interesting and attractive to children and its flowers suggest wild petunias. The whole plant, and particularly the seeds, is violently poisonous, containing the two powerful alkaloids, atropin and hyoscyanin. Many cases of poisoning of children by the seeds have been reported, especially of youngsters playing "Indian" and attempting to eat wild things which attract them. The trumpet-shaped flowers are pretty, and children have been poisoned by sucking the trumpets; while the fresh, angular-toothed leaves have been mistaken for spinach and have been eaten with disastrous results. The plant rarely produces vomiting, so that, if a child is suspected to have eaten it, emetics should be given without delay.

Mexican Tea
Dysphania ambrosioides (L.) Mosyakin & Clemants

Family Amaranthaceae (Amaranth Family)
Synonym *Chenopodium ambrosioides*
Poisonous Part shoots, leaves.

See p. 94.

Horsetail
Equisetum

Family Equisetaceae (Horsetail Family)
Poisonous Part all.

For discussion see p. 64. Since the **Horsetails** contain aconitic acid and are known to poison grazing animals it is very unwise, if one could possibly be tempted to do so, to eat the new sprouts.

Burning-bush, Strawberry-bush
Euonymus atropurpureus Jacq.
Euonymus americanus L.

Family Celastraceae (Bittersweet Family)
Poisonous Part fruits.

The brilliantly colored fruits, especially of the **Strawberry-bush** *(E. americanus)* of woodlands, are likely to be tempting. Muenscher states that children have been seriously poisoned by trying to eat the seeds of this genus.

BURNING-BUSH *(Euonymus atropurpureus)*

English Ivy
Hedera helix L.

Family Araliaceae (Ginseng Family)
Poisonous Part berry.

The generally cultivated and sometimes naturalized **English Ivy** has attractive red berries. Children should be taught that they are poisonous.

Velvet-grass
Holcus lanatus L.

Family Poaceae (Grass Family)
Poisonous Part shoots, leaves.

The velvety grass of fields with leaves and culms temptingly soft to the touch should not be chewed, as the young bases of some grass-joints are nibbled. Both in the fresh and dry condition it contains the poisonous hydrocyanic acid.

VELVET-GRASS *(Holcus lanatus)*

Henbane
Hyoscyamus niger L.

Family Solanaceae (Nightshade Family)
Key-characters annual weed, with the stem and sharply angled and cleft leaves covered with a slimy, foul-smelling hairiness; the flowers, borne from the upper leaf-axils, with lurid, buff or yellowish, flaring corolla (about an inch broad) strongly veined with black or dark purple; fruit urn-shaped, surrounded by the firm, 5-toothed dry calyx, about 1/2 inch long.
Habitat and Range roadsides and waste grounds, locally abundant in the province of Quebec and occasionally elsewhere, west to Michigan and south into the northern states.
Poisonous Part all, especially seeds.

On account of its slimy hairs and disgusting odor **Henbane** is not likely to tempt adults; but in many parts of Quebec (as, for instance, about the city of Quebec), it is so common that every one should be informed of its poisonous properties. The plant is the source of the hypnotic poison, hyoscyanin, which in its action strongly resembles atropin. In case children are known to have eaten the seeds they should promptly be given a powerful purgative and the physician got with all speed.

Jewel-weed, Touch-me-not
Impatiens, four species

Family Balsaminaceae (Touch-Me-Not Family)
Poisonous Part all (if eaten).

The watery young stems and tender upper leaves of **Jewel-weed** might seem succulent enough to eat. It should be borne in mind that the plants have the reputation of being emetic and poisonous to stock. However, the juice of the stems does provide relief from the itch of **Stinging Nettle** and the rash of **Poison-Ivy** when rubbed on the skin.

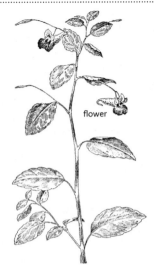

flower

JEWEL-WEED *(Impatiens capensis)*

Blue Flag
Iris versicolor L., and other species

Family Iridaceae (Iris Family)
Poisonous Part rootstock.

The common **Blue Flag or Iris** of meadow-lands has a bad reputation, the rootstock when eaten often causing fatality. The root is violently emetic and cathartic, containing the poisonous irisin, and great care should be taken not to confuse it with the edible **Sweet Flag or Calamus** (see p. 118), which superficially resembles it and grows in similar habitats. At flowering time there is no danger of confusion, but in the young, sprouting stage or in fruit the differences are less conspicuous.

Sweet Flag has yellowish-green foliage and when bruised gives off an aromatic fragrance; Blue Flag has darker-green foliage and no pleasant aroma. Sweet Flag has minute flowers in dry, drab, finger-like spikes, borne from the side of a leaf-like stalk; Blue Flag has the

flower large, showy

BLUE-FLAG *(Iris versicolor)*

familiar purple Iris flower, succeeded by an ellipsoid 3-valved pod. The rootstock of the Sweet Flag is gingery in odor and taste; that of the Blue Flag is essentially odorless and with a strong, disagreeable flavor.

Red-root
Lachnanthes caroliniana (Lam.) Dandy

Family   Haemodoraceae   (Bloodwort Family)
Synonyms   *Gyrotheca   tinctorium*, *Lachnanthes tinctorium*.
Key-characters leaves grass-like or iris-like; rootstock and subterranean runners as thick as a pencil, bright red; flower-stem somewhat leafy, bearing at the summit a flat-topped, white-woolly cluster of creamy-white 6-parted flowers 1/2 inch long.
Habitat and Range wet sandy or peaty pond-margins, cranberry-bogs, etc., Florida to Louisiana, northward, chiefly on the coastal plain, to southeastern Massachusetts; also western Nova Scotia.
Poisonous Part rootstock.

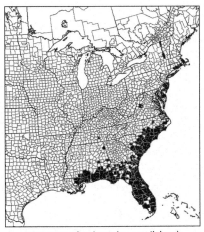

RED-ROOT *(Lachnanthes caroliniana)*

The succulent red rootstocks and runners of **Red-root** might prove attractive to the searcher for edible roots, especially since it is often associated with *Lycopus* (see p. 272) or with *Stachys hyssopifolia* (p. 272) and could easily be gathered with them. It is well recognized in the South as poisonous to hogs, animals which are not always too fastidious about their diet. It is generally stated, however, that in Australia the natives roast and eat the fleshy roots of the closely related genus *Haemodorum*. The rootstocks of our Red-root, roasted, may prove to be harmless, if anyone wishes cautiously to make the test.

Privet
Ligustrum vulgare L. and other species

Family Oleaceae (Olive Family)
Poisonous Part berry.

The **Privets**, now naturalized in rocky woods of the eastern states, have py-

PRIVET *(Ligustrum ovalifolium)*

ramidal or roundish clusters of blackish berries, which are likely to be tasted by children. Several cases are definitely recorded of children being poisoned by eating the berries.

Lupines
Lupinus perennis L. and other species

Family Fabaceae (Pea Family)
Key-characters plants with erect or sprawling stems, bearing alternate long-stalked leaves with numerous elongate leaflets radiating from a common point; pods numerous, in long clusters, resembling pea-pods; peas somewhat flat.
Habitat and Range dry, open soils, common southward, extending northward to Minnesota and Prince Edward Island.
Poisonous Part all, especially seeds.

The seeds of **Lupines** have sometimes been recommended as substitutes for peas but they should be used with extreme caution or probably not at alL It has been fully demonstrated that the

LUPINE *(Lupinus perennis)*

seeds of many species contain a powerful alkaloid and cause a disease of domestic animals, long known in Europe as "lupinosis."

Pimpernel
Lysimachia arvensis (L.) U. Manns & A. Anderb.

Family Primulaceae (Primrose Family)
Synonym *Anagallis arvensis*
Poisonous Part all.

Although **Pimpernel** (see p. 327) has been advocated by some as a salad or potherb, it is sometimes said to be poisonous. We do not know.

Pride-of-India, China-tree, "Mahogany"
Melia azedarach L.

Family Meliaceae (Mahogany Family)
Poisonous Part berry.

Pride-of-India or, as it is locally known, "Mahogany," is very familiar, either planted or wild, in the South. No one who has tasted its large, thin-fleshed drupes is apt to do it again. They are wholly unpalatable, but children who do not discriminate are often poisoned by eating them.

Melonette
Melothria pendula L.

Family Cucurbitaceae (Gourd Family)
Poisonous Part berry.

See p. 191. The berries are not likely to be eaten twice. They are said to be "a drastic purgative."

Moonseed
Menispermum canadense L.

Family Menispermaceae (Moonseed Family)
Poisonous Part berry.

The twining shrub, **Moonseed**, so strongly suggests a grape-vine that the unobservant might mistake it. Its stems do not become strongly woody nor covered with dark and shreddy bark; its leaves are attached to the footstalk a

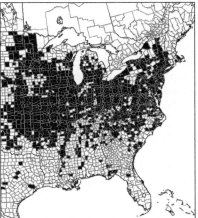

MOONSEED *(Menispermum canadense)*

grape-like
fruit

MOONSEED
(Menispermum canadense)

little way in from the margin, and the drupes have a single crescent-shaped stone. They are bitter and unpalatable but have poisoned children eating them.

Apple-of-Peru
Nicandra physalodes (L.) Scop.

Family Solanaceae (Nightshade Family)
Synonym *Physalodes physalodes*
Poisonous Part all

The old-fashioned garden plant, **Apple-of-Peru**, is now-a-days comparatively rare but it still persists in some country gardens, where it is allowed to grow for its rather attractive, blue, petunia-like flowers and its curious fruits with dry, 5-angled, bladdery husk. It should be generally known, then, that the plant is so poisonous as sometimes to be used as a fly-poison. Children should be taught not to eat the seeds.

Star-of-Bethlehem
Ornithogalum umbellatum L.

Family Liliaceae (or Hyacinthaceae, Lily Family)
Poisonous Part bulb.

Although sometimes advocated for food (see p. 262), the bulbs should not be eaten. They and the foliage are poisonous, either dry or fresh, to herbivorous animals.

Cowbane
Oxypolis rigidior (L.) Raf.

Family Apiaceae (Parsley Family)
Key-characters somewhat suggesting the parsnip plant, but the flowers white instead of yellow; leaves simply pinnate, with 3-9 lance-shaped or more slender coarsely toothed leaflets 1 to 5 inches long; root a cluster of slender-stalked thickened fibers resembling small sweet potatoes in form but with the odor of parsnip.
Habitat swamps, wet woods, springy meadows and sloughs.
Range New York to Minnesota and southward.

STAR-OF-BETHLEHEM (*O. umbellatum*)

Poisonous Part fleshy roots.

Cowbane has a bad reputation, having been charged with the death of cattle. Its roots, from their resemblance to sweet potatoes with the odor of parsnips, are likely to prove tempting to those unaware of the danger of eating them.

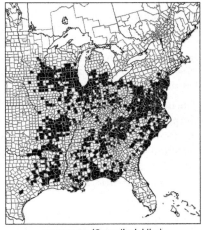

COWBANE *(Oxypolis rigidior)*

capsule

COWBANE
(Oxypolis rigidior)

Mistletoe
Phoradendron leucarpum (Raf.) Reveal & M.C. Johnston

Family Santalaceae (Sandalwood Family)
Synonym *Phoradendron flavescens*
Poisonous Part berry.

The white berries of the **American Mistletoe** might prove tempting to children; but it should be known that, in the Southern states several deaths of children have been attributed to the eating of these berries.

Pokeweed, Pigeon-berry, Garget
Phytolacca americana L.

Family Phytolaccaceae (Pokeweed Family)
Synonym *Phytolacca decandra*
Poisonous Part root

The new shoots of **Pokeweed** are much eaten as a substitute for asparagus and the plant is described and fully discussed in the next chapter (p. 295). The large tap-root, however, often as large as the human leg, is poisonous and, although very fleshy and succulent and many times larger than a good-sized parsnip, is not safe to experiment with as food. The root has long been reputed in medicine a powerful narcotic, emetic and cathartic, frequently causing death.

May-Apple, "Mandrake" or Wild Jalap
Podophyllum peltatum L.

Family Berberidaceae (Barberry Family)
Poisonous Part rootstock

The fruit of the **May-Apple** is edible, the plant being discussed under the edible species, p. 154. The rootstock, however, is poisonous, producing a fatal prostration. It somewhat resembles the rootstock of the common **Solomon's-seal** and the plant grows in rich woods where Solomon's-seal abounds. Especial care should therefore be taken in gathering the latter to guard against including rootstocks of the May-Apple. The rootstock lacks the circular scars which characterize that of Solomon's-seal; and its taste is said to be repugnant—strong and bitter, the rootstock of Solomon's-seal being slightly acrid but not bitter.

Cherry, Plum and Peach
Prunus

Family Rosaceae (Rose Family)
Poisonous Part leaves.

See p. 340. No one should attempt to make tea of the leaves. As soon as wilted they develop hydrocyanic acid and they have long been known to kill browsing animals.

Buckthorn
Rhamnus (various species)

Family Rhamnaceae (Buckthorn Family)
Key-characters shrubs or trees with alternate, finely toothed and itrongly veined leaves somewhat resembling cherry-leaves; bearing clusters of black, juicy berries along the branches and branchlets, the berries with 2-4 hard nutlets and persisting over winter.
Habitat various species, indigenous or introduced, in swamps or rocky woods.

Range Newfoundland to British Columbia and southward.
Poisonous Part berry.

The **Buckthorns** have handsome but often disagreeably bitter-sweet berries, which are not likely to be eaten in quantity. The berries of some are poisonous, though of others they are said to be palatable, but the juice of probably all members of the genus may be cathartic. One closely related species, *Frangula purshiana* (DC.) Cooper (formerly *Rhamnus purshiana*), of the Pacific slope, is an important source of cascara; and the commonly introduced *R. cathartica* L., which is abundantly naturalized in many parts of New England and other eastern states, was thus described by Dodoens in the 16th century: the berries "be not meete to be ministered but to young and lustie people of the countrie which doe set more store of their money than their lives." In northern Maine and New Brunswick the country children look with well founded terror upon the berries of the native *R. alnifolia* L'Hér of the swamps, a small boy once pointing them out to one of the writers with the remark: "Them is terrible things for the guts."

Castor-bean, Castor-oil-plant
Ricinus communis L.

Family Euphorbiaceae (Spurge Family)
Poisonous Part all, especially raw seeds.

Everyone should be aware of the violently poisonous properties of the **Castor-bean**, one of the popular ornamental plants of gardens and found throughout the southeastern USA. Belonging to a family notorious for its poisonous properties, the plant is chiefly famous as the source of the well-remembered castor oil. Although Ochse states that the Javanese cook and eat the young foliage and inflorescence of Castor-bean, it is wise not to imitate them. All parts of the plant, but especially the raw seed, contain the blood-poison, ricin. The plant poison sdomestic animals and three seeds have proved fatal to humans.

CASTOR-BEAN *(Ricinus communis)*

Locust
Robinia (various species)

Family Fabaceae (Pea Family)
Poisonous Part all, especially seeds.

Although the flowers and roots of the **Locust** tree have been advocated by some as food (see p. 229), the bark and leaves of some species have proved fatal to people eating them, and it has sometimes been stated that the root is also a dangerous poison. The seeds, when eaten, cause violent poisoning.

Bloodroot
Sanguinaria canadensis L.

Family Papaveraceae (Poppy Family)
Poisonous Part rootstock.

Bloodroot is too well known to all lovers of early spring flowers to need description, but a word of caution is wise lest some enthusiast should attempt to cook and eat its large, succulent root-stock. Few are likely to attempt this, however, for it is bitter and acrid. In small quantities it is said to stimulate gastric secretions and to aid digestion, but in large quantities it produces poisoning, with vomiting, dizziness and paralysis.

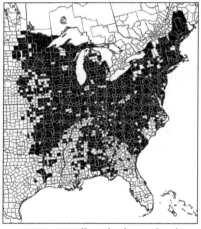

BLOODROOT *(Sanguinaria canadense)*

Bittersweet or Nightshade
Solanum dulcamara L.

Family Solanaceae (Nightshade Family)
Key-characters a climbing, vine-like shrub with the old branches woody; bearing alternate, irregularly lobed or cleft, or sometimes uncut, leaves, with the principal divisions oval and somewhat one-sided; producing from the stem, below or opposite the leaves, loose clusters of bright red, many-seeded, ovoid berries 1/3 inch long, with a 5-toothed green calyx at base.
Habitat rich thickets, especially in damp ground.

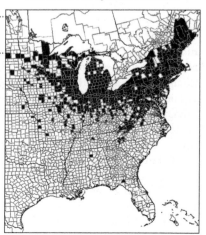

BITTERSWEET *(Solanum dulcamara)*

Range naturalized in most civilized regions of temperate America.
Poisonous Part berry.

The berries of **Bittersweet** (not to be confused with *Celastrus*, p. 182) have long been the subject of controversy, since by some people they have been thought poisonous, by others harmless. Experiments have shown that the juice fed to rabbits is fatal and, although there are evidently some people who can eat them (if they wish) without harmful results, it is wisest for most people, and especially children, to let them alone. The foliage of these plants contains the poisonous glucoside, solanine. Muenscher, in his *Poisonous Plants of the United States*, is reassuring, however, for he states that "Boiling apparently destroys the toxic principle."

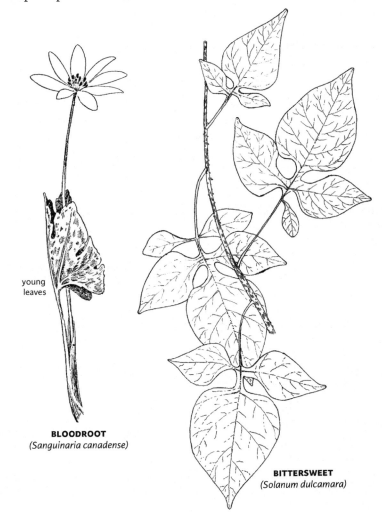

young
leaves

BLOODROOT
(Sanguinaria canadense)

BITTERSWEET
(Solanum dulcamara)

Black-berried Nightshade
Solanum nigrum L.

Family Solanaceae (Nightshade Family)
Poisonous Part berry.

The **Black-berried Nightshade** is discussed under edible plants (p. 334). For several years a large-fruited strain of this affinity was exploited by Luther Burbank (as a substitute for Blueberries!). It should be stated, however, that the berries of this species, like those of the Bittersweet, are harmful to some people and have been demonstrated to poison sheep, goats and other domestic animals. It is wisest, then, to be cautious about eating the berries, and children should be taught to leave them alone.

Ground-Hemlock
Taxus canadensis Marsh.

Family Taxaceae (Yew Family)
Poisonous Part berry.

See p. 77. The pulp of the bright red fruits is edible, but the stone is very poisonous, containing the toxic alkaloid, taxine.

Hoary Pea, Goat's Rue, Cat-gut
Tephrosia virginiana (L.) Pers. and several other species

Family Fabaceae (Pea Family)
Synonym *Cracca virginiana*
Key-characters a silvery-hairy plant about a foot high, with numerous wiry stems from a stout root, bearing many alternate leaves with numerous narrow leaflets; flowers like pea-blossoms, showy, clustered at the tops of the stems, variously colored with yellow, pink and purple; pods like long, flat and slender bean-pods; beans flat, like lentils.
Habitat and Range dry sandy barrens or open, oak or pine woods, common in the southeastern states, extending north to Minnesota and southern New Hampshire.
Poisonous Part all, especially seeds.

HOARY PEA *(Tephrosia virginiana)*

On account of its abundant, lentil-like seeds, the **Hoary Pea** (*Tephrosia virginiana*) is apt to be tempting; but it should be borne in mind that the juice of the plant was used by the Indians as a fish-poison, just as its close relative, *Tephrosia toxicaria*, is still used by the Mexican Indians. The roots fed to guinea pigs have proved highly poisonous.

Arrow-grass
Triglochin

Family Juncaginaceae (Arrow-Grass Family)
Poisonous Part all, if uncooked.

See p. 247. Although the scale-like seeds of **Arrow-grass** have been parched and used as coffee, it should be remembered that the fresh plant contains hydrocyanic acid and is harmful to grazing animals. The fruit, however, contains little, probably less than the large seeds in peach-stones, and may be harmless if one is forced to use it.

Indian Poke or White Hellebore
Veratrum viride Ait.

Family Liliaceae (or Melanthiaceae)
Key-characters leafy-stemmed plant with large, at first overlapping, oval or elliptic, alternate, longitudinally fluted or corrugated leaves conspicuous in early spring and tempting on account of the succulence of the quickly heightening shoots which soon produce long and loosely branched, open-pyramidal inflorescences of greenish flowers with 6 perianth-segments.
Habitat and Range meadows, low woods, banks of streams, etc., from eastern Quebec to western Ontario and southward.
Poisonous Part all.

INDIAN POKE (*Veratrum viride*)

Indian Poke, on account of its attractive appearance in early spring and its abundance in places where edible new shoots, such as those of **Marsh-Marigold**, **Water-Cress** and **Skunk-Cabbage** abound, should be known to every one, since it is so easy accidentally to include a bit of it in a hastily gathered basket of greens. The plant is violently narcotic, containing poisonous alkaloids, and in a few cases has been demonstrated as the source of death, although ordinarily quick treatment with cardiac and respiratory stimulants is likely to prove beneficial, especially since the poison is spontaneously vomited.

Atamasco Lily
Zephyranthes atamasca (L.) Herbert and other species

Family Amaryllidaceae (Daffodil Family)
Synonym *Atomasco atamasca*

Key-characters bulb suggesting an onion but without its odor; leaves similar to those of Narcissus; flower a handsome erect Amaryllis, a white to pinkish funnelform 6-parted flower 3-5 inches high, with 6 stamens, the flower on a naked stem with a 2-parted bract at summit.

Habitat and Range *Z. atamasca* in rich woods and damp clearings from Florida to Mississippi, north to Virginia, flowering in spring; other species southward.

Poisonous Part bulb.

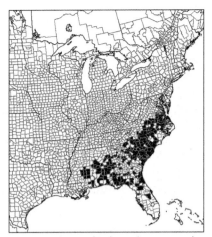

ATAMASCO LILY (*Zephyranthes atamasca*)

In the South "staggers" of horses are often supposed to be caused by eating the foliage of **Atamasco Lily**. The plant is related to **Amaryllis**, **Narcissus** and some other genera which have toxic alkaloids. It is safest to avoid it.

pleated leaves

INDIAN POKE
(*Veratrum viride*)

ATAMASCO LILY
(*Zephyranthes atamasca*)

INDIAN POKE *(Veratrum viride)*, young plants in spring.

POISON HEMLOCK *(Conium maculatum)*, the purplish splotches on the stem are characteristic.

CHAPTER THREE

Edible Plants of Eastern North America

In this Chapter, plants are first ordered by group—Ferns and Fern Relatives, Conifers, and Seed Plants (the 'Monocots' and 'Dicots'). Within each group, plant families are arranged alphabetically (by the scientific name of the family); within each family, genera and species are listed in alphabetical order, again by their scientific name.

Dennstaedtiaceae BRACKEN FERN FAMILY

Pasture-Brake, Bracken
Pteridium aquilinum (L.) Kuhn

Key-characters a coarse fern with solitary or scattered young stalks often 1/2 inch thick at base, nearly cylindric and heavily covered with rusty felt; the uncoiling frond (crozier) distinctly 3-forked, usually with a purplish spot at the angles which secretes a sweetish juice; old fronds of last year coarse and conspicuously 3-forked; rootstock extensively creeping and branching, blackish and almost woody, about 1/4 inch thick.

Habitat dry open woods, recently burned clearings, pastures, etc.

Range throughout America, from Newfoundland to the Rocky Mountains and southward; other closely related Brackens northwest to Alaska and southward into Mexico.

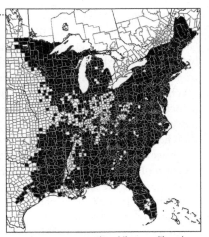

PASTURE-BRAKE *(Pteridium aquilinum)*

Season of Availability spring, before the croziers (young fronds) are unrolled.

Uses cooked vegetable, substitute for asparagus, nibble, masticatory (but see **Caution**, p. 62).

The **Pasture-Brake** is by all means the most widely known and generally the commonest of our ferns. Nevertheless, it is surprising how very few people know of its value and unlimited availability as a green vegetable in early spring, before the garden asparagus and peas are ready to use. In some regions, as New Zealand and Japan, closely related varieties of Bracken have long been used and are highly valued; but in Europe and America the use of the new uncoiled fronds is decidedly modern and as yet only a few people appreciate them.

Select the stouter stalks when very young and not more than 6 or 8 inches high; break as low down as tender, draw through the closed hand to remove the wool, wash and bunch like asparagus and boil in salted water or steam until tender (usually half-an-hour to an hour), season with salt and pepper and dress with melted butter or oil or with a cream sauce; serve with or without toast, as preferred. Or break or cut like string beans into short pieces, taking care to use only the tender, upper parts, cook in a little salted water, and season and dress as above, serving like string beans.

The raw stalks have very mucilaginous juice, so that some people enjoy eating the uncooked stalks as a relish or a masticatory. The juice is somewhat altered in cooking, but the boiled vegetable retains some of the mucilaginous quality. On this account the Pasture-Brake is not attractive to some palates, but to most people who have tried it properly prepared it has proved an interesting and palatable novelty. Surely there is an unlimited supply and until the Pasture-Brake becomes more generally used there is no danger of its extermination—a danger the Japanese have found it necessary to forestall by drastic laws.

The close relatives of our Bracken, in New Zealand, in the southwestern United States and in Europe, have a starchy layer in the rootstock, which is broken up by crushing, the starch being sufficiently abundant to be of economic importance. The rootstock of our plant has too little starch to be of value.

When the fronds of Bracken are full-grown and tough they develop toxic principles which sometimes poison grazing animals. No one in his right mind, however, would think of eating old, dry and hard Pasture-Brake any more than he would eat the foliage of his beans, squashes or tomatoes. When young and uncoiling the croziers seem to be wholesome.

Caution Bracken fern fiddleheads contain the carcinogenic terpene *ptaquiloside* and large quantities of these fiddleheads should probably not be eaten. However, as ptaquiloside is water-soluble, soaking Braken fiddleheads in cool water (to keep them crunchy) and changing the water several times, will greatly reduce ptaquiloside levels. Also, cooking, especially in salted water, almost completely destroys the carcinogen. Both of these techniques are employed in Korea, Japan and parts of China, where Braken is a very popular vegetable (for more information, see *The Atlantic* magazine online, June 30, 2011, at *www.theatlantic.com*).

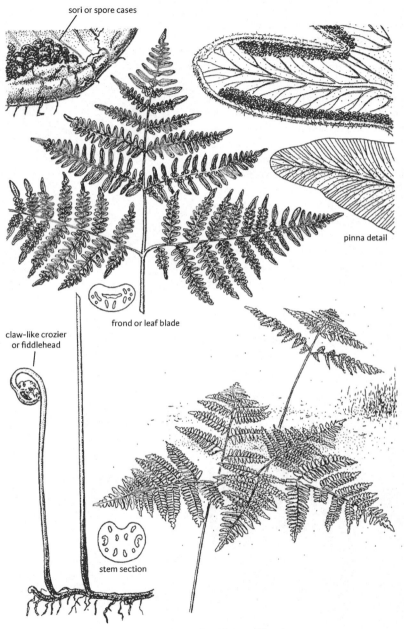

sori or spore cases

pinna detail

frond or leaf blade

claw-like crozier or fiddlehead

stem section

PASTURE-BRAKE *(Pteridium aquilinum)*

Equisetaceae HORSETAIL FAMILY

Water Horsetail, Pipes, Joint-grass
Equisetum fluviatile L.

Sturtevant states that this plant was eaten by the Romans, and he quotes Coles (17th century) as stating that "the young heads are dressed by some like asparagus, or being boyled are often bestrewed with flower and fried to be eaten." Johnson ascribes the same use to the more highly silicious **Scouring Rush**, *Equisetum hyemale* L.; but, were we forced to eat either, we should select *Equisetum fluviatile* as the less gritty. It is better to avoid the group as food, for the plants, which develop a powerful nerve-poison (aconitic acid), are well known to poison grazing animals. See p. 44.

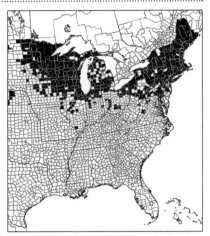

WATER HORSETAIL (*Equisetum fluviatile*)

WATER HORSETAIL (*Equisetum fluviatile*)

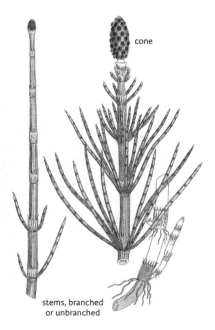

cone

stems, branched or unbranched

Onocleaceae SENSITIVE FERN FAMILY

Ostrich-Fern
Matteuccia struthiopteris (L.) Todaro

Key-characters young fronds forming dense, vase-like clumps borne from a long deep-creeping and freely forking rootstock; the old persistent remnants of last year's fruiting fronds resembling thick, dark-brown feathers, with numerous crowded, ascending, dry, necklace-like rows of rounded lobes; new fronds with stout stalks (stipes) bearing brown, papery, quickly deciduous, broad scales and with a feather-like leafy summit.
Habitat rich alluvium of streams, or northward in rich woods or on fertile slopes.
Range Newfoundland to British Columbia, south to upland Virginia, the Great Lakes States, Missouri and South Dakota.
Season of Availability spring, just before the uncoiling of the frond.
Uses as asparagus, escalloped vegetable.

OSTRICH-FERN *(Matteucchia struthiopteris)*

Few other substitutes for asparagus ever graced a slice of toast with as much promise of furnishing a substantial meal as lies in the thick, succulent, young unrolled fronds of the **Ostrich-Fern**. Abounding in the alluvial woods of the northern states and Canada and following many of the fertile valleys from near their sources quite to the lower reaches, the plant is sufficiently abundant to be gathered without fear of extermination, especially if some fronds are left to develop on the depleted crown. On a fishing or tramping trip in May, or northward in June, or in the mountains of Gaspé or in Newfoundland even in July, it makes a readily available and satisfying vegetable, quickly gathered and prepared; while two or three of the vase-like young crowns, when carried home, furnish an abundant meal for an average family. The tender young croziers are of dryish texture as contrasted with the mucilaginous quality of the **Pasture-Brake**, although the flavor of the two is similar. It is probable that bleaching by covering the newly pushing crowns with litter would render them of even better quality, but it would be an exceptional and squeamish individual who would object, at least when camping, to the well-cooked green croziers.

The tall plume-like fronds of the Ostrich-Fern are familiar along rich valleys in midsummer, when they form almost impenetrable thickets from 1 to 3 yards in height; but at that season they are tough and quite inedible. They are, however, easiest detected when in full development and good foraging grounds for the spring harvest may then be advantageously noted.

PREPARATION

The young croziers should be washed thoroughly, removing the dry papery scales (including those in the tightly coiled leafy tip) and the hard bases of the stalks, sprinkled with salt rather freely and boiled or steamed until tender (rarely more than half an hour), drained, seasoned with pepper (and salt if needed) and served in lengths with oil, butter, cream or a cream sauce, on toast or not as preferred. Or they may be cut or broken and treated like string beans. When thus prepared, a creamy sauce or straight cream or plenty of butter or oil is desirable, to counteract the dryish quality. Cut into small pieces, mixed with buttered (or oiled) bread- and cracker-crumbs, with milk, beaten egg and seasonings, and then baked until browned they make a superior escalloped dish. The vase-like crowns develop so early that crowns at the tips of the freely branching rootstocks can be brought, in the autumn, into the cellar after freezing in boxes of earth and forced for winter use. Canned Ostrich-Fern has recently come into the market. In one case, at least, a novice, eating the canned product, was somewhat poisoned. He suggests that some people may be sensitive to the protein in this unusual food. The senior author with eighteen students has eaten it freely on a long field-trip. All lived happily ever after.

Other Ferns Few of the ferns have poisonous young shoots and any which are sufficiently tender could be used as emergency-food, although the Pasture-Brake and the Ostrich-Fern have so much larger shoots and are so abundant where they occur that there is rarely any occasion to cook the smaller and inferior species, some of which are bitter or otherwise unpalatable.

Caution No one who is not perfectly sure that he knows a true fern from other delicately cut leaves should venture to eat the smaller ferns. Many plants, such as the notorious **Poison Hemlock** (*Conium maculatum*) and the related **Water-Hemlock** or **Beaver-poison** (*Cicuta maculata*), both deadly poisonous, have delicately cut leaves which by the untrained are often called "ferns."

OSTRICH-FERN (*Matteucchia struthiopteris*), harvested fiddleheads at market.

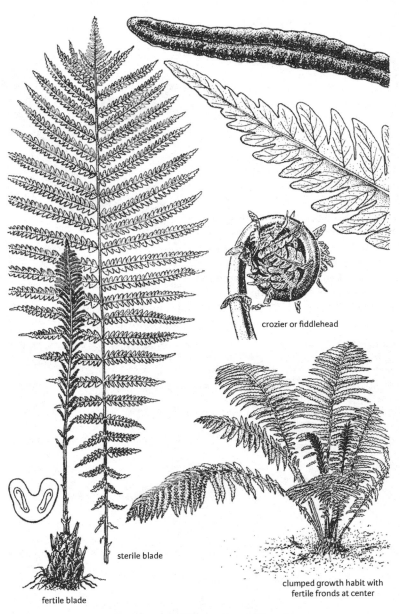

crozier or fiddlehead

sterile blade

clumped growth habit with
fertile fronds at center

fertile blade

OSTRICH-FERN *(Matteucchia struthiopteris)*

Osmundaceae CINNAMON-FERN FAMILY

Cinnamon-Fern, Buckhorn
Osmunda cinnamomea L.

Synonym *Osmundastrum cinnamomea*
Habitat wet woods and thickets.
Range throughout the eastern states, southeastern Canada and Newfoundland.
Season of Availability early spring, when beginning to sprout.
Use nibble.

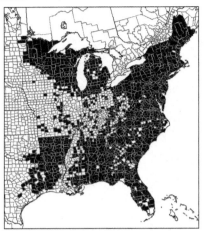

CINNAMON-FERN *(Osmunda cinnamomea)*

Every country boy in New England and eastern Canada knows and seeks for the heart of the newly unrolling crown of the **Cinnamon-Fern**. The Buckhorns or white, central, unexpanded fronds are crisp and tender, with a nutty flavor, but likewise with an acridity, overlooked by the small boy but usually detected by those who have left their boyhood behind. The stalks 6-8 inches high have been commended by some as a cooked vegetable. We have not found them attractive.

CINNAMON-FERN *(Osmunda cinnamomea)*

Cupressaceae CYPRESS FAMILY

Northern White Cedar, Arbor Vitae
Thuja occidentalis L.

Habitat woods and swamps.
Range eastern Quebec to Manitoba, south into the northern states and along the mountains to North Carolina and Tennessee.
Uses tea, soup.

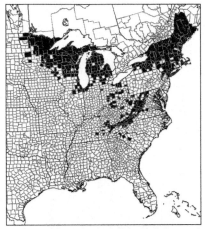

The twigs and chips of wood, bearing the familiar cedar-oil, furnish a camp-tea, by some considered palatable but not so by Thoreau, who, in *The Maine Woods*, wrote: "This night we had a dish of arbor-vitae, or cedar-tea, which the lumberer sometimes uses when other herbs fail,—

'A quart of arbor-vitae,
To make him strong and mighty.'

NORTHERN WHITE-CEDAR *(Thuja occidentalis)*

but I had no wish to repeat the experiment. It had too medicinal a taste for my palate." In the northern forest the idea is general, that one who drinks cedar-tea will not have rheumatism. The late Cyrus G. Pringle, famous for his botanical explorations in Mexico and more recently through the publication of his diary, "The Record of a Quaker Conscience," shortly before his death spoke in terms of envy to one of the writers, who was starting for the Canadian forests, saying: "I wish I could go with you. If I could drink cedar-tea I should soon be rid of my rheumatism." Kephart states that the Ojibwe make a pleasantly sweet soup from the pith of the young shoots.

Ground-Juniper
Juniperus communis L.

Habitat open slopes, hilltops, pastures.
Range Labrador to Alaska, southward into the northern states.
Uses fruit (as a pleasant nibble), masticatory, coffee-substitute.

The berries of the common **Juniper** are well known as an essential ingredient of gin, but ordinarily they are quite inedible. A trailing variety, however, found in northeastern New Brunswick, on the Magdalen Islands, on Sable Island and in western Newfoundland, has an unusually large berry, about 1/2 inch in diameter, with a sweetish pulpy coat, which makes an attractive nibble. The juniper of northern Europe seems also to have edible pulp, as indicated in Bryant's *Flora Diaetetica*, in 1783, where we read: "The Swedes make an extract from the berries of this tree, which they generally eat with their bread for breakfast, as we do butter."

The berries have sometimes been roasted and used as a poor substitute for coffee.

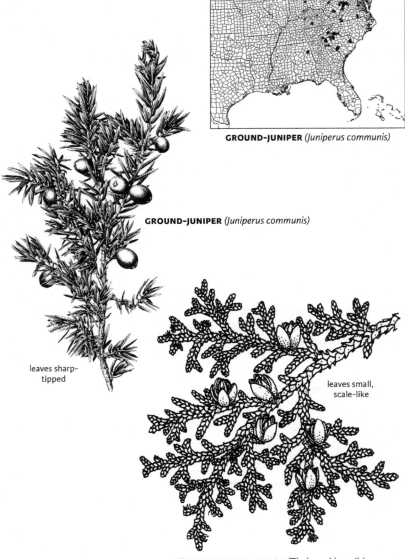

GROUND-JUNIPER *(Juniperus communis)*

GROUND-JUNIPER *(Juniperus communis)*

leaves sharp-tipped

leaves small, scale-like

NORTHERN WHITE-CEDAR *(Thuja occidentalis)*

Pinaceae PINE FAMILY

Fir, Fir Balsam, Balsam-Fir
Abies balsamea (L.) P. Mill

Key-characters bark smooth, furrowed only in age, bearing blisters filled with pitch (Canada balsam); branches nearly horizontal, forming a rather open summit resembling a many-storied pagoda; leaves flat, spreading horizontally from the branchlets; cones erect, disintegrating in the autumn, leaving naked nail-like axes.
Habitat woodlands.
Range Labrador, westward across eastern Canada and southward to the northernmost states and in the mountains to Virginia.
Use emergency-food.

The inner bark, like that of the Pines, Spruces, etc., may be used in emergency. The balsam or pitch, in extreme

FIR (*Abies balsamea*)

emergency, forms a highly concentrated though disagreeable food. Presumably the southern *Abies fraseri* (Pursh) Poir. has similar possibilities.

Larch, Hackmatack, Tamarack
Larix laricina (Du Roi) K. Koch

Habitat swamps and thin woods.
Range Labrador to Alaska, southward into the northern States.
Season of Availability spring and early summer.
Use emergency-food.

Sturtevant states that the natives of northern Siberia grate the inner bark of a related species and from it make a broth with fish and milk. The young shoots are nutritious and may serve as a possible emergency-food.

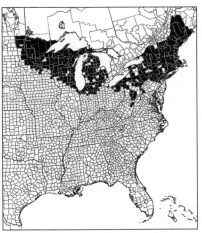

LARCH (*Larix laricina*)

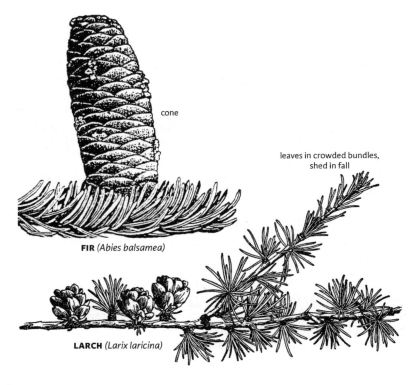

cone

leaves in crowded bundles, shed in fall

FIR *(Abies balsamea)*

LARCH *(Larix laricina)*

Spruce
Picea (3 or 4 species)

Key-characters Bark flaky, becoming furrowed, branchlets more or less drooping, forming a dense crown; needles nearly square in cross-section, spirally arranged on the twigs; cones drooping, persisting over winter.
Uses spruce-beer, spruce-gum, emergency-food.

The inner bark may be used in spring and early summer as an emergency-food in the same manner as that of the pines. The young shoots, stripped, are nutritious and also serve in emergency. Spruce-gum is derived from the two **Black Spruces** (*Picea rubens* and *P. mariana*), the **White Spruce** (*Picea glauca* or *P. canadensis*) forming inferior and

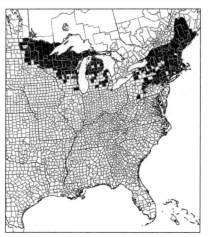

BLACK SPRUCE *(Picea mariana)*

usually brittle gum. The White Spruce is a decidedly northern tree, abounding on the better soils of Labrador, Newfoundland and Canada, extending into the northern borders of the United States. It is quickly recognized by its whitish-brown bark, as contrasted with the darker bark of the Black Spruces; by the whitish- or bluish-green foliage, as contrasted with the warmer-green of the other species; the perfectly smooth bark of the young twigs, the Black Spruces having minute hairs on the new shoots; and by its cylindric cones, the cones of the Black Spruces being egg-shaped to nearly globose. The bruised shoots and foliage of the White Spruce have a strongly disagreeable odor (whence the local names, Skunk- or Cat-Spruce); but the young shoots of the Black Spruces were the important ingredient in the formerly popular and still locally made spruce-beer.

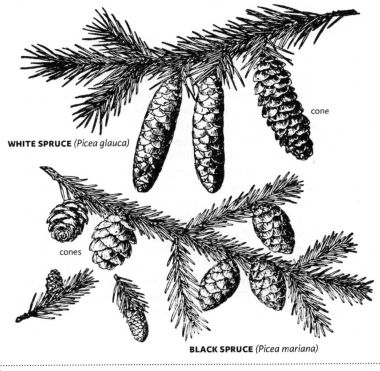

WHITE SPRUCE *(Picea glauca)*

cone

cones

BLACK SPRUCE *(Picea mariana)*

Pines
Pinus (a dozen species)

Uses bread, masticatory, nuts (seeds), emergency-food, cooked vegetable.

The juicy inner bark (cambium) of the pines (with us especially of the **White Pine**, *Pinus strobus* L.) in spring has apparently been an emergency-food, as well as a popular morsel for most northern country boys, in all regions where the trees are known. The "slivers" or strips of succulent inner bark of White

Pine, gathered in May or early June, are well known to farmer-boys of the northern states; and the stripped young shoots of the White Pine were formerly candied by the New Englanders. This inner bark has a more important food possibility, however, long recognized by Europeans as well as by the American Indians. The people of some portions of northern Europe early acquired the habit of laying aside a store of the "**Fir**" or **Scotch Pine** (*P. sylvestris* L.) against possible winter needs. Thus the immortal Linnaeus, tramping in 1732 through Lapland, found the Laplanders largely subsisting on the inner bark of the Fir. Briefly, their method

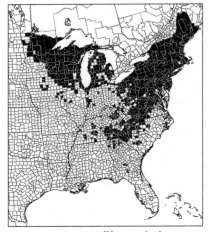

WHITE PINE (*Pinus strobus*)

was as follows. In spring they cut strips of the inner bark, which were fastened on the barn to dry over summer, and then, as necessity demanded, this dried bark was ground and mixed with other flours as material for famine-bread. Linnaeus stated that the bread was nutritious and that the ground bark when fed to cattle and swine proved fattening; but to his taste the bread was not attractive! Doubtless the inner bark of other pines would be as good a source of meal and, although the gathering and preparation of the bark is, naturally, a disagreeable and sticky process which few will be tempted to undertake, the importance of pine-bread as an emergency-food should be kept in mind. Those who may care to try it will be interested in the directions given by Linnaeus:

"Some people make bread of the bark of fir-trees. For this purpose they choose the bark of such trees as are of a large size, with but few branches, because the branches, as well as the younger trees, are more resinous, and therefore more strongly flavoured. The bark taken from the lower part of the tree is esteemed the best. The hard external coats require to be carefully removed. Stores of this bark are often laid by for winter use. Previously to its being ground into flour, it is laid over a slow fire in order to be warmed through, and rendered more friable, for it becomes by this means much thickened and very porous. It is next ground and baked, in the same manner as the barley. . . . The dough made of fir bark is more compact than barley dough, and almost as much so as that made of rye; but the bread has a bitterish taste."

The use of pine-bark by the American Indians was so extensive that early explorers frequently recorded large areas of trees stripped of their bark; and in this connection it is interesting to note that the name Adirondack means "tree-eaters."

More attractive food is to be found in the seeds of the pines, although none of the eastern species bears seeds comparable with the delicious fruit of some of the Nut Pines of the West. The seeds of the White and Norway Pines, are, however, sweet and nutritious, and Kephart suggests roasting to remove the resinous taste. The resin is less evident if the seeds are gathered in August, at about the time of the opening of the cone.

The Ojibwe Indians, according to the distinguished student of American ethnology, the late Huron H. Smith, gathered the firm and unexpanded aments of White Pine and stewed them with their meats. The cooked aments are said to be sweet and not pitchy.

Hemlock
Tsuga canadensis (L.) Carr.

Habitat dry woods.
Range eastern states, north to Minnesota, Ontario and New Brunswick.
Uses emergency-food, tea, beer, bread.

The inner bark may be eaten in emergency; and the young tips were used by the Iroquois to make a tea and were one of the ingredients of old-fashioned root-beer. According to several writers, the inner bark of the western species of Hemlock was extensively used by the Indians for bread.

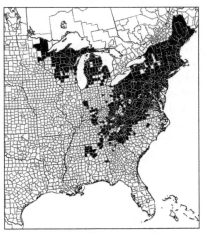

HEMLOCK *(Tsuga canadensis)*

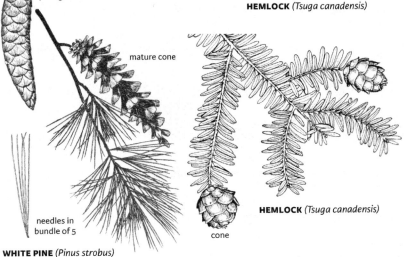

young cone

mature cone

HEMLOCK *(Tsuga canadensis)*

cone

needles in bundle of 5

WHITE PINE *(Pinus strobus)*

Taxaceae YEW FAMILY

Ground-Hemlock, American Yew
Taxus canadensis Marsh.

Habitat rich woods.
Range Newfoundland to Manitoba, southward into the northern States, and in the mountains to Virginia.
Season of Availability midsummer.
Uses fresh fruit as a nibble, masticatory.

The pulpy red portion of the berry is sweet and honey-like and perfectly edible. The nut-like seed is reputed to be poisonous, although we are unaware that any one has actually experimented with our species. It is well demonstrated, however, that the wilted foliage is poisonous to grazing animals, although the stiff and fresh foliage is harmless and often nibbled with relish by those who know it. The wilted leaves develop a heart-depressing alkaloid. See p. 56.

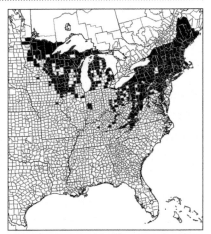

GROUND-HEMLOCK *(Taxus canadensis)*

needles

fruit

GROUND-HEMLOCK *(Taxus canadensis)*

Acanthaceae ACANTHUS FAMILY

Dicliptera

Dicliptera brachiata (Pursh) Spreng.

Use salad or potherb.

Ochse states that species of *Dicliptera* in the Dutch East Indies are eaten, the young leafy tips used either raw as salad or cooked. Our species is an opposite-leaved, smoothish, ascending, perennial herb 1-2 feet high, with thin and pliable long-pointed ovate leaves, the well developed pink gaping corollas 1/2-1 inch long and with 2 stamens or replaced by tiny closed corollas, the flowers subtended by pairs of opposite leafy bracts, the fruit a rigid 2-valved pointed capsule, each valve with clasps embracing the large flat seed. It occurs on wooded bottomlands from Florida to Louisiana, north to southeastern Virginia, southern Indiana, Missouri and eastern Kansas. We have not tried it, but the family is an extensive one without noxious properties. The juice is mucilaginous, the herbage somewhat bitter. It should be tested.

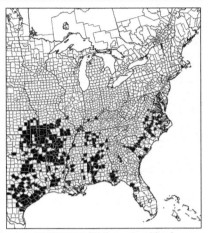

DICLIPTERA *(Dicliptera brachiata)*

DICLIPTERA *(Dicliptera brachiata), flowers.*

Adoxaceae MUSKROOT FAMILY

Elderberries, Black-berried Elder
Sambucus canadensis L.

Synonym *Sambucus nigra*
Uses cooked berries, preserves, pies, jelly, beverage, soup, breadstuff, pickles, asparagus-substitute, tea.

Although **Elderberries** have always been popular as a source of domestic wine, their possibilities as unfermented food are often little realized. To many people the flavor of Elderberries is disagreeable but to others it is palatable, and in preparation the flavor is often modified by seasonings. The berries, boiled with a small amount of sugar with lemon-rind, may be canned to use for pies and in this form will keep indefinitely. Or, mixed with grape or other tart fruit, the Elderberries make a delicious jelly.

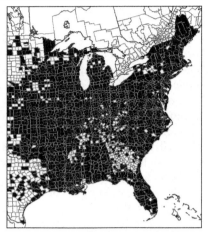

ELDERBERRY *(Sambucus canadensis)*

Possibly the limited area over which elderberry-pie is popular may be due to improper preparation. At least, the following note by Clute in The American Botanist for 1905 indicates the trouble.

"The Use of Elderberries.—In a discussion of the subject recently in pie-eating New England, the editor was surprised to find that many people are still ignorant of the fact that the berries of the common elder (Sambucus canadensis) make excellent pies. Others who have tasted so-called elderberry pie were inclined to call it a nauseating mixture. The trouble is not so much in the pie itself as in the way it is put together. Pies made of fresh elderberries are scarcely likely to appeal to many palates. The fruit still retains some of the rank eldery flavor possessed by the entire plant and made evident when the stem is broken; but if one will collect the berries when fully ripe and dry them in flat trays in the sun or in a warm oven he will have a cheap and appetizing material from which to manufacture pies all winter—and pies that are not inferior to huckleberry pies in flavor. The eldery flavor seems to be dissipated by drying. The berries stewed and sweetened are also in demand in some households as sauce. The berries are also of some medicinal value and thus have an additional claim to our attention as a winter food."

The following recipe for preparing Elderberry rob, for which we are indebted to *Berry's Fruit Recipes*, is well worth trying. Boil the fruit with spices (1 quart of juice with 1 tablespoon each of cloves, nutmeg and cinnamon); after half-an-hour strain and add 1/2 lb. sugar; boil a few minutes, skim, and seal while hot.

In *New England Herbs*, published by the New England Museum of Natural History, Mr. S. N. F. Sanford gives the following interesting recipe for "Elderberry Chutney. To two pounds of elderberries add one large onion, a pint of vinegar, a teaspoonful of salt, a teaspoonful of ground ginger, two teaspoonfuls of sugar, one saltspoonful of cayenne and mixed spices. The elderberries should have been freed from their stalks, weighed and washed, then put in a pan and bruised with a wooden spoon. Chop the onion, add the other ingredients and vinegar, bring to a boil, and simmer until thick. Stir well, put in a jar, and cover."

The juice cooked with sugar makes a pleasant beverage, which may be bottled for winter use and served with water and lemon; while in some parts of Europe, the berries of a related species are dried by the peasants and used in the winter to make a soup, the juice or the extract from the berries being thickened with flour.

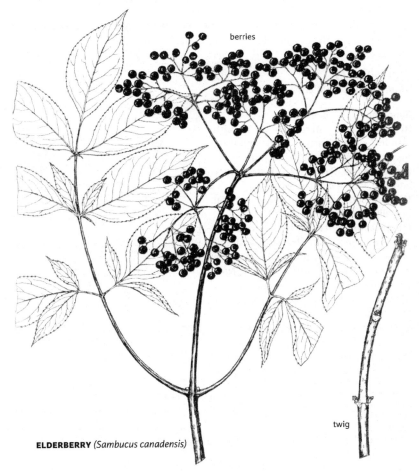

berries

twig

ELDERBERRY *(Sambucus canadensis)*

Elder-flowers, especially when very young, are likewise used in various ways: beaten into the batter and thus lightening the muffins or pancakes and giving them a distinctive flavor; and the unexpanded flowers and green fruits have sometimes been pickled to use like capers. According to Berry, the young shoots may be cooked and eaten, although by some writers it is stated that the green parts of the shrub are poisonous.

Although plain elder-flowers or these toned up by the addition of mint are familiar diet-food and diet-tea for dyspeptics, elder-flowers through the following recipe, published by Elizabeth Remsen Van Brunt, enter a field beyond the reach of most dyspeptics:

"And the umbels of creamy blossoms make a delicious fritter. Cut at the very height of bloom, soak in brandy with a stick of cinnamon for an hour. Dip each cluster (coarse stem removed) into rich egg batter and drop in deep hot fat, frying until a light brown. Drain on brown paper, serve sprinkled with powdered sugar and orange or lemon juice."

The brilliant red berries of the **Red-berried** or **Stinking Elder**, *Sambucus racemosa* L., with rhomboid clusters of fruit, are inedible.

Squashberry
Viburnum edule (Michx.) Raf.

Synonym *V. pauciflorum*
Key-characters straggling shrub with slender, gray branches and opposite, maple-like leaves; the large red berries borne in small, flat-topped clusters, juicy and acid, with a large flat stone.
Habitat cool woods and thickets or on gravelly or rocky banks.
Range Labrador to Alaska, south across Newfoundland, Cape Breton Island and eastern Quebec, and locally on the mountains of northern New England, New York and Pennsylvania, and in cool regions of northern Michigan, Wisconsin and Minnesota.
Season of Availability late summer to winter, the fruit softening after frost and persisting over winter.
Use fruit, fresh or cooked, jellies, etc.

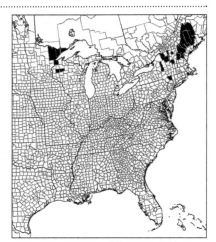

SQUASHBERRY *(Viburnum edule)*

Squashberries are smaller and less acid than Highbush-Cranberries and borne in smaller clusters. In Newfoundland and Cape Breton especially they are in high repute for "squash" or sauce, and jellies. The fresh berries being only mildly acid when ripe are pleasant to eat raw, in spite of the large, flat stone.

Hobblebush, Moosewood
Viburnum lantanoides Michx.

Synonym *Viburnum alnifolium*
Use fruit as nibble or masticatory.

The oblong, blue-black berries of the Hobblebush of cool, Canadian and Alleghenian forests, when thoroughly ripe, are sweet and palatable, in taste suggesting dates or raisins. On account of the very large stone the berries are not generally gathered for table-use. The **Striped Maple** (*Acer pensylvanicum* L.) of Canadian and upland forests is also known as Moosewood and because it bears no berries is often considered by Maine guides the male of the species, the berry-bearing *Viburnum lantanoides* being considered the female.

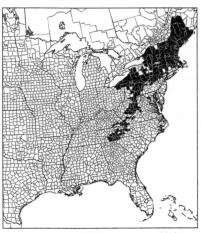

HOBBLEBUSH (*Viburnum lantanoides*)

Wild Raisin, Sweet Viburnum, Sheepberry
Viburnum lentago L. and *V. nudum* L. (synonym: *V. cassinoides*), and Black Haw, *V. prunifolium* L.

Key-characters large shrubs or small trees with opposite, entire or finely toothed oblong to ovate, thickish leaves, and with terminal, flat-topped clusters of white flowers, followed by blue-black or dark-purple "plums," which are usually elongate but sometimes spherical, in *V. lentago* 1/2 inch or more long, in the other species somewhat smaller; stone large, flat.
Habitat and Range swamps, riverbanks or open pastures and thickets, one species or another throughout eastern America, north to Quebec and Newfoundland.
Season of Availability late summer and autumn.
Use fruit as nibble or masticatory.

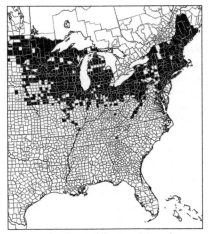

WILD RAISIN (*Viburnum lentago*)

The fully ripe bluish or blackish "plums" have a thin and rather dry, sweet pulp, which is palatable raw, although the stone is disagreeably large. The cooked pulp has not proved attractive, but it is possible that by adding some tart fruit to it a palatable sauce might be prepared.

fruit

opposite leaves

WILD RAISIN *(Viburnum lentago)*

High-bush Cranberry, Cranberry-tree
Viburnum opulus L. var. *americanum* Ait.

Synonym *Viburnum trilobum*
Key-characters large shrub or small tree with pale, ashy-brown bark; the opposite leaves 3-lobed above the middle, somewhat suggesting maple-leaves; the large, red berries borne in flat-topped, terminal clusters, very acid, with a large flat stone.
Habitat rich thickets, especially along streams or at borders of low woods or by walls and fences.
Range Newfoundland to British Columbia, south rather generally through northern New England and eastern Canada, more locally to New Jersey, Pennsylvania, the Great Lakes States, northeastern Iowa, the Black Hills, etc.

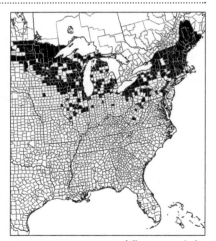

HIGH-BUSH CRANBERRY *(Viburnum opulus)*

Season of Availability late summer to winter, the berries softening after frost and lasting over winter.
Uses cooked fruit, preserves, jellies.

In the northern states and Canada High-bush Cranberries are generally known and in many regions where the Bog-Cranberries are unknown the fruit is regularly cooked and served under the name "Cranberry." The fruit is acid and of pleasant flavor, but on account of the large, flat stones, it is desirable to strain the sauce. Jelly made from High-bush Cranberries is of beautiful color and delicious flavor.

Caution Do not confuse with the northern native High-bush Cranberry the introduced and cultivated (sometimes escaped) **Wayfaring Tree**, *Viburnum opulus* var. *opulus* of Europe. The fruits of the latter are bitter and sadly disappointing to those who suppose it to be the Canadian species.

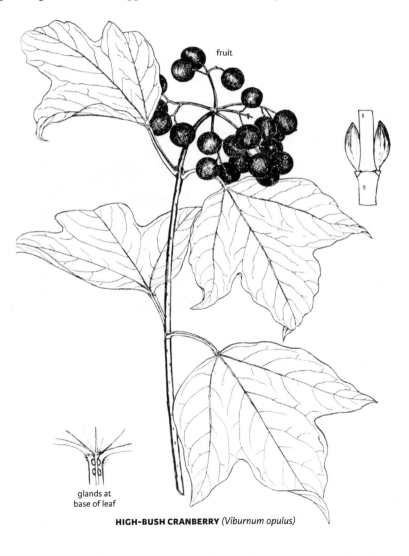

fruit

glands at
base of leaf

HIGH-BUSH CRANBERRY *(Viburnum opulus)*

Aizoaceae FIG-MARIGOLD FAMILY

Sea-Purslane
Sesuvium maritimum (Walt.) B.S.P.

Key-characters an annual, freely forking, mostly prostrate, fleshy herb, with opposite, round-tipped slender-stalked leaves (mostly 1/4-3/4 inch long) and short, strongly divergent, axillary branches crowded with flowers; flowers greenish, sessile in the leaf-axils, less than 1/4 inch long, with 5 erect, ovate, pale-margined sepals and a capsule opening by n circular slit near the base.
Habitat and Range Sea-beaches of the Atlantic, north to Long Island, local.
Season of Availability early summer.
Uses potherb, pickles.

The **Sea-Purslane** may be eaten as a potherb, though it is said to be pretty salty; and its succulent stems are sometimes pickled like Samphire. It is so local, however, that it is relatively unimportant.

Sea-Purslane
Sesuvium portulacastrum (L.) L.

Use potherb, pickles.

A coarser species than the preceding, differing chiefly in size of parts and numerous (instead of 5) stamens, following seashores from the Tropics northward to North Carolina. It is pantropical in range. In eastern Asia it is raised as a garden vegetable, said to be regularly sold in the markets of China and the Dutch East Indies.

SEA-PURSLANE *(Sesuvium portulacastrum)*

New Zealand Spinach
Tetragonia tetragonioides (Pallas) Kuntze

Synonym *Tetragona expansa*
Use potherb.

New Zealand Spinach, now so familiar as a summer spinach, is becoming naturalized as a weed southward. It is useful as a cooked green.

Alismataceae WATER-PLANTAIN FAMILY

Mud-Plantain, Water-Plantain
Alisma (2 species)

Key-characters plants of wet places, with rosettes of long-stalked erect and smooth leaves with round-based or heart-shaped, broad, pointed blades with 3 to 9 parallel ribs; the flowers with 3 small white petals and 3 green sepals, borne in compound, long-stalked, branching clusters, the smaller clusters with slender flower-stalks radiating like rays of an umbrella; flowers ripening into little disks of thin scale-like fruits.
Habitat muddy shores and margins of ponds and streams.
Range: southern Canada and southward throughout our area.
Season of Availability autumn to spring, when the roots are well filled.
Use starchy vegetable.

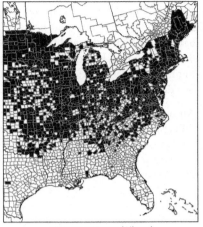

MUD-PLANTAIN *(Alisma)*

The solid bulb-like bases of the plant are farinaceous and it is stated that after thorough drying, to rid them of an acrid taste, they are eaten by the Calmucks. The species are so closely allied that it is probable that any of them might be used.

Arrow-head, Arrow-leaf, Duck-Potato, Swan-Potato
Sagittaria (various species, about 7 with large tubers).

Key-characters plants of pond- or river-margins, with rosettes of erect or rarely floating leaves with arrow-shaped blades; readily recognizable in flower by having circles of flowers (mostly in threes) near the summit of the flower-stalk, each with 3 filmy white petals; in fruit bearing near the summit of the flower-stalk circles (usually in threes) of rounded heads of flat seeds.
Habitat wet swamps or shallow waters.
Range eastern Quebec to British Columbia, south to the Gulf of Mexico.
Season of Availability late summer and autumn.
Use starchy vegetable.

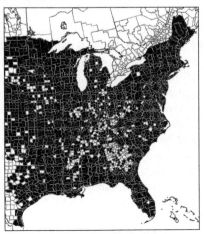

ARROW-HEAD *(Sagittaria)*

Likely to be confused with: (1) **Arrow-Arum, Green Arum** or **Tuckahoe** (*Peltandra*), having arrow-shaped leaves but a stout and deep vertical root, the Arrow-heads having the root fibres springing directly from the base of the tufts of leaves, without a strong deep rootstock. The fruits of the Arrow-Arum are rounded, bean-like seeds in masses within a leathery pouch (spathe). (2) **Wild Calla** (*Calla palutris* L.) with heart-shaped or rounded leaves springing from stout, widely creeping and horizontal rootstocks, and bearing heads of red berries. (3) **Pickerel-weed** (*Pontederia cordata* L.), with leathery heart-shaped or arrow-shaped blades; the mature plant bearing one heart-shaped leaf high upon the flower-stalk; the flowers blue-purple spotted with yellow and borne in a dense spike; the dry fruits also in a dense spike.

All our species of Arrow-head produce late in the autumn hard, potato-like tubers at the ends of long subterranean runners, but those most available as food are, naturally, the larger species, *Sagittaria latifolia* Willd. and *S. cuneata* Sheldon (synonym: *S. arifolia*) and a few others. The tubers of these plants have been used by the native races of North America and of related species by those of Asia, and at the present day they form a food of some importance with the Chinese, cultivated at the borders of rice-fields and sometimes to be seen in the markets of San Francisco and New York. The tubers of our species were the Wapato of the northwestern Indians, referred to by Lewis and Clark and other explorers, and the Katniss of the Algonquin. The tubers are borne often several feet away from the parent plant and are available only after mid-summer, and chiefly in the autumn. The larger tubers are an inch or two in diameter, containing a somewhat milky juice which, when raw, is unpleasant to the taste, but which is said by many explorers to be dispelled on cooking, the tubers after roasting or boiling becoming sweetish and palatable.

Kalm's account, written in New Jersey in 1749, was as good as any: "Katniss is another Indian name of a plant, the root of which they were likewise accustomed to eat. . .; The Indians either boiled this root or roasted it in hot ashes. Some of the Swedes likewise eat them with much appetite, . . . A man of ninety-one years of age, called Nils Gustafson, told me, that he had often eaten these roots when he was a boy, and that he liked them very well . . . I afterwards got some of these roots roasted, and in my opinion they tasted well, though they were rather dry: The taste was nearly the same with that of the potatoes."

A more recent verdict is that of Professor Milton Hopkins: "the tubers . . . are as toothsome a morsel as anyone could hope to enjoy. I have eaten them baked and boiled, as one cooks potatoes, and found them eminently satisfactory. They should be cooked about 30 minutes and are best if they are peeled afterward. The mealy quality of the potato is not present, and the texture is somewhat more smooth. The arrowhead tuber makes a superb dish for picnic suppers and lunches, and if the picnic grounds are not too far distant from a colony, one can make the event outstanding by asking the guests to dig their own tubers and roast them in a bed of hot smouldering coals." Professor

Hopkins has the right idea. Ordinarily the tubers are so remote from the parent-plant that the Indians depended largely upon the stores of them which they found already assembled by muskrats. One needs a bathing-suit if he goes for them.

Some of the Indian tribes, after boiling the tubers, sliced them and strung them on strings (like dried apples) to dry for winter use.

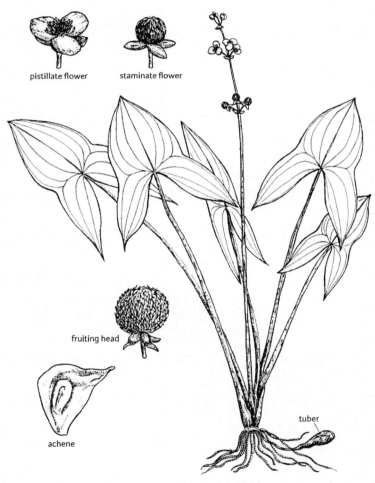

pistillate flower   staminate flower

fruiting head

achene

tuber

ARROW-HEAD *(Sagittaria latifolia)*

ARROW-HEAD *(Sagittaria latifolia)*

Altingiaceae SWEET-GUM FAMILY

Sweet Gum
Liquidambar styraciflua L.

Use chewing gum.

The fragrant gum, which exudes from cracks and bruises in the bark, tastes somewhat like spruce-gum and is enjoyed in our southernmost states. The gum is scarce as far north as North Carolina, but is occasionally found in Virginia and northward. From one of the once popular books of Maurice Thompson, Clute dug out the statement that he "once went to school where everybody chewed sweet gum, except the teacher, who chewed tobacco."

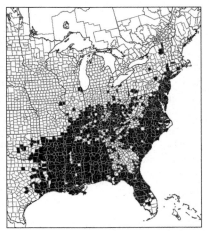

SWEET GUM *(Liquidambar styraciflua)*

palmately
lobd leaves

SWEET GUM *(Liquidambar styraciflua)*

fruit

Amaranthaceae AMARANTH FAMILY

Amaranth, Pigweed, Wild Beet
Amaranthus (about 10 species)

Uses potherb, breadstuff.

The **Amaranths** are very similar to the Pigweeds, *Chenopodium*, and are often called "Pigweed." They differ in having scaly inflorescences and more veiny, often hairy leaves and stems, and former members of the Chenopodiaceae have now been merged into the Amaranth Family. The young plants are sometimes used as a potherb, and the seeds as a breadstuff, these uses having been especially practiced by the southwestern Indians. In the North their use has not been general; but as potherbs we can thoroughly commend the larger species. They are often very common as garden-weeds and, gathered young, are as good as spinach.

Orach
Atriplex patula L.
Atrplex glabriuscula Edmondston

Key-characters resembling the Pigweeds and differing from them only in technical characters of the flowers and fruits: the flowers being imperfect or unisexual and the fruits having two large, wing-like sepals.
Habitat and Range seashores from Labrador to Virginia and rich open soil across the continent.
Season of Availability late spring and summer (sometimes autumn).
Use potherb.

As a potherb *Atriplex* is superior to Lamb's-Quarters or Pigweed, but can sometimes be somewhat bitter. The succulent leaves or young tips, especially

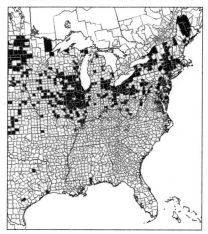

ORACH *(Atriplex patula)*

when the plant grows along the seashore, are juicier and somewhat impregnated with salt. The plant is often so abundant on seashores that it might supply many families throughout the season.

Another personal experience shows the importance of **Orach** where fresh vegetables are scarce. Entertained at one of the great cod-fishing "rooms" on the coast of Labrador, where vegetables are the products of tin-cans, a party of botanists, delighted with the thickets of *Atriplex glabriuscula* growing 6 feet high and freely branching on the refuse from the fish-cleaning sheds, brought in a large bundle of leafy tips and requested to have them cooked. After the meal the genial host, native of southern Newfoundland, said to his daughter, "This is a godsend. Now we can induce Mother to come down to the Labrador if she can have fresh vegetables." Similarly, the fisher-folk on the Newfoundland coast have evinced their delight when shown how to recognize Orach, Goose-tongue, Scurvy-grass, and other neglected foods which surround them. Even in October, when Harvard or Radcliffe classes in taxonomy make their trips to Cape Cod, enough young tips of *Atriplex patula* are found regularly to furnish the vegetable for dinner.

Summer-Cypress
Bassia scoparia (L.) A.J. Scott

Synonym *Kochia scoparia*
Use potherb, cereal.

The familiar annual **Summer-Cypress**, popular with us as a bedding-plant with rich purple coloring in autumn, was introduced from Asia. It spreads freely from cultivation. In China and Japan its young tips are used as a potherb; but it is there raised chiefly for its abundant seeds, used by themselves or in bread, and for the dried bushy-branched plant for brooms—essential for clearing up after a meal.

Pigweed, Goosefoot, Lamb's-Quarters
Chenopodium album L. and ca. 14 other species

Key-characters annual herbs, the young growth whitened with a close mealiness; the alternate long-stalked leaves more or less angulate-toothed, especially near the base, somewhat fleshy, 1-4 inches long; the older plants bearing many insignificant scalloped green flowers in clusters forming spirelike inflorescences; seeds black, rarely 1/8 inch broad, shaped like a biconvex lens.
Habitat several closely related species so similar as to be separated only with difficulty; some native along seashores, others abundant as garden weeds, or about rubbish, in roadside ditches, and other disturbed soils.
Range throughout temperate North America.

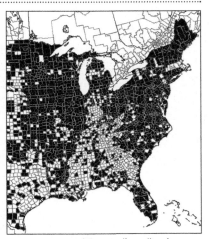

PIGWEED (*Chenopodium album*)

Season of Availability for potherb, early summer, and the young tips to midsummer; seeds in autumn and early winter, the fruiting plants usually holding the seeds until after heavy frosts.

Uses potherb, breadstuff.

The common **Pigweed**, so familiar in rich garden soil, in barnyards, and similar habitats, has always been a popular potherb; under the more appetizing name, **Lamb's-Quarters**, highly prized by European peoples.

In spite of a spendthrift American prejudice against it because it is so common, the Pigweed, which annually appears in all good garden soils, is really one of the most valuable, though promptly destroyed crops of the garden before the planted vegetables are in season. Cooked and eaten like spinach, the tender

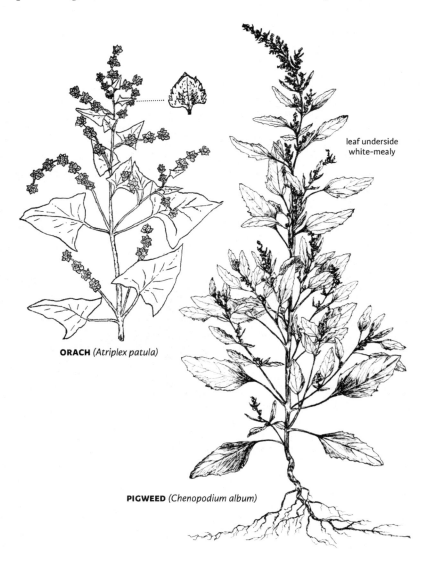

leaf underside
white-mealy

ORACH *(Atriplex patula)*

PIGWEED *(Chenopodium album)*

shoots and leaves are often called delicious, and nearly every one who tries it, unprejudiced by the knowledge that it is an every-day weed, is enthusiastic. Some years ago one of the writers planted the garden at his summer home in early May, and when in June he moved his family to the country, he found the garden full of Pigweed. For two weeks before the peas were ready, and for a month before the New Zealand spinach could be used, the family enjoyed the abundant Pigweed, and under the sophisticated name "spinach," presented pans of it to the local residents, who returned with the suggestion that if the crop was abundant they would like another mess, little guessing that they had been enjoying despised Pigweed, which grew even more luxuriantly in their own barnyards. In cooking, Pigweed reduces considerably in bulk and it is necessary to gather two or three times the bulk that is wanted when cooked. The fresh leaves readily shed water but, as soon as steamed, lose this peculiarity. The boiled Pigweed is a comparatively dry potherb and it is particularly good if mixed with Dock-greens which are unusually wet or mucilaginous.

The seeds of the Pigweeds can be gathered in great quantities and they were largely used by the American Indians as a source of bread or in gruel. They are very hard and slippery, inclined to jump and bounce while being ground; and, although they may be ground dry, we have found it advantageous to boil them for a couple of hours, then to mash, and then dry the mass before grinding. The flour and bread are very dark-colored on account of the black seed-coats but of good flavor and highly nutritious, tasting somewhat like buckwheat but with the characteristic "mousey" flavor distinctive of this group of plants.

Another incident in the experience of the senior author illustrates the prejudice against not too attractive or conventional foods. Planning for a meeting of botanists in his study, he set to work on the menu to follow the business meeting: puree of dried Fairy-ring mushrooms, escalloped canned Purslane, salad of cooked blanched Pokeweed and Sorrel from the cellar, etc. A bread of Pigweed-seeds was decided upon. Proceeding in January to the border of a frozen truck-farm, a peck of seeds with husks and other fragments was quickly gathered. Winnowed by pouring back and forth from containers out-of-doors, so that the lighter husks and debris blew away, a yield of a full quart of the black and drab fruits was left. When supper was served, Mrs. Femald brought in the soup which found favor, with thin biscuits of Jack-in-the Pulpit flour, then the Purslane and salad, with a plate of intensely black muffins. I explained that, having no cook, I had volunteered to make the muffins. The plate went around the table, regularly to receive a polite, "No, I thank you", until it reached the late Emile Williams, half-French and with more than usual Yankee consideration for others. Everyone else having declined my black muffins, Williams took one, put on his eye-glasses and inspected it, then sniffed at it. "Ah, *Chenopodium album*" was his immediate diagnosis. Asked how he guessed, he replied: "I've just been reading Napoleon's Memoirs. Napoleon at times had to live on it." The plate was promptly cleared and returned to the kitchen for more, to nibble with the Beach-Plum preserve.

Caution Certain species of *Chenopodium*, notably *C. ambrosioides* [now termed *Dysphania ambrosioides* (L.) Mosyakin & Clemants], Mexican Tea or Wormseed and *C. chenopodioides* (L.) Aellen (synonym: *C. botrys*), Jerusalem Oak or Feather-Geranium, the former a common weed of waste or cultivated ground, the latter often grown in herb-gardens for its aroma, should not be used as potherbs. They are covered with glandular or oily atoms, have a pungent odor, and are regularly avoided by grazing animals. In cases of fodder-shortage animals have been poisoned by them. A strong aromatic tea can be made from them by those who want it; it is popular in Mexico and parts of South America, where regularly raised for tea. For some centuries the oil of *Dysphania ambrosioides* has had repute in killing intestinal worms and it is now much used for hook-worm. Its connotation is not attractive but it might be advisable in some regions to use it regularly.

Strawberry-Blite, Strawberry-Spinach
Chenopodium capitatum (L.) Ambrosi

Key-characters similar to Pigweed, but with the mature flowers becoming fleshy and bright red.
Habitat recently burned clearings and borders of sandy fields.
Range across Canada to Alaska and locally southward into the northern states.
Season of Availability early summer (potherb); late summer (fruit).
Uses potherb, fruit.

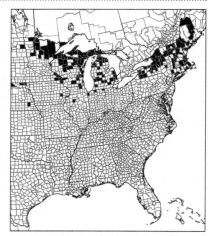

STRAWBERRY-BLITE *(Chenopodium capitatum)*

The **Strawberry-Blite**, one of the most striking plants of Canadian clearings, on account of its masses of brilliant red pulpy fruits, may be used as a potherb like spinach; or the succulent fruits, although insipid, may be eaten either raw or cooked. They are highly nutritious.

"Samphire," Glasswort, Chicken-claws
Salicornia (various species)

Key-characters fleshy herbs of the salt marshes and sea-strands, with leafless, conspicuously jointed, juicy stems bearing inconspicuous flowers hidden under closely appressed scales; plants bright green in summer, becoming red in autumn.
Habitat and Range three species: one a tough-stemmed perennial of sea-shores from Massachusetts southward (*S. ambigua*); the others annual, with soft stems usually branching from near the base, *S. europaea* and *S. bigelovii* (or *S. mucronata*) occurring

northward to the Maritime Provinces or Newfoundland, chiefly on salt marshes.
Season of Availability summer and early autumn.
Uses pickles and salad.

The name "**Samphire**" is in colloquial use in America for these plants, but they should not be confused with the quite different samphire of Europe. The Glassworts, being succulent and filled with brine, form a pleasant salty salad (especially while the plant is young), and have long been popular as a source of pickles, the tender stems and branches being first boiled in their own salted-water before being put into the spiced oil or vinegar. Of the confusion of Salicornia with the true Samphire of Europe Bryant, in his Flora Diaetetica, says:

"This plant is gathered by the country people, and sold about for the true Samphire, but it is very different from that plant (. . . *Crithmum maritimum*). This, however, makes an excellent good pickle, which renders the cheat the less to be regretted."

Loudon, too, thought so favorably of it that he suggested that it "might be cultivated in the garden, by imitating a small portion of salt-marsh."

Sea-Blite
Suaeda (ca. 5 species)

Use potherb.

The **Sea-Blites**, succulent plants of saline soil from Labrador to Florida and Texas, and inland in salt-licks, differ from the pigweeds in having the fleshy leaves slenderly cylindric or thick-linear. The tender branches and leaves may be boiled but they are so full of salt as to need two or three waters.

SAMPHIRE *(Salicornia)*

Anacardiaceae CASHEW FAMILY
....
Sumach
Rhus (various species)
....

Key-characters shrubs or small trees with coarse, soft branches and feather-like leaves with numerous pointed leaflets, and bearing somewhat pyramidal or rhomboidal terminal clusters of red, berry-like hard fruits.

Habitat and Range dry open soil; the Staghorn Sumach, *Rhus typhina* L. (or *R. hirta*), with the branches covered with long, velvety hairs and the berries with long, acidic red hairs, occurring from Rimouski Co., to western Ontario, south to Georgia, the Great Lakes States and Iowa; Smooth Sumach, *Rhus glabra* L., with smooth branchlets and with the leaf-stalks not winged, from central Maine to Manitoba and southward; Dwarf Sumach,

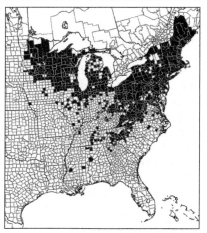

STAGHORN SUMACH *(Rhus typhina)*

Rhus copallinum L., with minutely downy branchlets and with a broad wing extending between the leaflets and down the leaf-stalk, from southern Maine to southern Ontario and southward.

Season of Availability throughout the year, but chiefly from midsummer to early winter.

Use a cool, acidic drink.

The hairs on the surface of the **Sumach** "berries" contain malic acid and, on account of their pleasant acid taste, the berries are familiar to most children. The Indians, and after them the Europeans, used the fruit as the source of a cool, summer drink, which is prepared by bruising the fruit in water, thus freeing the acid, then straining off the acidulated water through cloth, to remove the hairs, and adding sugar. This drink in color resembles the familiar pink lemonade and in flavor is quite as palatable. The fruiting heads are likely to be inhabited by numerous insects and care should be taken to select· the heads which are not disagreeably worm-eaten. By various tribes of Indians the dried berries are stored to supply an acid drink in winter.

In some statements we find the boiling of the berries recommended, but boiling is to be avoided, since the hard seeds contain abundant tannin, which is extracted by boiling and which renders the "rhusade" astringent and somewhat unwholesome. In fact, in many country districts the brew from boiled Sumach berries is a familiar cure for sore throats. The berries of Staghorn Sumach are less acid than those of the other species.

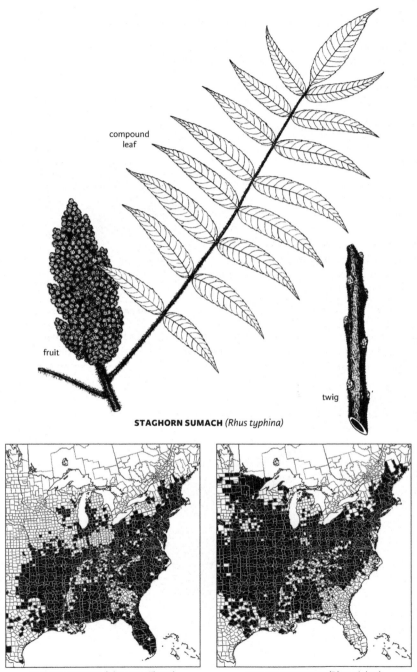

compound
leaf

fruit

twig

STAGHORN SUMACH *(Rhus typhina)*

DWARF SUMACH *(Rhus copallinum)*   **SMOOTH SUMACH** *(Rhus glabra)*

Annonaceae CUSTARD-APPLE FAMILY

Pawpaw
Asimina triloba (L.) Dunal (other species southward from southeastern Virginia)

Habitat and Range shrub or small tree of rich woods and banks of streams in the Southern and Central States.
Season of Availability autumn, in the North usually after light freezing.
Use fruit (raw or cooked).

The fully ripe fruit of the American **Pawpaw** has long been famous among those who have the fortune to live where it occurs, the fruit when fully ripe (northward often after slight freezing) being sweet and luscious. It is eaten either raw or baked or as a filling for pies, or is combined with eggs, cornstarch and gelatine for a dessert.

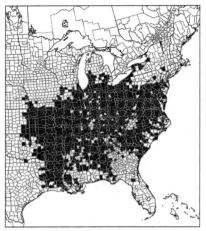

PAWPAW *(Asimina triloba)*

Some European writers, presumably not knowing pawpaws at their best, have said, "the fruit is relished by few except negroes"; but Timothy Flint knew better: "The pulp of the fruit resembles egg-custard in consistence and appearance. It has the same creamy feeling in the mouth and unites the taste of eggs, cream, sugar and spice. It is a natural custard, too luscious for the relish of most people." The fruits usually fall while green, hard and acrid. They must be harvested (mostly from the ground) and kept until ripe.

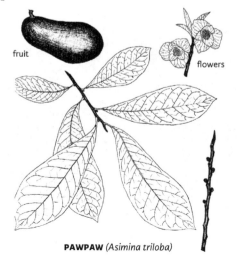

fruit

flowers

PAWPAW *(Asimina triloba)*

Apiaceae PARSLEY FAMILY

Caution This family contains many of our well known garden vegetables, such as carrot, parsnip, celery, fennel, parsley, etc., but unfortunately many members of the family are among the most notorious of poisons: **Poison Hemlock, Water-Hemlock (or Beaver-poison),** and several others. The genera of the family so closely resemble one another that it is entirely unsafe for any but the most expert botanist or those who, through training or special experience, are absolutely familiar with the plants, to experiment with the wild species. Among the wild members of the family there are several which make possible or even desirable food. The more important of these are enumerated below. *Also see Chapter II, Poisonous Plants.*

Angelica, Purple Angelica
Angelica atropurpurea L.

Key-characters a tall and stout, purple-stemmed plant often 6 or 8 feet tall, the stems smooth; the leaves divided on a plan of 3, having a broad and leathery, sheathing base, the leaflets ovate to rhombic, coarsely toothed, 1-3 inches long: flowers greenish-white and small, borne in nearly globular umbels 3-6 inches in diameter: whole plant pleasantly aromatic.

Habitat and Range rich, low grounds, oftenest in the alluvium or terraces of streams or in limy swamps, southern Labrador to western Ontario and Wisconsin, south to Delaware, Pennsylvania, West Virginia, Ohio, Indiana and Illinois; ascending along mountain-brooks in Quebec and northern New England.

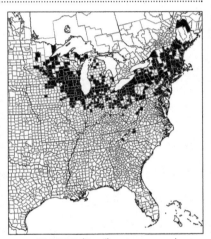

ANGELICA *(Angelica atropurpurea)*

Season of Availability leaf-stalks and young stems, late spring and early summer; roots, autumn and early spring.

Uses salad, cooked vegetable, confection.

The common northern **Angelica** has the same uses as the Old World species and from colonial days has been popular, especially through its candied roots and young shoots, which, after thorough boiling, are again boiled in sugar and allowed to cool. The tender, new stems and leaf-stalks when peeled are relished by many as a salad, but they have a rather strong flavor which is removed by boiling in two waters, when the cooked vegetable strongly suggests stewed celery. The very similar European species has long had the same uses.

Seacoast Angelica
Angelica lucida L.

Synonyms *Coelopleurum lucidum, C. actaeifolium*
Key-characters a coarse plant from 1-4 feet high, with large leaves having a conspicuously inflated base, the blade green and 3-forked, these |eetions again divided on a plan of 3, the leaflets ovate, green on both sides, coarsely toothed, from 1-3 inches long; stem coarse and green, often dotted with sticky spots, bearing round-topped umbels 3-5 inches broad, with small, white flowers followed by squarish, oblong, scale-like, ribbed dry fruits about 1/4 inch long.
Habitat and Range sandy, gravelly or ledgy sea-shores or seaside thickets, Labrador and the lower St. Lawrence to Long Island Sound.
Season of Availability early summer, while tender.
Use like stewed celery.

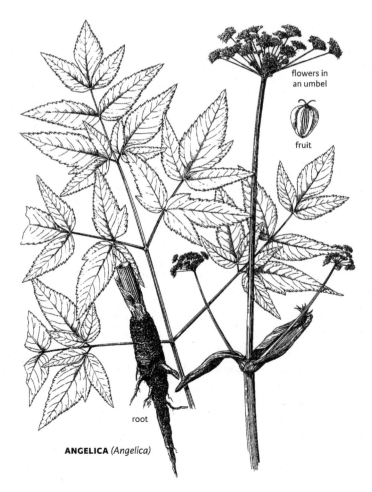

flowers in
an umbel

fruit

root

ANGELICA *(Angelica)*

The young stems and tender stalks of the young leaves, when peeled, are very juicy and with the characteristic odor and flavor of unbleached celery, although rather too strong for the European palate. When cooked like celery in two waters the young stems and leaf-stalks make a palatable and wholesome vegetable and on the shores of the Gulf of St. Lawrence and of Newfoundland-Labrador might become an important food. In his notes from the Aleutian Islands Dr. E. C. Van Dyke of the University of California made the significant entry on the labels of *Angelica lucida* of the North Pacific: "Natives eat the leaf-stalks of this raw."

Caraway
Carum carvi L.

Uses seasoning, salad, potherb, root-vegetable.

The familiar **Caraway**, now thoroughly naturalized in Newfoundland, eastern Canada, and many parts of the northern United States, has many uses available to those who are perfectly familiar with the plant but unsafe for those un-certain of its identity. The seeds are familiar seasoning, either in cookies and bread or sometimes with cheese or, after the German method, mixed with ginger, salt and butter and spread on bread. But the other uses are less familiar in America.

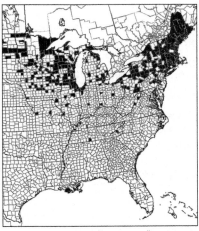

CARAWAY *(Carum carvi)*

The tender, new leaves are highly recommended by European writers as a salad, while the slightly more mature foliage is said to make a good potherb (presumably by cooking in two waters). The plant, like the carrot or parsnip, is a biennial, making a vigorous tuft of leaves and a well-filled root the first year; and upon the authority of the seventeenth century apothecary, John Parkinson,

"the roote thereof is better foode then of the Parsnep, and is pleasant and comfortable to the stomacke helping digestion." Parkinson further informs us that "the seede is conducing to all the cold greefes both of the head and stomacke; . . . the seede is much used in Bread, Cakes, &c. to give a rellish and warming qualitie to them as of a spice, and in Comfits, to eate with fruit to breake the windinesse of them."

In Parkinson's time, as above noted, the root of Caraway was fully appreciated. A century later it had already become neglected, as indicated by Bryant's statement in 1783: "The roots of the cultivated Caraways were formerly in great esteem when boiled; how they have fallen into neglect is not easy to guess, as they certainly merit a place at table, as much as some that come there."

Centella
Centella asiatica (L.) Urban

Key-characters Centella, like the Water-Pennyworts, is a low creeping herb. It differs in having the erect long-stalked ovate leaf with a broad open sinus and the 2—4-flowered basal umbels subtended by 2 conspicuous bracts.
Habitat and Range It abounds in low meadows or wet sands of the coastal plain from Mexico and Texas to Florida, thence north to Virginia and more locally to Delaware.
Uses salad and potherb?

The Asiatic species, according to Ochse, is sold in the markets of Java as raw salad or to be steamed. Ours should be tried; the succulence of the leaves is inviting.

Honewort, Wild Chervil
Cryptotaenia canadensis (L.) DC.

Key-characters stem becoming 1-3 feet tall, with remote, alternate, long-stalked, 3-parted leaves, the leaf-stalks dilated at base and somewhat clasping the stem, the leaflets oval, with a double toothing of rather coarse and broad teeth bordered by much finer slender teeth; flowers tiny, white, borne in slender-stalked irregular umbels from the summit of the plant and the upper axils; mature fruits spindle-shaped, about a third of an inch long, dry and seed-like, splitting lengthwise into halves.
Habitat and Range rich woods, and thickets or banks of streams, western New Brunswick to western Ontario, south to Georgia and Texas.
Season of Availability late spring and early summer, while young and tender.
Uses soup, potherb, salad, root-vegetable, seasoning.

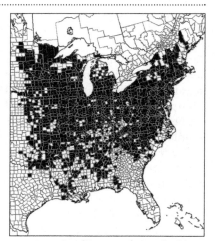

HONEWORT *(Cryptotaenia canadensis)*

The discerning Swedish explorer, Pehr Kalm, who was sent to North America by his government during the first half of the 18th century, to discover useful plants, wrote in his journal of 1749 from Fort St. Frederic (Crown Point), that this plant "abounds in the woods of all North America. The French call it cerfeuil sauvage, and make use of it in spring, in green soups, like chervil. It is universally praised here as a wholesome, anti-scorbutic plant, and as one of the best that can be had here in spring." We find few if any modern references to the use of Honewort in America except such as bear the earmarks of derivation from Kalm's statement.

How different, however, is the situation in Japan where the identical species occurs. It is there an important vegetable:

"It prefers a moist, loamy soil. The seed is sown in May between the rows of ripening grain, and covered with straw for mulch. When the grain is removed it becomes the sole occupant of the ground, and is manured and cultivated during the summer. The next following January it is usually manured with rice bran, and the earth is hilled-up over the roots so the leaves can bleach when they shoot through. The leaves appear in March, when they are pulled off at the roots, tied in bundles, and marketed. The tops are used for greens and to flavor soups, and the blanched stems are used both as a salad and boiled, and they are really a very desirable vegetable. Old plants are often lifted in the fall, and placed on gentle hot-beds made of rubbish, where they produce leaf stems for early use. These are some seven or eight inches long and quite slender. The root is also eaten when boiled and dressed with oil."

Wild Carrot, Queen Anne's Lace, Bird's-nest
Daucus carota L.

Range throughout eastern North America
Use root-vegetable.

The **Wild Carrot**, which is such a pest in many old fields, belongs to the same species as the garden carrot but its root is small and tough and there are conflicting traditions which indicate that it is scarcely edible, some people stating that it is actually poisonous. Mrs. Morrell, who writes from a large experience with edible wild plants in Maine, states that the roots raised from the seeds of the Wild Carrot are remarkably sweet.

Harbinger-of-Spring, Pepper-and-Salt
Erigenia bulbosa (Michx.) Nutt.

Use edible root.

The tiny **Harbinger-of-Spring**, growing in rich hardwood from southern Ontario and western New York to Minnesota and southward, is familiar to all lovers of Nature where it grows. Its small bulb-like root is edible.

Fennel
Foeniculum vulgare P. Mill.

Key-characters tall, smooth perennial herb with pale and very smooth cylindric stems; leaves with foot-stalk embraced by a large pair of sheaths (stipules) 1-5 inches long, the leaf itself dissected into innumerable threadlike segments; the yellow flowers in large umbrella-like clusters, suggesting those of parsnip, but more open; whole plant strongly aromatic. **Uses** seasoning, condiment.

FENNEL *(Foeniculum vulgare)*

Fennel, originally cultivated in this country, is widely naturalized in waste lands, on roadsides, etc., in the Southern States, and more locally northward to southern New England, New York, Michigan, etc. It is not greatly appreciated with us but with peoples of southern European stocks is a favorite seasoning. This has long been so. Thus, Parkinson (1640) wrote:

"the Italians especially doe much delight in the use thereof, and therefore . . . transplant it and whiten it, to make it more tender to please the taste, which being sweete and somewhat hot and comforting the stomacke, helpeth to digest the crude flegmaticke qualitie of Fish, and other viscous meats which they much inure themselves unto. We use it to lay upon Fish or to boyle it therewith and with divers other things, as also the seede in breads and other things."

Evelyn, in his Acetaria (1706), stated that it:

"recreates the Brain; especially the tender Umbrella, and young Seeds annex'd to them. The Stalks, white, plump, and soft, are to be peel'd, and then dressed like Sellery. The early tender Tufts of the emerging Leaves, being minc'd, are eaten alone with Vinegar, or Oyl and Pepper, and to correct the cooler Materials, enter properly in Composition [of Ballets]."

When one contemplates the vast wastes of Fennel about some of our more southern cities and recollects that it "recreates the Brain," it seems a pity that it is not more often used.

Cow-Parsnip, Masterwort
Heracleum maximum Bartr.

Synonym *Heracleum lanatum*
Key-characters one of the coarsest of the family, with stout stems, 3-10 feet high,

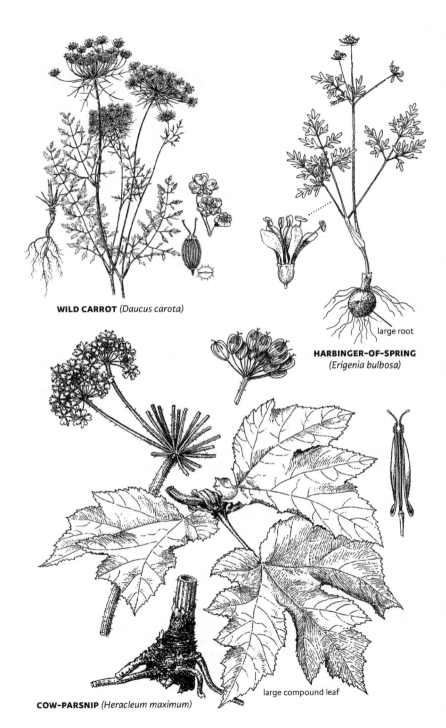

WILD CARROT *(Daucus carota)*

large root

HARBINGER-OF-SPRING
(Erigenia bulbosa)

large compound leaf

COW-PARSNIP *(Heracleum maximum)*

covered at least when young with dense whitish wool; leaves as large as those of burdock or rhubarb, divided into 3 main divisions, the leaf-stalk with a conspicuously inflated and clasping base, the coarse and irregularly toothed leaflets suggesting large maple leaves, whitened with wool on the under surface; flower-clusters umbrella-like, very large, often 6 inches to a foot across, flat-topped, with many of the uneven, white, marginal flowers 1/2 inch broad.
Habitat and Range rich ground, alluvial thickets and seashores, Newfoundland to Alaska, south to upland North Carolina, Kentucky, Kansas, and in the western mountains.
Season of Availability late spring and early summer.

COW-PARSNIP *(Heracleum maximum)*

Uses salad, cooked vegetable (as stewed celery), root-vegetable, substitute for salt.

Although the **Cow-Parsnip** is a picturesque but coarse and ill-smelling plant not generally recognized among the whites as a food-plant, its young leaf-stalks and young stems, before the expanding of the flowers, when properly prepared are quite as wholesome and almost as palatable as stewed celery. The tender stalks are as coarse as large stalks of celery, of an aromatic and sweetish flavor, though when green with a strong and disagreeable taste. Among the northern Indians, who eat the peeled stalks either raw or cooked, they have always been in high repute. In our own experience, the raw stalks, on account of the disagreeable odor and taste, are not attractive, but when boiled in two waters (the first water thrown off) they are an agreeable or even delicious vegetable.

Chestnut, writing of the food-plants of the Indians of Mendocino County, California, says: "Mr. George Grist who has had an extended experience with the Indians of Bound Valley, and who in 1892 was the Government farmer for the reservation, informed me that he had seen the hollow basal portion of the plant used as a substitute for salt. It was dried in short cylinders and eaten either in the dry state with other food or placed in the frying pan and cooked into the substance to be eaten."

Some Indians also cooked the large root. Dr. H. H. Smith wrote: "This is another of the Meskwaki potatoes, of which there is an unlimited supply on the reservation. It is cooked like the rutabaga and tastes somewhat like it. We had always supposed the root to be poisonous, but they experience no ill effect from its use. The Meskwaki called our attention to the resemblance of the side roots to the ginseng root, and also to the fact that it smells the same as ginseng when fresh or dried. The white man so often mulcts the Indian that it seems poetic justice when the tables are turned. Many of the Meskwaki sold these side roots dried and tied like ginseng for ginseng to a white buyer who used to visit the reservation buying ginseng, and he never discovered the difference. Doubtless the Chinese, the ultimate consumers, never found out the difference, either. The first Meskwaki name given is the one used when mentioning it for medicinal use, and for the table the name 'skipwa'ok' is given. They say the roots are like sweet potatoes."

European Cow-Parsnip, Hogweed, Eltrot
Heracleum sphondylium L.

Key-characters similar to the native *Heracleum maximum*, but greener and with harsh hairiness; the leaves with 3-7 bluntly toothed leaflets only 2-5 inches long. A weed of fields and roadsides in southeastern Newfoundland, and locally from Cape Breton to northern New York and southern New England (naturalized from Eurasia).
Use cooked vegetable, beer.

In Eurasia their **Cow-Parsnip** is used, by those who understand its value, as a vegetable. Thus we find the English student of plant-lore, Phoebe Lankester, saying:

"This is one of our common wayside plants, which might really be usefully employed, if our peasantry were better informed as to the nature and properties of the wild vegetation surrounding them. It is generally looked upon merely as a noxious weed, though in some districts where it grows, the leaves are collected and given to pigs, who quickly fatten upon them; hence the plant is called Hogweed. The stalks when stripped of their rind, which is somewhat acrid, are edible, and are used as food in some parts of Asiatic Russia. In Siberia and Russia the stalks are dried in the sun, when a sweet substance exudes from them, which resembles sugar, and is eaten as a great delicacy. A spirit is distilled from the stalks thus prepared, by first fermenting them with water and either mingling bilberries with them or not. Gmelin says this spirit is more agreeable to the taste than spirit distilled from corn. The young shoots and leaves may be boiled and eaten as a green vegetable, and when just sprouting from the ground resemble asparagus in flavour. This experiment is, however, seldom tried, owing to the ignorance of those to whom such an addition to the table would be a benefit and luxury."

Where it abounds, as near Trepassey in southeastern Newfoundland, it is despised because it taints the milk. Mrs. Lankester suggests a better use for it.

Water-Pennywort
Hydrocotyle, 6 species.

Key-characters small, soft-stemmed creeping herbs with round, scallop-edged leaves half an inch to 4 inches across, either with a deep sinus at the junction with the leaf-stalk or centrally attached; flowers small, greenish-white in umbels or clusters or

sometimes in small bunches along a slender axis, maturing into 2-parted ribbed fruits.
Uses salad and potherb?

We know nothing of the desirability of the **Water-Pennyworts** for food. Ochse states that in Java the native species, very similar to ours, "are eaten whole, raw or steamed . . . They are frequently sold in the markets." It should be easy to test our species.

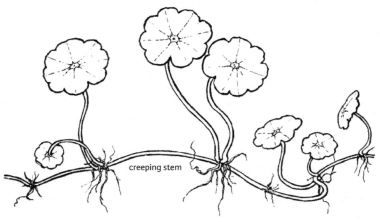

WATER-PENNYWORT *(Hydrocotyle)*

Scotch Lovage, Alexanders (Newfoundland)
Ligusticum scoticum L.

Key-characters a rather stout plant of sea-shores, with long-stalked leaves in basal clusters; the leaf-stalk crimson or purple at the broad, sheathing base, with 3 forks bearing ovate, rather coarsely toothed, glossy leaflets 1-3 inches long; the flowering stems arching, bearing flat-topped, somewhat umbrella-shaped clusters of white flowers, followed by pale-brown, dry, oblong fruits nearly half an inch in length.
Habitat and Range ledgy, gravelly or sandy sea-shores, Labrador to New York, common northward, becoming rare southward.
Season of Availability early summer.
Uses potherb, celery-substitute, confection.

In America **Scotch Lovage** has never come into general favor, but in the Hebrides and other maritime sections of Scotland it has long been used, either as a cooked potherb or, when blanched by covering with litter, the leaf-stalks have found use as a substitute for celery. The whole plant has an aromatic odor, but when raw a strong flavor, and it is probable that to most palates it would be acceptable only by cooking in two or more waters. The young shoots are sometimes candied like Angelica.

Sweet Cicely
Osmorrhiza, ca. 4 species

Key-characters leaves fern-like, very delicately dissected, with 3 primary forkings to the leaf-stalk; fruits borne in umbels (the branches or rays of the cluster spreading like the rays of an umbrella), elongate, seed-like, becoming 1/2-3/4 inch long, and covered with strong, stiff hairs by which the 2 halves of the fruit readily catch upon the clothes.

Habitat and Range rich woods, various species from southern Labrador and Newfoundland across the continent, south through the eastern and central states.

Season of Availability year-round.

Use anise-flavoring.

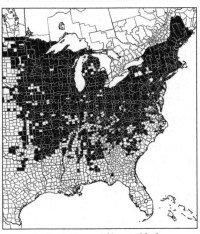

SWEET CICELY *(Osmorrhiza)*

The stout, fleshy and forking roots of these plants have a considerable amount of anise-oil, some species more than others, and for those who care for that flavor make a readily available camp-seasoning.

Wild Parsnip
Pastinaca sativa L.

Use cooked vegetable.

There is an impression that the roots of the **Wild Parsnip** are poisonous but, as Halsted has well said, it is probable that all cases of poisoning by "Wild Parsnip" are due to the mistaking for it of other plants such as **Water-Hemlock** (*Cicuta*), which has large roots smelling like parsnips. Wild Parsnip is a common weed of rubbish heaps, waste lands and rich roadsides, where it has been introduced by seed from the cultivated strains of the species. When these wild plants grow in sufficiently rich soil outside the garden, there should be no reason why the roots should not be used by those who are certain of the identity of the plant.

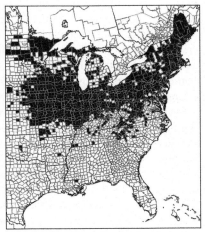

WILD PARSNIP *(Pastinaca sativa)*

Caution use care when handling these plants as they are skin-irritants.

Water-Parsnip
Sium suave Walt.

Synonyms *Sium cicutifolium*
Uses root-vegetable, relish.

The **Water-Parsnip** grows in habitats similar to those occupied by **Water-Hemlock or Beaver-poison** (*Cicuta*); and since the roots of the latter plant are deadly poisonous to eat, only those who are thoroughly familiar with the two plants at all stages of development should venture to try the roots of *Sium*— and then first on a rabbit or guinea-pig. Our authority for the use of roots of our Water-Parsnip (*Sium*) as food by the Indians is Sir John Richardson, who certainly knew his plants and who wrote:

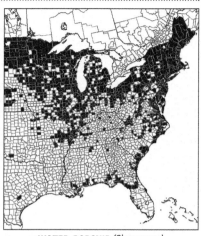

WATER-PARSNIP *(Sium suave)*

"From a party of Chepewyans who were encamped on the Otter Lake, we procured a quantity of a small white root, about the thickness of a goose quill, which had an agreeable nutty flavor. I ascertained that it was the root of the *Sium suave*. The poisonous roots of *Cicuta virosa, maculata,* and *bulbifera,* are often mistaken for the edible one, and have proved fatal to several laborers in the Company's [Hudson Bay Co's.] service. The natives distinguish the proper kind by the last year's stem, which has the rays of its umbel ribbed or angled, while the Cicutae have round and smooth flower-stalks. When the plant has put out its leaves by which it is most easily identified, the roots lose their crispness and become woody. The edible root is named *uskotask* by the Crees, and *queue de rat* by the Canadians. The poisonous kinds are called *manito-skatask,* and by the voyageurs *carrotte de Moreau,* after a man who died from eating them."

It is interesting that the Chippewayans should independently have discovered the food-value of *Sium* roots, for the closest relative of our plant is the Old World Skirret, *Sium sisarum*. The Skirret has had some popularity as a garden vegetable, especially in Europe, where it has been called "the sweetest, whitest, and most pleasant of roots." Bryant compares it to parsnip and gives a detailed account of extraction of sugar from the roots.

By Coville it is stated that the Klamath Indians eat the aromatic foliage of our plant as a relish. The white man's taste is hardly up to that.

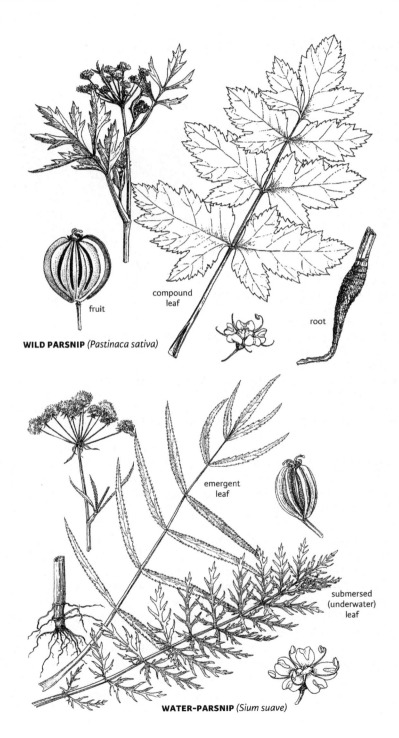

fruit

compound
leaf

root

WILD PARSNIP *(Pastinaca sativa)*

emergent
leaf

submersed
(underwater)
leaf

WATER-PARSNIP *(Sium suave)*

Apocynaceae DOGBANE FAMILY

Milkweeds, Silkweeds
Asclepias (a dozen useful species)

Key-characters steins stoutish, unbranched, with milky juice, bearing opposite, oblong to ovate and entire leaves with a broad midrib; in summer familiar to every one because of the showy clusters of flowers, each with 5 tubular hoods, followed by the large greenish pods bearing plumose or silky seeds. **Habitat and Range** the common Milkweed or Silkweed, *A. syriaca*, the species most generally gathered, in dry, open soil, roadsides, fence-rows or borders of fields, New Brunswick to Saskatchewan and southward; other species more localized. **Season of Availability** new shoots, late spring and early summer; sugar from flowers, through summer; young pods, summer and early autumn.

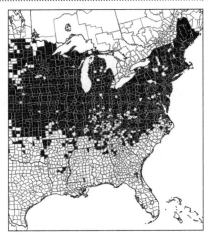

COMMON MILKWEED *(Asclepias syriaca)*

Uses potherb, asparagus, cooked vegetable, sugar, chewing-gum. **Caution** other plants with upright habit and milky juice but inedible stems are to be guarded against, especially the Spurges (Euphorbia) in which the leaves are scattered and alternate, plants reputed to be poisonous; and the Dogbanes (see p. 34).

The use of Milkweed-shoots while the leaves are still young and unexpanded is somewhat general in eastern America, the shoots when a few inches high being rubbed through the hand to remove the wool and cooked and served like asparagus. The leaves before they become tough and bitter are sometimes used like spinach, care being taken to throw off the first water which has extracted the bitter from the milky juice.

The Indians likewise cooked the young flower-clusters while still in bud as greens, and Gilmore tells us that, among the Dakotas the young seed-pods while very immature and green are boiled and eaten, usually with meat. We are ready, from careful experimentation, to commend most highly this important discovery of the Dakotas. The pods when almost full-grown but still solid make, when cooked, a most palatable green vegetable, comparable with okra. Singularly enough, if the pods are gathered at just the right stage, the seeds and silk within cook up as a soft and delicate mass. If, however, the pods have become in the least elastic (under pressure of the fingers) they will cook up tough and stringy and the silk will be too obvious. The young and firm pods boiled in salted water, with a pinch of soda, may likewise be canned like

any other vegetable and make a novel and delicious addition to the winter supply.
The most surprising use of Milkweed is one that is not generally practiced and which needs verification. In his journal of explorations in America, the famous Swedish traveller, Pehr Kalm, wrote in the 18th century:

"The French in Canada make a sugar of the flowers, which for the purpose are gathered in the morning, when they are covered all over with dew. This dew is expressed, and by boiling yields a very good brown, palatable sugar."

Common Milkweed *(Asclepias syriaca* L.) is the species generally used for cooking, but it is probable that several other similar species are just as good. The only one, apparently, which has found its way into the literature of edible plants, except **Swamp Milkweed**, *A. incarnata* L. (which is good) seems to be the **Butterfly-weed**, *A. tuberosa* L., but on account of its shaggy-pubescent and slender stems it is not inviting. Furthermore, its roots are a demonstrated poison. For that matter, the raw shoots of any Milkweed may be toxic.

We have tried the young pods of Asclepias incarnata and some of the smaller species. These have not proved attractive. Some of the larger species more closely related to *A. syriaca* should be tested: such species as *A. sullivantii*, and *A. latifolia* and *A. speciosa* of the western states.

The following item by H. C. Skeels, published in the American Botanist, vol. vi. 77 (1904), should interest typical modern Americans.

"Milkweed Chewing Gum.—The boys of the prairies who pull off flower heads of rosin-weed, are matched by the children of Grand Rapids, Michigan. These children break the midribs of the leaves of the common milkweed *(Asclepias syriaca)* and the milky juice oozes out. In a few minutes it hardens, is collected and used for gum. I cannot vouch for its flavor, not having tried it, but have the assurance of one who has that 'it was good.'"

Barrows, in his account of the ethnobotany of southern California, states that by the Indians of that region the sap of some of the Milkweeds is collected and allowed to stand over night near a fire. It soon coagulates and is then used as a chewing-gum, the bitter taste soon disappearing.

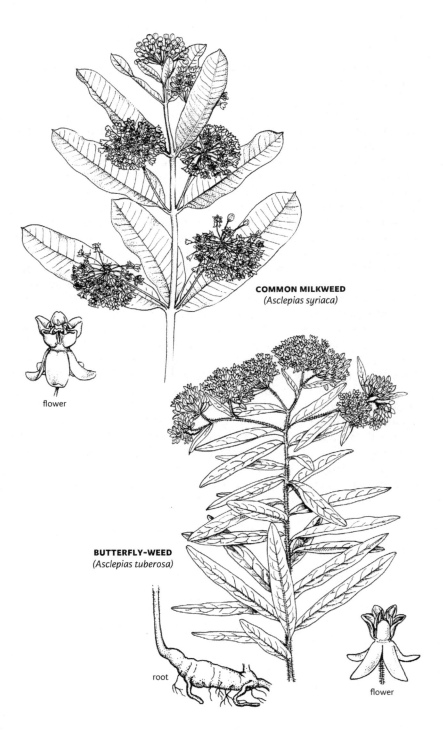

COMMON MILKWEED
(*Asclepias syriaca*)

flower

BUTTERFLY-WEED
(*Asclepias tuberosa*)

root

flower

Aquifoliaceae HOLLY FAMILY

Cassina (or Cassena) or Yaupon

Ilex glabra (L.) Gray (Black Alder)
Ilex laevigata (Pursh) Gray (Holly)
Ilex opaca Ait. (American Holly)
Ilex verticillata (L.) Gray (Holly)
Ilex vomitoria Ait. (Gall-berry or Inkberry)

Use tea.

Without question **Cassina or Yaupon** is the most desirable substitute we have for tea; it is, therefore, most unfortunate that it should be handicapped by the technical name *Ilex vomitoria*. Fortunately, however, the country people of the southern coastal plain, from Texas to Florida, thence northward into the flat part of Arkansas and around the coast eastward to the region of Cape Henry and the lower James River, know it only by its old Indian names and harvest it, unprejudiced, as a delicious and slightly tonic tea. The offensive name came from the old custom of southern Indians of drinking a very strong brew, supposed by some to be of Cassina, in ceremonial assemblies until it produced results never thought of in ordinary and temperate use of properly made tea.

The invidious charges against Cassina which resulted in an uninviting specific name may, after all, have been too hastily made. At least, Porcher, who intimately knew Cassina, published the following defense of it, written by his correspondent, Simmes, in 1863:

"I think there is some mistake among the authorities you quote when they assert this to be the material out of which the Indians manufacture the famous 'Black Drink' used at their most solemn festivals, and which I have always understood, while travelling among them forty years ago, to be compounded of

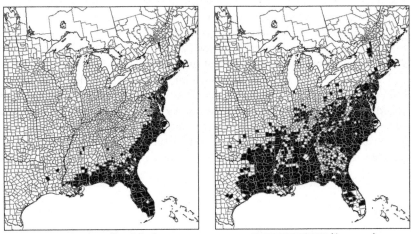

BLACK ALDER *(Ilex glabra)*   **AMERICAN HOLLY** *(Ilex opaca)*

various roots, by decoction, and acting as a powerful emetic. The leaves used moderately as tea have never, as I believe, acted thus upon the system."

The leaves, like those of oriental tea, contain an appreciable amount of caffeine, this rendering the decoction from them mildly stimulating. I. vomitoria is a stiffly branched shrub or small tree with close whitish-gray bark and small, leathery and evergreen bluntly scalloped leaves, and black, seedy berries along the branchlets. Every one in the Southeast knows it. The leaves are not simply harvested and brewed; if they were they would make an unpalatable drink, with strong herby taste. They must, like oriental tea-leaves, be properly prepared. Here are Porcher's directions, based in part on the preparation of the related South American mate or Paraguay Tea, *Ilex paraguayensis*:

"It can be gathered during the whole year. It is collected in the woods—'a process of kiln-drying is resorted to upon the spot, and afterward the branches and leaves are transported to some crude mill and powdered in mortars. The substance, after this operation, is almost a powder, though small stems, denuded of their bark, are always permitted to remain.' A small quantity of the leaf, either with or without sugar, is placed in a common bowl, upon which cold water is poured; after standing a short time, boiling water is added, and it is at once ready for use. It must be imbibed through a tube on account of the particles of leaf and stem which float upon the surface of the liquid." In practice, however, a simple strainer, bit of fine cheese-cloth or a filter-paper have been found perfectly practicable!

Ilex cassine, a more southern evergreen with much larger and entire leaves, may be similarly used, as are some other evergreen-leaved species of the South.

The common **Inkberry or Gallberry**, *Ilex glabra*, a low evergreen shrub of peaty or sandy soils from Louisiana to Florida, thence north on the coastal plain to Massachusetts, and common in bogs or on pond-margins of western Nova Scotia, has shining oblong to narrowly wedge-shaped leaves an inch or two long, and hard black berries along the branchlets. Its leaves also contain caffeine and are said to yield a good tea.

Other species of *Ilex*, the evergreen **Holly**, *Ilex opaca*, a tree with spiny-margined and very stiff evergreen leaves and red berries, and **Black Alder or Winterberry**, *Ilex verticillata*, a shrub of swamps with deciduous toothed leaves and with red berries persisting into winter along the branches, have often been commended for tea-making, doubtless chiefly because of their generic affinity to Cassina and Inkberry, but the note by Dr. Lee, quoted under Sassafras, states that the leaves of *I. opaca* were in the South "the most common substitute for tea during the Civil War." Neither of these species contains caffeine, which gives the others their tea-like quality.

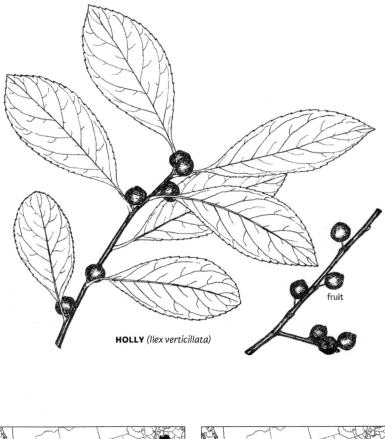

HOLLY *(Ilex verticillata)*

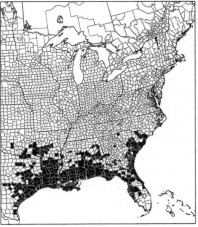

fruit

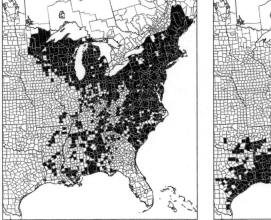

HOLLY *(Ilex verticillata)*   **GALL-BERRY** *(Ilex vomitoria)*

Araceae ARUM FAMILY

All the members of this family contain acrid and usually peppery principles which reside in minute crystals (raphides) of calcium oxalate scattered through the fresh tissue. The peppery and puckering qualities of these crystals are familiar to all country boys of eastern America in the rounded rootstock of the Indian Turnip or Jack-in-the-Pulpit. These properties are dispelled by heat and drying through the breaking up of the crystals, although it is doubtful if the crystals are much, if at all, affected by boiling. After thorough and prolonged drying the plants become mild and pleasant to the taste. It is surprising to find that quite independently the native peoples of remote parts of the world have discovered this fact and have come to rely upon members of the Arum family as sources of food.

Sweet Flag, Calamus

Acorus americanus (Raf.) Raf. (native)
Acorus calamus L. (introduced)

Key-characters leaves resembling Iris, but yellowish-green in tone, and when bruised giving off an aromatic fragrance; flowers minute, borne in a dense, drab, dryish, finger-like spike from the side of a leaf-like stalk; root stout, horizontal, covered with shreddy bases of old leaves; with a gingery odor and taste.
Habitat shallow water of river- and pond-margins or inundated meadows and swamps.
Range Prince Edward Island to the Great Lakes Region, locally to Idaho, south to Florida and Texas.
Season of Availability spring.
Uses confection, salad.

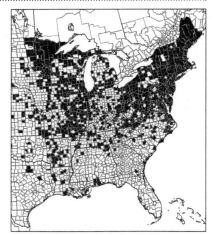

SWEET FLAG *(Acorus)*

Candied Sweet Flag roots have long been popular both in Europe and America as an aromatic confection; and the making of candied flag-root was one of the few frivolities of our great-great-grandmothers. The candied roots have been much sold by the Shakers and others in New England. The fresh root is gingery or peppery and with a peculiar, distinctive soapy taste unpleasant to some, and the confection is too strong for wholesale consumption, though forming a pleasant and tempting nibble. To candy the root, give it two or three days of continuous boiling, cut it into small pieces and finally boil a few minutes in sugar with only enough water to make a rich syrup.

The young shoots in the spring have a very delicate and tender inner portion (the innermost partly developed leaves surrounded by the tough bases of the outer leaves) which forms a pleasant nibble on a tramping trip and an unusually palatable salad for an out-of-door lunch.

Green Dragon
Arisaema dracontium (L.) Schott

The **Green Dragon** is related to Jack-in-the-Pulpit, but has the leaves cut into several leaflets. The root has undoubtedly similar properties (see description below).

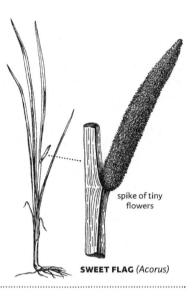

spike of tiny flowers

SWEET FLAG *(Acorus)*

Jack-in-the-Pulpit, Indian-Turnip
Arisaema triphyllum (L.) Schott

Key-characters familiar at its flowering season in spring and early summer on account of the "Jack"; recognizable in the autumn, when the root is well filled, by the 3-parted old leaves on succulent leaf-stalks, by the fruit consisting of scarlet berries borne in a dense egg-shaped cluster; and by the round root, varying in size from that of a small nut to a diameter of 2 or 3 inches.
Habitat rich, low woods, chiefly near streams.
Range eastern Quebec to Manitoba and southward.
Season of Availability early spring and late autumn, when the plant is resting.
Use breadstuff.

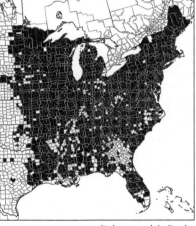

JACK-IN THE -PULPIT *(Arisaema triphyllum)*

The root of **Jack-in-the-Pulpit** seems to have been much used by the Indians as a source of flour. Jacob Bigelow, one of the pioneers in New England botany and a conspicuous figure in American medical history, was much interested in the use of these roots; and he stated that the acrid principle has "no affinity for water." Consequently, as many experiments have shown, the acridity is not dispelled by boiling, although dry heat or prolonged exposure to the air breaks up the crystals. After experimenting with the roots, Bigelow concluded that, when properly dried, they furnished a great store of fine white starch. The root, according to him, should be peeled, mashed, grated or pulverized, put into a strainer, and repeatedly washed to take out the starch. These washings, thoroughly pulverized, contain, according to Bigelow, approximately one-quarter of the weight of the original root and are a wholesome and palatable flour. Kephart's recipe differs from Bigelow's only slightly, Kephart first roasting the roots, then powdering, heating again and letting stand a few days until it becomes bland. The native treatment of the roots of related Himalayan species is still different, for Masters tells us that in the Himalayas the roots are "beaten into a pulp with water, and allowed to ferment, a process which destroys their acridity."

The Fernald family has secured a very palatable cake, biscuit or bread from the fleshy roots of Jack-in-the-Pulpit without this washing-out of the starch. By cutting the roots into very thin slices and then forgetting about them they have been found after some weeks to be crisply dry and wholly mild. Then ground to flour they have a mild suggestion of cocoa-flavor.

It is stated by some authors that the berries were eaten by the Indians; but this statement should be taken with caution (or "with a good deal of salt" to overcome the pepperiness of the berries). After prolonged drying, however, the berries may prove to be as palatable as those of the Arrow-Arum, discussed below.

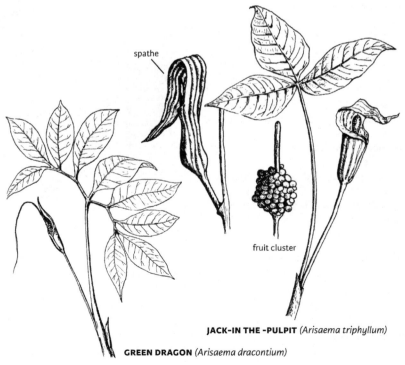

spathe

fruit cluster

JACK-IN THE -PULPIT *(Arisaema triphyllum)*

GREEN DRAGON *(Arisaema dracontium)*

Wild Calla, Water-Arum, Water-Dragons
Calla palustris L.

Key-characters stems trailing and rooting freely in shallow water or muck, 1/2-1 inch in diameter, greenish and succulent, terminated by tufts of heart-shaped leaves on long stalks; the flowers forming an egg-shaped mass in the axil of an open, greenish-white bract or spathe, suggesting a miniature calla lily; berries scarlet, in a head.
Habitat quagmires, quaking bogs and edges of swamps.
Range across the cooler parts of temperate North America, extending locally south to New Jersey, Pennsylvania and the Great Lakes region.
Season of Availability late autumn and early spring while the rootstocks are filled.
Use breadstuff.

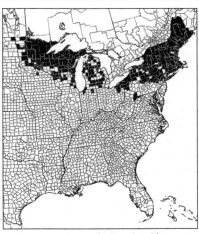

WILD CALLA *(Calla palustris)*

The fame of **Wild Calla** as a bread-food seems to have originated with Linnaeus's account of its use in Scandinavia. The original account was in the Flora Lapponica, but many years later there was published a more available English account from which we quote:

"Missen bread is made of Water Dragons *(Calla palustris)*. The roots of this plant are taken up in spring, before the leaves come forth, and, after being extremely well washed, are dried either in the sun or in the house. The fibrous parts are then taken away, and the remainder dried in an oven. Afterwards it is bruised in a hollow vessel or tub, made of fir wood, about three feet deep; as is also practised occasionally with the fir bark. The dried roots are chopped in this vessel, with a kind of spade, like cabbage for making sour kale (sour crout), till they become as small as peas or oatmeal, when they acquire a pleasant sweetish smell; after which they are ground. The meal is boiled slowly in water, being continually kept stirring, till it grows as thick as flammery. In this state it is left standing in the pot for three or four days and nights. Some persons let it remain but twenty-four hours; but the longer the better, for if used immediately it is bitter and acrid; both which qualities go off by keeping. It is mixed for use, either with the meal made of fir bark, or with some other kind of flour, not being usually to be had in sufficient quantity by itself; for the plant is, in many places, very scarce, though here in such abundance that cart loads of it are collected at a time. This kind of flammery, being mixed with flour, as I have just mentioned, is baked into bread, which proves as tough as rye-bread, but is perfectly sweet and white. It is really, when new, extremely well-flavoured."

The seeds of Wild Calla may likewise be ground into flour, but the meal should be dried for a long time to rid it of the acrid and biting pepperiness.

Golden-club, Tuckahoe
Orontium aquaticum L.

Key-characters and Habitat an aquatic plant with long-stalked oblong leaves in rosettes at the summit of the large rootstock, bearing in spring finger-like, spongy, yellow spikes on naked fleshy stalks, afterward followed by bean-like greenish seeds.

Range southeastern and central Massachusetts to Florida, chiefly on the coastal plain.

Season of Availability roots, autumn and spring when well filled; seeds in summer.

Uses breadstuff, starchy vegetable.

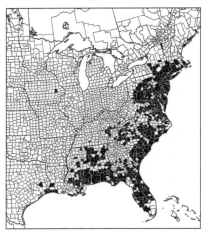

GOLDEN-CLUB *(Orontium aquaticum)*

The **Golden-club** was used by the American Indians somewhat interchangeably with the **Green Arum** (*Peltandra*) under the name *Tawkee or Tuckahoe*, the roots and seeds being prepared in the same way and apparently having similar properties. (See discussion of **Green Arum**, p. 86).

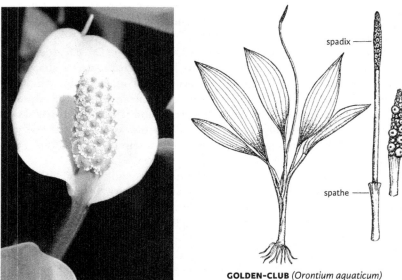

spadix

spathe

WILD CALLA *(Calla palustris)*

GOLDEN-CLUB *(Orontium aquaticum)*

As enthusiastic an account as any was that of the Swedish botanist, Pehr Kalm, in his journal of March 17th, 1749: "Taw-kee is another plant, so called by the Indians, who eat it. Some of them call it Taw-kim, and others Tackvim. . . The cattle, hogs and stags, are very fond of the leaves in spring; . . . The Indians pluck the seeds, and keep them for eating. They cannot be eaten fresh or raw, but must be dried. The Indians were forced to boil them repeatedly in water, before they were fit for use; and then they ate them like pease. . . . Sometimes they employ these seeds instead of bread. Some of the Swedes likewise ate them; and the old men among them told me, they liked this food better than any of the other plants which the Indians formerly made use of. This Taw-kee was the Orontium aquaticum."

Arrow-Arum, Green Arrow, Tuckahoe
Peltandra virginica (L.) Schott '

Key-characters and Habitat plant of pond-margins, quaking bogs and boggy thickets, with rosettes of ascending leaves with succulent long stalks and arrow-shaped blades; readily recognizable in flower and fruit by its leathery green to whitish cup or spathe (suggesting that of the calla lily), which surrounds the dense spike of minute flowers, or in fruit a mass of slightly pulpy, green to dark-brown globular berries; root large and perpendicular, difficult to dig.
Range southern Maine to the Great Lakes, south to the Gulf; a related species, *Peltandra sagittifolia* (Michx.) Morong, with broader white spathe and crimson berries, in the Southern States.

ARROW-ARUM *(Peltandra virginica)*

Season of Availability root, in spring or autumn, while stored with food; seeds in autumn or spring (in the spring found floating as slightly gelatinous, globular, amber-colored berries about half-an-inch in diameter, with the hard seed inside).
Uses breadstuff, starchy vegetable.

In historical writings and in the literature of Indian foods, the **Green Arrow** has received a large share of attention, chiefly on account of the discussion by Captain John Smith. Whether Captain Smith based his observations on the root of Green Arrow or upon the related **Golden-club**, *Orontium*, is not clear; for both plants have similar roots and similar seeds and both were apparently used indiscriminately by the Indians. In his Historie of Virginia, Captain Smith wrote in 1626:

"We had more Sturgeon, than could be devoured by Dog and Man, of which the industrious by drying and pounding, mingled with Caviare, Sorell and other wholesome hearbes would make bread and good meate: others would gather as much Tockwhogh roots, in a day as would make them bread a weeke, so that of those wilde fruites, and what we caught, we liued very well in regard of such a diet. But such was the strange condition of 150, that had they not beene forced nolens, volens, perforce to gather and prepare their victuall they would all have starued or have eaten one another."

"The chiefe root they have for food is called Tockawhoughe. It groweth like a flagge in Marishes. In one day a Salvage will gather sufficient for a weeke. These roots are much of the greatnesse and taste of Potatoes. They use to cover a great many of them with Oke leaues and Ferne, and then cover all with earth in the manner of a Colepit; over it, on each side, they continue a great fire 24 houres before they dare eat it. Raw it is no better than poyson, and being rosted, except it be tender and the heat abated, or sliced and dryed in the Sunne, mixed with sorrell and meale or such like, it will prickle and torment the throat extremely, and yet in sommer they vse this ordinarily for bread."

Although Captain Smith found that the root "being roasted, . . . will prickle and torment the throat extremely," Pehr Kalm, the Swedish traveler, writing from New Jersey in 1749, gave it a more favorable estimate: "Taw-ho and Taw-him was the Indian name of another plant, the root of which they eat. Some of them likewise call it Tuckah; but most of the Swedes still knew it by the name of Taw-ho. . . . Hogs are very greedy of the roots, and grow very fat by feeding on them.... When they are fresh, they have a pungent taste, and are reckoned a poison in that fresh state. Nor did the Indians ever venture to eat them raw, but prepared them in the following manner: They gathered a great heap of these roots, dug a great long hole, ... into which they put the roots, and covered them with the earth . . .; they made a great fire above it, . . . and then they dug up the roots, and consumed them with great avidity. These roots, when prepared in this manner, I am told, taste like potatoes." Later writers seem to have depended very largely upon Smith's account; but in a manuscript letter preserved at the Gray Herbarium, the late Albert Commons, who during his long life of active botanizing was recognized as the leading

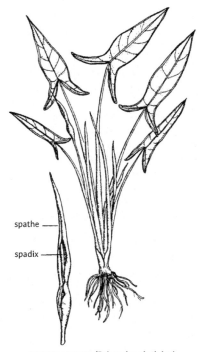

spathe

spadix

ARROW-ARUM *(Peltandra virginica)*

field-botanist of Delaware, presents a different story. Mr. Commons states that, although the fresh seeds are slightly acrid, the roots and leaves are not so. This divergence from the account by Smith would indicate that occasionally the roots lack the peppery quality which is generally found in the family. The root contains a large amount of starchy matter and when thoroughly dried it quite lacks the pungent taste. The root should be carefully experimented with, for, if it proves to be a source of palatable meal, its abundance and size would make it of considerable importance.

The seeds were stated by Rafinesque, one of the most picturesque and erratic writers on natural history and every other field of learning, to be used as a substitute for pepper; but other observers have stated that by the Indians the boiled berries were considered a great dainty. It is noteworthy that seeds which have been kept for several years are perfectly palatable, slightly sweetish, suggesting in taste parched Indian corn; and seeds which have soaked over winter in the water of ponds have only the slightest suggestion of pepperiness, which is readily dispelled by heat or prolonged drying. From these seeds a palatable but unsightly bread can be made, blackish-brown in color, and tasting like corncake with a strong flavor of cocoa. In our experiment one-and-a-half quarts of the water-soaked berries, when dried and ground, furnished only one gill (½ cup) of meal.

Skunk-Cabbage, Swamp-Cabbage
Symplocarpus foetidus (L.) Salisb. Ex Nutt.

Key-characters familiar to most people on account of the peculiar mottled and striped, leathery, shell-shaped spathe in the early spring, surrounding a globular mass of insignificant flowers, and from its skunk-like odor when bruised; after flowering the leaves developing rapidly into a clump slightly suggesting a cabbage, the individual leaves having an outline suggesting the familiar burdock leaf, but smooth and moist to the touch; the root often as large as the human forearm, perpendicular, and strongly anchored by pale, cord-like fibres.
Habitat swampy woods.
Range Quebec to western Ontario, south to Georgia and Missouri.
Season of Availability roots in late autumn and early spring while well filled; leaves in the spring while tender.
Uses breadstuff, potherb.

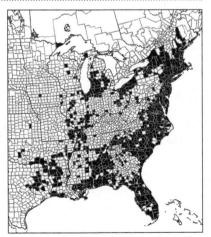

SKUNK-CABBAGE *(Symplocarpus foetidus)*

The roots of the Skunk-Cabbage have had repute among the eastern Indians as a source of bread. In regions where the plant thrives the roots are abundant but difficult to dig; and obviously, for many reasons, only an enthusiast will try to secure them. It is probable that drying or baking before final use will dispel the acrid properties, as in *Peltandra* and *Arisaema*, but our own experience shows that three weeks of drying is insufficient to dispel the peppery quality. The bread made from the flour dried for three weeks is palatable, having a suggestion of cocoa-flavor, but a few minutes after it has been eaten the mouth stings with the peculiar burning and puckering sensation familiar to all who have tasted the fresh root of Jack-in-the-Pulpit. One average root gives about half a cup of flour.

A more available food is found in the "cabbage" or young tuft of leaves, which, in spite of inevitable prejudice on account of the odor of the bruised plant, makes a not wholly unpalatable vegetable. During boiling no trace of the characteristic, disagreeable odor is given off, but the cabbage should be cooked in several waters to which has been added a pinch of baking soda. Serve with vinegar and butter or other sauce. Our Italian immigrants often make use of these greens which, if prejudice were forgotten, might abundantly serve a large population. Our experience indicates that the plants vary, sometimes being quite mild, sometimes peppery. If one is in luck he will cook only the former.

Caution In gathering the young cabbages extreme caution must be taken not to include the **White Hellebore** or **Indian Poke** (*Veratrum viride* Ait.) which grows with the Skunk-Cabbage and is a violent poison. *Veratrum* (see p. 57) has an upright, elongating stem becoming several feet high; and the elliptic, sessile leaves are strongly pleated or fluted; the Skunk-Cabbage has the leaves all from the top of the root, with no elongate stem, and the leaves are rounded at base, on definite leaf-stalks, and not pleated.

young leaves

SKUNK-CABBAGE (*Symplocarpus foetidus*)
flower, left; spring scene, facing page

Araliaceae GINSENG FAMILY

Wild Sarsaparilla
Aralia nudicaulis L.

Uses ingredient in root-beer, emergency-food.

The long rootstock of the common **Wild Sarsaparilla** of dry woods is often used as an ingredient of root-beer. We have the statement of the pioneer New England botanist, Manasseh Cutler, that during their wars or hunting expeditions, the Indians subsisted for long periods of time on these roots.

Spikenard, Life-of-Man, Pettymorrel
Aralia racemosa L.

Uses root-vegetable, cooked green vegetable, ingredient in root beer, jelly.

The familiar **American Spikenard**, found in rich woods from eastern Quebec to Manitoba, south to Virginia, in the upland to Georgia and Alabama, and to Missouri and eastern Kansas, has long, cylindric, often branching clusters of purplish berries which have a pleasant aromatic flavor, but are not considered edible. The stout root is pleasantly aromatic and in the northern states is one of the popular ingredients of root-beer.

Dr. Huron H. Smith told of the Menomini Indians cooking the "Indian Spikenard" roots. "An aboriginal Menomini dish was spikenard root, wild onion, wild gooseberry and sugar. This is described as being very fine." Mrs. Morrell, writing from Maine, says: "Each year I make jelly with berries of Life-of-Man, a great favorite." The closely similar Aralia cordata of Japan is there very important. Seeds are sown in any unused and fertile corner. When the plants

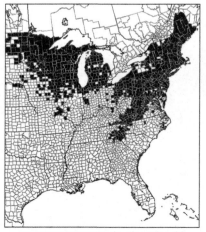
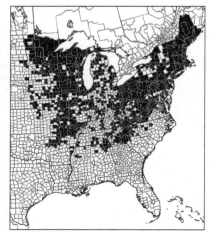

WILD SARSAPARILLA *(Aralia nudicaulis)*　　　**SPIKENARD** *(Aralia racemosa)*

are three or four years old the roots are covered with soil or litter and the blanched new stems, like asparagus, are harvested and sold in the market. "Stewed and served with sauce . . . an agreeable and palatable dish." Our common Spikenard has great possibilities.

Angelica-tree, Hercules'-club
Aralia spinosa L.

Use potherb.

Our very prickly shrub or low tree, **Angelica-tree**, growing up to 30 feet high in borders of woods or on river-banks of the Gulf States, north to New Jersey, Pennsylvania, western New York, Ohio, Indiana, Illinois and Iowa, with very large and very compound leaves and umbels of whitish flowers forming a gigantic panicle, may have some use after all. In Japan their representative of our species furnishes a secondary food. The young expanding leaves, before their prickles become hard, are gathered and cooked as a green, served with vinegar.

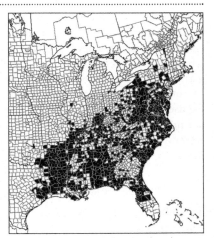

ANGELICA-TREE *(Aralia spinosa)*

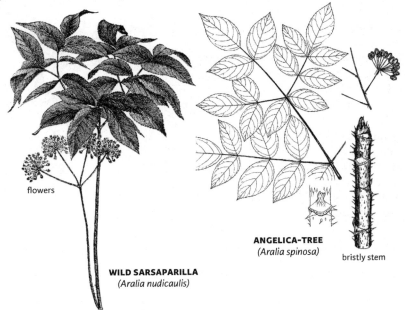

flowers

WILD SARSAPARILLA
(Aralia nudicaulis)

ANGELICA-TREE
(Aralia spinosa)
bristly stem

Ginseng
Panax quinquefolius L.

Habitat rich deciduous woods
Uses emergency-food, tea.

Ginseng, long famous as the great Chinese panacea, has, on account of the Chinese demand for the roots, become nearly exterminated as a wild plant in eastern America where it formerly abounded in rich woods. Its deep, parsnip-like root is aromatic and, like the other members of the family, may be used as an emergency-food, while an infusion of the leaves is stated by several authors to make a palatable tea.

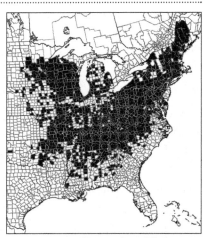

GINSENG *(Panax quinquefolius)*

Dwarf Ginseng, Groundnut
Panax trifolius L.

Use starchy vegetable, eaten like nuts.

The globular, bulb-like root of the **Dwarf Ginseng**, which occurs in rich, deciduous woods throughout the northeastern United States and adjacent Canada, is familiar to most children on account of its starchy and somewhat nutty quality. Eaten raw it is disagreeably starchy, but when boiled a few minutes in salted water it becomes very palatable, either as a hot vegetable or eaten cold like salted nuts. Ordinarily the plant is too scattered or too deep-rooted among strong fibres for the roots to be secured in abundance.

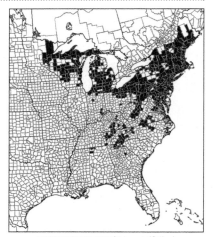

DWARF GINSENG *(Panax trifolius)*

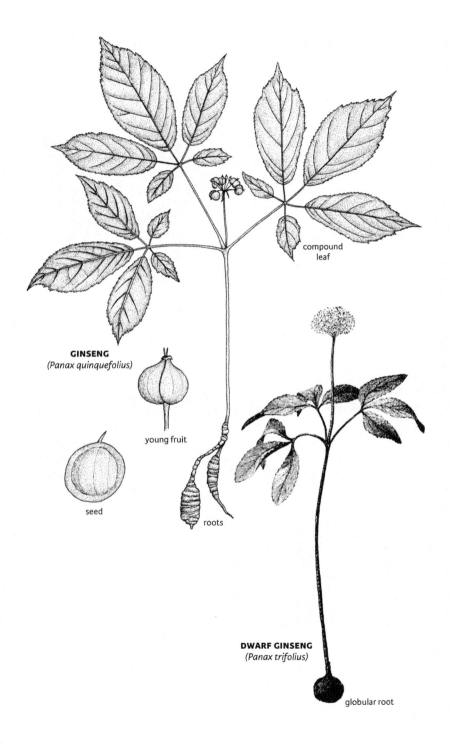

compound
leaf

GINSENG
(Panax quinquefolius)

young fruit

seed

roots

DWARF GINSENG
(Panax trifolius)

globular root

Aristolochiaceae BIRTHWORT FAMILY

Wild Ginger
Asarum canadense L.

Uses nibble, condiment, substitute for preserved ginger.

The rootstock has a fragrance and taste suggestive of ginger and is an agreeable nibble. It may be used either fresh or dried as a substitute for ginger in seasoning.

The long and nearly superficial rootstocks of **Wild Ginger**, cut into short pieces, boiled until tender and then cooked in a rich sugar-syrup and canned or not (as preferred) make a palatable substitute for preserved ginger. Although the rootstocks are reputed to be somewhat medicinal, no discomfort has been experienced from using this substitute in moderate quantity. Inordinate eating of it might be detrimental, a point which those who are sufficiently inquisitive might well determine.

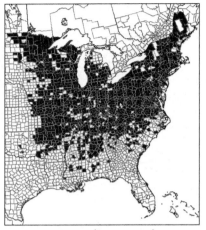

WILD GINGER *(Asarum canadense*

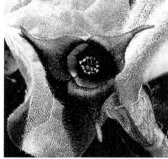

flower

WILD GINGER *(Asarum canadense)*

Asteraceae ASTER FAMILY

Burdock
Arctium (4 species)

Uses salad, cooked vegetable, potherb, soup, confection.

As a food-plant the usually common and much despised **Burdock** has greater possibilities than the neglected **Pigweed**. In fact, in Japan an esculent garden variety has been developed and, according to some authors, it is in that country "as important as potato is here"; and a century ago the great French botanist, Poiret, expressed astonishment that Burdock was not generally found in French kitchens.

In many parts of Europe Burdock-roots, young leaves and young stems have been much used for food. The

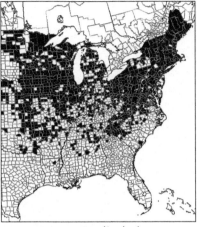

BURDOCK *(Arctium)*

roots, at the end of the first season, are described as tender, nutritious, of excellent flavor, in this as well as in form and size resembling salsify, like which they are cooked. Our experiments, following this suggestion, have been surprisingly successful. The tender pith of the root and the leaf-stalks when young, before the stem has begun to lengthen, boiled in two waters (with a little soda in the first water, to break the tough fibers, salt in the second water), make a really palatable and unusual potherb.

The young stems, which are often an inch or more in diameter, are gathered before the flower-heads are well formed, in late spring or early summer, and carefully peeled, great care being taken to remove every shred of the tough, strong-smelling and bitter rind. The remaining pith is a half-inch or more thick, tender and succulent and, when cooked in two or more waters (to remove the strong taste), makes a superior vegetable, in flavor like salsify.

According to some writers, the young tops, including the stems, leaves and young branches, are good as a potherb, the first waters, naturally, being thrown off as in cooking the pith. Others even state that the pith of the young stems is eaten raw, with a dressing of oil and vinegar, or sometimes candied; and Waugh tells us that by the Iroquois the roots of this plant (introduced into America by the European) are dried and stored for winter and, when required, are soaked out for use as a soup.

Surely, when our sophisticated tastes have been trained to favor the Burdock, there should be no trouble in exterminating this now obnoxious weed from many back yards.

root

BURDOCK *(Arctium minus)*

Mugwort, Wormwood
Artemisia vulgaris L. *and other species*

Use condiment.

The leaves of **Mugwort** and of some of the other **Wormwoods** are sometimes used as aromatic, bitter condiments much like tansy.

Spanish Needles
Bidens bipinnata L.

Use potherb.

The semicosmopolitan **Spanish Needles**, one of the annual species of **Beggar-ticks**, too abundant in most tropical and warm-temperate regions, is usually looked upon only with disgust on account of its exceptionally slender and adhesive "ticks." The natives of Tropical West Africa have found a way to keep it from fruiting, for Dalziel tells us that there the leaves are used as a potherb. To the European nose the odor of *Bidens* is rather offensive.

Plumeless Thistle
Carduus (several species)

Uses rennet, cooked vegetable.

The **Plumeless Thistles** are with us rather locally naturalized from Europe. They differ from our common thistles chiefly in having the long individual hairs of the "thistle-down" simple instead of covered with minute branches or plume. They have the same use as rennet, Lightfoot saying of *Carduus nutans* L.: "The dry'd flowers . . . are used in some countries as a rennet to curdle milk." In late spring and early summer, when the flowering stem has well grown, the thick pith, with all the rind cut off (very easily) is delicious boiled a few minutes in salted water and dressed.

Chicory, Blue Sailors
Cichorium intybus L.

Key-characters leaves mostly clustered at the top of a strong taproot, in form resembling dandelion-leaves but thicker and usually harsher: stems tall, loosely branching, rather rigid, bearing in late summer and autumn bluish "flowers" (heads) in form resembling dandelions and followed by loosely cylindric fruiting clusters.

Habitat fields, roadsides and waste places, especially in clay soils or ashes.

Range generally introduced from Europe, found from Newfoundland to Manitoba and southward, often, as in eastern Massachusetts, excessively abundant but sometimes local or absent over considerable areas.

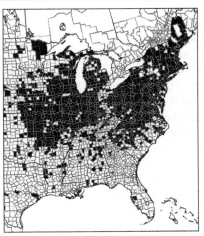

CHICORY *(Cichorium intybus)*

Season of Availability for salad and potherb, spring and winter (indoors); roots, autumn to spring.
Uses potherb, salad, coffee-substitute.

Chicory has always been more or less popular in European countries, having been well known, apparently, to the early Romans. In the spring the leaves are gathered somewhat indiscriminately with dandelion-greens, having the same excessively bitter quality which some people find palatable in a potherb. The bitterness is somewhat reduced by cooking and may be further withdrawn by cooking the leaves in several waters.

Under the name "Barbe du Capucin," the blanched leaves have long been popular as a salad in continental Europe, and are more and more seen in American markets, although the closely related endive is, perhaps, more generally cultivated. An economical and decidedly attractive bitter salad is easily secured by digging the larger, wild Chicory-roots during late autumn or in mild periods during winter, boxing them in earth in a dark and warm cellar, preferably with a cover to keep out any rays of light. The roots, frequently watered, soon send up an abundant, crisp white foliage which, by judioious handling, may be continued for several weeks.

The use of the ground and roasted roots of Chicory as an adulterant in coffee has long been practiced and, according to some authors, coffee containing a large proportion of Chicory is not only more palatable but more wholesome than true coffee. For, although discriminatingly referring to some frequently cooked plants as "not, however, valued by persons of refined taste", Lindley enthusiastically wrote of Chicory, "whose tap roots are cultivated as a substitute for Coffee, which they certainly improve when torrefied and added in small quantities." Lindley was an Englishman.

Johnson tells us that in parts of Europe the demand for Chicory-coffee often exceeds the supply and that the ground Chicory has sometimes been mixed with sawdust, roasted beans, dried horse-liver, and other substances used to add bulk. Thus it is easy to understand the scarcity of good coffee in most tourist-hotels of Europe.

Since through many decades Chicory-root has maintained its place as the chief substitute for or adulterant of coffee and is now being urged as an official substitute, the following passage, written by Porclier in South Carolina when the South was suffering from the privations caused by the Civil War, may be of value:

"By the combination of a little chiccory with coffee the flavor of the coffee is not destroyed, but there is added to the infusion a richness of flavor, and a depth of color—a body, which renders it to very many people much more welcome as a beverage. The cheapness of chiccory enables a grocer, by the combination of chiccory powder with good coffee, to sell a compound which will yield a cup of infinitely better stuff than any pure coffee that can be had at the same price. Any one with a sensitive taste, and a sufficient purse, would of course buy coffee of the finest quality, and never think of bettering with chiccory the enjoyment of its delicate aroma. The majority of the people, however, are by no means in this position. Coffee, with an admixture of genuine chiccory, (which we take care to procure by purchasing the article in its raw state, and having it roasted the same as coffee,) was preferred to coffee in its pure state. The reason of this we can clearly understand, and will explicitly state. We can afford to sell, and do sell a finer coffee wThen mixed with chiccory than we can sell in its pure state at the same price; and the superiority of the coffee in conjunction with the fulness of the chiccory, in our opinion, decidedly gives greater satisfaction to the public."

The "fillers" now being exploited contain chicory and various types of parched beans.

ray flower

root

CHICORY *(Cichorium intybus)*

Thistle
Cirsium, about ten species

Habitat and Range disturbed places throughout eastern North America
Uses cooked vegetable, rennet.

Several writers, both in Europe and in America, advocate the utilization of young elongating stems of **Thistles** as potherbs. Thus, Lightfoot says of *Cirsium palustre* (L.) Scop.: "The tender stalks of this and most of the thistles are esculent, being first peel'd and boil'd. In this manner the inhabitants of Smoland in Sweden, as Linnaeus informs us, often eat them." Writing from Alabama of "Giant Thistle . . ., a winter annual, forming a round mat of leaves fully 15 or 20 inches in diameter, very spiny," Dr. Carver said "This plant is delicious when young, cooked just like turnip greens. . . . Nearly all the leaves can be used if the sharp spines are clipped off with a pair of scissors before cooking."

Most of our thistles are biennial; from the rosette, formed the first season, the upright flowering stem arising the second season. It will require enthusiasm and hunger to start our people gathering and trimming the spines from thistle-leaves. Our experiment shows that from May through June, when the new leaves are succulent, the flavor is good but the return not worth the discomfort and labor. Lightfoot's recipe is better: the young stems, stripped of their leaves, then peeled (taking off all the shreddy rind), cut in pieces and boiled a few minutes in salted water, are a vegetable of great delicacy, tender and with a mild flavor of French Artichoke. Withering says of **Bull-Thistle**, *Cirsium vulgare* (Savi) Ten.: "The flowers, like those of the Artichoke, have the property of Rennet in curdling milk."

leaf

BULL-THISTLE *(C. vulgare)*

Cosmos
Cosmos bipinnatus Cav.
Cosmos sulphureus Cav.

Use salad or potherb.

The familiar orange- or golden-rayed **Cosmos** of gardens is beginning to establish itself as a plant of waste lands and roadsides from New Jersey and Pennsylvania southward. *C. sulphureus*, a native of Mexico, is naturalized in many tropical and warm-temperate regions; and Ochse tells us that in the Malayan region "The young tops and the leaves of this species are eaten, either raw or cooked. . . . Sometimes it is sold for this purpose on the native markets." Raw it has a slightly unpleasant, oily flavor. This is, perhaps, modified in cooking. It will be easy to secure a sample.

Eclipta
Eclipta prostrata (L.) L.

Use potherb.

The insignificant weedy annual, **Eclipta**, of damp soils, alluvium, ditches, etc. from Tropical America to southern New York, southern Ontario, Indiana, Illinois, Iowa and Nebraska, is a semi-cosmopolitan weed with rough-hairy, slender but depressed stems, sessile and opposite, lanceolate to oblong toothed and pointed leaves, and small axillary heads with tiny white rays. We find no indication that it has been used in America as food but Dalziel states that in Africa "The plant can be used as a potherb."

Large-leaved Aster
Eurybia macrophylla (L.) Cass.

Synonym *Aster macrophyllus*
Use potherb.

The large, heart-shaped leaves of this Aster, which occur in tufts in dry woods and thickets, have sometimes been used as a potherb, especially in Maine and Quebec. They quickly become tough and leathery and, if they are to be tried, should be gathered when very young.

Galinsoga
Galinsoga parviflora Cav. , *G. quadriradiata* Ruiz & Pavón, and several less common species.

Key-characters small opposite-leaved annuals, the succulent, 3-nerved, ovate, toothed leaves 1-4 inches long; tiny heads of flowers, with short, white to pinkish rays borne at the tips of the branches; the chaff at summit of the nutlets of small, oblong, cut-fringed, pale scales.
Habitat and Range aggressive weeds of cultivated or disturbed soils northward to southern Canada.
Season of Availability summer and autumn.
Use potherb.

Galinsoga in the last half-century has rapidly spread and has now become, as Small properly characterizes it, "A particularly pestiferous weed of such

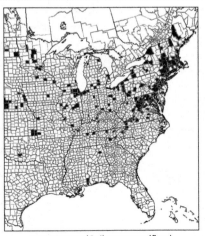

GALINSOGA (*Galinsoga parviflora*)

rapid growth and seeding as to make eradication extremely difficult." It has invaded most tropical and temperate regions; but in southeastern Asia it met a hungry population who cook the young plants (all but the roots) as greens. It belongs in a group of edible and, gastronomically, quite wholesome plants (Sunflowers, etc.). If our people take to eating it the problems of backyard vegetable-gardens will be partly solved.

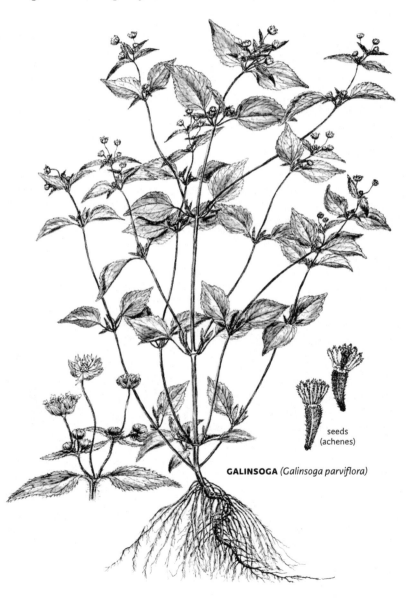

seeds
(achenes)

GALINSOGA *(Galinsoga parviflora)*

Sunflower
Helianthus (various species)

Uses breadstuff, oil, soup, coffee-substitute.

Long before the coming of the white man and the exploitation of Sunflower oil, the American Indians were using the seeds of the larger species of **Sunflowers** as important sources of food. Slightly parched and ground into flour, they serve in making bread, cakes and rich soups; or the oil, separated by boiling the crushed seeds and skimming the oil from the surface of the water, was used by the Indians, as it is now by the whites, as a table-oil.

Several explorers state that the roasted shells, after the starch has been removed by roasting, crushing and sifting, or the roasted seeds were used in preparing a drink "tasting just like coffee."

Jerusalem Artichoke
Helianthus tuberosus L.

Uses root-vegetable, salad, pickle, purée.

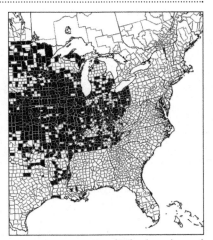

The **Jerusaleum Artichoke**, which is a species of Sunflower with large tubers, is indigenous in the central part of North America and was cultivated by the Indians who introduced it to the Europeans. The tubers have been in considerable repute in parts of continental Europe, but, although often found in our markets, they are not greatly appreciated by the whites in America. The flesh is watery and sweet and with a peculiar flavor which is palatable to some tastes, disagreeable to others. Many persons like the tubers as a salad or pickle. When cooked they

JERUSALEM ARTICHOKE *(Helianthus tuberosus)*

are prepared as a puree or peeled and baked, with liberal oil or butter, or escalloped with crumbs which absorb the mucilaginous juice. The tubers have been extensively cultivated in the past and the plants are now thoroughly naturalized along roadsides, in borders of fields or in town-dumps throughout the Eastern States and southern Canada.

The discussion of the waning use of the Jerusalem Artichoke in Europe, given by W. B. Booth, three quarters of a century ago, is worth quoting:

"They are used either boiled and mashed with butter, or baked in pies, and when nicely cooked are not only well flavoured, but considered to be both wholesome and nutritious—more so even than the potato, as they may be eaten by invalids when debarred from the use of other vegetables. On the continent they are in considerable demand for soups, and before the potato became plentiful, they were a good deal used in this country [England]. Parkinson, writing in 1629, says they were then so common in London 'that even the vulgar began to despise them: they were baked in pies with marrow, dates, ginger, sack, &c. and, being so plentiful and cheap, rather bred a loathing than a liking for them.' Hence it appears that, as the culture of the potato extended, it gradually displaced the Jerusalem Artichoke, and at the present time the latter is only grown to a very limited extent in first-class gardens. Since the failure of the potato crops, the Jerusalem Artichoke has been strongly recommended as a substitute for that vegetable; but notwithstanding all that has been said and written in its favour, it is still far from common, and by no means esteemed so much as it deserves to be."—W. B. Booth in The Treasury of Botany.

The name "Jerusalem" applied to this plant is likely to lead to misconception. The tubers, early introduced into Europe, were soon popular in the Mediterranean countries and in Spanish were called girasol, in Italian girasole. True to their genius in such matters the English promptly changed it to "Jerusalem."

JERUSALEM ARTICHOKE
(Helianthus tuberosus)

tuber

Elecampane
Inula helenium L.

Use confection, substitute for soda-mints.

It is generally stated that the young leaves of **Elecampane** were eaten as a potherb by the Romans, but by those who have tried them the leaves are found to be bitter and disagreeably aromatic. A more general use in Europe, not well known in America, is the candying of the cooked roots, making, according to Mrs. Lankester, "A sweetmeat, very popular with schoolboys." It would be rash to assume that the prowess of English schoolboys in athletics is in any way due to their eating this confection; but note what Parkinson, in 1640, thought of it and how closely his account accords with that of Pliny:

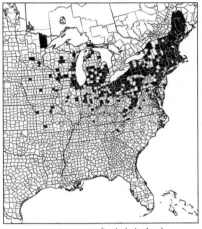

ELECAMPANE *(Inula helenium)*

"The fresh rootes of Elecampane preserved with Sugar . . are very effectuall to warme a cold & windy stomack, and the pricking and stitches therein, or in the sides . . ., and to helpe the cough, shortness of breath . . . Pliny writeth . . . let no day passe without eating some of the rootes of Enula condited, which it may be . . . to helpe digestion, to expell melancholy and sorrow; and to cause mirth."

It sounds like a substitute for bicarbonate of soda.

ELECAMPANE *(Inula helenium)*

Wild Lettuce
Lactuca, several species

Use potherb.

The species of **Wild Lettuce**, although of the same genus as garden lettuce, resemble the latter only in technical characters: milky juice, tall and leafy flowering stem and yellow, coppery or bluish little strap-shaped flowers borne in elongate or urn-shaped heads, the flowers surrounded by green to purple bracts. One species or another is found from Newfoundland to British Columbia, south throughout the United States. Belonging to the genus *Lactuca*, they are beyond suspicion and the vigorously growing leafy stems (before flowering, after which they are tough) and the unexpanded inflorescences can be cooked. Dr. Carver praised the tender kinds as salad.

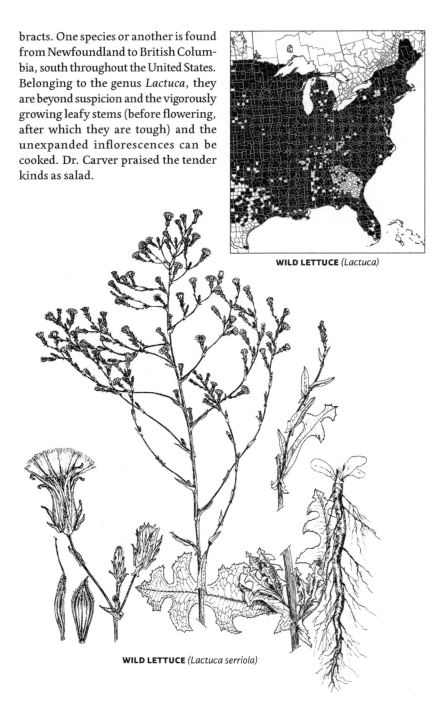

WILD LETTUCE *(Lactuca)*

WILD LETTUCE *(Lactuca serriola)*

Nipplewort
Lapsana communis L.

Uses salad, potherb.

Nipplewort, a small-leaved lettuce-like plant with milky juice, is locally and sometimes abundantly naturalized as a weed—for instance, for 20 miles or more along the Chesapeake and Ohio Railroad east of Richmond, Virginia. In view of the fact that every helpless infant has been forced to feed at a nipple it is comforting to learn that Nipplewort is edible. Withering stated that "Before it goes into flower it is eaten raw"; and Mrs. Lankester said that it can be cooked as greens.

Ox-eye Daisy, Whiteweed, Marguerite
Leucanthemum vulgare Lam.

Synonym *Chrysanthemum leucanthemum*
Use salad.

Some European authors state that the young leaves of the **Ox-eye Daisy** make a palatable salad, and in China several related species are used as salads. The odor of our plant suggests, however, that fondness for this particular salad is an acquired taste.

Tarweed
Madia (various species)

Use meal.

The **Tarweeds**, viscid and heavy-scented herbs (ours annuals), with narrow leaves, the yellow flowers borne in small heads which are crowded into dense clusters, the seeds nut-like, each more or less embraced by a bract, are native from Pacific America across the plains to Minnesota, and three of them are appearing in waste places in the Atlantic States and eastern Canada. They are not likely to be of much service to us but the oily and nutritious nutlets are (or were) used by western Indians for meal.

Scotch Thistle, Cotton Thistle
Onopordum acanthium L.

Uses substitute for French artichoke, salad.

The true **Scotch Thistle** is only rarely naturalized in North America and few people will be situated to experiment with it. But English writers state that the fairly large receptacle or base of the head is cooked and eaten like the artichoke, and that the vigorous young shoots stripped of their rind and then boiled are also edible.

Sweet Coltsfoot
Petasites frigidus (L.) Fries (includes *P. palmatus*)

Key-characters Extensively creeping herbs, flowering before the leaves expand, the flowering stem stout and 4 inches to a foot and a half high, sheathed its whole length by leaf-like bracts, the creamy-white flowering heads fragrant and borne in a large cluster; leaves expanding later and arising along the creeping rootstocks, rounded or triangular in outline, cut and cleft into coarse lobes, the blades becoming 2-9 inches broad.

Habitat and Range low woods, damp clearings and boggy meadows, Labrador to northern Alberta, south through Newfoundland and eastern Canada to northern and western New England, northern New York, Michigan, Wisconsin and Minnesota.

Season of Availability spring and summer.

Use potherb.

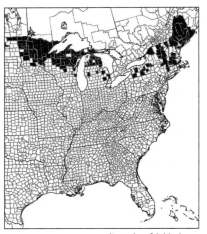

SWEET COLTSFOOT *(Petasites frigidus)*

The foliage and young inflorescences of Eurasian species are frequently cooked; those who have tried our own report them to be "very good."

Fireweed
Senecio hieraciifolius L.

Synonym *Erechtites hieracifolia*
Uses salad or potherb.

The very familiar leafy- and simple-stemmed, annual plant of the Aster Family, with stems 1-3 feet high, the narrow leaves abundant and toothed, the inflorescence a group of cylindric heads with many tubular creamy-white flowers, the nutlets capped by long white hairs, abounds in rich low ground or after fires, in burned clearings, whence the name Fireweed. It is common from Florida to Texas, northward to Canada, with closely

SWEET COLTSFOOT *(Petasites frigidus)*

related species in tropical America and from eastern Asia to New Zealand. In Asia the young tops and tender foliage are eaten, either raw or cooked. There is no reason, except the odor, to prevent our using it. Cooking may make it palatable to us.

Rosin-weed, Compass-plant
Silphium laciniatum L.

Use chewing-gum.

Gilmore states that by the Omaha Indians the resinous exudations of the **Rosin-weed** of the Prairies are used as chewing-gum; and Clute noted (*American Botanist* for 1903) that "Country boys are wont to pull the flower-heads from the plant and to return later for the hardened juice." This experiment should be tried on related species, *S. terebinthinaceum* Jacq. of prairies and openings from southern Ontario to Minnesota, south to Georgia, Alabama and Missouri, and *S. compositum* Michx. of the southeast, northward into Virginia.

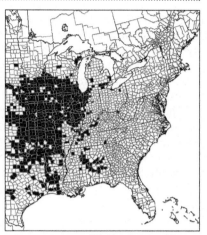

ROSIN-WEED (*Silphium laciniatum*)

Sweet Goldenrod
Solidago odora Ait.

Key-characters a Goldenrod with one-sided inflorescences and strictly entire, widely spreading, elongate, smooth leaves 3-4 inches long, which are conspicuously dotted with translucent spots (when held to a bright light); the bruised foliage and other fresh parts giving off a delicate odor suggestive of anise.
Habitat and Range dry, sandy, gravelly or other sterile plains or borders of thickets and open woods, from Texas to Missouri and Florida, and northward to southern New Hampshire.
Season of Availability summer and early autumn.
Use tea.

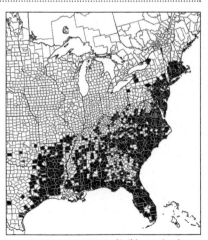

SWEET GOLDENROD (*Solidago odora*)

One of the first Europeans to record the use of the **Sweet Goldenrod** in making tea was Johann David Schoepf, who was chief surgeon of one of the bodies of German troops sent to America by George III during our Revolution. Writing from Bedford Co., Pennsylvania, Schoepf said:

"Here we were introduced to still another domestic tea-plant, a variety of *Solidago*. The leaves were gathered and dried over a slow fire. It was said that around Fort Littleton many 100 pounds of this Bohea-tea, as they call it, had been made as long as the Chinese was scarcer. Our hostess praised its good taste, but this was not conspicuous in what she brewed."

The account given only a few years later by the globetrotting botanist, Frederick Pursh, was very different; and, in view of the facts that nowadays we are wont to despise all native substitutes for tea and to demand that our tea come from China or adjacent regions, it is worth while to repeat Pursh's statement:

"The flowers, gathered when fully expanded, and carefully dried, give a most agreeable substitute for tea, which for some time has been an article of exportation to China, where it fetches a high price."

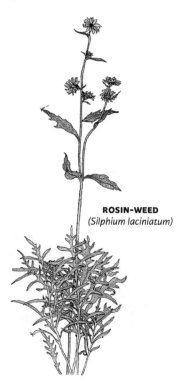

ROSIN-WEED
(Silphium laciniatum)

SWEET GOLDENROD *(Solidago odora)*

Sow-Thistle
Sonchus (various species)

Key-characters bristly or prickly-leaved thistles with heads of yellowish flowers, and a milky, bitter juice.
Habitat and Range weeds of cultivated lands, barnyards, roadsides, etc., throughout temperate America.
Season of Availability early summer, before flowering.
Uses potherb, salad.

The common **Sow-Thistles** have a milky juice and a bitter taste very similar to those of dandelion and chicory, and in Europe the young foliage has sometimes been used as a potherb or salad, although the plants have rarely appealed to the English taste. Consequently we find John Parkinson, in 1640, saying:
"They are usually eaten as salat herbes in the "Winter and Spring, while they are young and tender by those beyond the seas familiarly."
Our own tests show the succulent species to be fairly good but not superior potherbs.

Muster John-Henry
Tagetes minuta L.

Use seasoning.

Muster John-Henry, as it is universally called in southeastern Virginia and eastern North Carolina, is a tall aromatic annual with feathery leaves and large terminal flat-topped inflorescences of innumerable slenderly cylindric, tiny yellowish heads. The whole plant is pleasantly aromatic, from the oil-dots which freely cover it. It is seen in the yards of most colored families and has spread freely to roadsides, open bottomlands and dumps; it is generally used to season soups and broths and might well find a place in modern herb-gardens.

Costmary
Tanacetum balsamita L.

Synonym *Chrysanthemum balsamita*
Uses salad, condiment.

The old-fashioned **Costmary**, now somewhat established about towns as a relic of cultivation, has an agreeable smell, which to many is far preferable to that of any of the Mints. "Costmary was formerly cultivated in gardens for the purpose of mixing with sallads, and it is a pity it is not continued, as from its sensible qualities it seems superior to many aromatic plants now [1783] in credit."

Tansy, Bitter Buttons
Tanacetum vulgare L.

Use condiment, cooked vegetable.

Gerarde, in the sixteenth century, wrote:
"In the spring time are made with the leaues hereof newly sproong up, and with egs, cakes, or Tansies, which be pleasant in taste, and good for the stomacke;" and among the devout in England similar cakes and puddings with Tansy as the "bitter herb" are used during Lent. In Maine occasionally Tansy-cheese is made by steeping the herb and pouring the extract into the milk before the curds are made.

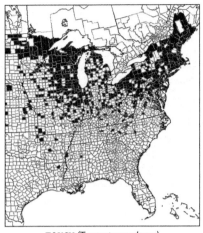

TANSY *(Tanacetum vulgare)*

In these times, when aromatic and other strong herbs are in vogue, this paragraph from Evelyn's Acetaria of two and a half centuries ago might be appreciated:
"Tansy, *Tanacetum*; hot and cleansing; but in regard to its domineering Kelish, sparingly mix'd with our cold Sallet, and much fitter (tho* in very small quantity) for the Pan, being qualify'd with the Juices of other fresh Herbs,.Spinach, Green Corn, Violet, Primrose-Leaves, &c. at entrance of the Spring, and then fry'd brownish, is eaten hot, with the Juice of Orange and Sugar, as one of the most agreeable of all the boil'd Herbaceous Dishes."

Dandelion
Taraxacum officinale G.H. Weber ex Wiggers and about ten local native species.

Range throughout North America.
Uses potherb, salad, coffee-substitute.

The use of young Dandelion-leaves as a potherb is so familiar that it hardly needs discussion. Nevertheless the novice should be particularly cautioned that the leaves at first should be covered with boiling, not cold, water, thus removing much of the herby taste. Like Chicory the leaves of the Dandelion may be blanched by covering during their rapid growth and then prepared as a salad; but the best salad from these plants is prepared from the cold, cooked greens thoroughly chilled, chopped, and served with a proper dressing. Strong plants (crowns and 2 or 3 inches of root) brought into the cellar and raised in winter, covered with litter or coal-ashes, furnish a splendid salad.

On the continent of Europe and in this country dandelion-greens have long been recognized as having a decidedly wholesome effect on the digestion, but in England the value of this bitter potherb was tardily appreciated. Thus, after enumerating the virtues of the plant and its popularity on the continent, good old Dr. Culpepper wrote in 1770:

"You see here what Virtues this common Herb hath, aiul that's the reason the French and Dutch so often eat them in the Spring; and now if you look a little farther, you may see plainly, without a pair of Spectacles, that Foreign Physicians are not so Selfish as ours are, but more communcative of the Virtue of Plants to People."

The ground roots, like those of chicory, can be used to adulterate coffee or used alone to make a palatable, bitter drink; and in times of famine the roots themselves, cooked, have been used for food. We thus find tho statement made by various authors that, during a famine on the island of Minorca caused by a destruction of tho harvests by locusts, many of the inhabitants subsisted on tho roots of Dandelions.

Goat's-beard, Salsify, Oyster-plant
Tragopogon, three species

Key-characters tall biennials with tap-roots; leaves like broad grass-blades, with milky juice, the first year forming broad rosettes or tufts, the second shriveling as the tall, leafy flowering stem develops; flowers resembling large dandelion-heads, yellow or purple, the involucre or leafy cup without the outer curling series of the dandelions; the long fruits with long firm beaks, with the slender, terminal beard of plumose hairs. Three species with us: Salsify or Oyster-plant, *Tragopogon porrifolius* L., with purple flowers, the fruits 5/16 of an inch long; Goat's-beard, *T. pratensis* L. and *T. dubius* Scop., both yellow-flowered, the former with the long terminal flower-stalk slender to summit, the green involucre from 3/4 to 1-1/4 inches high, the fruits scarcely an inch long, *T. dubius* with the flower-stalk thickened above, the involucre 2 to 3 inches long and the fruits 1 to 2 inches long.
Habitat fields and roadsides.
Range one or more species often abundant in southern Canada, thence south to Georgia, Tennessee, Missouri, etc.
Season of Availability for green vegetable, spring; for root, autumn to earliest spring.
Uses potherb, cooked root, salad.

Salsify or Oyster-plant is more or less familiar as a winter-vegetable; the root, variously prepared, is appreciated by many. When it grows wild the roots, unless in very rich soil, are smaller than in the highly cultivated plant but perfectly good, remembering always that they are useless after the flowering stem has developed. The young stems when a few inches high and the bases of the lower leaves make a delicious cooked vegetable.

Many people like the roots of the yellow-flowered weedy species better than those of the cultivated Salsify. The latter has larger roots, therefore it alone is in the gardens. The cultivation of Salsify apparently is not very old. Note Evelyn's indignation in 1706:

"Goats-beard, Tragopogon; but of late they have Italianiz'd the Name, and now generally call it Salsisix; and our Seed-Sellers, to disguise it, being a very common Field Herb, growing in most Parts of England, would have it thought (with many others) an Exotick, and call it Salsify and Sassify; whilst, by whatever Name dignify'd or distinguish'd, it must be own'd to be an excellent Sallet-Root, and very nutritive, and may be stew'd and dress'd as Sorzonera, exceedingly amicable to the Breast."

As to the superiority (except in size) of the yellow-flowered Goat's-beard, Bryant, writing in England, said: "This plant [the bell-flowered *Tragopogon porrifolius*] is cultivated in gardens by the name of Salsafy, and its roots are dressed and served up at table in a variety of forms. They are of a pleasant, nutritious nature, but though these are at present in the greatest esteem, they are much inferior to those of the pratense."

Coltsfoot
Tussilago farfara L.

Use confection.

The familiar **Coltsfoot**, naturalized from Eurasia and abounding in damp clay soils of brooksides and roadsides from Newfoundland to Minnesota and in parts of the Northeastern States, is, of course, famous as a supposed cough-medicine. Coltsfoot-candy, is a delicious confection.

Caution Because of the content of pyrrolizidine alkaloids (toxic to the liver), Coltsfoot is no longer recommended for internal use.

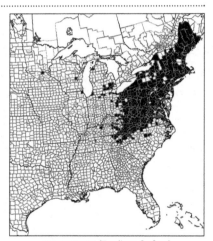

COLTSFOOT *(Tussilago farfara)*

Cocklebur or Clot-bur
Xanthium (various species)

Range throughout North America.
Use breadstuff.

Although it is sometimes stated, as by Sanford, that "The seeds . . . were ground and mixed with corn meal and with squash seeds, by the western Indians, and eaten as food", it should be noted that Muenscher classes *Xanthium* seeds among the poisonous group. The forbidding burs and the rank odor and taste are not inviting.

fruit in globe-
shaped head

GOAT'S-BEARD
(*Tragopogon dubius*)

creeping
root

TANSY (*Tanacetum vulgare*)

COLTSFOOT (*Tussilago farfara*)

Berberidaceae BARBERRY FAMILY

Barberry
Berberis vulgaris L.

Habitat and Range dry thickets, fence-rows, rocky pastures and rocky borders of woods, especially abundant in southern New England and adjacent New York, and occasional elsewhere. Originally introduced from Europe, but now thoroughly naturalized.
This species is at once distinguished from the introduced *B. thunbergii* by its forking spines and long cluster of very juicy berries, *B. thunbergii* having simple spines and the dry, inedible berries few in a cluster.
Season of Availability fruit, autumn and winter; leaves, spring.
Uses cooked fruit, jelly, jam, pies, drink, nibble or masticatory.

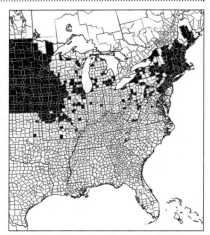

BARBERRY *(Berberis vulgaris)*

In the regions where it abounds the **Barberry** has always been a favorite fruit for spiced preserves, jellies and other similar preparations. The juice should be extracted without the addition of water (when there are plenty of berries) or water may be added, and with an equal bulk of sugar it makes a very tart, distinctly flavored jelly. When water is used it is necessary to add apple to make the juice jell. Barberry-juice is especially desirable to mix with sweet or insipid fruits in preserves or jellies. The berries are also used like cranberries as an acid sauce of fine flavor, but full of "shoe pegs," or in tarts or pies, or cooked in a spiced syrup. New England housewives often put Barberries into the cans of other preserved fruits to which they lend a tart flavor. The syrup from the barberry mixed with water and other juices, makes a pleasant, cooling drink.

The young leaves in spring make a palatable acid nibble; and the berries "are boiled in soups to give them a tart flavour."

The **native Barberry**, *Berberis canadensis* P. Mill., occurring in dry woods and on bluffs from western Virginia to Georgia and Missouri, has equally good fruit, which is used like that of the introduced species.

May-Apple, Hog-Apple, Wild Lemon, "Mandrake"
Podophyllum peltatum L.

Habitat and Range rich woods of the Central States, eastward to western Quebec and western New England and southward.

Season of Availability late summer.
Uses fruit, marmalade, summer drink.

The fully ripe fruit of the **May-Apple**
(because flowering in May) is familiar
to every country boy of the regions
where the plant abounds and, although
Asa Gray described it as "mawkish,
eaten by pigs and boys," in its fresh
state it has a peculiar flavor very agreeable to most human grown-ups. It
makes a luscious marmalade and a
beautiful jelly, and, being abundant
where it grows, should be experimented
with cooked in other ways. In the South
a drink is prepared from the juice of

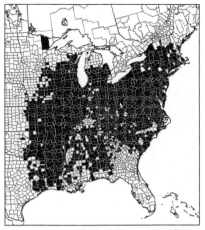

MAY-APPLE *(Podophyllum peltatum)*

the fruit with Madeira and sugar, and
a less ardent beverage may be prepared by squeezing the juice into lemonade or
other fruit-drinks.

Caution the foliage and root of the plant are poisonous to eat (see p. 52).

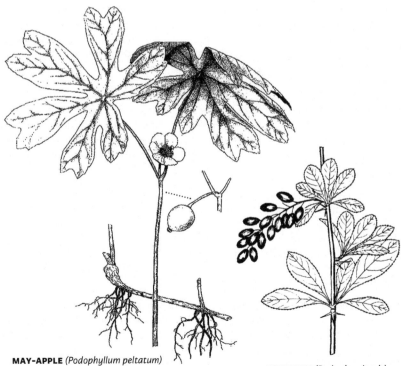

MAY-APPLE *(Podophyllum peltatum)*

BARBERRY *(Berberis vulgaris)*

Betulaceae BIRCH FAMILY

....

Alder
Alnus (various species)
....

Uses emergency-food, nibble.

According to Kephart, the inner bark is a possible emergency food. The young bark and winter-buds are popular nibbles with country boys, not alone for their tolerable flavor, but particularly for the beautiful, olive-brown saliva produced, which makes very emphatic spots on the lingering snow of early spring.

....

Birch
Betula (various species)
....

We have two distinct groups of **Birch** trees. The most important are distinguished by the following key.

1 Leaves rounded or heart-shaped at base, with 8 or more pairs of veins furrow-like or impressed into the upper surface; the cone-like fruiting catkins 1/2 inch thick, of a short, cylindric form, with scales which persist over winter; bark not white 2
1 Leaves rarely heart-shaped, those of the fruiting branches with 7 or fewer pairs of veins prominent or standing out above; the slender, finger-like fruiting catkins with quickly falling scales; bark white, creamy or pinkish (sometimes brown in young or exposed trees) 3
2 Bark dark brown and close, resembling that of a cherry-tree; scales of the cones not hairy on the margins................... **Sweet, Cherry or Black Birch** (*B. lenta* L.).
2 Bark yellowish-gray, with a lustre, very shaggy; scales of cones finely hairy on the margins........................ **Yellow or "Black" Birch** (*B. alleghaniensis* Britt.).
3 Bark dull, chalky-white or dirty-white, close, the layers not readily separating; leaves smooth and shining on both sides, with very slender, elongated tips ....
.... **White, Gray, Wire- or Old-field Birch** (*B. populifolia* Marsh.).
3 Bark somewhat lustrous, creamy- or pinkish-white or brown, freely splitting into papery layers; leaves with hairy tufts beneath in the axils of the veins, not very slender-tipped .... **Paper-, Canoe- or White Birch**, (*B. papyrifera* Marsh.).

There are other species but these are the most widely distributed, except for the relatively southern **Red or River-Birch** (*Betula nigra* L.), which is a "Black" birch with shaggy, terra-cotta, thin bark, downy new growth, and somewhat rhombic leaves pale beneath.

Habitats and Ranges Sweet Birch (*B. lenta*), dry woods of the Alleghenian region, extending from the mountains of Tennessee to southwestern Maine and northern New York; **Yellow Birch** (*B. alleghaniensis*), rich woods, Newfoundland to Manitoba, south into the northern states and locally to the mountains of Tennessee and North Carolina; **Red or River-Birch**, river-swamps and lowlands of the South, north to New Jersey

(locally to southeastern New Hampshire) and up the Mississippi Valley; the small **White or Gray Birch** (*B. populifolia*), sterile soils, either wet or dry, Prince Edward Island to Delaware and the Thousand Islands; **Paper- or Canoe-Birch** (*B. papyrifera*), Labrador to Alaska, south into the northern states and locally to the Carolina mountains.
Uses tea, cooling drink, syrup, sugar, oil of wintergreen, vinegar, bread, beer.

The bark, young buds, leaves and twigs of the **Sweet Birch** and the **Yellow Birch** contain an aromatic oil which is essentially identical with the oil found in the Checkerberry plant and some others of the Heath family. When not prepared synthetically, "oil of wintergreen" of commerce is extracted from these birches, especially from the Sweet Birch which is the more aromatic of the two. The oil-bearing twigs, leaves, etc., make a pleasant flavoring and the dried leaves, especially of the Yellow Birch, were commended by Michaux and others for tea. The sap is said to make a pleasant drink, and, when boiled down, to furnish sugar. Birch beer, made by fermenting the sap, is made chiefly from Sweet Birch.

The **White Birches** lack the aromatic oil found in the Sweet Birches, but their sap, secured in early spring before the unfolding of the leaves, was prized by the northern Indians and travellers as a pleasant, sweet drink, and by boiling it can be reduced to syrup or, finally, sugar; it is also sometimes used in making vinegar. Although in North America birch beer is usually made from the Black Birches, it is probable that the sap of the Paper- or Canoe-Birch could be used. * Our species is so close to the White Birches of Europe that the following recipe of a "Fair Lady" of the 17th century in England may interest those who desire their beer:

"To every Gallon of Birch-water put a quart of Honey, well stirr'd together; then boil it almost an hour with a few Cloves, and a little Limon-peel, keeping it well scumm'd. When it is sufficiently boil'd, and become cold, add to it three or four Spoonfuls of good Ale to make it work . . . and when the Test begins to settle, bottle it up . . . it is gentle, and very harmless in operation within the body, and exceedingly sharpens the Appetite, being drunk ante pastum."

The inner bark of various White Birches, ground to flour, has often been used as emergency bread-stuff.

Ironwood, Hornbeam, Water-Beech
Carpinus caroliniana Walt.

Use emergency-food.

Kephart states that the nuts are edible, but they are so very small, rarely 1/3 inch long, that only in emergency would they be gathered for food.

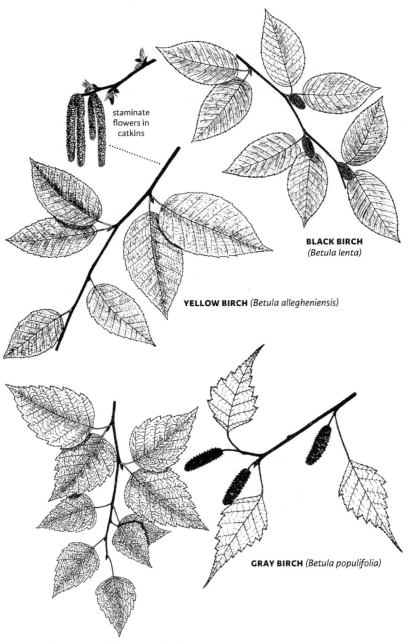

staminate
flowers in
catkins

BLACK BIRCH
(Betula lenta)

YELLOW BIRCH *(Betula allegheniensis)*

GRAY BIRCH *(Betula populifolia)*

PAPER BIRCH *(Betula papyrifera)*

Hazel, Filbert
Corylus (two species)

Key-characters shrubs with leaves somewhat suggesting those of Yellow Birch or Alder, with filbert-like nuts borne in a leafy husk. Two species in eastern America: *Corylus americana* Marsh., with the husk open and somewhat flaring at the summit and usually bearing stalked glands on its surface, the nut-shell brown and generally thick and hard; and *C. cornuta* Marsh. (or *C. rostrata*), the Beaked Hazel-nut, with the very bristly husk conspicuously contracted above into a long neck, the bristles making the fruit difficult to gather; the shell of the nut whitish-brown, comparatively thin and usually easily cracked between the back teeth.

Habitats and Ranges *C. americana*, in thickets, common southward, extending north into southern Ontario and Quebec and central New Hampshire and central Maine; *C. cornuta*, thickets, borders of woods and banks of streams, Newfoundland to British Columbia, and generally through the northern states, south, chiefly in the mountains, to Georgia and Missouri.

Season of Availability late summer and early autumn.

Uses fresh nuts, bread and cake.

The nuts of both species are sweet and similar in quality to the European filbert, and are popular with children and adult residents of country districts, where the nuts are gathered for winter use. When ground into meal they make a delicious cake-like bread comparable only to filbert bread.

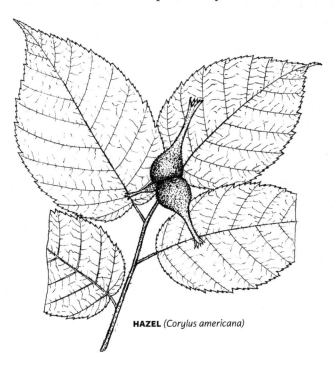

HAZEL *(Corylus americana)*

Boraginaceae BORAGE FAMILY

Waterleaf, John's Cabbage
Hydrophyllum virginianum L.
Hydrophyllum canadense L.

Use potherb.

In 1843, Dr. John Torrey stated that the leaves of both the smoother species of **Waterleaf**, *Hydrophyllum virginianum* and *H. canadense*, were used in New York state as potherbs under the name of John's Cabbage. Waugh likewise stated that by the Iroquois the young leaves were used, while Kephart records the commendable virtue, that the plants stand repicking and that the leaves do not quickly become woody. Loudon, discussing the plant as "Shawanese Salad," says the leaves are eaten either raw or cooked; but Dr. Huron H. Smith, long familiar with Indian customs,

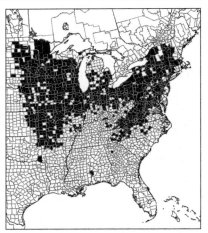

WATERLEAF *(Hydrophyllum virginianum)*

stated that, in cooking, the first water should be thrown off. Our own test was wholly satisfactory. The young leaves and tender summits of stems cook in five minutes and are a delicate potherb.

Comfrey
Symphytum officinale L.

Use potherb.

The old-fashioned garden **Comfrey** occasionally escapes from cultivation to roadsides and ditches. By some European writers it is stated that the young leaves when boiled make "a tolerable vegetable," and that the blanched stalks make an "agreeable asparagus." Lindley, however, while tolerating it said, "not, however, valued by persons of refined taste."

COMFREY *(Symphytum officinale)*

Brassicaceae MUSTARD FAMILY

To this family belong many of the cultivated vegetables; the so-called brassicaceous crops (turnips, cauliflower, Brussels-sprouts, cabbage, etc.), the mustards, radish and various cresses. Practically all the members of the group have qualities suggestive of the crops, but the following are the most important of the wild species to use as food.

Garlic-Mustard
Alliaria officinalis (Bieb.) Cavara & Grande

The old-fashioned garden plant, **Garlic-Mustard**, a tall biennial with heart-shaped or somewhat triangular stem-leaves smelling like garlic, and with white flowers with 4 petals, borne in a simple terminal cluster, has spread to roadsides and moist forests. It is available for those who like the combination. Evelyn, hiding the identity under the old English names, Jack-by-the-Hedge and Sauce-alone, said, "eaten, as other Sallets, by all Lovers of Garlickand Bryant, nearly a century later, said: "The poor people in the country [England] eat the leaves of this plant with their bread, and on account of the relish they give, call them Sauce-alone. They also mix them with Lettuce, use them as a stuffing herb to pork, and eat them with salt-fish."

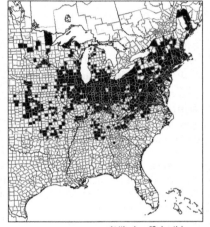

GARLIC-MUSTARD *(Alliaria officinalis)*
upper, below

Alpine Cress
Arabis alpina L.

Key-characters a matted perennial with slender and branching crowns, with loose rosettes of fleshy but hairy coarsely toothed, inversely egg-shaped leaves about an inch long; loose flowering stems with a few somewhat clasping leaves, the stems with a loose elongating cluster of white flowers of 4 petals 1/3 inch long.
Habitat cool rocks, gravelly shores, borders of rills.

Range eastern Arctic America, south to western Newfoundland and the Gasp6 Peninsula, Quebec; often cultivated in rockeries.
Season of Availability spring and summer.
Uses salad and potherb.

The fresh foliage and flowers are as agreeable to eat as any of the wild cresses.

Horseradish
Armoracia rusticana P.G. Gaertn., B. Mey. & Scherb.

Synonyms *Radicula armoracia, Rorippa armoracia*
Uses condiment, potherb.

The familiar **Horseradish** is abundantly naturalized in the northeastern United States and southern Canada, especially in ditches and other damp open spots, but like the **Water-Cress** it is not found in more primitive districts. The use of its root as a condiment is familiar, and it has been stated that the young foliage makes a palatable potherb.

Winter-Cress, Yellow Rocket
Barbarea vulgaris Ait. f.
Barbarea verna (P. Mill.) Aschers. (Belle-Isle Cress)

Key-characters perennial mustards, with large clumps of bright-green and glossy leaves remaining fresh all winter; the terminal lobe of the leaf rounded, the lateral 1-4 pairs similar, but much smaller; stem stoutish, angled, shooting up early in the spring and bearing elongating clusters of golden-yellow flowers with 2 pairs of opposite petals.
Habitat *Barbarea vulgaris* in rich low grounds, especially near streams and barn-yards; *B. verna* in fallow fields.
Range throughout temperate eastern America.
Season of Availability late autumn, winter and early spring.
Uses potherb, salad.

The **Winter-Cress** has the unusual habit of growing vigorously during warm periods in winter and it derived its Latin name Barbarea from the fact that its young leaves are green and can be eaten on St. Barbara's day, in early December. The young foliage and new young stems, while still tender, are quite as good a potherb as dandelion-greens, having a similar bitter quality. They should be cooked in two or more waters, the first water removing the strongest bitter. In French Canada the young leaves are eaten as a salad, but they are too bitter for the average palate.

The closely related *Barbarea verna* is the cultivated **"Scurvy-Grass," Belle-Isle Cress or Winter-Cress** of the market, especially in the Southern States. It is an abundant weed of fields and roadsides in early Spring, but, although readily available, is mostly unknown to or ignored by the people who might use it.

WINTER-CRESS
(Barbarea vulgaris)

Sea-Rocket
Cakile edentula (Bigelow) Hook.

Key-characters a succulent-stemmed and fleshy-leaved annual of sea-strands, with the fleshy, somewhat wedge-shaped leaves wavy-margined; the flowers lavender, with 2 pairs of opposite petals; the seed-pods plump, consisting of 2 joints, the upper joint beaked.

Habitat sandy and gravelly seashores and lake-strands.

Range Atlantic coast, northward to southern Labrador, and locally on the strands of the Great Lakes.

Season of Availability early summer to autumn.

Uses potherb and salad.

According to Dr. Harold St. John, one of the few botanists familiar with southern Labrador, the fisherman of that Coast gather great quantities of young **Sea-Rocket** to cook as a green. The cooked plants are of good quality, but without a very distinctive taste, although when cooking they give off a strong odor as of turnip. The succulent young foliage and young capsules are palatable when mixed as a salad with other milder leaves or, when eaten raw by themselves, have a flavor of horseradish.

Shepherd's-purse, Pick-pocket
Capsella bursa-pastoris (L.) Medik.

Key-characters familiar garden weed, with the elongate leaves of the basal rosette varying from entire to coarsely toothed; the white flowers forming elongating clusters, with 2 pairs of opposite petals; seed-pod flat, forming an inverted triangle (broad base up).
Habitat and Range gardens, lawns, paths and waste places, in all civilized regions.
Season of Availability leaves, late winter and early spring, before becoming tough; seeds, summer and autumn.
Uses potherb and salad, breadstuff.

The vigorously growing new foliage is sometimes cooked like spinach and, although its turnip-like odor and flavor are disagreeable to some, it is relished by many people. Barton, in 1818, writing from Philadelphia, said:

"The young radical leaves are brought to market and sold for greens, in the spring of the year" and Correa de Serra in 1821 wrote to the Horticultural Society of London: "The Capsella bursa pastoris, or common Shepherd's purse . . . is an esculent plant in Philadelphia, brought to market in large quantities in the early season. The taste, when boiled, approaches that of Cabbage, but is softer and milder. This plant varies wonderfully in size and succulence of leaves, according to the nature and state of the soil where it grows. Those from the gardens and highly cultivated spots near Philadelphia come to a size and succulence of leaf scarcely to be believed without seeing them. They may be easily bleached by the common method, and certainly in that state would be a valuable addition to the list of delicate culinary vegetables."

By 1837 Darlington, writing from neighboring West Chester with special emphasis on "domestic and rural economy," did not seem to know of the phenomenal plant of the Philadelphia market and spoke of Shepard's-purse, as others have ever since, merely as "a troublesome weed."

Chestnut states that by California Indians the seeds are sometimes gathered and ground into meal.

Spring-Cress
Cardamine bulbosa (L.) Crantz

Key-characters an early spring plant, with bulbous or tuberous, thickened white rootstock, and upright stem with scattered, alternate oval leaves; the upper leaves

sessile, the lower slender-stalked and more rounded; flower-cluster elongating, with the 4 white petals inch long.
Habitat wet or springy woods.
Range southern New Hampshire to Minnesota and southward.
Season of Availability as salad, early spring; rootstocks, throughout the year.
Uses salad, condiment.

The tender young plants have the flavor of horseradish and make a very pleasant salad. The bulbous rootstock has a similar flavor and when grated and mixed with vinegar makes a good substitute for horseradish, as do the tender young leaves and stems, chopped fine and mixed with vinegar. Lady's-smock is equally good.

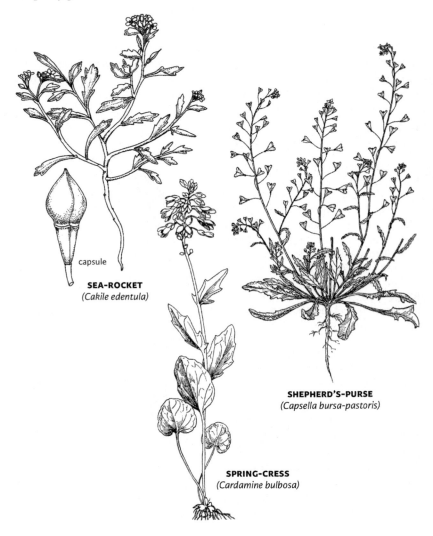

capsule

SEA-ROCKET
(Cakile edentula)

SHEPHERD'S-PURSE
(Capsella bursa-pastoris)

SPRING-CRESS
(Cardamine bulbosa)

Crinkle-root, Pepper-root
Cardamine concatenata (Michx.) Sw.
Cardamine diphylla (Michx.) Wood, plus several other species.

Synonyms *Dentaria concatenata, Dentaria dissecta*
Key-characters plants of early spring, bearing stalked, hand-shaped leaves midway on the stem; the leaves 2 or 3, with 3-5 toothed, finger-like divisions; inflorescence a loose, elongating cluster of white or pink flowers about 1/2 inch long; rootstock crisp and fleshy, whitish, elongate, peppery.
Habitat rich woods.
Range various species throughout the deciduous forest region of eastern America, from eastern Quebec to western Ontario and southward.
Uses salad, condiment.

The crisp, white rootstock is a popular nibble with children and makes a palatable ingredient in salads or a (pleasant radish-like relish when eaten with salt. Its flavor suggests horseradish and the grated rootstock, when mixed with vinegar, makes a satisfactory camp-horse-radish.

Native Water-Cress
Cardamine pensylvanica Muhl. Ex Willd.

Key-characters resembling Water-Cress, but without the creeping or prostrate stems; the leaves forming circular, basal rosettes, and the flowering stem upright; divisions of the leaves usually more numerous or narrower than in the true Water-Cress, and flowers smaller.
Habitat wet or springy places or in shallow water.
Range throughout temperate North America from southern Labrador to British Columbia, south to northern Florida and Texas.
Season of Availability spring and early summer and sometimes through the winter (young rosettes).
Use salad.

Our **Native Water-Cress** so closely re-sembles the market plant that by many people it is not readily distinguished from it, and it makes almost as good a salad or ingredient of a salad. The stems and leaves are, however, less succulent. It is safest to disinfect the plants before

NATIVE WATER-CRESS
(C. pennsylvanica)

eating raw. (See note under Water-Cress.)

Other species of *Cardamine*, of which there are several, doubtless have similar qualities.

Scurvy-Grass
Cochlearia (3 species)

Key-characters leaves slender-stalked, forming a circular rosette a few inches across; the roundish blades more or less coarsely angled, fleshy and almost veinless, with a strong odor or taste of cress or horseradish; flowering stems branching, arising from the old rosettes, a few inches high, bearing elongate clusters of small white flowers with 4 petals, followed by flattened, roundish seed-pods.
Habitat and Range seashores and sea-cliffs from the Magdalen Islands, Anticosti and the Mingan Islands in the Gulf of St. Lawrence around the coasts of Newfoundland and outer Labrador.
Season of Availability throughout the open season, while the leaves and stems are tender.
Uses salad, potherb.

Scurvy-Grass has very palatable, crisp foliage and forms one of the most agreeable of salads, suggesting water-cress. It is an important addition to the diet of northern peoples, and in the early days of navigation was much sought as a preventive of scurvy. Bryant says that "the best way of eating them [the leaves] is between bread and butter."

Peppergrass
Lepidium (about 6 species)

Key-characters leaves in spring forming rosettes, the individual leaves deeply cut or toothed and with the characteristic cress-flavor; flowers minute, white or whitish, in elongating slender spike-like clusters, with 4 petals (these sometimes wanting) in opposite pairs; seed-pod flat, circular or nearly so, notched at the summit.
Habitat roadsides or dry, open soils.
Range temperate regions generally.
Uses salad, condiment.

The vigorously growing young shoots in spring make a good substitute for water-cress or garden-cress, and the peppery pods or seeds through the summer are an excellent seasoning for salads or soups. These seeds mixed with vinegar and salt (very little) make a tasty dressing for meats.

Water-Cress
Nasturtium officinale Ait. f.

Synonyms *Rorippa nasturtium-aquaticum*
Use salad.

The familiar **Water-Cress** of the markets is naturalized in America, in clear streams or pools or about springs, rarely far from the haunts of man. As a salad it needs no discussion here, but certain cautions should be emphasized. In gathering Water-Cress great care should be taken not to confuse other plants with it, since the deadly **Water-Hemlocks** (see p. 39) grow in habitats where the cress is often found. Beware also of contaminated water, too near farms or towns, or, in the woods, flowing by remote piggeries. In using Water-Cress it is safest always to disinfect it by using some harmless, disinfecting wash, such as "chlorazene" (see p. 11). One can't be sure of the water in which it grew.

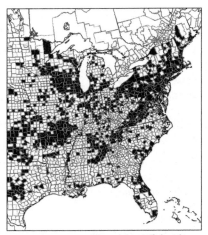

WATER-CRESS *(Nasturtium officinale)*

Those who make wry faces when they taste mustard-oil or Water-Cress should appreciate the generic name *Nasturtium*, from the latin nasus tortus, a convulsed nose. This generic name, for centuries belonging to Water-Cress, has, in popular usage, been transferred to the wholly different South American *Tropaeolum*, so popular in the flower-gardens. The transfer came about through the similar taste of the centrally attached round leaves, the showy flowers and the plump fruits of the latter. Ask any non-botanical seedsman for Nasturtium; you will surely get *Tropaeolum!*

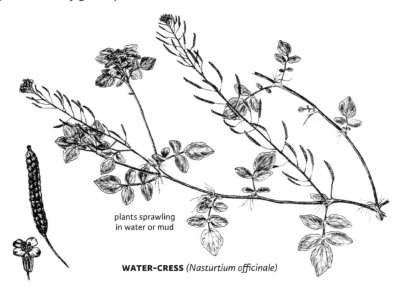

plants sprawling
in water or mud

WATER-CRESS *(Nasturtium officinale)*

Amphibious Yellow Cress
Rorippa amphibia (L.) Bess.

Uses salad and potherb.

This coarse perennial species, with elongate rooting branches and entire or shallowly toothed to jagged oblanceolate leaves, small yellow flowers and ellipsoid pods, is naturalized in wet places in Quebec, New England and New York. In Europe and Asia the young shoots are eaten either raw or cooked. Doubtless other species could be similarly used.

Mustard, Hedge-Mustard
Brassica (about 10 species)
Sisymbrium officinale (L.) Scop.

Uses potherb, salad.

The **Mustards** are familiar weeds of cultivated ground or waste land and the young plants are popular as potherbs. The leaves of the smoother-leaved species are sometimes used in salads. The powdered mustard of the table comes from seeds of this genus. The **Hedge-Mustard**, *Sisymbrium officinale*, one of the commonest weeds of manured lands, barn-yards, etc., makes a particularly good potherb, if gathered young.

Penny-Cress, Mithridate-Mustard
Thlaspi arvense L.

Key-characters a common annual weed with oblong, pale leaves along the stem; white flowers with 4 petals a third of an inch long, and deeply notched flat, roundish many-seeded pods about half an inch long, these in simple elongate clusters, each pod on a slender, spreading stalk and, when ripe, with the 2 flat valves falling away from a thin membrane which separates them. **Habitat and Range** a common roadside- and field-weed from Labrador to Alaska, south through the Northern States and locally in the South. **Uses** salad, condiment.

The young leaves are edible, tasting somewhat mustardlike, with a suggestion of onion. The seeds can be eaten as a mustard-like condiment.

The name Mithridate, long applied to this and some other possibly medicinal plants, comes from an ancient physician, Mithridate, who tried his concoctions on himself.

PENNY-CRESS
(Thlaspi arvense)

Butomaceae FLOWERING-RUSH FAMILY

Flowering-Rush
Butomus umbellatus L.

Key-characters tall marsh plant with erect, sword-shaped leaves and flowering stem 3 feet or more high, the latter terminated by an umbrella-like cluster of showy rose-colored and green flowers, with 3 large purple-tinged bracts at base; the flowers with sepals and petals an inch long, 3 of each; fruit-pods inflated, with a long beak, about half an inch long; rootstock thick and fleshy, late in the season bearing many grain-like and promptly deciduous tubers.

Habitat swampy shores and river-flats.

Range along the St. Lawrence from above Montreal to below Quebec and about Lake Champlain, thence westward to southern Michigan.

Season of Availability autumn to spring, when the rootstocks are well filled.

Uses starchy vegetable, bread.

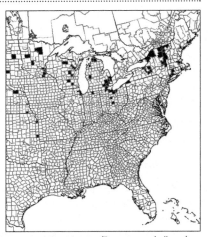

FLOWERING-RUSH *(Butomus umbellatus)*

Both Professor Balfour and Rev. C. A. Johns state in the *Treasury of Botany*, that in northern Asia the rootstock is roasted and eaten; and Unger adds that in Norway it "often serves as material for bread." Others speak of the rootstocks as acrid and bitter. Drying or roasting may dispel the acridity as it does that of the Araceae. The plant has only recently naturalized itself along the St. Lawrence and about Lake Champlain but it has spread so rapidly that it has become something of a nuisance; under these circumstances it may be fortunate that it can be used as food.

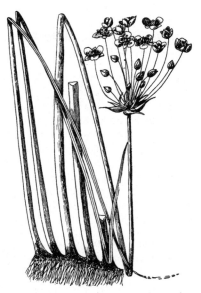

FLOWERING-RUSH *(Butomus umbellatus)*

Cabombaceae WATERSHIELD FAMILY

Watershield
Brasenia schreberi J.F. Gmel.

Key-characters a branching aquatic with the stems, leaf-stalks and ¡under surfaces of the leaves slippery with a colorless gelatinous coat; leaves oval, attached at the middle to the stalk; flowers about 1 inch across, with 3 or 4 narrow mauve-purple petals; fruits a cluster of club-shaped small pods inclosed in the calyx.

Habitat ponds, quiet streams, etc.

Range general at low altitudes northward into southern Canada.

Season of Availability autumn to spring.

Uses starchy tuberous roots, salad.

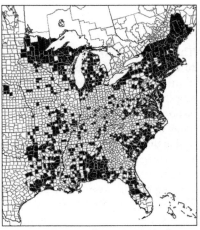

WATERSHIELD *(Brasenia schreberi)*

We have never dug the roots, but it is stated on good authority that the California Indians ate the tuberous roots.

Professor Georgeson stated that in Japan "The leaf-stems and young leaves, before they expand, with the adherent mucilage or slime, are eaten as a salad with vinegar."

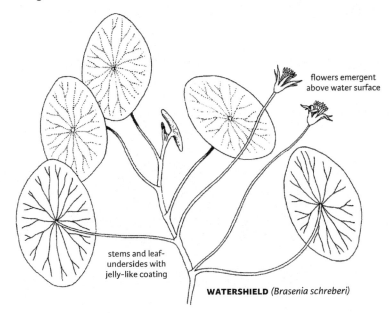

flowers emergent
above water surface

stems and leaf-
undersides with
jelly-like coating

WATERSHIELD *(Brasenia schreberi)*

Cactaceae CACTUS FAMILY

Prickly-Pear, Indian Fig
Opuntia (several species)

Uses fruit, soup-thickening, cooked vegetable.

The fruit of the **Prickly-Pear** is familiar to all who live within the range of these plants and some of the better fruits of southwestern or Mexican species occasionally come to the eastern market. They have a sweet and succulent pulp and in the Southwest are highly valued. Unfortunately the surface is covered with tufts of deciduous, extremely irritating bristles. Nevertheless, the Indians and many whites in the Southwest and in Mexico have conquered this difficulty. They prize them not only as fruit but as a thirst-quencher; and the

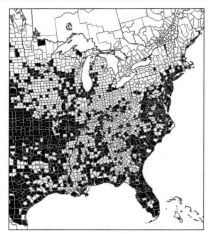

PRICKLY-PEAR *(Opuntia)*

parched seeds, after being pulverized, are used as a thickening for soup. Even the thick, leaf-like branches supply food, being roasted in hot ashes and peeled, leaving a palatable but slimy pulp. Our own species are relatively unimportant and practically never used.

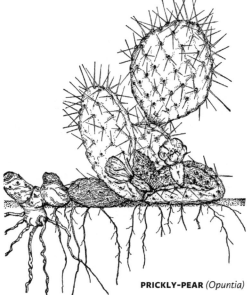

PRICKLY-PEAR *(Opuntia)*

Campanulaceae BLUEBELL FAMILY

Purple Bellflower
Campanula rapunculoides L.

Key-characters stem 1-3 feet high, leafy; the lower leaves long-stalked and heart-shaped, the upper gradually becoming more narrow and sessile, all coarsely toothed and stiffly hairy beneath; flowers blue-violet, bell-shaped, nodding, in very elongate, spire-like, one-sided clusters.
Habitat and Range roadsides and thickets about towns, escaped from old-fashioned gardens and borders.
Uses salad, root-vegetable.

The widely creeping rootstocks send off late in the season at irregular intervals fleshy, subterranean cord-like branches which are full of succulence and make a palatable, slightly sweetish salad or, when cooked, have a flavor suggestive of parsnip. In Europe, whence we derived our plant, it seems not to have been used, doubtless because of the large-rooted and superior **Rampion**, *Campanula rapunculus* L., which was formerly a garden-vegetable there.

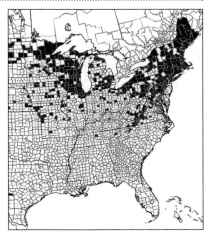

PURPLE BELLFLOWER *(C. rapunculoides)*

flowers in elongate spikes

PURPLE BELLFLOWER
(Campanula rapunculoides)

Cannabaceae HEMP FAMILY

Hemp
Cannabis sativa L.

Use parched seeds eaten.

The **Hemp** is an occasional weed about rubbish of towns. In eastern and southern Europe its seeds are much eaten after being parched or, according to some authors, they are made into cakes and fried. The seeds contain much oil and are nutritious or even stimulating. A famous oriental intoxicant is derived from the resin of the plant, the narcotic marijuana. See p. 37.

Hop
Humulus lupulus L.

Uses potherb, asparagus.

The young shoots of **Hop**, especially if blanched, have been somewhat popular as a substitute for asparagus. Only very young shoots should be gathered, the older ones being tough and bitter. The flavor is unique and to many tastes delicious; the texture dry and slightly gritty. Chopped very fine and well dressed with butter or cream the young shoots are excellent.

Hops are raised chiefly for their fruit, used in brewing beer and ale. During the temporary period of national prohibition the inimitable Clute remarked of the "delicious nutty flavor" of the boiled shoots, that "Further experiments will doubtless be necessary before hop growers turn from brewing to boiling."

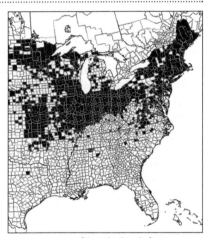

HOP *(Humulus lupulus)*

spike of pistillate flowers

HOP *(Humulus lupulus)*

Cannaceae CANNA FAMILY

Golden Canna, Indian Shot
Canna flaccida Salisb.

Use starchy rootstock?

The beautiful yellow-flowered **Golden Canna** of swamps from Florida to South Carolina (casually escaped northward) presumably has edible young corms. The new corms of some tropical species, developed on the rootstock, are cooked and eaten as starchy food. Porcher thought it probable that a good "arrowroot"-starch would be found in the root. We have seen no verification of this.

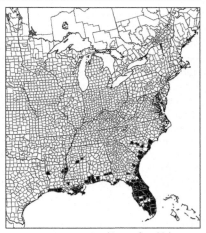

GOLDEN CANNA *(Canna flaccida)*

flowers yellow,
large and showy

GOLDEN CANNA *(Canna flaccida)*

Caprifoliaceae HONEYSUCKLE FAMILY

Waterberry, Swamp Fly-Honeysuckle
Lonicera villosa (Michx.) J.A. Schultes

Synonym *Lonicera caerulea*
Key-characters shrub 1-3 feet high, with stiffly ascending branches covered with very shreddy but persistent bark; the new sprigs with pale-brown, smooth bark; leaves opposite, nearly sessile, oblong to oval, about 1 inch long, rather firm, entire, dark-green above, paler beneath, rounded at tip; flowers and fruits borne in the leaf-axils; berries blue, resembling blueberries but with 2 slender and spreading, leaf-like bracts at base, very juicy and with many fine seeds (shrub quickly distinguished from the true blueberries by opposite leaves).
Habitat peaty and wet, rocky soils northward; cold peat-bogs and swamps southward.

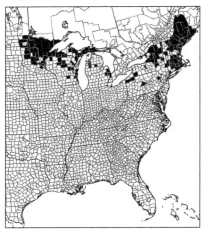

WATERBERRY *(Lonicera villosa)*

Range Labrador to Manitoba, south to bogs of southern New England, northern Pennsylvania, Michigan, Wisconsin and Minnesota.
Season of Availability berries, late May (southward) to early August (northward).
Use berries.

Although but little known as edible fruit, the **Waterberries**, as they have been appropriately named in eastern Maine, are delicious, in flavor somewhat suggesting blueberries. On account of their early ripening, long before true blueberries are ripe, Waterberries should be better known. By some who have learned to prize the berries it has even been suggested that the shrub should be cultivated and the fruit improved. Thus the distinguished Wisconsin naturalist and scholar, Increase A. Lapham, long ago wrote to Asa Gray: "Is not this worth cultivating for its abundant fine-flavored fruit? I will send you a root." The American shrub was long confused with the Eurasian *Lonicera caerulea* (now treated as a variety of *L. villosa*) but differs in certain striking characters from the European species, and it is noteworthy that we have found no reference to the use of the fruit for food in Europe.

Wild Coffee, Tinker's-weed, Feverwort
Triosteum (three species)

Key-characters coarse herbs with simple, erect, usually bunched, more or less hairy stems 1-1/2 to 3 or 4 feet high, with coarse, opposite, entire leaves rather abruptly narrowed at base and often joining around the stem; fruits clustered in the leaf-axils,

2-8 at each node of the stem, orange to dark red, ovoid to nearly globose, about 1/2 inch long, crowned by the 5 narrow and leaf-like sepals, and containing 3 large, bony stones.

Habitat and Range open woods and rocky slopes or thickets, frequent southward, more locally northward to western New Brunswick, southern Quebec and southern Ontario.
Season of Availability late summer and autumn.
Use coffee-substitute.

Barton, a distinguished botanist of Philadelphia a century and more ago, wrote: "I learned from the late Rev. Dr. Muhlenberg, that the dried and toasted berries of this plant, were considered by some of the Germans of Lancaster county, as an excellent substitute for coffee, when prepared in the same way. Hence the name of wild coffee, by which he informed me it was sometimes known."

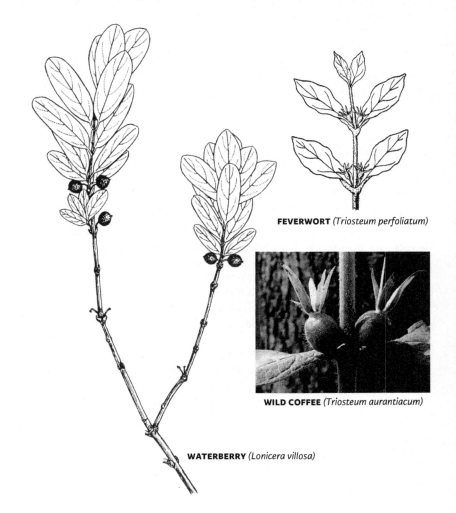

FEVERWORT *(Triosteum perfoliatum)*

WILD COFFEE *(Triosteum aurantiacum)*

WATERBERRY *(Lonicera villosa)*

Caryophyllaceae PINK FAMILY

Mouse-ear Chickweed
Cerastium semidecandrum L.

Use potherb.

The **Mouse-ear Chickweeds** are chiefly weeds of cultivated land, and differ from the true Chickweeds in having oblong, finely hairy leaves of thick texture. Most of them are too hairy and tough to be attractive, but the small, annual species, *Cerastium semidecandrum*, which abounds in early spring as a weed on Cape Cod, thence locally southward, grows very rapidly and, gathered before flowering, makes a thoroughly palatable potherb.

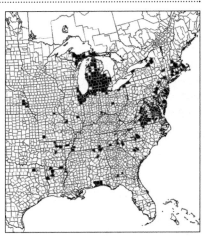

MOUSE-EAR CHICKWEED *(C. semidecandrum)*

Sea-Purslane, Seabeach Sandwort
Honckenya peploides (L.) Ehrh.

Synonym *Arenaria peploides*
Uses salad, potherb, pickle, drink.

This fleshy, coarse chickweed-like plant of sea-strands from Virginia northward is very succulent when young and, according to some European writers, may be made into pickles which are "said to have a pleasant pungent taste." In Iceland the plant is steeped in sour whey and allowed to ferment; the liquor is then strained off and fresh water added to it, when it is said to taste like olive-oil and is used as a beverage. As a salad or relish it may be eaten, picked fresh as one follows the shore; and it is also a very tolerable potherb if gathered before it is too old and stringy.

In his account of Sable Island, off Nova Scotia, Dr. Harold St. John said: "This succulent, free-growing plant is the choicest fodder of the 'gangs' of wild ponies that roam the island. . . . Taking the hint from the ponies, I myself tried munching a sprig of the *Arenaria*, and found it of good texture, juicy and with a strong but not unpleasant taste resembling that of cabbage."

Moss-Campion
Silene acaulis (L.) Jacq.

Use cooked vegetable.

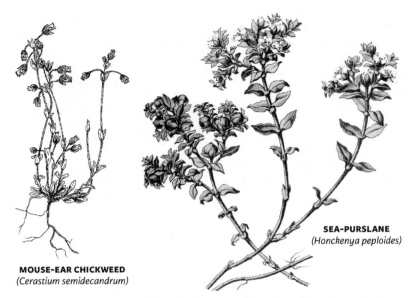

SEA-PURSLANE
(Honckenya peploides)

MOUSE-EAR CHICKWEED
(Cerastium semidecandrum)

This densely-tufted moss-like pink of the arctic realm abounds on the barrens of Newfoundland and eastern Quebec and is found on Mt. Washington, New Hampshire; and, with its tough, closely forking stems and masses of persistent dead leaves, it hardly suggests culinary possibilities. Nevertheless, in his *Tour in Iceland*, Sir William Hooker states that the plant is "boiled and eaten with butter by the Icelanders." The great profusion of the plant in some areas suggests the desirability of testing it as a cooked vegetable; but its habitat in gravels and its habit of retaining for years the half-decayed old branches and leaves indicate that, in order to render it acceptable to a fastidious palate, considerable preparation is necessary.

Bladder-Campion, Maiden's Tears, Snappert
Silene vulgaris (Moench) Garke

Synonyms *Silene cucubalus, S. latifolia*
Uses potherb, soup.

The **Bladder-Campion**, so named from its inflated, thin-textured calices, is one of the commonest roadside- and railroad-weeds in some regions of northern New England, eastern Canada and Newfoundland, thence west to British Columbia and rather locally southward to Virginia, Tennessee, etc. The young shoots when about two inches long are a palatable cooked green, having a flavor suggestive of green peas, but with a slight bitter taste. This bitter is due to saponin, a bitter principle present in many members of the Pink family and in large quantity poisonous. The amount present in the young shoots of Bladder-Campion is not harmful, and some English authors have suggested the cultivation of the plant as a garden vegetable, the bitter of the new shoots being checked by blanching with litter. A puree made from the boiled shoots is nearly equal to the best puree of spinach. Bryant, in the 18th century, was so enthusiastic about this plant, that he wrote:

"Our kitchen-gardens scarcely furnish a better flavoured sallad than the young, tender shoots of this plant, when boiled. . . . If the plant were under cultivation, no doubt but it would be improved, and would well reward the gardeners labour."

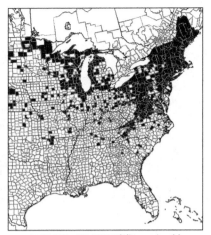

BLADDER-CAMPION *(Silene vulgaris)*

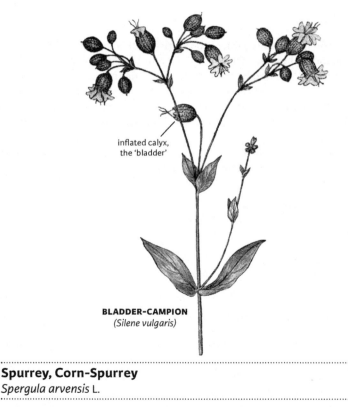

inflated calyx, the 'bladder'

BLADDER-CAMPION
(Silene vulgaris)

Spurrey, Corn-Spurrey
Spergula arvensis L.

Use breadstuff.

The only use of **Corn-Spurrey** seems to have been as a source of famine-bread in Scandinavia, and all the accounts are obviously derived from the original one of Linnaeus who, toward two centuries ago, wrote: "In times of great scarcity, when nothing better is to be had than seeds of Spurrey (*Spergula arvensis*) from the fields, these seeds, after being dried, are ground and baked, along with a small proportion of corn [wheat]. The bread thus made proves blackish, but not bad."

Spurrey is such an abundant weed of grain-fields and of sandy open soil throughout the Northern States and Canada, that it should be a very simple experiment to try the quality of this Norwegian famine-bread. All the members of its group contain saponin, a bitter and somewhat poisonous principle, so that only under stress is it desirable to use the seeds.

Chickweed
Stellaria media (L.) Vill.

Synonym *Alsine media*
Use potherb.

The common **Chickweed** of gardens and damp, shaded dooryards is not to be despised as a mere weed, for many European authors are enthusiastic in their praises of it as a substitute for spinach. Thus Mrs. Lankester went so far as to say: "When boiled, it forms an excellent green vegetable resembling spinach in flavour, and is very wholesome." Others speak of it as having little taste (as we have found out), but as being a good padding to add bulk to other spinaches. Only the young, vigorously growing tips should be used, since the older bases of the plant become stringy in age.

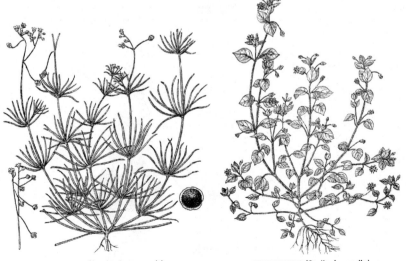

SPURRY (*Spergula arvensis*)   **CHICKWEED** (*Stellaria media*)

Celastraceae STAFF-TREE FAMILY

Shrubby Bittersweet, Waxwork
Celastrus scandens L.

Use emergency-food.

Dr. Edward Palmer and some other writers on Indian foods state that the tender branches and the sweetish bark of **Bittersweet or Waxwork** were used by the Chippewas as food, the poisonous saponin which is contained in the bark being dispelled by cooking; the boiled bark being sweet and palatable.

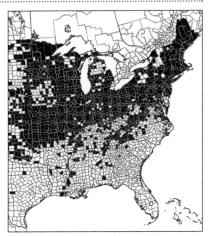

SHRUBBY BITTERSWEET *(Celastrus scandens)*

fruit

SHRUBBY BITTERSWEET *(Celastrus scandens)*

Clethraceae SWEET-PEPPERBUSH FAMILY

Sweet Pepperbush
Clethra alnifolia L.
Clethra acuminata Michx.

Use cooked vegetable.

According to Dr. Georgeson the young leaves of the Japanese species are cooked, in times of scarcity of other greens, and eaten with rice in Japan. The Japanese species is so similar to ours that our own familiar species might be tried.

SWEET PEPPERBUSH *(Clethra alnifolia)*

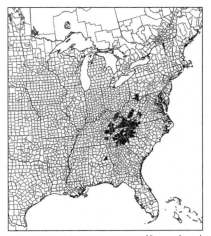

MOUNTAIN SWEET PEPPERBUSH *(C. acuminata)*

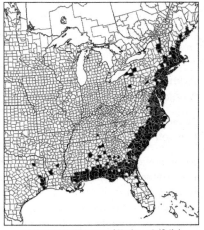

SWEET PEPPERBUSH *(Clethra alnifolia)*

Commelinaceae SPIDERWORT FAMILY

Day-flower
Commelina diffusa Burm. f.
Commelina communis L.

Use potherb.

The familiar succulent **Day-flowers** with creeping annual stems, alternate and long-sheathed narrowly ovate fleshy leaves, and evanescent blue flowers borne from semi-heart-shaped sheaths, are eaten in the East Indies as steamed vegetables, "very fit on account of succulence." The weedy *Commelina communis* which is too aggressive in door-yards, gardens, ditches, etc., may prove palatable to some. If the large-leaved perennial *C. virginica* L. with creeping rhizomes and leaf-blades up to 8 inches long and 2 inches broad can thus be used it would be easy to gather a good kettle-full from low woods and thickets, from Florida to Texas, north to southern New Jersey, southern Pennsylvania, Maryland, Kentucky, Missouri and eastern Kansas. The group is not considered poisonous and experiments are in order.

Erect Day-flower
Commelina erecta L.

Use starchy root-vegetable.

Lindley, writing from the viewpoint of medicine, states in his *Vegetable Kingdom* that "The fleshy rhizomes of Commelyna . . . angustifolia . . . contain a good deal of starch mixed with mucilage, and are therefore fit for food when cooked." We do not know of the fleshy roots of *C. erecta* (synonym *C. angustifolia*) actually being used. The plant occurs from Florida to northern Mexico, north to southeastern New York, Pennsylvania, West Virginia, northern Indiana, Illinois, Missouri and Nebraska, usually in sands or sandy loam. It should be investigated.

Aneilema
Murdannia keisak (Hassk.) Hand.-Maz.

Synonym *Aneilema keisak*
Use potherb.

Murdannia keisak resembles the creeping species of *Commelina* but does not have the semi-heart-shaped spathe, the pink axillary flowers borne in autumn in leafy-bracted racemes, the fleshy stems becoming greatly elongate (up to 6 feet long) and loosely ascending. It is primarily Asiatic, where it (and other species) is eaten as a potherb. With us it abounds in fresh tidal marshes of tidewater Virginia.

Spiderwort
Tradescantia (several species)

Uses salad, potherb.

The several species of *Tradescantia* have succulent stems and leaves. They are familiar in our Southern and Central States and spread from cultivation northward. The commonly cultivated "Wandering Jew" belongs to the group. The late Dr. Carver of Tuskegee Institute highly commended them as "rich flavored," "the one most highly prized . . . is *T. virginica.*"

flowers 3-petaled

SPIDERWORT *(Tradescantia virginiana)*

DAY-FLOWER *(Commelina virginica)*

Convolvulaceae MORNING-GLORY FAMILY

Man-of-the-Earth, Wild Potato-vine
Ipomoea pandurata L. G.F.W. Mey.

Key-characters a twining or trailing vine resembling the morning-glory; with heart-shaped leaves and with purplish and white morning-glory flowers usually clustered on long stalks from the leaf axils; the root a gigantic tap-root, which often weighs from 15 to 30 pounds, in appearance resembling the tropical yam.
Habitat dry or light alluvial soils or fields.
Range southern and central states, extending locally northward to Ontario and Connecticut.
Season of Availability autumn to spring while the root is well filled.
Use root-vegetable.

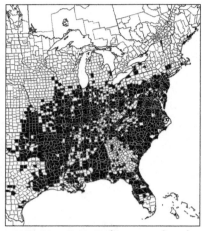

MAN-OF-THE-EARTH (*Ipomea pandurata*)

The tremendous, yam-like root of **Man-of-the-Earth** is reported by several writers on Indian foods to be used by the Indians, although it is to be noted that the fresh root is reputed to be purgative. The plant is related on the one hand to the sweet potato, on the other to the tropical, purgative *Ipomoea purga*. Caution should, therefore, be exercised in using it.

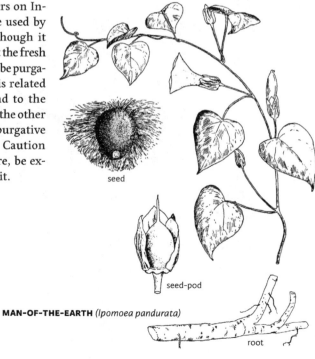

seed

seed-pod

MAN-OF-THE-EARTH (*Ipomoea pandurata*)

root

Cornaceae DOGWOOD FAMILY

Bunchberry, Crackerberry

Cornus canadensis L.
Cornus suecica L.

Uses pudding, masticatory.

The familiar, bright-red clusters of the **Bunchberry** always attract attention and, although the berries of the more southern species, *Cornus canadensis*, are insipid and dry, with a very large stone, the berries of the more northern *C. suecica*, which bears its clusters from the axils of the small opposite leaves, are slightly tart and more palatable. Linnaeus describes the use of the latter berries by the Laplanders in making a dessert which might well be prepared from our common Bunchberry, with the addition of lemon-juice. The Lapland method of making what Linnaeus described as a "dainty" was to mix the berries with whey, then to boil them until the mass was as thick as a "flummery." This pudding (preferably with the stones strained off) was eaten with cream.

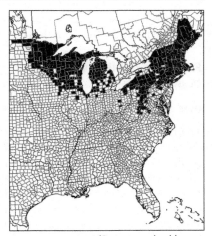

BUNCHBERRY *(Cornus canadensis)*

Ooeechee Lime or Ogeechee Plum

Nyssa ogeche Bartr. Ex Marsh.

Uses preserves, acid drink.

The well known **Ogeechee Lime** of wooded swamps from Florida to South Carolina has large red fruits up to 1-1/2 inches long. In his Travels William Bartram said: "I saw large, tall trees of the *Nyssa coccinea*, si[ve] Ogeeche, growing on the banks of the river . . . There is no tree that exhibits a more desirable appearance than this, in the

showy cream-colored bracts

BUNCHBERRY *(Cornus canadensis)*

autumn, when their fruit is ripe, and the tree divested of its leaves; for then they look as red as scarlet, with their fruit, which is of that colour also. It is of the shape, but larger than an olive, containing an agreeable acid juice . . . they are called Ogeeche limes, from their acid fruit being about the size of limes, and their being sometimes used in their stead." Stephen Elliott, in 1824, writing of "the pleasant acid of its fruit," said "but its last flavour is austere"; and another South Carolina botanist, Dr. Mellichamp, wrote of the "very delightful acid preserve . . . made from the large drupes."

Sour Gum or Black Gum, Tupelo
Nyssa sylvatica Marsh.

Uses acid fruit, masticatory.

The familiar **Sour Gum or Tupelo** got the first name from its pleasantly acid fruits. These are bluish stone-fruits with a very thin pulp, but sharply acid and pleasant to roll in the mouth in autumn and winter. The more southern var. *biflora* (or *N. biflora* Walt.) has the fruit juicier but intensely bitter. Similarly **Cotton Gum** (*N. aquatica* L.) of southern swamps has disagreeably tasting fruit as large as a small olive.

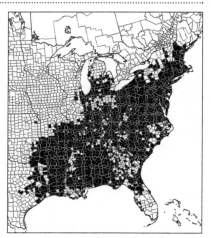

SOUR GUM (*Nyssa sylvatica*)

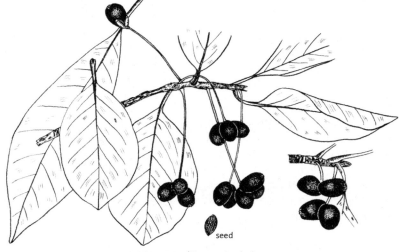

seed

SOUR GUM (*Nyssa sylvatica*)

Crassulaceae STONECROP FAMILY

Live-forever, Frog-plant, Aaron's-rod
Hylotelephium telephium (L.) H. Ohba

Synonyms *Sedum triphyllum, S. purpureum*
Key-characters a familiar, fleshy weed 1-2 ft. high, with the fleshy, cool, oblong, very succulent leaves, crowded but spirally arranged on the stem; in midsummer bearing a round-topped, broad cluster of crimson or magenta (sometimes whitish) small flowers; root stoutish, bearing numerous finger-shaped, crisp tubers.
Habitat damp fields, roadsides and rich, rocky banks, often a too abundant weed.
Range eastern Quebec to Maryland and Wisconsin.
Season of Availability as salad and potherb, late spring and early summer; tubers, spring to midsummer, again in autumn.
Uses salad, potherb, pickle.

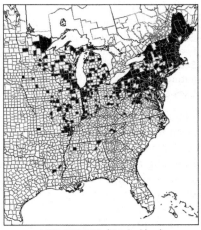

LIVE-FOREVER *(H. telephium)*

Live-forever or Frog-plant is familiar to most children in regions where it occurs on account of the readily loosened epidermis of the leaf, loosened by holding the leaf between the tongue and the roof of the mouth; after which, by blowing into the opening, the loosened epidermis may be distended like a frog's throat. It is, therefore, surprising how few people are familiar with the delicious quality of the tender, young leaves and stems as a salad. If the plant is to be used as salad, it should be gathered very young, but as a potherb (of indifferent quality) it may be used until July. The rounded or finger-like tuberous roots are crisp and succulent and after some days pickling in a salted vinegar, best put on the tubers while boiling hot, they form a tasty relish. After midsummer the tubers become stringy and tough, but again in late autumn crisp tubers may be found. They often occur in enormous masses and then furnish an abundant and easily obtained food.

Roseroot, Scurvy-Grass
Rhodiola rosea L.

Synonym *Sedum roseum*
Key-characters a tufted, succulent plant, with a large rough root which, when bruised, gives off a fragrance like attar-of-roses; stems 6-10 inches high, with crowded, fleshy, pinkish- or whitish-green, oblong, toothed leaves; flowers pale-yellow, in a dense terminal cluster, followed by reddish or purplish, 4- or 5-pronged capsules.

Habitat and Range ledges, rocky banks and cliffs, especially near the sea, rarely inland, abundant in the polar region and southward, especially on the coast of Labrador, frequent on the coast of Newfoundland, local on the outer coast of Maine, as far southwest as Monhegan Island, rare southward to northeastern Pennsylvania and the Carolina Mountains. **Season of Availability** early summer to autumn.
Uses salad, potherb.

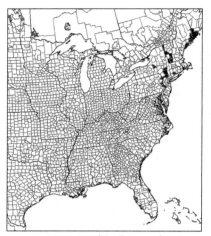

ROOSEROOT *(Rhodiola rosea)*

The succulent young leaves and stems of the **Roseroot** are an important salad in northern regions, and the stems and leaves up to the time of young fruit are cooked as greens. Where abundant the plant is of great importance, owing to the scarcity of green vegetables in northern countries.

Presumably other species of *Rhodiola* and the related *Sedum* when tried will prove to be good salads and potherbs, since various European species are thus eaten, but the creeping *Sedum acre*, as its name implies, is too pungent.

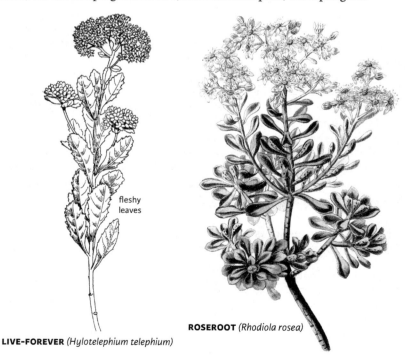

fleshy leaves

ROSEROOT *(Rhodiola rosea)*

LIVE-FOREVER *(Hylotelephium telephium)*

Cucurbitaceae GOURD FAMILY

Melonette
Melothria pendula L.

Use pickles.

The delicate climbing **Melonette** of our Southern States, extending northward into Virginia, southern Indiana and southern Missouri, is like a very slender and tiny cucumber-vine, with ovoid green to black berries about half an inch long. Although Bryant, in his *Flora Diaetetica*, said "The inhabitants of the West Indies pickle these berries, and use them as we do Capers," it should be noted that the West Indian species are quite distinct from our true Melothria pendula and that Porcher, who certainly knew our plant, said: "The seeds act as a drastic purgative— half a one is a dose for an adult. Martius states that three or four will act powerfully on a horse." With plenty of other pickles it is wise to go slow in using Melonette. In this case it would be unwise to take Bryant's statement even with the proverbial grain of salts! See p. 49.

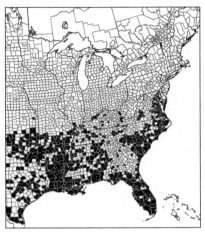

MELONETTE *(Melothria pendula)*

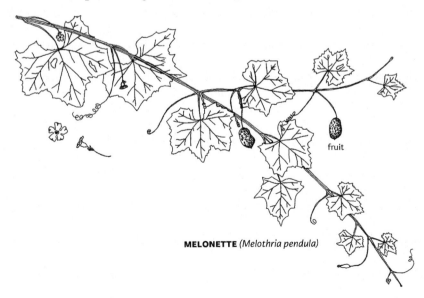

MELONETTE *(Melothria pendula)*

fruit

Cyperaceae SEDGE FAMILY

Chufa, Nut-Grass, Earth-Almond, Zulu-nuts
Cyperus esculentus L.

Key-characters grass-like plants with leaves all basal, except for a circle of similar long leaves at the base of the inflorescence; the latter with widely spreading rays, like the rays of an umbrella, and bearing numerous yellowish spikelets with saw-tooth edges; the base of the plant sending out long runners terminated by nut-like tubers inch in diameter.
Habitat alluvial soils or rich, cultivated or waste lands.
Range St. John valley, New Brunswick, to the Pacific, and southward to the Tropics.
Season of Availability late autumn or early spring, the tubers keeping over winter.
Uses farinaceous vegetable, flour, drink, coffee-substitute.

CHUFA *(Cyperus esculentus)*

Chufa has long been a popular food with the Ethiopians and a cultivated strain of *Cyperus esculentus*, brought from Africa, is now somewhat cultivated in the Southern States. Experiment has shown, however, that the cultivated strain, derived from tropical or subtropical Africa, cannot be cultivated with success in the Northern States, although we have a native plant which seems to differ only in its smaller tubers, which are borne farther from the parent plant and not in such abundance as in the cultivated variety. The tubers are slightly sweetish and nutty, but with a tough, dry rind which is not readily masticated; they are commonly boiled, sometimes candied, or they may be ground and made into a palatable and wholesome flour.

Chufa, as indicated by Sturtevant, was so valued in ancient times that its tubers were placed in Egyptian tombs dating back to more than 2000 years before Christ. In other parts of the Mediterranean region and northward as far as England they are sent to market, to be nibbled as dainties or prepared as a conserve; and Unger states that, in the 18th century, "it was employed as a substitute for coffee in the whole of Germany"; while Loudon speaks of it as grown in Hungary for this purpose.

A Spanish recipe for a refreshing drink from Chufa is to soak for 48 hours a half-pound of the tubers, mash, add 1 quart of water, 1/3 pound of sugar and then put the liquid through a sieve and serve as a drink or use to make ices.

spikelet

tuber

CHUFA *(Cyperus esculentus)*

Nut-Grass
Cyperus rotundus L.

Use farinaceous vegetable.

Cyperus rotundus differs from *C. esculentus* in having reddish-purple spikelets and firmer runners. It is a weed of the Southern States, coming north to Virginia and rarely to New York. Its small tubers have been used like those of Chufa.

Nut-Grass, Bulrush

Schoenoplectus maritimus (L.) Lye
Schoenoplectus robustus Pursh

Synonyms *Schoenoplectus maritimus* synonyms: *Scirpus maritimus, S. paludosus*
Schoenoplectus robustus synonym: *Scirpus robustus*
Uses farinaceous roots, flour.

The large **Bulrushes** of saline habitats and brackish, wet places along the coast and locally in the interior with long rope-like rootstocks bearing tuberous enlargements at intervals, are said by Blankinship to furnish food to some of the western Indians; and the rootstocks of closely related species are said by Royle to be ground and used for flour in India. The tubers of ours are as large as chestnuts or larger, and, upon grinding, may be found to furnish flour as good as that from **Chufa**.

Tule, Tall Bulrush

Schoenoplectus tabernaemontani (K.C. Gmel.) Palla
Schoenoplectus acutus (Muhl. ex Bigelow) A. & D. Löve

Synonyms *Schoenoplectus tabernaemontani* synonym: *Scirpus validus*
Schoenoplectus acutus synony: *Scirpus acutus*
Key-characters and Habitat tall plants of pond-margins or marshes, with naked, flexible stems several feet high, the larger stems 1/2 to 1 inch in diameter at base; terminated by a loose or dense cluster of small brown spikes (borne just below the tip of the stem).
Range one species or another from Newfoundland to British Columbia and Mexico.
Season of Availability rootstock, autumn and early spring, when the rootstock is filled with starch and sugar; pollen, June to September; seeds, July to winter.
Uses masticatory, breadstuff, syrup.

The rootstock of **Tule** has been in high repute among American Indians as a source of food; the young, leading tip in the autumn, from which next year's shoot will arise, is eatable and reputed to relieve thirst. It is tender, slightly sweetish, and crisp, but the labor of digging it precludes its becoming a popular food for those whose women are not inclined to gather it. In regions of alkaline waters it is said to be of importance as a thirst-quencher.

The dried rootstocks, when beaten, furnish a meal which was used by the Indians as a breadstuff; and the bruised young roots, boiled in water, furnish a sweet syrup. Some writers on American Indian foods state that the pollen, gathered in a cloth, is used for making cakes, and that the seeds are gathered for food.

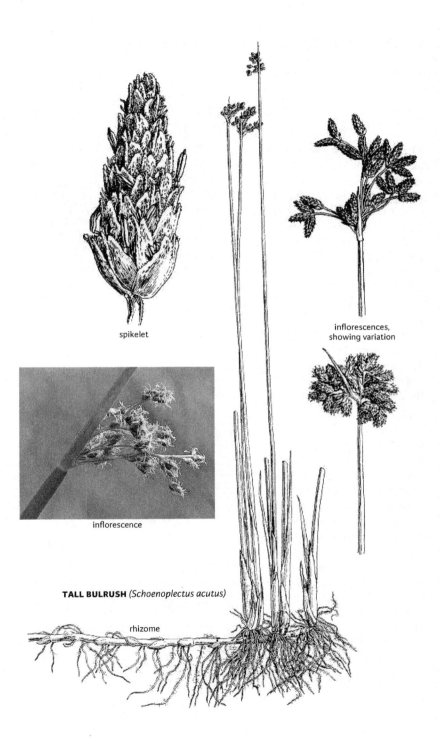

spikelet

inflorescences,
showing variation

inflorescence

TALL BULRUSH *(Schoenoplectus acutus)*

rhizome

Dioscoreaceae YAM FAMILY

Cinnamon-vine or Chinese Yam
Dioscorea polystachya Turcz.

Synonym *Dioscorea batatas* Dcne.
Use root-vegetable.

The **Cinnamon-vine**, so much cultivated as an ornamental in the South and northward as far as New England, climbs high by twining, and has attractive, strongly ribbed, rounded-triangular and long-pointed opposite leaves with small whitish bulb-like tubers borne in the axils. As far north as Pennsylvania it escapes and in waste lots, as about Richmond, Virginia, is often very abundant. Its deep subterranean potato-like tubers are said to become 2 or 3 feet long. Cooked like potatoes they are reputed to be excellent. They are extensively cultivated in southeastern Asia and when they were first brought to Europe nearly a century ago Decaisne and other French botanists and agriculturalists, as quoted in The *Gardeners' Chronicle* for July 22, 1854, commended the giant roots as "rich in nutritive matter, eatable when raw, easily cooked either by boiling or roasting . . . in cooking . . . it acquires the taste and quality of a Potato, for which it might be mistaken." The vigorous new shoots should not be eaten; they are purgative.

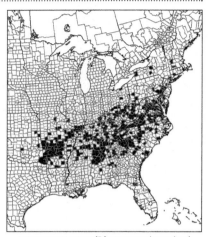

CINNAMON-VINE *(Dioscorea polystachya)*

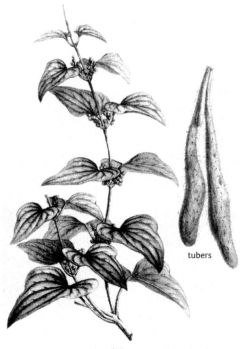

tubers

CINNAMON-VINE *(Dioscorea polystachya)*

Droseraceae SUNDEW FAMILY

Sundew
Drosera (ca. 7 species)

Use substitute for rennet.

According to Linnaeus and other European authors, the leaves of the **Sundews** have the power, like rennet, of curdling milk. In the words of our own Manasseh Cutler:

"If the juice be put into a strainer, through which the warm milk from the cow is poured, and the milk set by for a day or two to become acescent it acquires a consistency and tenacity neither the whey nor the cream will separate. In this state it is used by the inhabitants in the north of Sweden, and called an extremely grateful food."

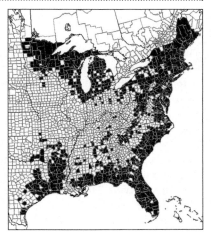

SUNDEW *(Drosera)*

ROUNDLEAF SUNDEW *(Drosera rotundifolia)*
leaf covered with gland-tipped hairs, above
habit, right

Ebenaceae EBONY FAMILY

Persimmon
Diospyros virginiana L.

Uses fruit, jelly, syrup, coffee-substitute, breadstuff, tea, vinegar, beer.

The **Persimmon** is so familiar to all natives of the southeastern United States as to need no introduction. The great fame of the fruit lies in the fact that, although intensely puckery before fully ripe, it becomes sweet and palatable, often delicious, when thoroughly mature. Those who know persimmons at their best will often travel many miles to secure the fruit. The qualities of the individual trees vary tremendously. Some of them produce small fruits; some, juicy fruits twice as large, while the "var. *pubescens*" of Missouri, eastern

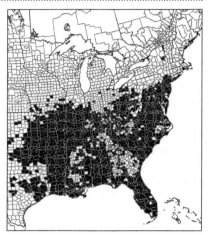

PERSIMMON *(Diospyros virginiana)*

Kansas, Arkansas and Oklahoma, may have fruits 3 inches in diameter. Some bear abundantly, some scantily. Some of the trees from southern Indiana southward and westward have their fruit ripe as early as the middle of August; but in that latitude most of the persimmons ripen in October and November, and a few trees not until December or even January. The raw fruit, when thoroughly ripe, is delicious and it should not be picked until it is almost as soft as a thin cake-batter. At that stage it is not marketable; consequently, market persimmons are picked when unripe.

One of the best ways of serving cooked persimmons is as a pudding: 2 cups persimmon pulp, 1 cup (scant) sugar, 1 egg, 2 cups milk, 2 cups flour, 1 teaspoon soda, 1/2 teaspoon salt, 1 teaspoon cinnamon, 1/2 teaspoon cloves, 1/2 teaspoon allspice.

Combine the ingredients, beating well. It is best to save about half the milk until all the flour has been added. Pour about 1-1/2 inches deep in well greased pans and bake about an hour in a 325° oven. The pudding turns dark brown when it is done. Serve either warm or cold with whipped cream. Soft, juicy persimmons make the best pudding.

Professor Milton Hopkins likes his pudding a little richer;

"3 eggs, ½ teaspoon salt, 2 cups sweet milk, 3-1/2 cups flour, 1 qt. seeded persimmon fruits, 1 pint cold water, 1 teaspoon soda, 1 cup granulated sugar.

"Wash and seed the fruit (to make 1 quart, about 3 quarts of whole fruit are required) and soak them in cold water for about an hour. Then run them through a colander. Mix the other ingredients in the order given, stirring thoroughly. Pour the batter into a greased pan and bake at 400° for one hour or until the pudding is a dark brown in color. Serve either hot or cold with whipped cream or hard sauce, and garnish with maraschino cherries. The pudding keeps well in the icebox for several days."

Porcher gives a recipe for Persimmon syrup: "The persimmons are mixed with wheat bran, baked in pones, next crashed and put in vessels, water poured on, and all allowed to stand twelve hours. Strain and boil to the consistency of molasses."

He also says: "A good vinegar, very much like, and equal to, white wine vinegar, is made as follows:

"Three bushels of ripe persimmons, three gallons of whiskey, and twenty-seven gallons of water. To those who can get the persimmons, the vinegar thus produced will be relatively cheap, even at any price which the most elastic conscience can ask for the spirits."

But, reaching the subject of spirits, we will stop, although the saintly Rev. M. A. Curtis, writing from North Carolina, gave the blessing of the Church to "Simmon Beer . . . by no means despicable"; and within a few months the value of dried persimmon-leaves, which heretofore have not been used for tea, has been announced. Vinson & Cross, as reported by them in *Science* for November 6, 1942, state that "Persimmon leaves have been found to give exceptionally high values in content of vitamin C . . . tea from green leaves was very acceptable . . . , as was also that made from leaves dried in a Bussler oven at 140° F. . . . The flavor . . . was similar to sassafras tea."

In the South at various times the seeds have been roasted and used as a substitute for coffee; while some of the southern Indian tribes dried the fruits and ground them into meal for bread-making.

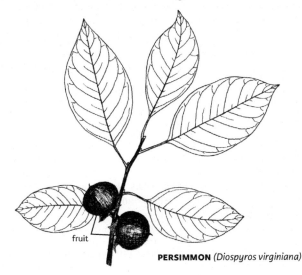

fruit

PERSIMMON *(Diospyros virginiana)*

Elaeagnaceae OLEASTER FAMILY

Silverberry
Elaeagnus commutata Bernh. Ex Rydb.

Synonym *Elaeagnus argentea*
Key-characters a shrub with alternate, silvery, scurfy entire leaves and scurfy branches; and roundish, dry and mealy berries about 1/2 inch in diameter, covered with silvery scales.
Habitat and Range dry rocky, mostly limestone slopes, in the Northwestern States and western Canada, extending locally east to eastern Quebec.
Season of Availability late summer and autumn.
Use fruit.

The **Silverberries**, although rather dry and mealy, are said to be edible but not of the best quality. Some of the Asiatic species in cultivation have more juicy fruit.

Buffalo-Berry, Bull-Berry
Shepherdia argentea (Pursh) Nutt.

Key-characters tall shrub with somewhat thorny, scurf-covered branches; the opposite leaves narrowly wedge-shaped, silvery on both sides with scales or scurf; axillary berries scarlet, pleasantly acid before frosts, afterward becoming sweet.
Habitat and Range banks of streams, Manitoba and northern Minnesota to Kansas and westward.
Season of Availability late summer and autumn.
Uses fruit, jelly, drink.

Buffalo-Berries are a staple wild fruit of the Northwest. After frosts they become sweet and are then eaten, raw or cooked. By the whites the sour berries, gathered before the frosts, are used to make a most delicious jelly, said to be preferred to currant jelly, the berries containing a considerable amount of pectin. The juice is also used in preparing a delicious summer drink.

Soapberry
Shepherdia canadensis (L.) Nutt.

Key-characters low shrub with opposite, oval leaves green above but silvery or rusty beneath with scurf or scales; branches rusty with scales; berries small, oblong, axillary, orange or reddish, disagreeable to the taste.
Habitat and Range dry, limy rocks and slopes, Newfoundland to Alaska, south to the northernmost states and along the Rocky Mountains.
Season of Availability summer and early autumn.
Use source of a creamy food.

Soapberries, though disagreeable to the European's palate, furnished a very popular food to the Indians. They contain a bitter principle, saponin, which foams in water. The thick, cream-like suds is tinged with red and, when sweetened, was held as a great delicacy by the Indians.

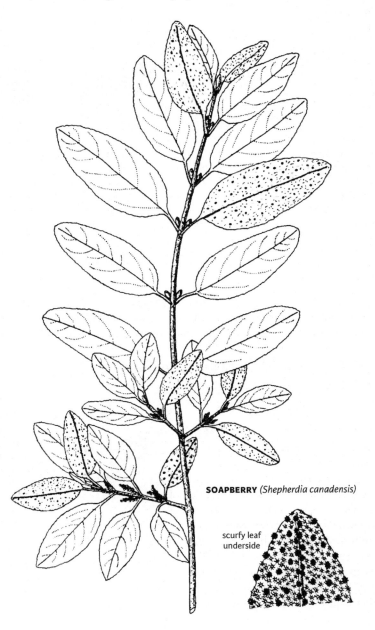

SOAPBERRY *(Shepherdia canadensis)*

scurfy leaf underside

Ericaceae HEATH FAMILY

Bog-Rosemary
Andromeda polifolia L.

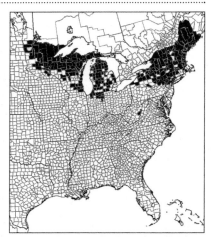

BOG-ROSEMARY *(Andromeda polifolia)*

Synonym *Andromeda glaucophylla*
Key-characters low and slender, aromatic evergreen shrub with bluish-gray stiff narrow leaves, with margins tightly recurved against the white lower surface; bud-scales with a bloom; flowers with delicate pink urn-shaped corollas, the foot-stalks recurving; fruit a depressed, turban-shaped capsule.
Habitat and Range mossy bogs, damp peat and quagmires, Labrador to Manitoba, south to Newfoundland, Nova Scotia, New England, northern New Jersey, Pennsylvania, West Virginia, Indiana, Wisconsin and Minnesota.
Season of Availability throughout the year.
Use tea.

Dr. H. H. Smith stated that **Bog-Rosemary** is used as a substitute for tea by the Ojibwe Indians. Its aroma is certainly delicious. Do not boil, simply draw the aroma with water. Boiling would extract the harmful andromedotoxin.

Bearberry, Kinnikinik, Mealberry, Hog-Cranberry
Arctostaphylos uva-ursi (L.) Spreng.

Use cooked fruit; emergency-food.

The dry and insipid red berries of the common **Bearberry** which forms extensive prostrate mats on sterile rock and sand from the Arctic regions south to the upland of Virginia, sands of northern Indiana and Illinois and rocks to South Dakota and New Mexico, are mildly medicinal but wholly uninviting to eat raw. Porsild, however, says that "the mealy berries are quite nourishing. They are rather tasteless when raw, but are quite palatable when cooked."

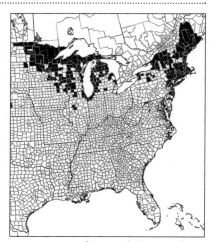

BEARBERRY *(Arctostaphylos uva-ursi*

capsule

BOG-ROSEMARY
(Andromeda polifolia)

urn-shaped flowers

BEARBERRY *(Arctostaphylos uva-ursi*

Alpine Bearberries, "Poisonberry" (in Newfoundland)

Arctous alpinus (L.) Niedenzu
Arctous ruber (Rehd. & Wilson) Nakai

Synonyms *Arctostaphylos alpina, Arctostaphylos rubra*

Key-characters prostrate, matted shrubs with pinkish-brown, papery bark, the trailing branches densely covered with crinkly-margined, very veiny, obovate leaves, which persist for many years as dried brown or gray masses of foliage; berries black (in A. alpinus) or bright-red (in A. ruber), very juicy and with 4 or 5 hard seeds, the berries more or less hidden among the newer leaves.

Habitat rocky barrens.

Range *Arctous alpinus,* throughout the arctic and sub-arctic barren region, extending southward to Newfoundland (where called "Poisonberry") and the higher mountains of Quebec, Maine and New Hampshire; A. *ruber,* limestone rocks and gravel, northern Newfoundland, Anticosti and the Mingan Islands of Quebec to Hudson Bay and the Canadian Rockies.

Season of Availability late July to October.

Use berries, fresh or cooked.

The fruit of the **Alpine Bearberries** is unattractive to many palates, but in the absence of more attractive berries this fruit is apparently wholesome and one soon acquires a taste for it. When thoroughly ripe the berries are juicy, with a pleasant acid but slightly bitter flavor, fairly good raw but better when cooked with sugar and eaten cold. Those of us who have had an opportunity to try both species prefer the red berries to the black.

Leather-leaf, Cassandra
Chamaedaphne calyculata (L.) Moench

Use tea.

According to Dr. H. H. Smith, the leaves of **Leather-leaf**, a familiar ever-green shrub of bogs of cooler parts of the Northern Hemisphere, are used, like those of **Bog-Rosemary** for tea by the Ojibwe Indians. The Ojibwe are famed as a stout people, but if one makes tea from Leather-leaf, the same care as in using Bog-Rosemary should be exercised. Steeping would probably extract the harmful andromedotoxin.

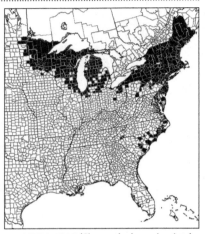

LEATHER-LEAF *(Chamaedaphne calyculata)*

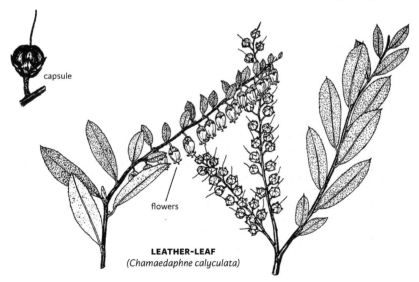

capsule

flowers

LEATHER-LEAF
(Chamaedaphne calyculata)

Pipsissewa or Prince's Pine
Chimaphila umbellata (L.) W. Bart.
Chimaphila maculata (L.) Pursh (Spotted Wintergreen)

Uses drink, nibble.

The familiar green-leaved **Pipsissewa** of acid woodlands from the Gaspé Peninsula to British Columbia, south, as one or more of its geographic varieties, to Georgia, the Great Lakes States and Mexico, is a regular ingredient in root-beer. Both it and Spotted Wintergreen are well known to most lovers of the woods as pleasant and refreshing nibbles.

Crowberry, Curlewberry
Empetrum nigrum L. and two other species.

Key-characters matted, evergreen shrubs, with slender, trailing branches covered with short needles, suggesting those of spruce or juniper; bearing on the branchlets black, purple or pink, very juicy round berries with 6-9 hard seeds.

Habitat and Range three species: the Black Crowberry (or Blackberry of Newfoundland), *Empetrum nigrum*, with branchlets smooth, the old leaves reflexed, and the small berries black, abundant on peaty, sterile soils throughout the Arctic regions and south to the coast of Maine, the higher mountain-summits of New England, Pictured Rocks, Michigan, and the mountains of Alberta, British Columbia and Washington; Purple Crowberry, *E. nigrum* ssp. *hermaphroditum* (synonym *E. atropurpureum*), with the young branchlets white with down, the old leaves spreading but not reflexed, and the large fruit purple or plum-colored, on sand hills about the Gulf of St. Lawrence and on granite gravels and ledges of the lower mountains of Maine and New Hampshire; Pink Crowberry or Rockberry, *E. nigrum* ssp. *eamsii* (synonym *E. eamesii*), with young branchlets covered with white wool, leaves scarcely spreading, and small berries bright coral-pink, on exposed sands, gravels and ledges, southern Labrador, Newfoundland and adjacent islands and Cape Breton.

Season of Availability midsummer to early spring.

Uses berries, fresh or cooked, beer.

The **Curlewberries or Crowberries** form an important fruit in northern regions for, although to a sophisticated taste they are slightly unpalatable, their disagreeable qualities are soon forgotten under the pressure of thirst and hunger. The berries are extremely watery, with a mildly medicinal flavor which is improved by freezing, and may be gathered from midsummer throughout the winter. The berries of the purple- and pink-fruited species are superior to those of the Black Crowberry or "Blackberry" but of more limited distribution. To some palates the flavor of the cooked berries is greatly improved by the addition of some tart berry and plenty of sugar. In puddings they make a good substitute for currants.

In his account of Sable Island, off Nova Scotia, Dr. Harold St. John says: "They are sometimes used by the residents of the island in the manufacture of a slightly alcoholic drink. The berries are crushed, then after the addition of sugar or molasses the juice is put in a dark air-tight receptacle until the fermentation takes place."

Trailing Arbutus, Mayflower
Epigaea repens L.

Use pleasant nibble.

The fragrant corollas of the **Trailing Arbutus** are spicy and slightly acid and are well known to children who eat them as a pleasant nibble and to relieve thirst.

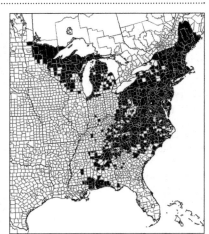

TRAILING ARBUTUS *(Epigaea repens)*

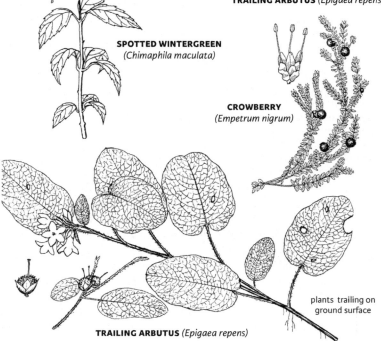

SPOTTED WINTERGREEN
(Chimaphila maculata)

CROWBERRY
(Empetrum nigrum)

plants trailing on ground surface

TRAILING ARBUTUS *(Epigaea repens)*

Moxie-plum, Creeping Snowberry, Maidenhair-berry, Capillaire
Gaultheria hispidula (L.) Muhl. ex Bigelow

Synonym *Chiogenes hispidula*
Key-characters fine, trailing vine with thread-like branches covered with small, roundish, pointed, finely bristly leaves about 1/4 inch long; whole plant highly flavored with "oil of wintergreen" or "checkerberry"; berries ellipsoid, ivory-white, very juicy, covered with minute hairs, borne along the lower sides of the trailing branches.
Habitat Mossy knolls and damp woods or thickets, chiefly under spruce or fir.
Range Labrador to British Columbia, south to the Maritime Provinces, northern and western New England, northern New York and the Great Lakes States, and in upland swamps locally to the mountains of North Carolina.

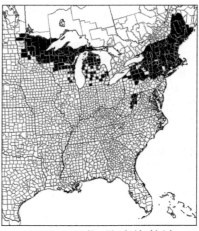

MOXIE-PLUM *(Gaultheria hispidula)*

Season of Availability herbage, throughout the year; berries, midsummer and early autumn.
Uses berries, fresh or cooked; tea.

The **Moxie-plum** (or **Moxie-vine**), as it is called in Maine, or the **Maidenhair-berry or Capillaire**, as it is called in Canada and Newfoundland, rarely fruits in abundance in the southern part of its range; but in the mountains of Gaspé and the woods of Newfoundland the trailing mats often fruit so heavily as to fleck with white the knolls where they grow. Under these circumstances the berries are gathered with ease by lifting and stripping the branches and a pint cup can be filled in a few minutes. Eaten fresh the berries are pleasantly acid, with a mild suggestion of checkerberry, but when eaten with cream and sugar they are one of the greatest delicacies of the northern woods, having, in addition to the mild, lemon-like acidity and the checkerberry-flavor, a suggestion in their aroma of heliotrope.

The danger to the uninformed which lurks in colloquial names is well illustrated by Capillaire and Maidenhair, the names universally used in Newfoundland for Chiogenes. In France and in French Canada Capillaire is the name of Maidenhair-Fem, Adiantum, the roots of which are used medicinally. But the names were too much for the globe-trotting Sir Bichard Bonnycastle who, having "a first-hand unfamiliarity with the facts", published an account of Newfoundland plants. Under the Ferns he had: "The maiden hair (Adiantum pedatum) is a little trailing plant, seeking sheltered places, and is one of the most beautiful of the family of Alices, or ferns. It bears a little fruit, white, and like an ant's egg, which contains so much saccharine matter as to be luciously sweet when made into a jam or preserve. It is occasionally brought to families here by the girls who follow the berry-picking trade; but is preserved, and not used for capillaire, as in Canada." Sir Richard's naive account was the basis for the record under "Newfoundland," in one of the recently revised encyclopedias, of the berry-bearing ferns of that Island.

The preserves prepared in Newfoundland from these berries are justly famous as the most delicious preserve known in the region. All travellers in Newfoundland who are vouchsafed a taste write with enthusiasm of the preserve, which is rarely offered for sale, the berries bringing the highest price of any wild fruit in the market (before the war a price of two dollars a gallon for the raw berries). Tea made from the leaves has a mild flavor of wintergreen.

Checkerberry, Wintergreen, Teaberry, "Ivry"-Leaves
Gaultheria procumbens L.

Uses tea, condiment, nibble, fruit.

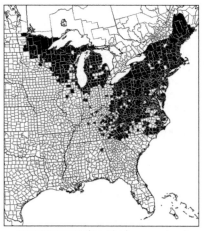

The berries and young, tender leaves of the **Checkerberry** are familiar to most country children (under very diverse colloquial names) on account of their pleasant, aromatic flavor. The berries, maturing in late summer, last over winter and in early spring, after the melting of the snow, become enlarged and much less dry than in the autumn. The young leaves in the spring while still red are tender and highly flavored with oil of checkerberry, but in mid-summer become tough and less palatable. Woodsmen esteem the mature leaves as a substitute for tea. In

CHECKERBERRY (*Gaultheria procumbens*)

the eighteenth century the plant was highly reputed as a tea-substitute; and we are told that the French Canadian court-physician, Dr. Hugues Gaultier (also spelled Gaulthier) "decouvrit le the du Canada . . . qu'il designa comme un breuvage excellent." On account of Gaultier's enthusiasm over the great possibilities of this tea, his friend, Pehr Kalm, the famous Swedish explorer, who visited him in 1748, proposed that the plant be named *Gaultheria*.

It should be noted that "oil of checkerberry" or "oil of wintergreen," used so much as a flavoring and in medicine, is derived (when not made synthetically) by distillation from the twigs of **Black Birch**.

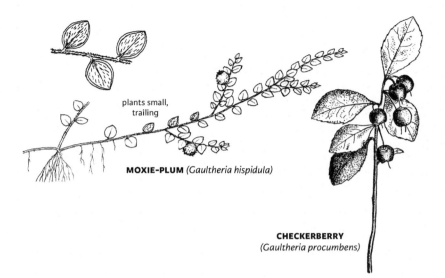

MOXIE-PLUM *(Gaultheria hispidula)*

CHECKERBERRY
(Gaultheria procumbens)

Black Huckleberry
Gaylussacia baccata (Wagenh.) K. Koch

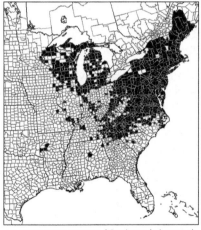

Key-characters a rigid, much-branched shrub a few feet in height; the alternate, oval to oblong leaves slightly varnished with yellowish-brown resin or wax, sticky when pinched; berries black and juicy, borne in small clusters along the branches, rarely blue with a bloom; seeds 10, hard and stone-like.
Habitat dry or rocky, occasionally boggy, open situations, clearings, pastures, etc.
Range Newfoundland to Manitoba, south to Georgia and the Great Lakes States.
Season of Availability June to September.
Use fruit.

BLACK HUCKLEBERRY *(Gaylussacia baccata)*

The **Black Huckleberry** is so abundant that it is known to most people but, singularly enough, there prevails in many regions a tradition that the berries are poisonous. This idea may have arisen through confusion with some similar fruit, like the **Chokeberries** [*Aronia arbutifolia* (L.) Pers.], which are puckery and nearly inedible when uncooked, or the **Buckthorns** (*Rhamnus*), which have poisonous berries. Although having hard seeds, the Black Huckleberries are deliciously spicy and sweet, in flavor superior to most of the small-seeded **Blueberries** or "huckleberries" (*Vaccinium*) and often mixed with them by the pickers.

Dwarf Huckleberry
Gaylussacia dumosa (Andr.) Torr. & Gray

Key-characters low shrub, rarely more than 1-3 feet high, with gland-dotted, narrowly obovate to oblong, sharp-tipped leaves; the blackish berries hairy or bristly, in short, leafy clusters, juicy and aromatic, with 10 stone-like seeds.
Habitat and Range peat-bogs and quaking, mossy pond-shores and wet thickets, Newfoundland to New Jersey, and in drier sands and peats from New Jersey southward.
Season of Availability August, September.
Use fruit.

On account of its habitat, in sphagnum bogs, the **Dwarf Huckleberry** is not generally known in the North; but its fruit is juicy and deliciously spicy. Southward, where it takes to dry sands, the fruit is readily accessible.

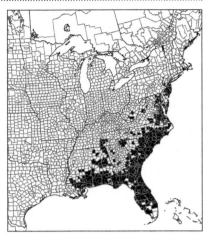

DWARF HUCKLEBERRY *(Gaylussacia dumosa)*

Dangleberry, Bleu-Tangle
Gaylussacia frondosa (L.) Torr. & Gray ex Torr.

Key-characters loosely branched shrub with whitish-green, elliptical or oblong, alternate leaves covered beneath by minute waxy atoms; berries blue and juicy, slender-stalked, borne in pendulous clusters; seeds 10, hard and stone-like.
Habitat and Range dry or moist woods, southern New Hampshire to Florida and Louisiana.
Season of Availability August, September.
Use fruit.

Although rarely gathered and by many people thought (erroneously) to be poisonous, **Dangleberries**, often found in abundance, make one of the most luscious of desserts, being remarkably juicy and with a rich, spicy and sweet flavor.

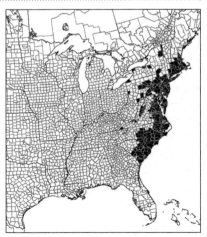

DANGLEBERRY *(Gaylussacia frondosa)*

Indian Pipe or Corpse-plant
Monotropa uniflora L.

Use cooked vegetable (for those who want it).

The members of the Heath Family in general contain rather powerful properties which render them more or less poisonous, some species known as "lambkills" being fatal to browsing animals. The **Indian Pipe** lacks the green coloring matter of most members of the family, and by its mushroom-like aspect has often suggested itself as possibly edible. So far as we are informed, the only person who has reported upon it is Prest, who states that the fresh plant is almost tasteless but that when parboiled and then boiled or roasted it is "comparable to asparagus." Our own single experiment was not gratifying in its result.

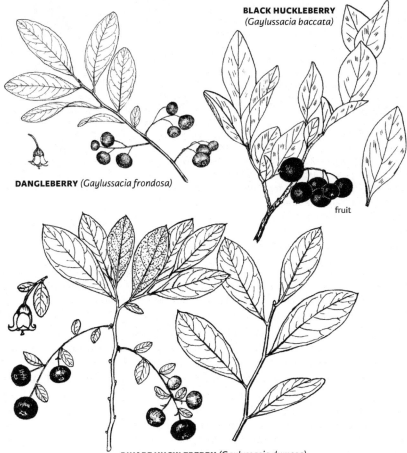

BLACK HUCKLEBERRY
(Gaylussacia baccata)

DANGLEBERRY *(Gaylussacia frondosa)*

fruit

DWARF HUCKLEBERRY *(Gaylussacia dumosa)*

Sorrel-tree, Sour-wood or Titi
Oxydendrum arboreum (L.) DC.

Uses masticatory, thirst-quencher.

The acid leaves of the **Sorrel-tree** of the Southern States when chewed are well known to allay thirst.

Labrador Tea or Bog-Tea
Rhododendron groenlandicum (Oeder) K.A. Kron & Judd
Rhododendron tomentosum Harmaja

Synonyms *Rhododendron groenlandicum* synonym: *Ledum groenlandicum*); *R. tomentosum* Harmaja synonym: *Ledum palustre* (including *Ledum decumbens*).
Key-Characters low straggling shrubs with evergreen, alternate, dryish leaves covered beneath with dense wool (at first whitish, afterward brown), the margins of the leaves rolled back; flowers white, in umbrella-shaped, terminal clusters, followed by ellipsoid to slenderly-oblong seed-pods.
Habitat and Range boggy or peaty soils throughout the arctic regions, one species, *R. groenlandicum*, extending south in cold bogs to southern New England, northern New Jersey, mountains of Pennsylvania, and the Great Lakes States.
Season of Availability throughout the year.
Uses tea, food-conservator.
Caution internal use should be limited due to toxic substances in this plant.

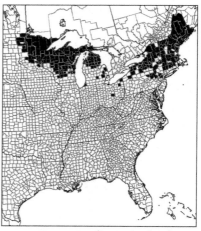

LABRADOR TEA *(R. groenlandicum)*

Through its suggestive name as well as the writings of northern travellers, **Labrador Tea** has gained a considerable reputation as a tea-substitute. Those who have tried the two species refer to the more northern *R. tomentosum* as superior to *R. groenlandicum*. The early explorer of western Canada, Dr. John Palliser, writing in his journal of 1866, thus noted it: "We encamped after passing the Long Muskeg, where we got a supply of the muskeg tea (*Ledum palustre*), which makes a capital beverage in absence of a better."

The shrub has a strongly aromatic fragrance due to an oil, and Linnaeus found that in Lapland, two centuries ago, *"Ledum (palustre) is laid among corn in the barns, to drive away mice."*

If the bristly spikes of *Setaria verticillata* (see p. 312) will keep away rats and the leaves of our *Rhododendron* will drive away mice, the housewife should be pretty well set, especially if there is good basis for the statement made by

Barton and Castle concerning the common **Water-Pepper**, *Persicaria hydropiper* (L.) Delarbre: "It is not eaten by any animal. In some parts of Germany this herb is kept in bedrooms for the purpose of dispersing fleas, as these insects, it is said, will not come where it is." **Fleabane**, *Erigeron*, has at least a good name in this connection. Unfortunately the housewives in many regions where it is much needed do not have a supply of **Bugbane**, *Cimicifuga*.

Lapland Rosebay
Rhododendron lapponicum (L.) Wahlenb.

Key-characters a depressed shrub forming dense mats; with oblong, dry, evergreen leaves about 1/2 inch long, dotted, especially beneath, with brown specks; flowers violet-purple, 1/2 inch broad, in terminal clusters, succeeded by ellipsoid, reddish capsules covered with minute scales.
Habitat dry, exposed, rocky or mountainous areas.
Range Arctic regions, south across the barren lands to Newfoundland, the mountains of Gaspé, Mt. Katahdin and Traveller Mt., Maine, the higher White Mts., Mt. Marcy, New York, and the Dells of Wisconsin.
Season of Availability throughout the year.
Use tea.

leaf under-
side densely
brown hairy

LABRADOR TEA *(Rhododendron groenlandicum)*

Sir John Richardson, writing of his famous expedition across the barren lands of Canada in search of traces of his former companion, Sir John Franklin, said: "An infusion of the leaves and flowering tops was drunk with us instead of tea, but it makes a less grateful beverage than the *Ledum palustre.*"

Blueberries, "Huckleberries," Whortleberries, Whorts, Hurts, Bilberries
Vaccinium (20 or more species)

Uses fruit, fresh, cooked or dried; jelly.

Our Blueberries belong to two quite distinct groups: one, with the berries borne in terminal clusters, the true Blueberries, confined to eastern North America; the other, with the berries borne in the leaf-axils, the Bilberries or Whortleberries, distributed rather generally in the northern half of the northern hemisphere. The **Blueberries and Bilberries**, often called "huckleberries," are readily distinguished from the true Huckleberries, *Gaylussacia*, by having very many, fine and soft seeds instead of 10 larger stones, and by having no waxy atoms on the foliage and new shoots.

The true Blueberries are roughly classified into the **High-bush** and the **Low-bush** species, each group containing several distinct shrubs. The **High-bush Blueberries** are essentially southern, abounding in the southeastern states but becoming local north of Massachusetts, coastwise Maine and Nova Scotia. These High-bush Blueberries are difficult of classification, consisting of possibly several distinct species, the exact characters of which are not clearly understood. The berries are either blue with a bloom or black, sometimes purple or amber-pink.

The **Low-bush Blueberries** fall into several well-marked species with fruit of quite different character. One of them, the **Sour-top** or **Velvet-leaf Blueberry** (*Vaccinium myrtilloides* Michx.) is easily distinguished by having both sides of the small, entire leaves and the young twigs downy and the berries acid and maturing late in the summer. The Sour-top Blueberry is rather northern, occurring from Newfoundland to Manitoba, southward into the northernmost states and along the mountains to Virginia.

The other two Low-bush Blueberries have smooth leaves and twigs and sweet berries. The **Low Sweet or Early Sweet Blueberry**, *V. angustifolium* Ait., has the leaves bright-green on both sides (or in one form grayish), comparatively narrow (lanceolate or oblong) and distinctly bordered with fine bristles; while the **Late Low Blueberry**, *V. pallidum* Ait., has the leaves often whitened beneath, more oval in outline and usually with an entire margin. The Early Sweet Blueberry is abundant northward, from Labrador to the Saskatchewan and through the northern states, in dry, open places, especially in recently cleared land where fire has run. It extends southward to Virginia, but in its best development and heaviest fruiting is characteristically northern, where the very sweet berries are the preferred fruit of the late summer. Southward the fruit matures in June or early July, northward into August or early September. The Late Low Blueberry is characteristic of thin oak woods, thickets and dry clearings of the southeastern states, extending north to Michigan, southern Maine and southern Nova Scotia. Its fruit is not so large and juicy as that of the Early Sweet Blueberry and matures several weeks later (in southern New England in August and early September). Other species are familiar in the South.

The **Bilberries or Whortleberries** are characteristic of Labrador, Newfoundland and the highest mountainous regions of New England, New York and the Lake Superior region. Although good or even sometimes superior, the berries are usually inferior to the true Blueberries, having a slightly bitter taste; but a single species, *V.* × *nubigenum* Fern. (pro sp.), confined to the mountains of western Newfoundland and Gaspé, has very richly flavored and large berries.

The use of Blueberries as fresh or stewed fruit is sufficiently general to need no comment, but the use of other fruits with Blueberries in making jams and jellies is less practiced than it should be. With the addition of sour apple, which supplies both tartness and pectin, a delicious jelly is made. The Indian practice of drying Blueberries in the sun later to be used like currants in puddings, cakes and pemmican, is decidedly worth imitating, the berries drying readily in a week or ten days and being immune to decay.

Bog-Cranberries
Vaccinium macrocarpon Ait.
Vaccinium oxycoccus L.

The two species of Bog-Cranberry are very similar, the common species of the southeastern United States, northward to Wisconsin and Newfoundland, the familiar Cranberry of the market, *Vaccinium macrocarpon*, having oblong leaves bis inch or so in length and berries about inch in diameter; the Northern Cranberry, *V. oxycoccus*, abounding in the cooler regions of the northern hemisphere and extending southward in bogs to New England and the Great Lakes States and locally to the Carolina mountains. The Northern Cranberry has smaller, nearly triangular leaves and much smaller berries which are usually spotted with drab or brown. The berries are good but too small to compete with the larger fruit of the southern species.
Uses cooked fruit, jelly, acid drink, pie, etc.

The use of **Cranberries** as an acid sauce is familiar, but the berries may be utilized in various ways not so generally known: in the making of jelly or refreshing drinks; the syrup whipped with gelatine or white of egg into a light desert; or in the making of the well known camouflage, mock cherry-pie. Cranberries ordinarily require a large amount of sugar, but some years ago a Philadelphia experimenter announced that, by adding salt to the cooking berries before the sugar is added, the acidity is counteracted and only a small amount of sugar is needed. In our own experience, a teaspoonful of salt is found to take the place of half the sugar (a cupful) ordinarily used with a quart of Cranberries.

Squaw-Huckleberry, Deerberry

Vaccinium stamineum L. (with 2 or 3 related species in the South).

Key-characters diffusely branched shrub 1-5 feet high, with alternate, oval leaves whitish beneath, and bearing pendulous, leafy clusters of globular or pear-shaped, greenish, yellowish or amber-purple, gooseberry-like berries which, when ripe, promptly drop to the ground and have a sour and bitter taste and very thick skin.
Habitat and Range dry, sandy woods, plains, and rock-crests of the southeastern states, extending northward locally into southern Ontario, and central and southeastern Massachusetts.
Season of Availability July (southward) to early October.
Uses raw or cooked fruit, jelly, marmalade.

Although the raw fruit of the **Squaw-Huckleberry** is often unpalatable to some people and often supposed to be poisonous, individual shrubs yield delicious raw fruit. When cooked and served cold they are by many people considered delicious, suggesting a combination of gooseberry- and cranberry-sauce, with the slight bitter taste of grapefruit-marmalade. Jelly or marmalade made by cooking the juice or pulp with an equal weight of sugar is novel in color (greenish-amber) and unique in its agreeable flavor. The freshly stewed berries, when warm, are disagreeable in taste. Thousands of bushels go annually to waste. Those who know their possibilities do what they can to prevent this catastrophe. The berries often drop before ripening.

Mountain-Cranberry, Rock-Cranberry, "Partridge-berry," "Pomme de Terre"

Vaccinium vitis-idaea L.

Key-characters creeping, evergreen shrub with glossy, box-like leaves covered beneath with scattered, black bristles; berries red, in terminal clusters, shaped like blueberries but acid like cranberries.
Habitat and Range rocky, open soil, abundant throughout the northern barren lands, south to Newfoundland, Nova Scotia, the eastern coast of Maine and the mountains of New England.
Season of Availability late summer and autumn, but preferably late autumn after the frost has touched them; also winter and early spring.
Use cooked fruit.

The **Mountain-Cranberry**, "**Partridgeberry**" of Newfoundland, or **Pomme de Terre** of French Canada and Labrador, needs no introduction to northern peoples, for it is one of the staple fruits of all northern lands. In fact, the Norwegians have so long depended upon this fruit that the Norwegian colonists who have settled in the Middle West import the berries in vast quantities from

Norway and from Newfoundland, preferring them to the larger bog-cranberries of the United States. Export of the Partridge-berries from Newfoundland alone to Minneapolis and neighboring markets has sometimes reached the annual total of more than 8600 barrels, valued at $40,000. In New England, where the berries are found chiefly on the rocky summits of granite mountains and on the eastern coast of Maine, they are commonly picked too soon, before the frost has had a chance to mellow them. All northern explorers insist that the berries are superior after the frosts.

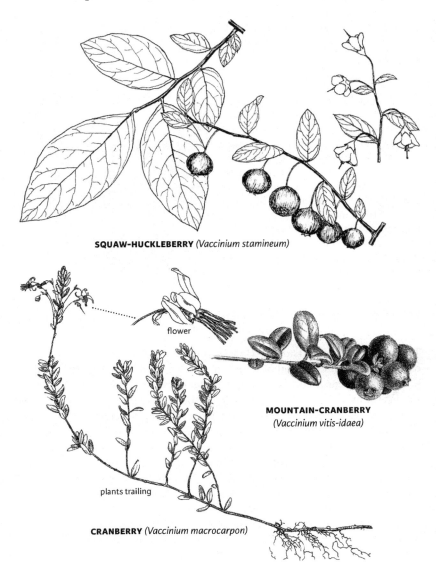

SQUAW-HUCKLEBERRY *(Vaccinium stamineum)*

flower

MOUNTAIN-CRANBERRY
(Vaccinium vitis-idaea)

plants trailing

CRANBERRY *(Vaccinium macrocarpon)*

Fabaceae PEA FAMILY

The young pods, young seeds and new herbage of many members of this family are succulent and so closely resemble similar parts in cultivated beans and peas, that it is a natural inference that they are all safe wild foods. Many species, however, contain actively poisonous principles, and in Europe the eating of various wild peas has caused serious nervous disorders. In our own country, the eating of the various loco-weeds, members of this family, causes similar nervous upheavals in browsing animals. The eastern American species of the family which furnish safe foods are described below.

Hog-Peanut
Amphicarpaea bracteata (L.) Fern.

Key-characters a twining vine with delicate, thread-like stems and branches; leaves alternate, with 3 ovate leaflets resembling those of a bean; flowers pea-like, whitish or lilac, in axillary clusters, succeeded by small bean-pods; producing from the lower axils slender runners which bear round, somewhat flattened, bean-like fruits 1/4 to 1/2 inch in diameter.
Habitat rich, moist thickets and woods, especially near streams.
Range New Brunswick to Manitoba, south to the Gulf States.
Season of Availability late autumn and early spring.
Use subterranean fruits like shelled beans.

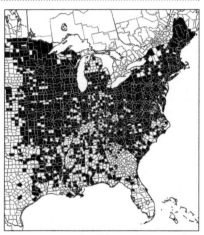

HOG-PEANUT *(Amphicarpaea bracteata)*

The subterranean fruits of the **Hog-Peanut** were well known to the Indians, particularly of the Central States; and, when boiled and properly seasoned with salt and pepper and dressed with butter or cream, they are not unlike the shelled beans of the garden, though of a rather dry quality. The "skin" or shell of the 1-seeded subterranean pod is somewhat leathery, but cracks off in boiling. The fruit is sufficiently abundant to repay the time spent in digging, especially when one is camping in the autumn. Voles or field-mice gather the fruit in quantities and their nests often contain several quarts of the beans. The canny Indian procedure was to depend upon these stores but, although it is commonly said that the Indians stole the stores from the voles, Gilmore comes to their defense and states that when they removed the beans from the nests the Dakota Indians, at least, always replaced them by an equivalent amount of corn other food for the rodents. The "skins" of the beans were removed by rubbing, after the beans had been soaked in warm water or lye.

Kudzu-Vine
Pueraria montana (Lour.) Merr.

Use edible starch.

The rapidly growing **Kudzu-vine** of eastern Asia, familiar as an ornamental vine with grape-scented purple flowers was previously much planted in the southern and eastern states, and has become naturalized, often in abundance, as far north as Pennsylvania, Indiana, and Illinois. The root usually forks into several branches with a tough outer coat but fleshy within; "the fleshy portion of each of the main branches being from four to five feet long, as thick as a man's arm." In Japan "the wild plants are dug for these roots, and often with great difficulty. When a sufficient quantity of them has been gathered, they are cleaned, cut in pieces, crushed, and the starch washed out and allowed to settle to the bottom of the tub. The starch is then purified by repeated washings and when dried is a fine, pure white article, which is much esteemed for food."

Groundnut, Indian Potato, Wild Bean, Hopniss
Apios americana Medik.

Key-characters a twining vine with very slender, rather soft stems, which become whitish and dry over winter; leaves alternate, with 5-9 narrowly ovate, slightly stalked leaflets; flowers in dense clusters from the leaf-axils, in late summer, chocolate-brown and paler, deliciously fragrant; pods resembling bean-pods, borne (rather infrequently) in clusters; root an elongate chain of tuber-like enlargements (the "nuts") which become 1-3 inches long.
Habitat rich thickets, chiefly in low grounds or along streams.
Range New Brunswick to western Ontario, south to the Gulf of Mexico.
Season of Availability throughout the year, but best from late sum* mer to spring.
Uses substitute for potato, seeds for beans.

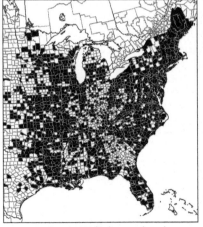

GROUNDNUT *(Apios americana)*

Probably no wild food-plant of temperate eastern America so soon attracted the attention of the European colonist as the **Groundnut**. It was one of the few eastern plants held in highest repute by the Indians, and the earliest European chroniclers in America wrote with enthusiasm of its virtues and possibilities. Thus Gosnold in 1602 recorded the "great store of ground-nuts on the Elizabeth Islands" and in Smith's Virginia the author tells of "Grounds nut as big as Egges, and as good as Potatoes, and 40 on a string not two inches under ground."

We are told by Young in his *Chronicles*, that during their first winter in New England the Pilgrims were forced to live upon Groundnuts. The great value to the colonists of this ready food is further indicated by a reputed town law, which in 1654 ordered that, if an Indian dug Groundnuts on English land he was to be set in stocks, and for a second offense to be whipped.

As early as 1635 the plant was cultivated in France but it was soon forgotten. In 1845, however, it was re-introduced into Europe, this time as a possible substitute for the potato, which was becoming subject to diseases. But attempts at cultivation were soon abandoned, since the plant proved to be an impracticable crop. For the roots to reach a size fit for use requires two or three years at least, and its habit of producing the strings of "nuts" just beneath the surface of the soil renders cultivation of ground about the plant impossible.

The raw tubers are somewhat tough, with a very viscid, milky juice, but of a pleasant sweetish, turnip-like taste. The young tubers may be eaten raw, but the viscid juice leaves an unpleasant rubber-like coating on the teeth and lips. This disagreeable quality is removed by roasting or by parboiling, with salt, and then roasting for a few minutes; but a satisfactory method of preparation is to cut the tubers (skin and all) into thin slices and fry and season like fried potatoes. These fried slices should be eaten hot for on cooling they become tough and uninteresting.

Or, better still, slice the "nuts" and simmer with butter, pork or bacon in a sauce-pan until tender; then dry off rapidly, cooking in such salt and pepper as is desired in the last few minutes.

Various Indian tribes are said to have used the seeds as beans; but ordinarily they are too scarce to supply much food.

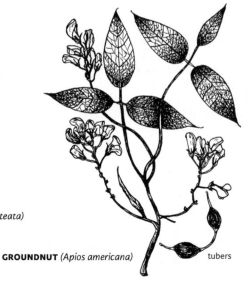

bean

HOG-PEANUT *(Amphicarpaea bracteata)*

GROUNDNUT *(Apios americana)*   tubers

A very local relative of our groundnut, *Apios priceana* B.L Robins., known only from Kentucky and southward, has a single irregularly turnip-shaped root 6 inches or so in diameter.

Peanut
Arachis hypogaea L.

The familiar and in the South extensively cultivated **Peanut** spreads from cultivation or sprouts spontaneously from waste or rejected seed and is found wild by roadsides and in waste places northward to Virginia, Tennessee, Missouri and Kansas. Its many uses are familiar.

Ground-Plum, Indian Pea
Astragalus crassicarpus Nutt. and related species

Uses fruit, raw or cooked.

The **Ground-Plums** are well known plants of the western prairies, extending eastward to Illinois and Missouri. They were formerly in much demand for the young plumlike fruits which were eaten either raw or cooked.

Caution other species of *Astragalus* have been recommended on account of their abundant pea-like seeds, but they should be eaten with great caution, since many of the western species are known to be "loco-weeds," poisonous to browsing animals.

Red-bud, Judas-tree
Cercis canadensis L.

Uses salad, pickle, cooked vegetable.

The brilliant pink flowers of the **Red-bud** are acid and are said to have been used by the "French Canadians" for salads and pickles. This statement, made by Torrey, has been repeated by Loudon and others, although the range of the tree is almost entirely south of the region of the French Canadians. It is probable that the idea was borrowed from European writers, for Bryant, in 1783, said of the related species of France, Spain and Italy: "The flowers have a sharp, acid flavour, and are not only mixed with salads to render them more grateful, but are also pickled in the bud, in the manner of Capers."

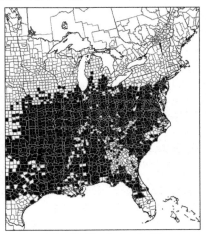

RED-BUD *(Cercis canadensis)*

Kephart states that the buds, flowers and young pods are good fried in butter or made into fritters and at least the junior author can vouch for their goodness.

Broom
Cytisus scoparius (L.) Link

Uses coffee-substitute, pickle.

Broom, a stiffly green-branched shrub with handsome pea-like yellow flowers is abundantly naturalized in Shelburne County, Nova Scotia, and locally (often abundantly) from southern Maine to West Virginia and Georgia. Many European writers state that the roasted seeds are a good substitute for coffee (in view of what is so often served in Europe as "coffee" it is well to try a little before stocking up too heavily with it). The fresh seed-pods are poisonous (intoxicating) but the flower-buds and pods, pickled, have a good reputation. Here is Evelyn's recipe:

"Broom-Buds and Pods. Make a strong Pickle, as above ["Put them into a strong Brine of White-wine Vinegar and Salt able to bear an egg"]; stir it very well, till the Salt be quite dissolved, clearing off the Dregs and Scum. The next Day pour it from the bottom; and having rubbed the Buds dry, pot them up in a Pickle-Glass, which should be frequently shaken, till they sink under it, and keep it well stop'd and cover'd.

"Thus may you pickle any other Buds."

Honey-Locust
Gleditsia triacanthos L.

Uses nibble, sugar, beer.

The hard seeds in the long twisting pods of **Honey-Locust** are surrounded by a thin pulp which remains sweet for some time after the ripening of the pod, and wherever the tree is native or planted is a well known pleasant nibble. Loudon states that sugar was formerly extracted from this pulp, but the amount secured would be very limited. Porcher stated that a beer is made in the South by fermenting the fresh sugary pods.

Soy-Bean
Glycine max (L.) Merr.

Soy-Bean, now recognized as indispensible in the arts as well as in the diet, is becoming naturalized along roadsides, in old fields, etc., in the South. Its virtues are too well known to need recapitulation here.

Wild Licorice
Glycyrrhiza lepidota Pursh

Uses root, raw or cooked.

The **Wild Licorice** of the prairies is well know on account of its sweet, licorice-like root. This was popular with the Indians who chewed the roots either raw or roasted in ashes.

Kentucky Coffee-tree
Gymnocladus dioicus (L.) K. Koch

Uses coffee-substitute, nut, pickle.

The seeds of the **Kentucky Coffee-tree** were said by Michaux to have been used by "the early emigrants to Kentucky and Tennessee, who hoped to find in its seeds a substitute for coffee; but the small number of persons who made the experiment abandoned it, as soon as it became easy to obtain from the seaports the coffee of the West Indies."

Gilmore states that the Pawnee Indians roast the seeds and then eat them like chestnuts; H. H. Smith found the Meskwaki Indians doing the same.

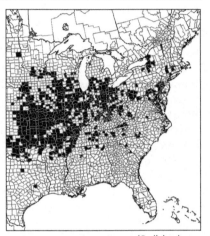

KENTUCKY COFFEE-TREE *(G. dioicus)*

Loudon states that "the pods, preserved like those of the tamarind (to which this genus is nearly allied), are said to be wholesome, and slightly aperient."

Licorice-root
Hedysarum alpinum L.

Key-characters handsome bushy-tufted herb with numerous upright, smooth stems 1-3 feet high, bearing many spreading, pinnate, green leaves with numerous small leaflets; flowers lilac to flesh-pink, pea-like, in long, one-sided clusters, followed by drooping pods made up of several flat, roundish segments.
Habitat and Range limy gravels and damp ledges, Newfoundland and Labrador to Alaska, extending south in abundance to eastern Quebec, New Brunswick and Aroostook Co., Maine, and locally to northern Vermont, and the north shore of Lake Superior.
Season of Availability autumn to early summer.
Uses sweetish root-vegetable.

Sir John Richardson, writing of his experiences in northern Canada, while searching for signs of the ill-fated John Franklin, said: "*Hedysarum boreale* furnishes long flexible roots, which taste sweet like the liquorice, and are much eaten in the spring by the natives, but become woody and lose their juiciness and crispness as the season advances. The root of the hoary, decumbent, and less elegant, but larger-flowered *Hedysarum mackenzii* (now classified as *H. boreale* ssp. *mackenzii*) is poisonous, and nearly killed an old Indian woman at Fort Simpson, who had mistaken it for that of the preceding species."

Richardson further stated that Sir William Hooker had been in error when, apparently on Richardson's authority, he had previously stated that the root of *H. boreale* ssp. *mackenzii* was edible and that of *H. boreale* poisonous. Our North American varieties of *Hedysarum alpinum* (formerly included within *H. boreale*) are so abundant in sections of Newfoundland and Canada that the verdict of the very experienced explorer of northern Canada, Mr. Erling Porsild, is significant:

"*Hedysarum boreale* is widely distributed throughout northern Canada, and is found as far north as the shores of the Arctic ocean.

"The root is mature in August and may be gathered in quantities with very little trouble until the ground freezes. In the spring before the new growth has started the roots are even better than in the autumn. During summer the roots become tough and woody.

"The root when cooked, in taste resembles that of young carrots, but is more nourishing.

"This root during early summer forms the principal food of the barren ground brown bears. Several species of meadow mice and lemmings in the autumn * harvest* the roots and place them 'en cache' for the winter. The caches are found in subterranean runways near the surface. The Eskimo, with the aid of a dog, has no difficulty locating these mouse caches, and frequently obtains his own supply for the winter in this manner."

Hyacinth-Bean
Lablab purpureus (L.) Sweet

Synonym *Dolichos lablab*
Uses as beans, potherb, salad.

The ornamental **Hyacinth-Bean**, with showy purple or white flowers in long and interrupted spike-like clusters and large pods about 1 inch broad, is cultivated chiefly for ornament southward and has escaped to roadsides and thickets northward to the District of Columbia and Ohio. In the Far East, where it is native, the young foliage, tender young pods and fresh inflorescences are eaten either raw or steamed, while the beans are cooked.

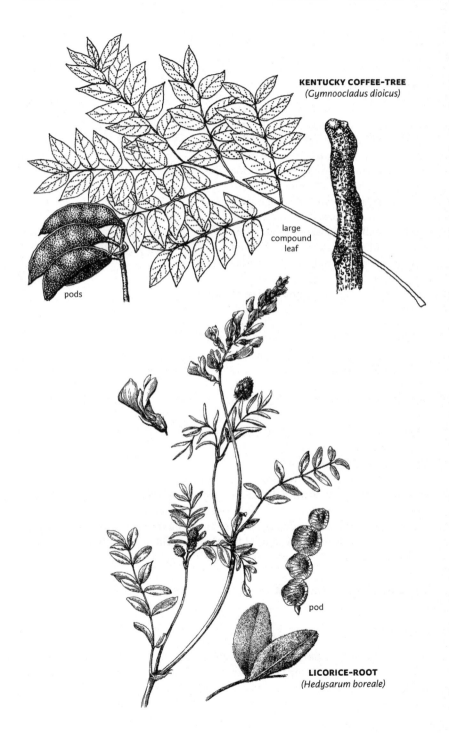

KENTUCKY COFFEE-TREE
(Gymnocladus dioicus)

large
compound
leaf

pods

pod

LICORICE-ROOT
(Hedysarum boreale)

....
Beach-Pea
Lathyrus japonicus Willd. (includes *Lathyrus maritimus*)
....

Uses young peas, salad.

The tender young seeds of the **Beach-Pea** used like green peas are a tolerable vegetable, although the peas are dry and have a slightly disagreeable taste. In various northern regions the ripe peas have served as a famine-food; but they are said to be almost indigestible and they are supposed to contain the poisonous alkaloid which characterizes the seeds of various species of this and related genera. In England, "in the year 1555, being a year of great dearth, the people collected large quantities of these peas between Orford and Aldborough, in Suffolk, upon a barren heath, where even grass would not grow; and as they never had observed any such plant as this there in the time of their fullness, when the eye is careless, they attributed their springing up then as a pure miracle, to keep the poor from starving, though in all probability they had been growing thereabouts for centuries before."

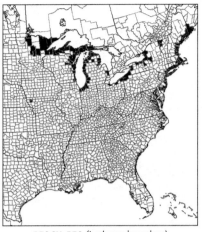

BEACH-PEA *(Lathyrus japonicus)*

Dr. Harold St. John, returning from a summer on the Labrador coast, stated that there the pips or young shoots coming through the sand and looking like the shoots of garden peas, (but often red or purple), are gathered and boiled and after cooking are made into salads. Since the herbage of many species of Lathyrus is poisonous, care should be taken carefully to test this food before extensively using it.

....
Tuberous Vetch, Earthnut
Lathyrus tuberosus L.
....

Use tubers.

Tuberous Vetch is a European species beginning to appear as an introduced plant in America. In Europe the tubers are gathered from the wild plant, or in some cases the plant is cultivated for them. Bryant stated that: "This plant, though a weed in France, is cultivated in Holland for the roots, which are carried to the markets there for sale. They have an agreeable pleasant taste, much resembling that of the Sweet Chestnut."

Lupine
Lupinus perennis L. and other species

Uses cooked vegetable.

It has been stated that the seeds of the **Lupines** may be used as a substitute for peas, but owing to the presence in the seeds of many lupines of a well recognized alkaloid, lupinine, it is wisest to avoid eating the seeds of our Wild Lupine. Many cases of poisoning (lupinosis) have been recorded from eating the pods and seeds.

Prairie-Turnip, Wild Potato, Indian Bread-root, Pomme Blanche
Pediomelum esculentum (Pursh) Rydb.

Synonym *Psoralea esculenta*
Use farinaceous vegetable.

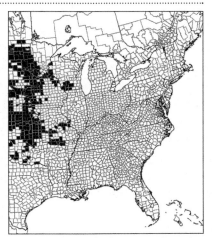

The famous **Prairie-Turnip or Pomme Blanche** of the Great Plains extends only locally into the western edge of our range, but in the West it has always been well known because of its starchy root. The chronicles of early explorers are full of references to its use by the Indians, and attempts were even made to cultivate it as a substitute for the potato. Because of its "wholesome, toothsome, and nutritious" qualities and its peculiar adaptability to arid regions, its improvement by cultivation is desirable. The roots are used in as many ways as potatoes, the raw root having a somewhat starchy and sweetish turnip-like taste.

PRAIRIE-TURNIP *(Pediomeum esculentum)*

Wild Bean
Phaseolus polystachios (L.) B.S.P.

Key-characters a slender twining perennial of thickets and woods with 3 rounded-ovate leaflets 2—4 inches long, small purplish flowers numerous in slender racemes, the keel-petal spirally coiled, the style bearded along the upper side, the drooping pods 2 to 3-1/2 inches long and containing 4 or 5 blackish kidney-shaped beans less than half an inch long.
Habitat and Range dry pine or oak woods and sandy thickets, Florida to Texas, north,

rather locally, to southern Connecticut, southeastern New York, Pennsylvania, West Virginia, Ohio, Indiana, Illinois, southern Minnesota and Nebraska.
Season of Availability late summer and autumn.
Use as beans.

Our native **Wild Bean**, belonging in a group with many species cultivated for their beans, can be used, although the crop, in the native habitat, is usually limited.

enlarged root

PRAIRIE-TURNIP *(Pediomeum esculentum)*

Locust
Robinia pseudacacia L.

Uses emergency-food, cooked vegetable, drink (doubtful, somewhat poisonous).

Kephart states that the inner bark can be used as an emergency-food; and other writers, Loudon, Merat, et al., have stated that the flowers may be fried or a pleasant drink made by infusing them. Loudon also states that the roots are sweet and licorice-like. The bark and roots, however, should be used with extreme caution since they are reported to be somewhat poisonous (see p. 62). Children have been made seriously ill by chewing the cambium.

Wild Senna, Coffee-Senna
Senna occidentalis (L.) Link

Synonym *Cassia occidentalis*
Use coffee-substitute, potherb, salad.

Senna occidentalis is a weedy tropical species of Wild Senna, naturalized in the South, northward to Virginia, Indiana and Iowa. Other species (natives) extend northward to New England and Wisconsin. The seeds of *Senna occidentalis* have been roasted and used as coffee, Porcher, writing in 1869, calling it Florida Coffee and saying "Once thought to be very valuable as a substitute for coffee," Vestal and Schultes reported it, in 1939, as "Coffee Senna . . . Coffee Weed," saying "The Kiowa formerly ground the seeds which were then boiled to make a coffee-like beverage." It is striking that in both these records the use as coffee was in the past.

In the Dutch East Indies the young leaves and immature pods are cooked as a potherb or the young pods eaten as a salad.

Our native species, *Senna marilandica* (L.) Link. and *S. hebecarpa* (Fern.) Irwin & Barneby, occurring northward to New England, New York, Ohio, Michigan and Wisconsin, might be tried.

Wild Bean
Strophostyles, 3 species.

Key-characters Native annual or perennial herbs, resembling cultivated beans, distinguished by having the few flowers crowded, the keel-petal merely incurved and not spiraling, the beans with squared ends and angled back.
Habitat and Range Damp or wet thickets, gravelly or sandy shores or open sands, one or more species from Florida to Texas, north to southern Quebec, southern Ontario, Michigan, Wisconsin, Minnesota, South Dakota and Colorado.
Season of Availability late summer and autumn.
Use beans.

The beans of *Strophostyles* are often abundant enough to gather. Their quality we have not tried.

Hoary Pea, Goat's Rue, Cat-gut
Tephrosia virginiana (L.) Pers. and several other species.

Key-characters a silery-hairy plant about a foot high, with numerous wiry stems from a stout root, bearing many alternate leaves with numerous narrow leaflets; flowers like pea-blossoms, showy, clustered at the tops of the stems, variously colored with yellow, pink and purple; pods like long, flat and slender bean-pods; beans flat, like lentils.

Habitat and Range dry sandy barrens or open, oak or pine woods, common in the southeastern states, extending north to Minnesota and southern New Hampshire.

On account of its abundant, lentil-like seeds, the **Hoary Pea** is apt to be tempting; but it should be borne in mind that the juice of the plant was used by the Indians as a fish-poison, just as its close relative, *Tephrosia toxicaria*, is still used by the Mexican Indians. The roots fed to guinea pigs have proved highly poisonous.

Clover
Trifolium (various species).

Uses breadstuff, salad, potherb, tea.

The seeds and dried flowers of various **Clovers** have been used in times of famine as a bread-food; and Lightfoot, writing of the use of the common White Clover, *T. repens* L., in Scotland, says that the bread made from it is very nutritious and wholesome. In western America the Indians have used the young herbage of various species as either a salad or potherb, and, among the eastern whites, clover-tea, made by brewing the dried flower-heads, is esteemed a wholesome and supposedly medicinal drink. It is stated that excessive eating of clover is likely to produce bloating.

Vetch
Vicia (many species)

Use emergency-food.

The seeds (peas) of **Vetch** (*Vicea sativa* L., etc.) have been tried as human food. They are asserted to be not palatable and rather indigestible. As food for domestic animals they, like hay, are invaluable; that does not, as some think, demonstrate them good food for man.

Broad- or Windsor-Bean, *Vicia faba* L., popular in Eurasia and in Newfoundland and eastern Canada, often occurs on rubbish and in waste-lots northward but is not really naturalized with us.

Cow-Pea, Black-eyed Pea
Vigna unguiculata (L.) Walp.

Synonym *Vigna sinensis*
Uses beans or "peas," young pods.

The **Asiatic Cow-Pea**, so much cultivated, has become naturalized by roadsides, in old fields or in thickets in the Southern States, northward into Virginia, Indiana and Missouri. The value as food and inevitableness of the "peas" on menus in the South is quite familiar. The young pods may be cooked as snap-beans.

Wisteria
Wisteria

Range native species, *Wisteria frutescens* (L.) Poir., from Florida to Texas, north to Virginia, Kentucky and Missouri; cultivated species often escaped and naturalized.
Uses salad and fritters.

It is frequently stated that the fresh flowers, properly dressed, make a good salad, and that mixed in batter they make good fritters.

pods

WILD BEAN *(Strophostyles helvola)*

Fagaceae BEECH FAMILY

Chestnut

Castanea dentata (Marsh.) Borkh. (American Chestnut)
Castanea pumila (L.) P. Mill. (Dwarf Chestnut, Chinquapin) and other species.

Key-characters *Castanea dentata,* originally the common American Chestnut, with leaves green on both sides, tapering to long slender tips; fruiting bur 2-3 inches in diameter; nut 1/2-1 inch broad. *C. pumila,* the Chinquapin, with leaves whitened beneath with down, merely acutish or blunt; mature bur 1 to 1-1/2 inches in diameter; nut 1/3 inch broad.
Habitat and Range *C. dentata,* originally common in sterile soils (though in recent years nearly exterminated by the ravages of the chestnut-bark disease) throughout eastern America, north to Ontario, central Vermont, north-central New Hampshire, and southwestern Maine; *C. pumila,* more southern, north to Indiana and New Jersey.
Uses nut, starchy vegetable, soup, breadstuff, confection, sugar, coffee-substitute, chocolate-substitute.

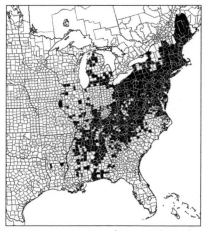

AMERICAN CHESTNUT *(Castanea dentata)*

ripe nut

The **Chestnut** was a very important food of the American Indians, and like the species of western Asia (long ago brought into Europe) served in scores of preparations unknown to the modern American, who, when they were common, ate chestnuts chiefly as a relish or as the accompaniment of a holiday. In Europe and Asia the Chestnut has from earliest times been an important source of bread, especially in southern Europe, where, among the peasants, chestnut-bread serves as a substitute for potatoes and wheat. Cooked in other ways, as roasting or boiling, it is eaten as a vegetable, or cooked with stewed meats, or in the form of flour made into a thick porridge.

The French usually boil the nuts with salt, and often with the leaves of celery, sage or other savory herbs, before cooking taking off the shells of all the nuts but one; when the shell of this odd one cracks it is known that all the nuts are cooked. The boiled chestnuts are mashed and eaten like mashed potatoes, and fritters made from chestnut-flour are considered a great delicacy. The

French marrons glaces are boiled chestnuts dipped in clarified sugar and then dried. In France, too, sugar is extracted from chestnuts, the nuts yielding 14% of sugar.

Owing to the ravages of the chestnut-bark disease, the possibility of extensively utilizing the American Chestnut is, temporarily at least, out of the question; but. should our Chestnut forests come back, they might easily afford great stores of now unappreciated food. The early settlers followed the European uses, and the American Indians had several uses which were distinctive. The nuts were cooked in their corn-bread or, when roasted, were used as coffee; and Thomas Ash, in his Description *of Carolina*, said of the Chinquapin: "Of the Kernel is made Chocolate, not much inferiour to that made of the Cacoa."

Beech
Fagus grandifolia Ehrh.

Uses nuts, table-oil, coffee-substitute, potherb, bread.

The triangular, thin-shelled **Beechnuts** are familiar to every country boy in our northernmost states and southern Canada, although south of our northern borders beechnuts do not seem, to mature with regularity, while in many regions where the trees abound the nuts are almost unknown. A few generations ago in central Maine, and presumably elsewhere, the gathering of beechnuts was a regularly awaited event of October, the boys watching anxiously for the clear, cold night which presaged a black frost. Then all was bustle to

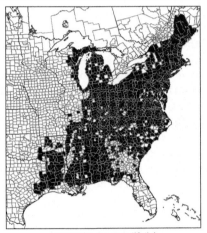

BEECH *(Fagus grandifolia)*

get out blankets, spreads, old sheets and other large cloths to spread carefully beneath the heaviest-fruiting trees to catch the abundant harvest of nuts which fell from the opening burs. The nut, readily opened by the thumb-nail, is one of the sweetest, most delicious products of the northern forests, and although, as a result of modern sophistication, it is rarely if ever seen in our markets, it is not many years since it was regularly brought in large quantities to the country grocery and even to the Boston market.

The American Beech is so similar to the European that by many competent botanists the two have been treated as one species (but now generally treated separately as *Fagus sylvatica* L., yet in Europe the beechnuts seem never to have been especially popular as human food. In fact, the following extract from quaint John Gerarde, of the 16th century, would lead one to suppose that only swine and invalids resort to this nut:

"The kernels or mast within are reported to ease the paine of the kidneies proceeding of the stone if they be eaten, and to cause the gravell and sand the easier to come foorth: with these mice and squirrels be greatly delighted, who do mightily increase by feeding thereon; swine also be fattened herewith, and certaine other beasts; also deere do feede thereon very greedily. They be likewise pleasant to thrushes and pigeons."

Unger, likewise writing from the European viewpoint, classifies Beechnuts among the vegetable products which would be eaten by man only when driven by extreme hunger.

In the early summer, in areas where the Beech fruits freely, the germinating nuts are abundant in the woods and these sweetish, nutty seedlings are sought by children. The young expanding leaves may also be cooked as a potherb.

The important use of Beechnuts in Europe is not one which has won much notice in America. In France, however, the preparation of Beech-oil has been so important that, according to Michaux (early in the last century), in some districts the Beech forests have yielded in a season more than 2,000,000 bushels of nuts, and from these nuts, when properly treated, oil equal to 1/6 the bulk of the original fruit can be extracted. The accounts of the preparation of Beech-oil for table-use are given by various European authors and we extract freely from the texts of Loudon and of Michaux. "When prepared for table-use the oil is treated with great care and by European writers, especially the French, it is said to be equal in delicacy to olive-oil.

The nuts are separated from the burs by shaking in sieves and then winnowing; they are then dried in an airy place to avoid possible mustiness or sprouting; and during the winter, whenever it is convenient to extract the oil, the nuts are heated in an oven to crack the thin brown shells which are then removed by beating or rubbing in the hands and winnowing.

"If labour is cheap, they may also be deprived of their inner skin, a very thin pellicle, which is very acrid. When blanched, they should, as soon as possible, be reduced into a paste by pounding them in a mortar, or by grinding them in a mill made on the principle of a coffee-mill." The implements employed should be kept scrupulously clean, in order to avoid making the oil rancid, cleaning them with alkaline ashes or lye and then thoroughly rinsing. The paste quickly dries, consequently water is added in the proportion of one pound to fifteen pounds of fruit. As soon as oil can be extracted from the paste by pressure of the hand it is sufficiently pulverized to go into the final press. It is then placed in perfectly clean linen bags or "bags of wool or hair."

The bags of paste are put under pressure, the force gradually applied, and continued for three hours or more, when most of the oil will have been pressed out. The paste is then prepared for a second squeezing by pulverizing, adding less water than at first, and warming carefully in a gentle heat, after which it is again pressed.

The oil is stored in casks or unglazed earthen vessels in a cool cellar; at the end of two or three months it is drawn off into fresh vessels, leaving the mucilaginous residue at the bottom of the first casks.

"This process is repeated three times during the first year; after which the oil is put into Florence oil flasks, and buried in sand in a cellar. The flasks should be always kept upright, and the oil drawn off from the mucilage which it will deposit into fresh flasks every year. Thus treated, it will keep 10 years, and improves by keeping, at least during the first 5 or 6 years; beech oil above 6 years old being reckoned the best."

In regions where Beechnuts can be gathered in abundance, it would certainly be an interesting experiment to prepare table-oil, although, from the preceding account, its preparation, like that of wines and brandies made from innumerable wild fruits, is to be regarded as a longtime investment, rather than as an emergency transaction. In view of the vast havoc wrought by the first World War in the Department of the Somme, it is interesting to find Michaux stating, that in 1779 the forests of Compiegne afforded oil enough to supply all the needs of that district for more than half a century! Whether in heavily fruitful areas our American Beechnuts would yield such supplies of oil has not been tested. A secondary use of Beechnuts is as a substitute for coffee, after being roasted; and in times of scarcity the inner bark has been used in Europe for bread-making.

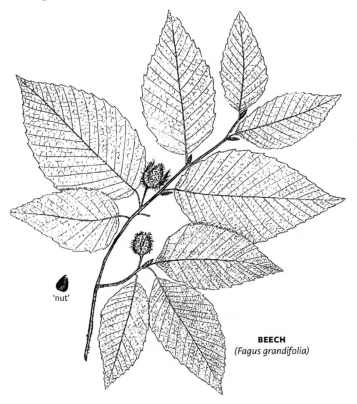

'nut'

BEECH
(Fagus grandifolia)

Acorns, Oaks
Quercus (many species)

Uses nuts, breadstuff.

We have many species of **Oak** in eastern America belonging to the well marked groups, with acorns of different quality: (1) the **White Oaks**, with the bark of the trunk usually scaly, the tips and lobes of the leaves without bristly elongations, the scales of the cup woody or corky, the inside of the nut-shell smooth, and the kernel usually sweetish; this group including the White Oaks, Post Oak, Bur Oak, and the Chestnut Oaks (about 10 species). (2) the **Black Oaks** or **Red Oaks** and the **Willow Oaks**, distinguished by darker, more furrowed and harder bark, br is tie-points to the tips of the leaves (and in lobed leaves at the tips of the lobes), thin scales of the cup, downy inner surface of the nut-shell, and very bitter kernel; this group including the various trees known as Black, Red, Yellow, and Scarlet Oak, the Willow Oaks and several others (about 15 species).

Acorns formed a very important portion of the breadstuffs of American Indians, some of the tribes of the arid regions of the Southwest depending largely on acorn-flour. Although bitter and somewhat astringent when raw, acorns lose these properties by being leached, and there is left a nutty meat rich in oil and starch, which is as nutritious as the meat of other nuts and thoroughly palatable.

In preparing acorns for bread-purposes, the Indians mixed the meats with hard-wood ashes and water, thus removing the bitter and astringent properties, or powdered the dried kernels and either poured boiling water through the flour, thus removing the tannin, or placed tho powdered mass in a basket or in a hollow pocket of sand and allowed running water to trickle through the mass. So general was this latter method among some of the southwestern tribes, who afterward ate the meal mixed with sand, that Dr. Valery Havard quoted a medical officer as stating that "he has seen an Indian 45 years old with the crowns of his otherwise healthy teeth half gone, while in Indians 60 years old, it is not uncommon to see all the teeth worn down even with the gums."

It is entirely unnecessary to mix sand with acorn-flour and thus to sandpaper the teeth. In our own experience we have found that the thoroughly dried kernels may be rid of the tannin by boiling for two hours, pouring oft the darkened water, and then allowing the commonly blackened kernels to soak in cold water, with occasional changes, until it is convenient to grind them into a paste (preferably within 3 or 4 days). The dried paste, powdered and treated according to conventional recipes for corn-cake ("fifty-fifty") makes a thoroughly palatable, dark bread or muffin, quite as good as any of the substitutes for all wheat to which, during the last war, we became accustomed. The Indians, having no yeast nor baking powders, made an unleavened, pasty bread which was unattractive to the whites, but there is no reason why, when properly prepared, acorn-bread may not become a cheap and wholesome food throughout temperate America. Although the sweet acorns of the White Oaks have less tannin than the acorns of the Black Oak series, the latter were used extensively by the Indians and their tannin is as readily removed. In some accounts it is stated that the acorns were boiled in ash-lye to remove the tannin and then boiled in several pure waters. In boiling or in long soaking much of the sugar is necessarily extracted from the acorn-flour. It has been suggested that this difficulty may be overcome by adding a small amount of gelatine (powdered) to the ground acorns, the gelatine removing the bitter taste without affecting the sugar.

It is and was not only the American Indians who used acorns for bread. Witness this from an English chronicler of the 17th century: "Acorns . . . (before the use of Wheat-Corn was found out) were heretofore the Food of Men, nay of Jupiter himself . . . till their Luxurious Palats were debauched . . . And Men had indeed Hearts of Oak; I mean, not so hard, but health, and strength, and liv'd naturally, and with things easily parable and plain."

The tender young oak-apples or oak-galls, produced by gall-wasps on the leaves of Red, Black and Scarlet Oaks in spring, contain a sweet juice which is often sucked out of the opened "apple" by children.

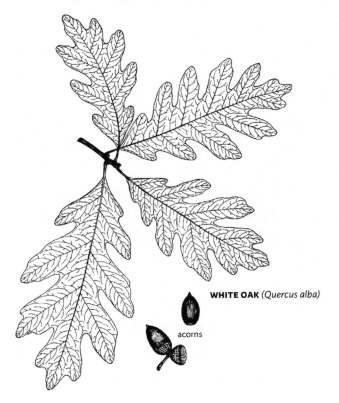

WHITE OAK *(Quercus alba)*

acorns

Geraniaceae GERANIUM FAMILY

Storksbill, Pin-grass
Erodium cicutarium (L.) L'Hér ex Ait.

Uses salad, potherb.

The **Storksbill** is an occasional weed around towns and especially in the neighborhood of woolen-mills, whence its seeds have been brought from the Southwest entangled in wool. The plant is extensively naturalized in the south-western states and several writers say that the young foliage is eaten raw or cooked by the Indians. In our Southwest it is raised as an important winter-forage under the name Alfileria.

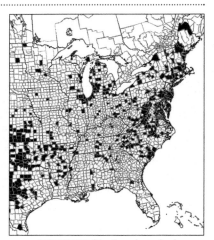

STORKSBILL *(Erodium cicutarium)*

seed

STORKSBILL *(Erodium cicutarium)*

Grossulariaceae CURRANT FAMILY
Gooseberries and Currants
Ribes, numerous species

We have many species of wild **Gooseberries** and **Currants**, the former abounding from Newfoundland across the continent, the latter extending into Labrador. The three commoner Gooseberries of the Northeast are: (1) *Ribes cynosbati* L., with bristly or prickly fruits, found from western Maine to Manitoba and southward, with the prickly berries thoroughly palatable when cooked; and (2) *R. hirtellum* Michx. and (3) *R. oxyacanthoides* L., which occur in southern Canada and the northern States, with smooth berries palatable when ripe and for preserves and jams considered superior to the cultivated species.

The most abundant Currants are four species, two black, two red. The common **Black Currant**, *Ribes americanum* P. Mill., through the eastern States (from western New Brunswick to Alberta, south to western Virginia, Illinois, Missouri and Nebraska), has smooth branches and smooth, thick-skinned berries in long drooping clusters, the skin covered with minute resinous atoms. The fruit of this species is somewhat like the black currant of the garden, musky in flavor and palatable only when cooked. The second Black Currant is a northern species, *R. lacustre* (Pers.) Poir., which abounds in damp woods from Newfoundland to Alaska, south into the northernmost states. This shrub is bristly, and the black, thin-skinned currants are covered with minute long bristles. The berries are very juicy and tart, with an odor, when crushed, suggesting the pole-cat, but when the berries are eaten by the handful the odor is inoffensive, and when cooked they make a good sauce.

The two native **Red Currants** are both northern, one with smooth berries, *Ribes triste* Pallas, the other with bristly fruit, *R. glandulosum* Grauer. The smooth berries of *R. triste*, which occurs in cool woods from Labrador to Alaska, south to New England, New York, Michigan and Wisconsin, are in appearance and flavor like the Red Currant of the garden, but they are inclined to drop before maturing. The bristly fruit of *R. glandulosum*, which occurs in rocky woods and swamps from Labrador to the extreme Northwest, south to New England, and along the mountains to North Carolina, and to Ohio, Michigan, Wisconsin and Minnesota, is known as **Skunk-Currant**, but, although the bruised shrub and berries have the polecat-odor, the berries are juicy and palatable. The bristliness and the odor are repulsive to novices, but those who have lived in the northern woods have learned to eat the berries with relish.

Some other species, both of Gooseberries and Currants, are more localized. They all supply good fruit.

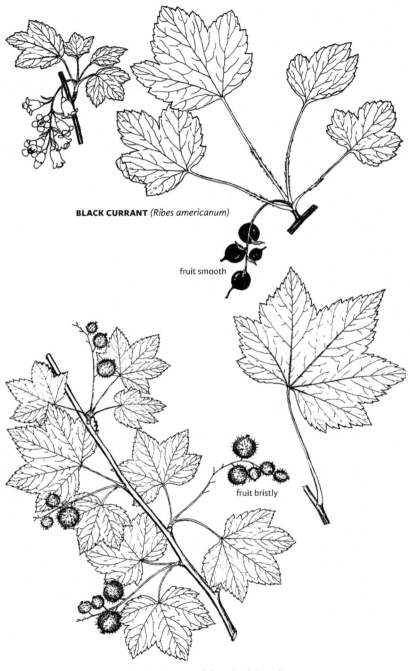

BLACK CURRANT *(Ribes americanum)*

fruit smooth

fruit bristly

SKUNK CURRANT *(Ribes glandulosum)*

Hamamelidaceae WITCH-HAZEL FAMILY

Witch-Hazel
Hamamelis virginiana L.

Use tea.

The familiar **Witch-Hazel**, which abounds in sterile woods through much of eastern America, depends for its reputation as an economic plant chiefly on its use in linaments, ointments, etc. But, according to Waugh, the Iroquois use a decoction of the leaves, sweetened with maple sugar, as a tea with their meals. It is probably quite as harmless to drink as to use as a "medicinal" lotion. Its action in the latter case is due to the tannin contained.

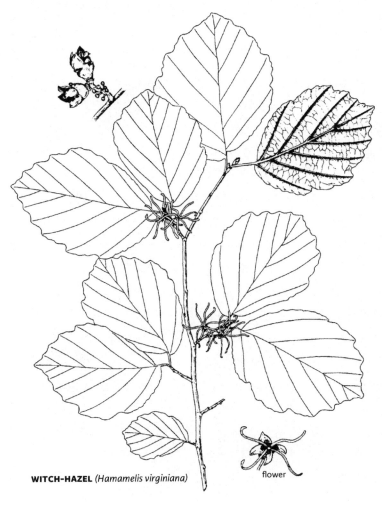

WITCH-HAZEL *(Hamamelis virginiana)*

flower

Hydrophyllaceae WATERLEAF FAMILY

Hydrolea
Hydrolea, several species.

Use potherb.

The **Hydroleas** with us are creeping-based perennial herbs with the ascending branches bearing entire, alternate, lanceolate to ovate leaves which often bear a sharp spine in the axil; the flowers handsome, with the blue corolla 5-cleft, 2 distinct slender styles and a 2-celled capsule. They grow in wet places in the South, some of them coming north to southern Virginia, southern Indiana, Illinois, Missouri and Oklahoma. The foliage is very bitter and in the South is often pounded to a pulp and used as a poultice. In the East Indies, however, where a species very similar to ours occurs, its young tips are cooked and eaten with rice, retaining "a slight bitter taste." Ours should be tested; *Hydrolea uniflora*, found in the lower Mississippi River valley, shown below.

Juglandaceae WALNUT FAMILY

Well known trees of temperate North America, being our only nut-bearing trees with long, pinnate leaves having numerous leaflets. The family includes **Walnuts, the Butternut, the Pecan, Hickory-nuts and Pignuts**. The nuts of many species are familiar in the markets and formed one of the most important foods of the Indians.

Uses fresh or dried nuts, bread, gravies, soups, butter, syrup, sugar.

The most obvious uses of the nuts are those at present practiced, the fresh or dried nuts eaten raw or ground into flour and used in nut-bread or -cake; but the Indians had other important uses for them, which were carefully worked up by "Waugh, from whom we freely extract. In the preparation of gravies, soups and butter the nuts were pounded (shells and all, shells subsequently separating and precipitating to the bottom of the kettle), boiled slowly in water, the oil skimmed from the surface, seasoned with salt, and used like butter on bread, potatoes and vegetables, or preserved for future use as food; or, the highest compliment in Indian practice, used as hair oil. In the boiling the fragments of shell sink to the bottom, and the meats rise to the top or swim slightly above the shells; and after skimming off the precious oil the Indians next skimmed off the meats which were seasoned and mixed with potatoes or meal. This mashed nut-meat was also often dried in cakes and preserved for winter use; and when needed the cakes were soaked in warm water and cooked.

Some of the earlier observers of Indians give such quaint and graphic accounts that they are well worth quoting. Thus Strachey, in The Historie of Travaile into Virginia Britannia, writes:

"This last kind the Indians beat into pieces with stones, and putting them, shells and all, into morters mingling water with them, with long woodden pestells pound them so long togither untill they make a kind of mylke, or oylie liquor, which they call powcohicora [whence our name hickory]."

Lawson, in his *History of Carolina*, states that one of their dishes was a soup made of the powdered nuts mixed with the broth, "which dissolves the Nut, and thickens, whilst the Shell precipitates, and remains at the bottom," naively adding, "this Broth tastes very rich." Thomas Ash, in his *Description of Carolina*, stated that the colonists' kitchens were frequently supplied with oil secured from the Indians, and that "whilst new it has a pleasant Taste; but after six Months, it decays and grows acid; I believe it might make a good Oyl, and of as general an use as that of the Olive, if it were better purified and rectified. " William Bartram, speaking of the vast quantities of nuts gathered by the Creeks, stated that he had seen more than a hundred bushels of the hickory-nuts belonging to a single family.

The sap of the Walnuts and Hickories is sweet, and when boiled down makes a syrup or sugar as delicious as that of the Maple. The trees should be tapped in early spring just before the unfolding of the leaves. It is definitely recorded that the Indians used the sap of both the Black Walnut and the Butternut, and practical experience of the writers has shown that at least the Shell-bark Hickory furnishes a delicious sugar.

Besides the general uses, discussed above, there are special uses and qualities belonging to the different species, which are enumerated below.

Hickory, Pecan
Carya, various species.

Key-characters distinguished from *Juglans*, the true Walnuts, by having the husk, when mature, crack into 4 valves, thus exposing the smooth-shelled nut.

We have 3 groups of Hickories: (1) the familiar Pecan, with an olive-shaped, thin-shelled nut, found in river-bottoms through the Mississippi valley; (2) the Sweet Hickories, including the Shell-bark or Shag-bark, Mocker-nut, etc., in which the 4 valves of the thick husk promptly split apart when the fruit is ripe, and in which the flesh of the nut is sweet and delicious; and (3) the Bitter-nuts or Pig-nuts, in which the thinnish husk cracks only above the middle, or very tardily to the base, and in which the flesh is often bitter, though sometimes (in *Carya glabra*) of good quality.

Range Pecan, southern Indiana to Iowa, and southward; the other species rather generally throughout the Eastern States, northward into southern Ontario, southern Quebec, and southwestern Maine.

The **Shell-bark** is the familiar white-shelled Hickory-nut of the markets, having a comparatively thin shell. The **Mocker-nut** has a much thicker, harder and darker shell and is not highly valued. The late W. E. Gerard offered an ingenious explanation of its name, saying: "The c in the word mocker is epenthetic, and the name mocker-nut stands for (New York) Dutch moker-noot, 'heavy-hammer nut,' i.e., one which, owing to the thickness of its shell, it takes more than a light hammer to crack."

Black Walnut and Butternut
Juglans nigra L.
Juglans cinerea L.

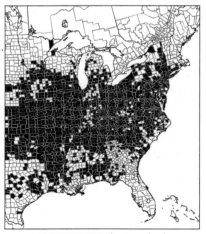

Key-characters distinguished from the Hickories by having the husk, which covers the nut-shell, close and tight and not cracking away from the nut. The fruit of the Butternut is elongate (ellipsoid) and the husk is covered with clammy or viscid short hairs; the fruit of the Black Walnut is spherical and without the viscid hairs.

Habitat and Range the Black Walnut in rich woods from the Mississippi basin eastward to New York and, southward, to the coast, the Butternut running farther northward and northeastward, extending

BLACK WALNUT (*Juglans nigra*)

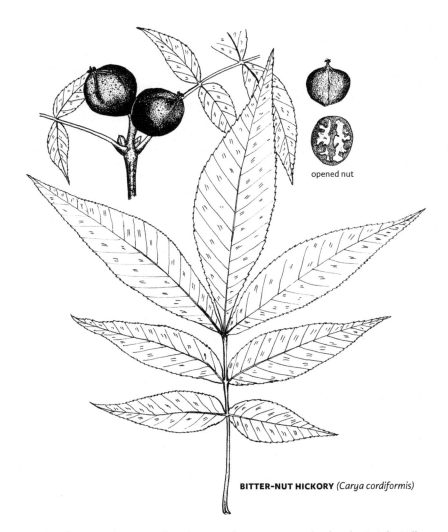

opened nut

BITTER-NUT HICKORY *(Carya cordiformis)*

in rich soil into southern Canada and eastward across New England to the St. John Valley in New Brunswick.

Uses (in addition to those enumerated on p. 243) pickles.

The young fruits are pickled by housewives in regions where they abound. The practice, dating back to colonial days and, obviously, brought from England, where pickled walnuts are still popular, is to take the halfgrown fruits, including the husks, plunge them into boiling, salted water; thoroughly wipe to clean off the down; then preserve in boiling vinegar spiced to taste.

Evelyn, in 1706, gave the following very detailed recipe for the preparation of pickled walnuts, so much used in England:

"Gather the Nuts young, before they begin to harden, but not before the

Kernel is pretty white: Steep them in as much Water as will more than cover them. Then set them on the Fire, and when the Water boils, and grows black, pour it off, and supply it with fresh, boiling it as before, and continuing to shift it till it become clear, and the Nuts pretty tender: Then let them be put into clean Spring-Water for two Days, changing it as before, with fresh, two or three times within this space: Then lay them to drain and dry on a clean coarse Cloth, and put them in a Glass Jarr, with a few Walnut Leaves, Dill, Cloves, Pepper, whole Mace and Salt; strewing them under every Layer of Nuts, till the Vessel be Three quarters full; and lastly, replenishing it with the best Vinegar, keep it well covered; and so they will be fit to spend within Three Months."

The husks of walnuts indelibly stain the fingers and clothes. Those who are experienced with them do not attempt to remove the fresh husks. Instead, the crop is put in piles to ferment. After fermentation has proceeded far enough the soft and brittle husks are easily removed. The nuts are then spread to dry very thoroughly before attempting to remove the deeply corrugated meat.

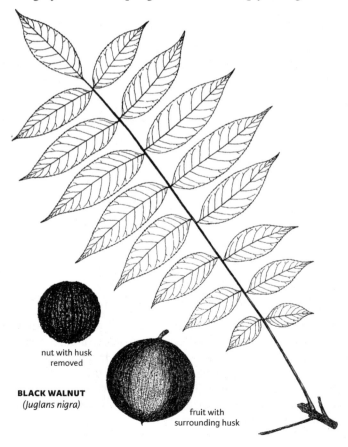

nut with husk
removed

BLACK WALNUT
(*Juglans nigra*)

fruit with
surrounding husk

Juncaginaceae ARROW-GRASS FAMILY

Arrow-grass
Triglochin maritima L.

Habitat swamps and sea-margins.
Range across the continent northward, along the coast southward to New Jersey.
Season of Availability late summer and autumn.
Uses parched grain, coffee-substitute.

Coville states that the dry, seed-like fruits of the **Arrow-grass** are parched and eaten by the Klamath Indians, or sometimes roasted and used as a substitute for coffee. The plant is abundant at the borders of salt marshes from southern Labrador to New Jersey, in saline or boggy spots across the continent northward, and southward in the saline areas of the Rocky Mountain region. It fruits very freely, bearing its flattish but strongly ridged, dry seeds in long spikes. The fresh seeds have a strong taste or odor suggesting watchmaker's oil or turpentine.

Caution the leaves of *Triglochin* often contain hydrocyanic acid and are poisonous to browsing animals. The fruit contains so little that, when roasted, it is probably harmless. See p. 57.

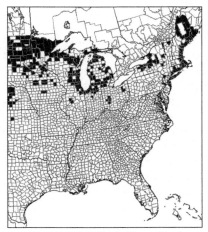

ARROW-GRASS *(Triglochin maritima)*

ARROW-GRASS
(Triglochin maritima)

stem
detail

Lardizabalaceae LARDIZABALA FAMILY

Chocolate-Vine
Akebia quinata (Houtt.) Dcne.

Use sweetish fruit.

Akebia quinata, a twining shrub with 5 digitate leaflets, purple flowers with 6 petal-like sepals and 3 or more ovaries, 1 or 2 of which ripen late in the autumn into oblong purple berry-like fruits 3 or 4 inches long, is commonly cultivated and tends to stray to roadside-thickets. Its ripe fruit cracks open and exposes the yellowish-green pulp with many black seeds. The pulp is sweetish and edible, appreciated by the natives of its home-region, China and Japan.

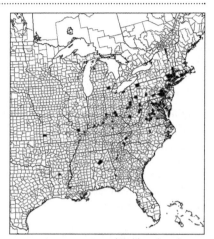

CHOCOLATE-VINE *(Akebia quinata)*

fruit

CHOCOLATE-VINE *(Akebia quinata)*

Lauraceae LAUREL FAMILY

Spice-bush, Benjamin-bush, Wild Allspice
Lindera benzoin (L.) Blume

Synonym *Benzoin aestivale*
Key-characters shrub with slender, grayish branches covered in early spring by dense sessile clusters of yellow flowers, later bearing elongate, bright-red berries and narrowly obovate, entire leaves; twigs, foliage and berries fragrant when bruised.
Habitat and Range swampy woods and brooksides, southern Maine to southern Ontario and southward; a similar specics, differing by having downy branchlets and leaves, found in the Southern States.
Season of Availability spring to autumn.
Uses tea, condiment.

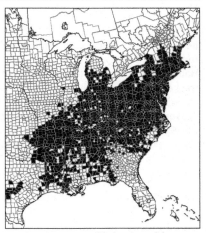

SPICE-BUSH *(Lindera benzoin)*

The young twigs, broken or cut, the leaves and the fruits all contain aromatic oil and make a very fragrant tea which is appreciated by some people. The new bark is pleasant to chew. The berries, dried and powdered, have been used as a substitute for allspice.

Red-Bay
Persea palustris Raf. Sarg.

Synonym *Persea pubescens*
Use condiment.

The familiar and handsome **Red-Bay** of the coastal plain from Texas to Florida, thence north in swamps and low, sandy woods to the lower James River, has firm evergreen leaves with the delightful odor of tropical bay. It is quite as good for seasoning soups and savory dishes.

SPICE-BUSH *(Lindera benzoin)*

Sassafras
Sassafras albidum (Nutt.) Nees

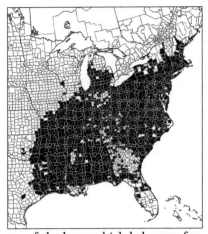

Key-characters tree or shrub with greenish branchlets; the leaves oval to fan-shaped, many of them often mitten-shaped or with two "thumbs"; berries blue, on thick, club-shaped, red fruit-stalks.
Habitat and Range dry woods and thickets, southern Maine to southern Ontario, Iowa, and south to the Gulf.
Season of Availability roots, throughout the year; leaves and pith, early summer.
Uses tea, soup, condiment (but see **Caution**, p. 251).

Very soon after the discovery of America, **Sassafras** became famous for its supposed medicinal virtues and it was one of the lures which led many for-tune-hunting and colonizing parties from Europe to America. As a source of great fortunes Sassafras proved a disappointment, but in the regions where it occurs it has always had a sort of popularity on account of its aromatic odor and flavor and its use as a tea and, in the South especially, as gumbo "filet." The tea is made by brewing the roots (some say the young shoots also), the brew being a deep red color. To many people this drink, served with cream and sugar, is decidedly palatable, though to others it is quite distasteful—perhaps as too suggestive of tooth-powder. The same roots may be brewed several times before the flavor is all extracted.

If any one doubts the appreciation of Sassafras-tea in the South he should note the following, sent by Dr. E. L. Lee of Bridgeport, Alabama, in 1907, to the American Botanist:

"We were a little amused by the statement in a recent number, that sassafras tea was used during the Civil War by the people of the South. So it was, but it was used from choice and a taste long cultivated. Long before the war, both whites and Indians made sassafras tea during the spring when the sap of the sugar maples was running. They boiled the sap a while then added the sassafras roots and boiled them a while longer and the tea was finished and a drink fit for the gods was the result. Was this fact alone not the cause of drinking sassafras tea in the spring of the year! The most common substitute for tea during the war was the leaves of Ilex opaca. It makes a very good tea."

The bark of the root is often dried and kept (the longer the better) to furnish an occasional nibble. This dried bark may be made into a strong-flavored condiment by grating it into boiling sugar and then cooling.

The young leaves and young pith are highly mucilaginous and, when dried

and powdered, form the famous gumbo "filet" of the South, where the whites
early learned the preparation from the Choctaw Indians. This powder is used
like gumbo to thicken soups. Dr. Carver gave the following directions: "The
young, tender stems and leaves . . . are cut, dried, and ground to a fine powder
and used in soups, broths. . . . It is especially useful in the preparation of
gumbo of various kinds. It can be cooked with the soup, etc.; or put in a salt
shaker and placed on the table to be used at will, like salt and pepper. It is most
wholesome and appetizing."

   Caution   An overdose of the oil may be narcotic in action. Modern reseach
has also shown that the essential oil in sassafras, primarily *safrole*, can lead to
liver damage and various types of cancer. As a precaution, taking sassafras in-
ternally should be avoided.

SASSAFRAS *(Sassafras albidum),*
leaf variation

Lentibulariaceae BLADDERWORT FAMILY

Butterwort
Pinguicula vulgaris L.

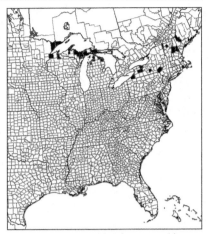

Key-characters leaves oblong, very fleshy and oily to the touch (as if buttered), pale yellowish-green, with the margins in-folded (thus trapping small insects); flower violet-like in form and color, borne on a glandular stalk from the center of the rosette of leaves.
Habitat boggy spots, wet, open ground or damp limy rocks.
Range Labrador and Newfoundland across the continent, south locally to northern New Brunswick, the White Mountains, the northern Green Mountains, northern New York, the Great Lakes region, and through the northern Rocky Mountains.
Season of Availability summer.
Use to curdle milk.

BUTTERWORT *(Pinguicula vulgaris)*

Linnaeus gives a detailed account of the use of **Butterwort** as a substitute for rennet. This account, much abbreviated and in English, instead of Latin, is re-peated by Loudon:

"*Pinguicula vulgaris* has the property of giving consistence to milk, and of preventing its separating into either whey or cream. Linnaeus says that the solid milk of the Laplanders is prepared by pouring it warm and fresh from the cow over a strainer on which fresh leaves of Pinguicula have been laid. The milk, after passing among them, is left for a day or two to stand, until it begins to turn sour; it throws up no cream, but becomes compact and tena-cious, and most delicious in taste. It is not necessary, that fresh leaves should be used after the milk is once turned: on the contrary, a small portion of this solid milk will act upon that which is fresh, in the manner of yeast."

Three other species, with violet, pink, white or yellow flowers occur in low pinelands from North or South Carolina to Florida. They could doubtless be used in the same way.

leaves sticky

BUTTERWORT *(Pinguicula vulgaris)*

Liliaceae LILY FAMILY

Members of the traditional, large Lily Family are now placed into a number of new families. However, as a convenience, we have maintained the traditional arrangement of the Liliaceae in this work.

Wild Onions, Garlic, Leek, Chives
Allium (8 or more species).

Key-characters readily recognized by the characteristic odor, the bulbs, and the slender, quill-like leaves, only the Wild Leek, *Allium tricoccum* Ait., having broad tongue-shaped leaves.
Habitats and Ranges *Allium canadense* L., the native Wild Garlic, with small bulbs borne among the greenish-white flowers, in rich meadows and alluvial woods and thickets from New Brunswick to Ontario, Florida and Texas; *A. tricoccum* Ait., the Wild Leek, with flat leaves 1-3 inches broad, in rich or alluvial woods and thickets from New Brunswick to Minnesota and Iowa, south to North Carolina; *A. cernuum* Roth, the Wild Onion, with nodding, loose clusters of pink flowers, from New York to South Carolina and westward; and *A. schoenoprasum* L., the Chives, with stiffly erect, dense pink heads resembling pink clover, on ledgy or gravelly riverbanks of Canada and the northern states.

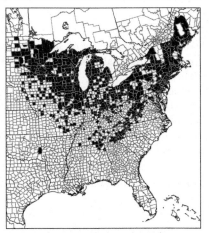

WILD LEEK *(Allium tricocum)*

Season of Availability bulbs, late autumn or early spring; bulblets of Wild Garlic, May or June; young leaves for seasoning, late spring or early summer.
Uses vegetable, seasoning, pickles.

The **Wild Onions** may be used as substitutes for the cultivated species, but the bulbs are usually very small, so that the supply is limited. The bulbs of *Allium canadense*, **Wild Garlic**, are sweet and very palatable, and Porcher and others state that the "top bulbs" are superior to the common onion for pickling. This species treated like leeks is a delicious vegetable; the whole plant, before flowering, merely stripped of the shriveled outer coats of the bulbs and trimmed to remove the wilted tips of leaves and then boiled in salted water. The water is the base for a delicate cream-of-onion soup. Various students of cultivated plants have surmised that the "Tree Onion" of the garden was derived from our American *A. canadense* or from a hybrid of it and some Old World species. Rusby speaks of the large, clustered bulbs of the **Wild Leek**, *A. tricoccum*, as one of the best, mildest and sweetest; and we are told that, in their journey in 1674 from Green Bay to the present site of Chicago, Marquette and his party subsisted largely on plants of *A. tricoccum* and *A. canadense*.

The late Dr. Huron H. Smith tells us that in the language of the Menomini Indians **Wild Leek** (*Allium tricoccum*), is *"pikwu'tc sikaku'shia"* (the skunk) and that "The word 'shika'ko' or 'skunk place' is the origin of the word Chicago, which in aboriginal times was the locality of an abundance of these wild leeks."

Field Garlic, *Allium vineale* L., the tough and very rank species which infests fields, pastures and roadsides of the Atlantic states and from New York southward so often flavors the late-winter and early-spring milk with garlic oil, is apparently not valued as human food. It belongs in the excessively strong-flavored series of species which were so feelingly characterized two centuries and a half ago by that learned and delightfully intelligent Englishman, John Evelyn:

"Garlick . .. and tho' both by Spaniards and Italians, and the more Southern People, familiarly eaten, with almost every thing,... we yet think it more proper for our Northern Rustics . . .: Whilst we absolutely forbid it entrance into our Salleting, by reason of its intolerable rankness, and which made it so detested of old, that the eating of it was (as we read) part of the Punishment for such as had committed the horrid'st Crimes. To be sure, 'tis not fit for Ladies Palates, nor those who court them, farther than to permit a light touch on the Dish with a Clove thereof ...

"Note, That in Spain they sometimes eat Garlick boil'd, which taming its Fierceness turns it into Nourishment, or rather Medicine.

Although Field Garlic is not used as human food but highly appreciated, when young, by cattle, another introduced species, *Allium ampeloprasum* L., the tall purple-flowered leek which is becoming dominant in fields about York-town, Virginia, is a perfectly possible food for man. If the people of Yorktown learn to eat it, it may be kept in restraint, for it now acts like an aggressive weed (and now well-established in the lower Mississippi River valley).

Asparagus
Asparagus officinalis L.

Asparagus occasionally spreads by seed to wild spots, but in the wild condition is not, naturally, so succulent as the cultivated plant. Its seeds, roasted and ground, have sometimes been advocated as a substitute for coffee. They are, however, often said to be poisonous.

Camass, Wild Hyacinth
Camassia scillioides (Raf.) Cory

Synonym *Camassia esculenta*

The eastern species was long confused with the western *Camassia quamash* (Pursh) Greene, which was recorded by nearly all the early explorers in the Northwest as an important article of food among the Indians. It is possible that the more eastern species is edible, but we have found no evidence of its being eaten.

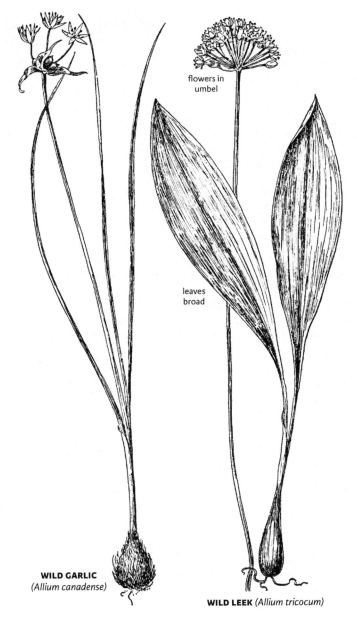

flowers in umbel

leaves broad

WILD GARLIC (*Allium canadense*)

WILD LEEK (*Allium tricocum*)

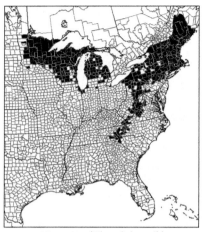

CORN-LILY *(Clintonia borealis)*

Corn-Lily, Straw-Lily, Cow-tongue
Clintonia borealis (Ait.) Raf.

Key-characters leaves 2-4, usually 3, in a basal rosette, oblong, fleshy and shiny, becoming 6-10 inches long, bordered with fine silky hairs; rootstock slender and extensively creeping; flower-stem (scape) rising a few inches to a foot, from among the leaves, bearing a terminal cluster of straw-colored, lily-like flowers from May to July, followed in late summer or autumn by livid-blue, globose berries.

Habitat cool woods northward, wet or swampy woods southward.

Range Newfoundland and southern Labrador to Lake Winnipeg, south across the northern states, and along the mountains to North Carolina.

Season of Availability spring, while the leaves are unrolling.

Uses potherb, salad.

The very young leaves of this plant are extensively used as a potherb by country people in parts of Maine under the name **Cow-tongue**; and the youngest leaves make a palatable salad, with a slightly sweetish, cucumber-flavor. Northward, where the plant abounds, it may well be used without danger of extermination; southward, where it is local, its use should be limited by discretion. The leaves must be gathered when just unrolling, for they quickly become tough and leathery.

The peculiar steel-blue berries are reputed to be poisonous, but so far as we can learn, no actual trials of them have been made.

The very similar Alleghenian species, *Clintonia umbellulata* (Michx.) Morong, can presumably be used in a similar way.

Dog-tooth Violet, Yellow Adder's-tongue, Trout-Lily
Erythronium americanum Ker-Gawl. (and several other species)

Key-characters readily distinguished by the two or three mottled, oblong-elliptic leaves, among which arises a single flower-stalk bearing a yellow, bell-shaped nodding lily; root bulbous, deep in the ground.

Habitat alluvial woods and rich terrace-lands, chiefly near streams.

Range New Brunswick to western Ontario and southward; other species westward.

Season of Availability for greens, early spring; for bulbs, early spring or late summer and autumn.

Uses potherb, cooked vegetable.

The leaves are occasionally used as a potherb, and where the plant is very abundant there can be no harm in occasionally gathering a mess. The small bulbs, shaped like slender tulip-bulbs, are nutritious and sweet but difficult to dig. Jacob Bigelow, who viewed plants from the standpoint of the physician,

CORN-LILY *(Clintonia borealis)*

leaves mottled

DOG-TOOTH VIOLET
(Erythronium americanum, left)
WHITE ADDER'S-TONGUE
(Erythronium albidum, right

stated that the bulbs are emetic. Our limited tests of them raw have shown no such property, but before using the bulbs for food care should be taken to try them in small quantity. Gilmore states that among the Winnebago the bulbs of more western species are eaten by the children "with avidity when freshly dug in springtime"; and two centuries ago the great traveller across Russia and Siberia, Gmelin, stated that the Tartars regularly use the bulbs of the Eurasian species for food.

Day-Lily
Hemerocallis fulva (L.) L.
Hemerocallis lilioasphodelus L.

Uses soup, cooked vegetable, root-vegetable.

The old fashioned **Day-Lilies** of the gardens differ from the true lilies in having long and broad grass-like or iris-like leaves arising from the crowns of the rootstocks and in having the closely clustered and erect brownish-orange or yellow flowers borne at the summit of a naked stalk; the large flowers shriveling and decaying after being open for a day. Both species, and especially the orange-flowered *Hemerocallis fulva*, are naturalized by roadsides and in thickets near old houses. Their availability for food is evident. Penhallow, writing of the superior quality of lily bulbs, universally used in Japan, says: "It is somewhat more difficult, however, to give testimony bearing upon the flavor and desirable qualities of flowers and buds from various species of *Hemerocallis*. . . . at the time of blossoming . . . the Aino women may be seen busily gathering the flowers which they take home and dry, or pickle in salt. They are afterwards used in soups." *H. graminea* is, perhaps, the most generally gathered species in Japan; the dried flowers come regularly to the Chinese markets in this country.

Penhallow missed a good thing. The fully grown buds or the freshly expanded flowers of *Hemerocallis fulva* immersed in a batter of beaten egg, milk, flour and seasoning and browned like fritters in oil or butter are a delicious and quickly prepared vegetable. They require only five minutes (long enough to brown, turned twice, on each side). The fleshy tuber-like roots, borne in clusters like dahlia-roots, boiled in salted water, taste like a blend of sweet corn and salsify.

In a detailed article on gum-jum or gum-tsoy, the dried perianths of Day-Lilies, the great authority on the genus, Dr. A. B. Stout, writes:

"In culinary uses the flowers of daylilies are employed chiefly in soups, in various meat dishes, and with noodles. In preparation the basal end of the dried flowers, consisting of the ovary, is removed and the rest is cut into several segments. Enough water is added to the quantity desired to insure complete soaking, which soon makes the parts become soft, pliable, and somewhat gelatinous. In this condition the material is added to soups that are already cooked, and when the whole is brought to a boil again, a matter of a few minutes, the dish is ready to be served. To various dishes of meats and noodles the soaked flowers are added during the final stages of cooking, or the flowers may be cooked separately for a few minutes and added as a garnish—somewhat as mushrooms are often employed.

"To these various dishes the flowers add substance of individual consistency and they supply a distinct and pleasing flavor that is best appreciated and realized by the eating. Flowers that are freshly collected may be used in quite the same way, but the flavor is somewhat different from that when dried flowers are used.

"Dr. Albert N. Steward of the University of Nanking states that in his experience in east central China the flowers may be collected for use as food after they have closed and begun to wither. A recipe which he reports is the following:

" 'Fry small pieces of pork until they are brown, then add a little soy-bean oil and water. After cooking for an hour add the flowers and cook until they are tender. The addition of a little salt improves the flavor.' "

DAY-LILY *(Hemerocallis fulva)*

Lilies
Lilium (ca. 8 species)

Use starchy vegetable.

The scaly bulbs of various species of true **Lilies** were eaten by the Indians and the bulbs of certain species are regularly cultivated by the Japanese and Chinese for table-use. Our native species all have edible bulbs, when cooked, starchy and slightly sweetish; but owing to the beauty of the flowering plants and their comparative scarcity, the digging of the bulbs is to be discouraged.

Two-leaved Solomon's-seal, Wild Lily-of-the-Valley, Scurvy-berries
Maianthemum canadense Desf.

Use berries.

The cherry-red berries in small, terminal clusters last over winter and have a not unpalatable bitter-sweet taste, but being somewhat cathartic, like the berries of *Maianthemum racemosum*, should be eaten with caution.

False Spikenard, False Solomon's-seal, Solomon's-zigzag, Scurvy-berries
Maianthemum racemosum (L.) Link

Synonym *Smilacina racemosa*
Uses starchy vegetable, pickle, asparagus, berries.

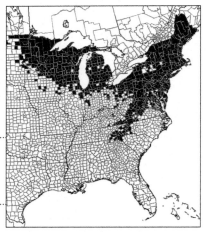

TWO-LEAVED SOLOMON'S-SEAL
(Maianthemum canadense)

The starchy and aromatic rootstocks make a pleasant pickle and we are told that the Ojibwe Indians cooked them like potatoes, first soaking the strong rootstocks in lye to free them of their disagreeable taste, then parboiling them to get rid of the lye. The young shoots make a possible asparagus. The comparative scarcity of the plant in most regions, however, makes it unwise to draw upon it when other vegetable food is available. The juicy red berries, borne in large, rhombic or pyramidal, terminal clusters, are somewhat palatable, bitter-sweet, suggesting bitter molasses, but they are cathartic and should be eaten with caution. John Josselyn, one of the earliest of New England chroniclers, said that they were "called treacle-berries, —having the perfect taste of treacle when they are ripe, —and will keep good a long while. Certainly a very wholesome berry, and medicinal." The related *Maianthemum stellatum* (L.) Link, with shorter stems and smaller leaves and shorter, simpler flower- and fruit-clusters, occurs in river-silts and on sandy shores and could be used when young as asparagus. The boiled young stems and leaves (before flowering-time) of the latter species are quite as palatable as dandelion-greens.

FALSE SPIKENARD (*M. racemosum*)

**TWO-LEAVED
SOLOMON'S-SEAL**
(*Maianthemum canadense*)

FALSE SPIKENARD
(*Maianthemum racemosum*)

Indian Cucumber, Cucumber-root
Medeola virginiana L.

Key-characters stems solitary, slender and erect, covered with cobwebby hairs, bearing near the summit a circle of 5-7 elongate leaves and often above that a smaller circle of 3 (rarely 4 or 5) leaves, from the axils of which are borne somewhat spider-like flowers with recurving straw-colored petals, the leaves in autumn becoming strongly Suffused with purple; berries black or purplish; root a horizontal, white tuber-like rootstock the size of a small thumb.
Habitat rich woods.
Range New Brunswick to western Ontario, south to Florida and the Great Lakes states.
Season of Availability throughout spring, summer and autumn.
Uses salad, pickle.

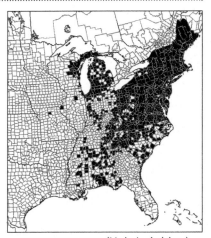

INDIAN CUCUMBER *(Medeola virginiana)*

The rootstock is crisp and starchy, with a delicate taste of cucumber, and forms a pleasant nibble in the woods, or, when dressed with vinegar or vinegar and oil, a pleasant salad or pickle. According to Manasseh Cutler, in the 18th century, the Indians ate the roots, but, in view of the attractive appearance of the root, it is surprising that it is not mentioned by other students of Indian foods.

Star-of-Bethlehem, "Dove's Dung" of the Old Testament
Ornithogalum umbellatum L.

Use roasted or boiled bulbs.

This familiar bulbous plant of old-fashioned gardens is introduced from Europe and is occasionally naturalized about door-yards and fields. European authors state that the bulbs are palatable

INDIAN CUCUMBER *(Medeola virginiana)*

and nutritious and that, when boiled or roasted, they form an important oriental food. This is supposed to be the bulb of ancient Scripture called "Dove's Dung." Its importance is attested by the following passage: "And there was a great famine in Samaria; and, behold, they besieged it, until an ass's head was sold for fourscore pieces of silver, and the fourth part of a cab of dove's dung for five pieces of silver."—2 Kings, Chap. VI, verse 25.

Star-of-Bethlehem, however, should be looked upon askance. All parts of the plant are poisonous to grazing animals. It is to be noted that the time of its great value in Samaria was during a great famine.

Solomon's-seal
Polygonatum (3 species)

Uses as asparagus, breadstuff.

The **Solomon's-seals**, characterized by the stout, fleshy rootstock with large circular scars or "seals," and the tubular, straw-colored bells hanging in spring from the leaf-axils and followed by drooping, blue, globular berries, have had some repute as a source of bread from the dried roots; while the larger, new shoots are sometimes gathered, when very young, as a substitute for asparagus. The scarcity of the plant makes it important that it should not be used except in emergency.

Caution If the roots are gathered great care should be taken not to confuse them with the rootstocks of **Mandrake or May-Apple**, *Podophyllum*, which often grows in similar rich woods and which has an elongate rootstock with enlarged nodes, but without the large, circular scars. The latter plant is reputed to be poisonous (see p. 52).

Twisted-stalk, Liver-berry
Streptopus (2 species)

Use berries.

The pulpy, pendulous, red or scarlet berries are eaten by the country people of northern Maine under the appropriate name of **Liver-berry**, and for similar reasons they are known to country boys in other parts of northern New England as Scoot-berries. Since the berries are cathartic they should

SOLOMON'S-SEAL *(Polygonatum biflorum)*

be partaken of with caution.' In taste they are somewhat insipid, with a cucumber-flavor.

Wake-Robin, Trillium, Benjamin
Trillium (6 or more species)

Use potherb.

The young, unfolding plants of **Trilliums** are eaten as greens by country people in Franklin County, Maine, under the name of "Much-hunger"; but on account of the scarcity and great beauty of the plants it is certainly to be hoped that, except in cases of "much hunger," they will not be gathered for food purposes. Trillium-roots are highly emetic. Their berries are open to suspicion.

Bellwort, Wild Oats
Uvularia (ca. 4 species)

Uses as asparagus, starchy vegetable.

Porcher states that the fleshy but small roots are edible when cooked. In 1785 Manasseh Cutler stated that the young shoots of the Bellworts might be eaten as asparagus and that the roots are nutritious and sometimes used in "diet drinks." Cutler's statements have been quoted in various forms by others, who have extended his words to cover all the species of the genus. Cutler was originally referring to *Uvularia sessilifolia* L., but there is presumably no difference in the qualities of the species. The plants are so uncommon that they can have no extensive use without danger of exterminating them. They should be used only in emergency.

Yucca
Yucca, various species, both native and cultivated.

Use Salad.

It is frequently stated that fresh flowers of **Yucca**, properly dressed, are a good salad.

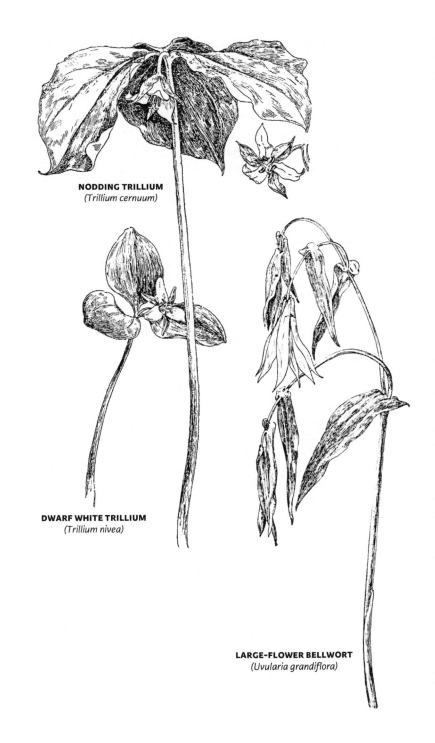

NODDING TRILLIUM
(Trillium cernuum)

DWARF WHITE TRILLIUM
(Trillium nivea)

LARGE-FLOWER BELLWORT
(Uvularia grandiflora)

Limnanthaceae FALSE MERMAID FAMILY

False Mermaid
Floerkea proserpinacoides Willd.

Use salad.

This weak annual herb of marshes and wooded riverbanks from western Quebec to Delaware and westward has a pleasant pungent flavor and is very tender. It may be eaten either as a nibble or dressed as a salad. It is so inconspicuous that only the technical botanist is apt to notice it.

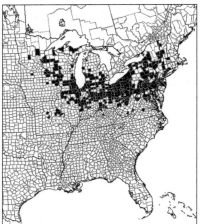

FALSE MERMAID *(Floerkea proserpinacoides)*

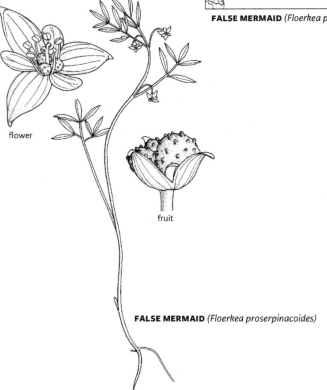

flower

fruit

FALSE MERMAID *(Floerkea proserpinacoides)*

Malvaceae MALLOW FAMILY

Mallows
Malva, Althaea, etc. (about a dozen species)

Uses potherbs, mucilaginous juice, soup.

The **Mallows** have mild, mucilaginous juices and throughout regions where they are found the smooth species have often been used as potherbs. In our own flora we have chiefly introduced species, which occur as weeds about barn-yards or on roadsides and in fields and, although these may be used as potherbs, they are chiefly known through their scalloped fruits, familiar to children as a nibble under the name of "Cheeses." Of more importance is the **Marsh-Mallow,** *Althaea officinalis* L., a European species rarely found in America, the root of which supplies the juice used as the basis of the well known confection.

Basswood, Linden
Tilia americana L. and three other species

Uses sugar, chocolate-substitute, tea, masticatory, emergency-food.

The sap of the **Lindens** is said to contain a considerable amount of sugar, but the most striking use of these trees is in the preparation of a substitute for chocolate. It has long been known in Europe, where it was first discovered by a French chemist, Missa, that the fruits of the Linden ground with some of the flowers furnish a paste which in texture and taste "perfectly" resembles chocolate. Various attempts have been made in Europe to produce this chocolate-substitute on a commercial scale but, owing to the liability of the paste

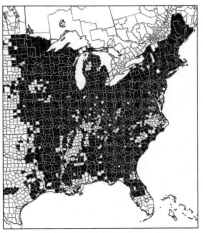

BASSWOOD *(Tilia americana)*

to decomposition, all have proved impracticable. The most conspicuous case was in the time of Frederick the Great, when that monarch engaged a German chemist to check the work of Missa. The results were entirely satisfactory but, as above stated, it was found that the new chocolate would not keep. "On this Ventenat [a distinguished French botanist of the time] remarks, that, if the subject had been pursued a little further, and the fruits of some of the American species of limes [Lindens] taken, the success would probably have been complete." Here is a great opportunity for some enterprising Yankee!

According to Waugh and some other writers on Indian foods, the Iroquois chewed the bast (inner bark)in the spring as a masticatory, and also the young buds in the spring as a thirst-quencher. The bast has also been recommended as a possible emergency-food.

The deliciously fragrant flowers of the Lindens have been popular in many countries as a substitute for tea, the tea prepared from them being "soft, well-flavoured, and sweet," so much so that Porcher, writing for the Southern Confederate families, said: "I would particularly recommend a larger use of these flowers in the Confederate States. It can be used wherever tea is required."

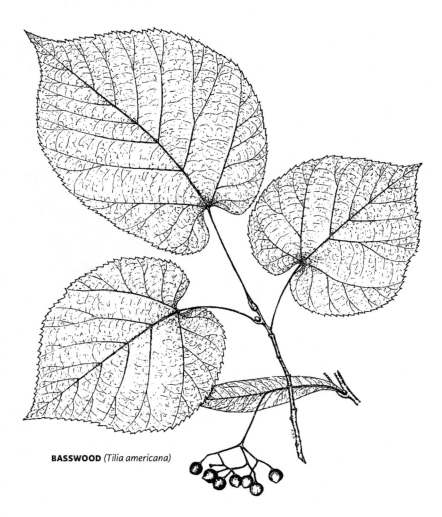

BASSWOOD *(Tilia americana)*

Martyniaceae MARTYNIA FAMILY

Unicorn-plant, Proboscis-flower
Proboscidea louisiana (P. Mill.) Thellung

Use pickle.

The **Unicorn-plant**, of riverbanks and waste places from the Gulf States northward to West Virginia, southern Ohio, southern Indiana (but now likely no longer present), Illinois and Iowa, is often cultivated for its beaked-fruit, used as a pickle.

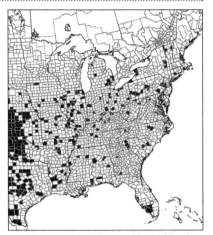

UNICORN-PLANT *(Proboscidea louisiana)*

fruit, above
flower, right

Melastomataceae MELASTOME FAMILY

Deergrass, Meadow-beauty
Rhexia virginica L. (and ca. 5 other species).

Uses salad, nibble.

The handsome **Deergrass** is too beautiful and local a plant to recommend for general use as a food, but in regions where it abounds it furnishes a pleasant salad, the leaves having a sweetish and slightly acid taste, while the tubers are pleasantly nutty in quality.

It is probable that other species of the genus have similarly palatable qualities.

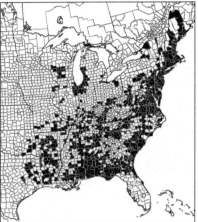

DEERGRASS *(Rhexia virginica)*

DEERGRASS *(Rhexia virginica)*

Menthaceae MINT FAMILY

In general the **Mints** are familiar on account of their aromatic oil; and, although it is extremely difficult for any but the most experienced botanist to recognize at sight the many species, the general relationship is quickly indicated by the square stem, opposite leaves, and definite aroma of most species. Many of the familiar savory herbs of the kitchen, sage, thyme, marjoram, summer-savory, hyssop, etc., are derived from this family. Some of these plants are wild in America and we have many other species the foliage of which might well be used in the kitchen and which are always acceptable in camp. A few species, furthermore, have tuberous roots which are available as salads or as cooked vegetables.

The most important of our wild Mints, besides those already enumerated, are the **Horehound** (*Marrubium*), a white-wooly, bitter herb of waste places, from which the familiar horehound-candy receives its name; the **Bee-balms** (*Monarda*), tall plants with the upper leaves brightly colored and with showy pink, purple or red, tubular flowers in crown-like heads; the **Pennyroyal** (*Hedeoma*), a common, small herb of dry fields and pastures, familiar to children in eastern America; the **Mountain-Mints** (*Pycnanthemum*), tall plants with minute flowers crowded in broad clusters of button-like heads; and the true **Mints** (Peppermint, Spearmint, etc.), familiar to most country children.

The plants with edible tubers and those used as greens are enumerated below.

Beauty-berry, French Mulberry
Callicarpa americana L.

Use berry as a nibble.

The familiar **Beauty-berry** of the South, in woods and thickets from Texas to Florida, northward into Oklahoma, Arkansas, Tennessee and Virginia, has the defoliated branches covered in late autumn and early winter with masses of small currant-like pinkish-purple berries. Of these Stephen Elliott said in 1816: "The fruit eatable, sweet at first, but pungent and astringent afterwards." In 1860, M. A. Curtis said: "These berries are juicy, slightly aromatic and sweetish, and are sometimes eaten, but are probably not very wholesome." Their best use is as a table-ornament for which they are almost unequaled.

Henbit
Lamium amplexicaule L.

Use potherb.

The little annual **Henbit**, which springs up in fallow fields in early spring, with rounded opposite leaves with scalloped edges, the upper ones clasping the succulent square stem and subtending branches of flowers with gaping purplish corollas and 5-toothed cup-like calices, is used in Japan as an ingredient of mixed potherbs. Our experiment shows it to be good when boiled and, when young in earliest spring, to be a pleasant nibble in the raw state. In Europe other species, like the perennial *Lamium album* of our gardens, are eaten either as salads or as potherbs.

Bugleweeds, Water-Horehounds
Lycopus americanus Muhl. ex W. Bart.
Lycopus amplectens Raf.
Lycopus uniflorus Michx.
Lycopus virginicus L.

Key-characters opposite-leaved, square-stemmed herbs; the leaves ovate or narrower, 1-2 inches long, bearing in their axils dense clusters of small, white flowers, followed by the greenish or finally drab fruiting clusters; plant almost odorless; roots bearing thickish, knobby, finger-like white tubers 3 inches long.
Habitat and Range *Lycopus uniflorus*, low grounds, Newfoundland to British Columbia, south to Virginia, the Great Lakes States and Nebraska; *L. amplectens* sandy pond-margins of the coastal plain, Mississippi and Florida to southeastern Massachusetts. *L. americanus* across much of North America. *L. virginicus*, eastern USA.
Season of Availability late autumn to spring, while the tubers are well filled.
Uses relish, root-vegetable, pickle.

The crisp, white tubers of the **Bugleweeds** are often very abundant but sometimes scarcely developed. They are mild in flavor and make a most attractive radish-like relish either out-of-doors or at the table. Boiled a short time in salted water, the tubers are an agreeable vegetable, much suggesting the crosnes of European markets. They are also good pickled. On peaty or turfy shores or in meadows the tubers are borne on long subterranean stolons and are distant from the parent-plant and hard to find. When the plants grow in open sand the tubers are often crowded, abundant and large, close about the bases of the old fruiting stems. This is the ideal place to secure them. The tubers of *Lycopus amplectens* are superior and might well be planted on open sandy shores to insure a good crop.

Woundwort
Stachys palustris L., *Stachys hyssopifolia* Michx., and several others.

Key-characters square-stemmed, erect herbs from creeping rootstocks, the stems covered on the angles with long spreading hairs and on the sides with softer and shorter hairs in *S. palustris*, the stems smooth in *S. hyssopifolia*; leaves opposite, nearly without foot-stalks, hairy and oblong in *S. palustris*, narrower and smooth in *S. hyssopifolia*; flowers in a series of circular clusters at summit of stem, forming an interrupted spike; the calyx bell-shaped and with sharp teeth; the corolla gaping, tubular, pink; in fruit 4 blunt nutlets at base of calyx.

Habitat and Range *S. hyssopifolia* on sandy or gravelly pond-margins, southeastern Massachusetts southward; *S. palustris* or close relatives in low grounds, Newfoundland to northwestern Canada, southward somewhat generally into the northern states; other species southward.
Season of Availability autumn to spring.
Uses salad, nibble, cooked root-vegetable.

Several species of *Stachys* develop in the autumn plump and crisp elongate white tubers from which new stems arise the following season. Those of *S. palustris* have been referred to by various European writers as, to quote Lightfoot, "sweet, and in times of necessity . . . eaten by men, either boiled, or dry'd, and made into bread." We have not tried them; but an Asiatic species has long been cultivated, especially in China and Japan and sometimes as a novelty elsewhere, for its edible tubers, as Chinese Artichoke.

The small and smooth plant of sandy shores on Cape Cod, Long Island and in New Jersey, thence southward, *S. hyssopifolia*, is worth attention. From October to early spring the sand about the colonies of shriveled fruting stems is full of crisp and nutty tubers and rootstocks, white and as good a nibble or salad as one could wish. On a winter's tramp where it abounds it tastes as good as crisp celery, though with an individual flavor.

leaves
opposite

**CUT-LEAF
WATER-HOREHOUND**
(Lycopus americanus)

WOUNDWORT *(Stachys palustris)*

Menyanthaceae BUCK-BEAN FAMILY

Buckbean, Bogbean, Water-Trefoil

Menyanthes trifoliata L.

Use breadstuff.

The familiar **Buckbean** of northern bogs and pond-margins has the strong, bitter principle which is found so generally in the gentians (Buckbean was formerly included in the Gentian Family). Nevertheless, the ground rootstocks have been used by the Laplanders and Finns in the making of missen-bread (famine-bread). Linnaeus gives an account of this bread, which is made by drying and grinding the thick rootstocks, then washing or leaching the meal to extract some of the bitter, after which a thoroughly unpalatable but nutritious bread may be made from the flour.

portion of flowering stem

BUCKBEAN *(Menyanthes trifoliata)*

Molluginaceae CARPETWEED FAMILY

Carpet-weed, Indian Chickweed
Mollugo verticillata L.

Use potherb.

The familiar **Carpet-weed**, with depressed, branching, slender stems and whorls of narrow leaves, with insignificant axillary flowers and 3-celled capsules, may be cooked and eaten. It is too small for most people to gather, except when very hungry.

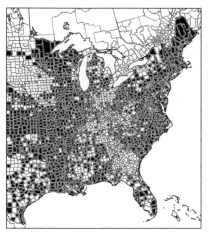

CARPET-WEED *(Mollugo verticillata)*

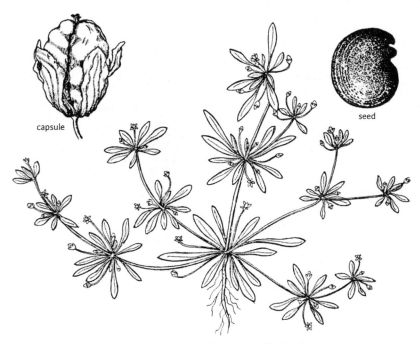

capsule

seed

CARPET-WEED *(Mollugo verticillata)*

Montiaceae CANDY-FLOWER FAMILY

Spring-beauty, "Fairy-Spuds"
Claytonia caroliniana Michx. *and Claytonia virginica* L.

Uses starchy vegetable, potherb.

The roundish, irregular roots of the **Spring-beauty**, varying from 1/2 to 2 inches in diameter, when boiled in salted water, are palatable and nutritious, having the flavor of chestnuts. The succulent, opposite-leaved young plants, which often abound in spring in rich woods and open glades, are a possible potherb. Only in regions where the plants are superabundant, however, would the quantity be sufficient to repay digging for the deeply buried roots. In some regions the plants cover many acres of wooded slopes or meadows and there in a few minutes it is possible to dig enough roots to furnish a pleasant change in the spring diet.

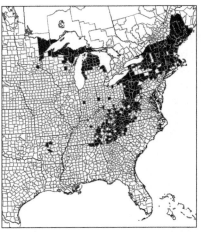

SPRING-BEAUTY *(Claytonia caroliniana)*

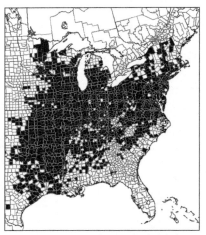

SPRING-BEAUTY *(Claytonia virginica)*

SPRING-BEAUTY
(Claytonia virginica)

Moraceae MULBERRY FAMILY

Fig
Ficus carica L.

The **Fig** is persistent about deserted old houses and in their neighborhood through the Southern States, northward into eastern Virginia. A fruiting colony of it in the borders of woods is often a godsend in late summer and autumn.

Red or Black Mulberry
Morus rubra L.

White Mulberry
Morus alba L.

Uses fresh fruit, pies, jellies etc., cooked vegetable.

No real out-of-door person living where the **Red or Black Mulberry** is found will fail to know the fruit, which is borne in an abundance allowing long and repeated feastings. The Indians and the early explorers west and southwest of New England counted the fruit of this native one of their most important berries. The perishable nature of the berries keeps them out of modern markets and the presence of an axis extending well into the fruit prevents its use fresh on the table. But neither disadvantage prevents its extensive use in

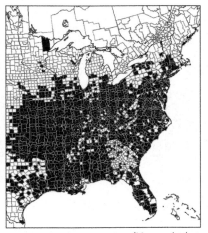

RED OR BLACK MULBERRY *(Morus rubra)*

regions where it abounds, either fresh from the tree or for pies, jellies (made from either immature or mature fruit), jams, marmalades, summer drinks, etc. The sugar contained in the fruit is said to be especially pure. The trees might well be cultivated over a wide area to serve for domestic uses.

The **White Mulberry** of Asia was extensively planted about a century ago as food for silk-worms. In favorable localities it has persisted and spread but, ripening at the time of larger and somewhat more preferred fruits of cultivation, its berries are largely ignored. As compared with those of the native Red Mulberry they are insipid. Asiatic writers, where *M. alba* is native, speak of the cooked young shoots as "a very good vegetable."

fruit

RED OR BLACK MULBERRY *(Morus rubra)*

Myricaceae SWEET GALE FAMILY

Sweet Fern
Comptonia peregrina (L.) Coult.

Key-characters small shrub with slender grayish branches, and elongate, deliciously fragrant, dryish leaves cut nearly to the midrib into 'oundish segments (hence the name "Sweet Fern"); the fruit forming bristly, globular burs with hard, glossy, olive-brown nutlets 1/8-1/4 inch long.
Habitat sterile pasture-lands and open sterile woods.
Range Prince Edward Island to Manitoba, south to northern Georgia and upland of Tennessee.
Season of Availability late spring, summer and autumn.
Uses tea, nibble.

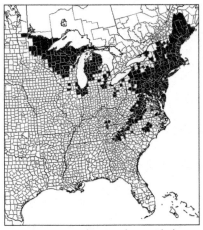

SWEET FERN *(Comptonia peregrina)*

The aromatic leaves of **Sweet Fern** make a palatable tea, and the young nutlets are a popular nibble with country children, especially during June and early July, while the small nutlets are still tender. The method of extracting the nutlet from the bur is the simple, childish device of inserting the thumb-nail under the nutlet, thus always staining the nail yellowish with the nearly insoluble resinous oil.

Wax-Myrtle, Bayberry
Morella pensylvanica (Mirbel) Kartesz
Morella cerifera (L.) Small
Morella caroliniensis (P. Mill.) Small, and other species southward.

Synonyms *Morella pensylvanica: Myrica pensylvanica; Morella cerifera: Myrica cerifera, M. pusilla; Morella caroliniensis: Myrica heterophylla*
Key-characters stocky shrubs or small trees with grayish bark and stiff branches, bearing oblong or narrower, entire or slightly toothed leaves 1-4 inches long; the fruiting branches covered with bunches of globular "berries" (nutlets), which are white or gray with waxy atoms; the leaves and wax of the fruit strongly aromatic.
Habitat sterile soils near the coast, extending locally inland on rocky barrens and plains or sometimes on bogs.
Range *M. pensylvania*, eastern North Carolina, north along the coast to the Gulf of St. Lawrence and southern Newfoundland, rarely inland to Lake Erie; *M. cerifera*, Gulf States north to Arkansas and around the coastal plain to Cape May, New Jersey; other species southward.
Season of Availability leaves, summer and autumn; berries, late summer to spring.
Use condiment.

pistillate
catkin

SWEET FERN *(Comptonia peregrina)*

WAX-MYRTLE *(Morella pensylvanica)*

Sweet Gale, Bog-Myrtle
Myrica gale L.

Key-characters and Habitat low shrub of swamps and boggy shores, with slender bronze branches; leaves alternate, strongly ascending, an inch or two long, narrowly wedge-shaped, grayish-green, with yellow resin-dots especially beneath, slightly toothed above the middle; fruiting branches bearing compact cones about half an inch long, made up of little yellow-green nutlets covered with granules of resin.

Range throughout the colder temperate regions of North America, extending south to New Jersey and the Great Lakes States, and in the mountains to Virginia.

Season of Availability leaves, late spring to autumn; nutlets, late summer to winter.

Uses condiment, tea.

SWEET GALE *(Myrica gale)*

The nutlets of **Sweet Gale** have been used in France and certainly should be used elsewhere, as an aromatic spice, having a delicious fragrance suggestive of sage. The leaves, when cured, make a delicate and palatable tea and are in much repute in country districts in northern Maine (under the name "Meadow-Fern" [in country districts in Maine there are two "Ferns": the shrubs, Meadow Fern and Sweet Fern; all members of the fern group are "Brakes."] as a cure for colds and catarrh, popular with the children if not always efficacious.

catkin

SWEET GALE *(Myrica gale)*

Nelumbonaceae LOTUS-LILY FAMILY

Water-Chinquapin, Nelumbo
Nelumbo lutea Willd.

Key-characters our largest Water-Lily, with large circular or shield-shaped leaves 1-2 feet across, usually raised above the surface of the water and with the center somewhat depressed or cup-like; the flower resembling that of the pond-lily, pale-yellow, 4-10 inches broad; the fruit-pod topshaped, perforated at the flat summit like a giant pepper-shaker, with the large nut-like seeds showing at the perforations.

Habitat and Range ponds and lake-margins from tropical America and the Gulf States northward locally to the Great Lakes region, and very locally in the coastal region to southeastern Massachusetts.

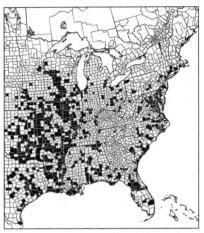

WATER-CHINQUAPIN *(Nelumbo lutea)*

Season of Availability tuberous rootstock, spring and autumn whlie well filled; seeds, summer and autumn; young leafstalks, early summer.

Uses tubers as a starchy vegetable; seeds as starchy vegetable and as breadstuff; young leaf-stalks and unrolling leaves as potherb.

Nelumbo, the **Water-Chinquapin**, has always been famous as an Indian food, and the whites who have tried it in its various preparations are enthusiastic about it. The very long rootstocks, often becoming 50 feet long, bear tuberous enlargements which become filled in autumn with starch; and these tubers or the crisp growing tips of the branches of the rootstock, when baked, are said to have a pleasant mealy quality suggestive of sweet potatoes. The seeds, which are as large as small acorns or marbles, have a hard, thick shell when ripe, but in their immature, half-ripe condition are said to be delicious either raw or cooked, in flavor like chestnuts. The ripe seeds have to be thoroughly parched to loosen the inner kernel. Then, after crushing and winnowing to dispose of the loosened hard shells, they may be again parched and eaten dry, or baked, boiled, or ground and used for bread.

The young leaf-stalks and unrolling leaves are said to form a palatable potherb.

The Omaha Indians are reported to gather the seeds in winter when the ice is firm. They also dry the tubers for winter use.

Caution The extreme rarity of the localities where Water-Chinquapin occurs in the North makes it inadvisable to raid the colonies for food. Farther south, however, where the plant is more abundant, little harm will be done, especially since the rootstocks are beyond the reach of all but the most enthusiastic.

The related oriental **Lotus** is extensively cultivated in southern China for its seeds, which are a regular food, and for the rootstocks, which are secured by draining the artificial ponds. Our own plant might similarly be propagated.

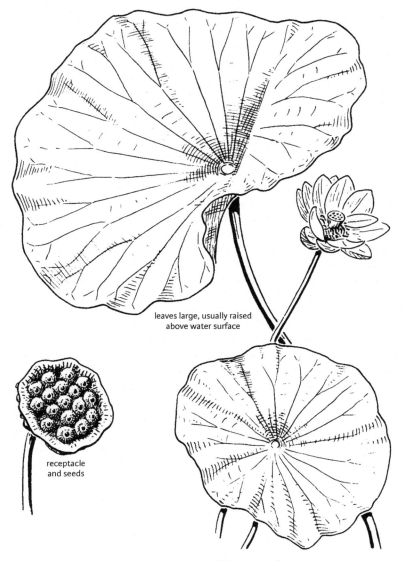

leaves large, usually raised
above water surface

receptacle
and seeds

WATER-CHINQUAPIN (*Nelumbo lutea*)

Nymphaeaceae WATER-LILY FAMILY

Cow-Lily, Spatter-Dock, Yellow Water-Lily, Pond-Collard
Nuphar, ca. 7 species

Key-characters leaves borne from the summits of a thick spongy rootstock, the blade elliptic to rounded, mostly 3-10 inches long, with a deep basal cleft or sinus, the leaf-stalk thick and spongy; flower nearly globular, yellow, or tinged with green or purple, with convex, leathery sepals and petals; fruit urn-shaped, an inch or two long, filled with seeds resembling kernels of popcorn.

Habitat and Range ponds, pools, quiet streams and bogholes; one species or another from southern Labrador to British Columbia, south to the Gulf of Mexico.

Season of Availability rootstocks, autumn to early spring while well filled; seeds, late summer and autumn.

Uses rootstocks as a starchy vegetable, seeds for bread, soups, and popped like corn.

To some of the northwestern Indians the seeds of the **Cow-Lilies** are a very important food and they spend several weeks each year in harvesting them. The northwestern species, *Nuphar polysepala* Engelm., is so important to the Klamath Indians, that a detailed bulletin on their use of the seeds and the preparation of the food "Wokas" was prepared by Coville. Very briefly: the seeds are extracted after the pods have thoroughly dried and have been pounded to loosen the seeds; although the pods which have thoroughly ripened in the water and have begun to disintegrate contain more valuable seeds. The seeds are parched for ten minutes to loosen the kernel contained within, then pounded or lightly ground and winnowed to get rid of the hard, firm shell. The remaining white kernels, after the hard shells of the seeds have been removed, may be parched, when they swell considerably but do not crack like pop-corn. Thus prepared they are said to be "a delicious food, particularly if slightly salted and eaten with cream." The white kernels are also ground into flour for bread-making or the dried seeds with their shells on may be stored for winter use, to be parched and ground as needed.

Although the seeds of this genus which have become most famous are those of the western *N. polysepala*, the large-flowered species of eastern America are so similar that it is highly probable that our eastern species would furnish as valuable seeds. In this connection it is noteworthy that the closely related European *N. lutea* has had a similar use. Thus, we find Mrs. Lankester stating that in England "Some persons boil the seeds, when they are said to have a pleasant nutty flavour."

The chief use of the eastern species by the Indians seems to have been of the rootstocks. These, like the rootstocks of the western species, contain considerable starch, in spite of their spongy texture, and were boiled or roasted as a vegetable. Quaint old John Josselyn, one of the first chroniclers of New England natural history, said "The Indians Eat the Roots, which are long a boiling, they tast like the Liver of a Sheep"; while Dr. Edward Palmer stated that, although the squaws often dove for these rootstocks, they found it simpler to steal them from muskrat-houses in which they were stored.

White Water-Lily
Nymphaea odorata Ait.

Synonym *Castalia odorata*
Use cooked vegetable.

Dr. Huron Smith stated that the flower-buds of the common fragrant **Water-Lily**, which abounds from Labrador to Manitoba, south to Florida and Texas, are cooked and relished by the Ojibwa Indians.

Tuberous Water-Lily
Nymphaea odorata ssp. *tuberosa*

Synonym *Castalia tuberosa*
Use starchy vegetable.

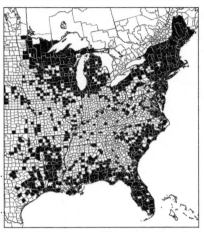

WHITE WATER-LILY *(Nymphaea odorata)*

The large white-flowered **Water-Lily**, with the flowers nearly odorless, the petals broadly rounded at tip, occurs in pond-margins and slow streams from southwestern Quebec to northern Ontario, thence southward to Maryland, Ohio, Indiana, Illinois, and Arkansas. Along its rootstock it bears egg-shaped or rhomboid brown tubers up to 3 or 4 inches long. These are freely broken off by wading among the plants late in the season and come to the surface in great quantity. In view of the general use of tubers and seeds of African members of this genus those of our own should be investigated. In his great volume, *The Waterlilies* (Carnegie Inst. Wash. 1905) Conard summarizes the uses as follows: "The use of waterlilies for food and ornament among the ancient Egyptians has already been referred to. This still continues to some extent in Egypt, but, on the West Coast of Africa, *Nymphaea* seeds constitute an important article of food. Travelers describe seeing the native women and children coming in at evening to the villages laden with the ripening fruits. These are laid in heaps until all of the soft parts decay. The seeds are then easily washed out clean, and are dried and stored away. They contain so much starch, oil, and proteid that they should form a very nutritious diet. When dry the seed coat is brittle and the kernel slightly shrunken, so that the two are easily separated. The kernels may be ground into a kind of flour or may be boiled whole. The resting tubers, in the dry season, are almost solid starch, and are eaten boiled or roasted like potatoes. The species used in West Africa are *N. caerulea* and *N. lotus*. In Madagascar, *N. lotus* and *N. capensis* are similarly used, and the seeds of *N. gigantea* are eaten by the Australians. In Central America also waterlily seeds are used for food."

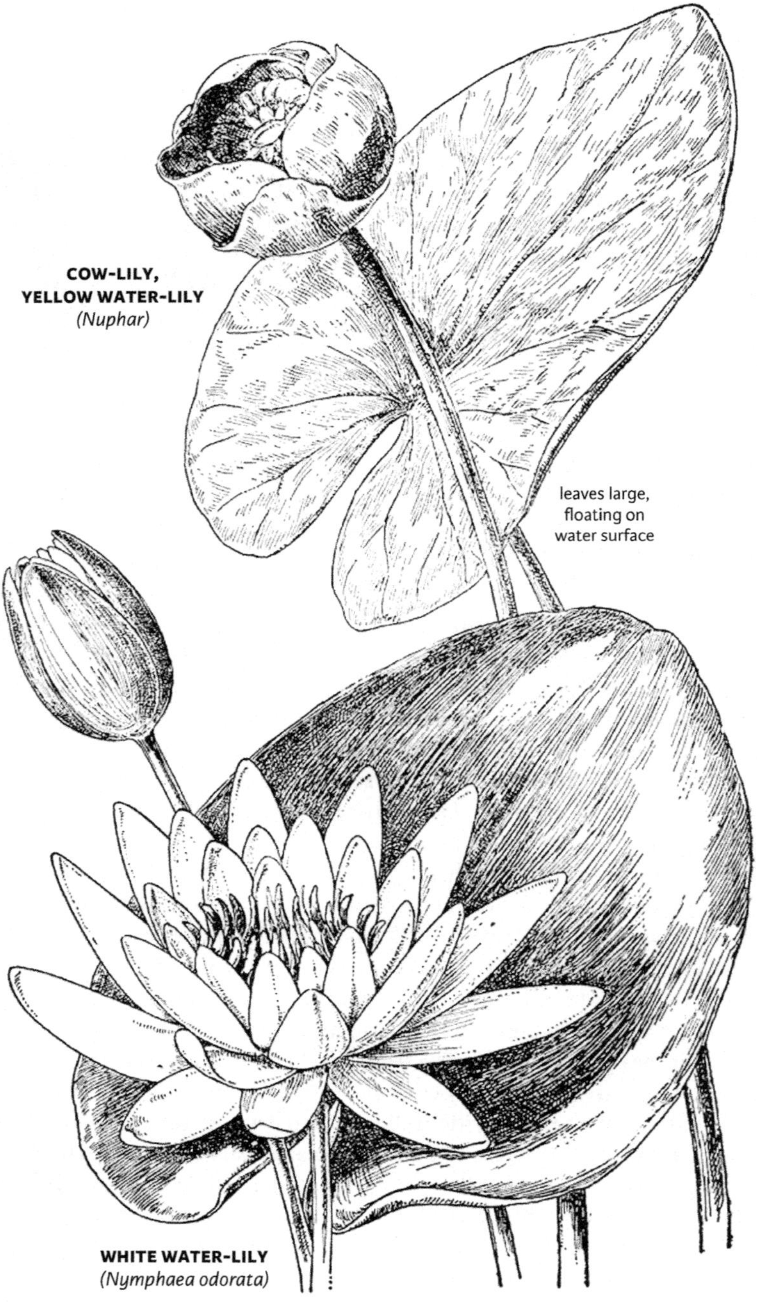

**COW-LILY,
YELLOW WATER-LILY**
(Nuphar)

leaves large,
floating on
water surface

WHITE WATER-LILY
(Nymphaea odorata)

Oleaceae OLIVE FAMILY

Ash
Fraxinus, seven species

Use pickle.

The winged fruits or "keys" of **Ash** are and long have been in vogue as a pickle in Europe and Asia. We have not met them in America, except as derived from European sources. Evelyn's 17th century recipe is detailed:

"Ashen-keys. Gather them young, and boil them in three or four Waters to extract the bitterness; and when they feel tender, prepare a Syrup of sharp White-wine Vinegar, Sugar, and a little Water. Then boil them on a very quick Fire, and they will become of a green colour, fit to be potted so soon as cold."

With a considerable variety from which to select we should certainly find some of our species quite as good for pickling as the keys of the European species.

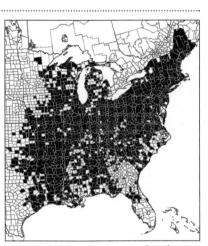

WHITE ASH *(Fraxinus americana)*

WHITE ASH
(Fraxinus americana)

samaras
(winged seeds)

Onagraceae EVENING-PRIMROSE FAMILY

Fireweed, Great Willow-herb
Chamaenerion angustifolium (L.) Scop.

Synonym *Epilobium angustifolium*
Uses potherb, asparagus, thickening for soup, tea.

The familiar **Fireweed** of the northern clearings has won some repute, especially in northern Europe and in western America, as a food plant. Various European writers speak with some enthusiasm of the use of the vigorous new shoots as a substitute for asparagus, and all agree that the leafy new stems make a wholesome and palatable potherb. In this connection it is interesting to note that the colloquial name of the plant among the French Canadians, at least of the Gaspé Peninsula, is "asperge."

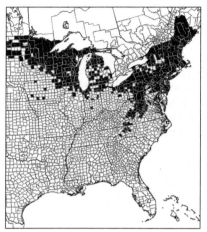

FIREWEED *(Chamaenerion angustifolium)*

Dawson states that the Indians of the Northwest scoop out the pith from the large stalks and cook this as a thick soup; and both Lankester and Johnson state that in England the leaves are used as an adulterant in tea.

River-beauty, Prostrate Willow-herb
Chamaenerion latifolium (L.) Sweet

Synonym *Epilobium latifolium*
Uses asparagus and potherb.

River-beauty, forming extensive carpets on the slaty or limy gravels of Labrador, Newfoundland and the Gaspé Peninsula, thence interruptedly across the continent and north to the Arctic, is closely related to the Fireweed, but has depressed, tufted stems, with whitish, fleshy, short and broad foliage and few terminal, very large and handsome rosy flowers. The new shoots are much more succulent than in the Fireweed and, although Unger, whose Germanic descendants are now thankful for much poorer fare, said that it makes "indifferent greens . . . , although sufficing for Northern Asia and Iceland," Mr. Erling Porsild, who knows Iceland, has long lived in Greenland and is familiar with other high-northern regions, finds it not "indifferent." He savs "The fleshy leaves are edible when cooked and in taste resemble spinach"; and the specialists on vitamins have recently discovered that spinach is wholesome food!

Evening-Primrose
Oenothera biennis L. and 4 or 5 related species.

Key-characters forming broad rosettes with many elongate, lanceolate or oblanceolate, entire or somewhat wavy-toothed, thickish leaves lying flat on the ground; the midrib conspicuous, whitish or reddish; root stout and fleshy, somewhat parsnip-like but more branching; flowering stems springing in summer from the winter-rosettes, becoming 1-4 feet high, bearing many crowded, alternate, entire leaves and showy yellow 4-petaled flowers followed by thickish horn-like, erect capsules.

Habitat and Range dry, chiefly gravelly open soils, Newfoundland to British Columbia and southward.

Season of Availability roots, late autumn, winter and very early spring.

Use root-vegetable.

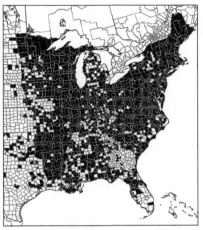

EVENING-PRIMROSE *(oenothera biennis*

The **Evening-Primrose** very early attracted attention in Europe, where it was introduced from North America and where it has been cultivated. The new plants produce rosettes and strong roots the first year, the flowering stems springing from the rosette the following summer and the fruiting plant dying in the autumn. Consequently, only the newly grown roots are available for food. The root is often disappointing to those who cook it, for if gathered too early in the autumn or too late in the spring it has a peppery, biting quality; but if caught at just the right stage of development, which has to be learned by experience in each locality, and cooked in two waters, it has a taste similar to that of salsify or oyster-plant, or some say like parsnip.

European authors state that the roots are used as salad, but the roots of our ordinary wild plants need cooking. It has also been stated that the young sprouts make a good salad but in our own experience they are altogether too puckery.

EVENING-PRIMROSE
(Oenothera biennis

FIREWEED
(Chamaenerion angustifolium)

Orchidaceae ORCHID FAMILY

Several of the orchids have bulbous or thick tuber-like roots and are said to have proved nutritious emergency foods. Owing, however, to the great rarity of most of the species, already fast becoming rare (and with many state or federally protected as endangered or threatened species), it is hoped that no one will experiment with these plants as food. In mediaeval times and even later the roots of most orchids were used medicinally, and at the present time in remote districts of the United States and Canada the roots, as "Nerve-roots," have a large reputation as nerve-tonics and heal-alls.

Caution Most members of the Orchid Family are legally protected due to their rarity. Also, plants of the various **lady's-slippers** (*Cypripedium*) can be irritating to the skin if handled.

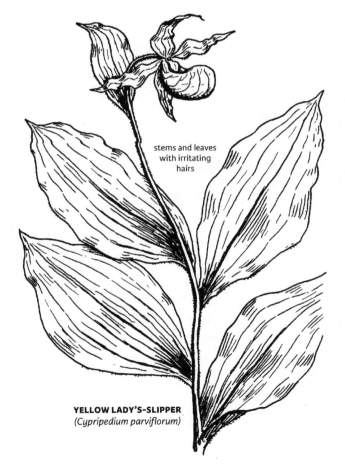

stems and leaves
with irritating
hairs

YELLOW LADY'S-SLIPPER
(*Cypripedium parviflorum*)

Oxalidaceae WOOD-SORREL FAMILY

Wood Sorrel, "Sour-Grass"
Oxalis (a dozen species)

Key-characters plants with clover-like leaves, having the 3 somewhat rounded leaflets notched at summit; the flowers with 5 spreading petals, whitish, pink, lilac or yellow; whole plant acid to the taste.
Habitat and Range in various habitats; the northern species, (*Oxalis montana* Raf., or "*O. acetosella*" of American authors) with pink and white striped petals, in cool woods across eastern Canada and south into the northern states; the lilac-flowered species (*O. violacea* L.) in open, rocky woods from Massachusetts to Minnesota and southward; the yellow-flowered, leafy-stemmed species (*O. stricta* L., etc.) in open soils throughout temperate North America.
Season of Availability late spring to autumn.
Uses salad, masticatory.

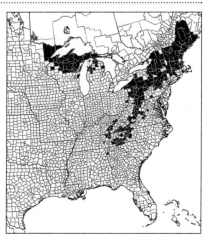

WOOD SORREL (*Oxalis montana*)

The familiar acid of the **Wood-Sorrels** is refreshing in warm weather and the leaves have long been popular with trampers and mountain climbers for their mildly tonic and refreshing properties. In small quantities the foliage is a wholesome addition to a salad, but, on account of the abundance of oxalic acid contained in the plant, it is unwise to eat the foliage in very large quantity. The woodland species is one of the several plants usually identified as the Shamrock and it was doubtless the European *Oxalis acetosella* to which Spenser referred when he wrote in the View of the State of Ireland during a Famine: "Out of every corner of the wods and glynnis they come creeping forth upon their hands, for their legs could not bear them; they looked like anatomies of death; they spoke like ghosts crying out of their graves; they did eat the dead carrions; and if they found a plot of water cresses or shamrocks they flocked as to a feast."

leaves
clover-like

WOOD SORREL *(Oxalis montana)*

Papaveraceae POPPY FAMILY

The poppies are unimportant in our wild flora. The European species, cultivated as ornamental plants, rarely become naturalized and the native yellow-flowered **Arctic Poppy**, *Papaver radicatum* Rottb., is unknown south of Labrador (and reported from the Rocky Mountains in the United States). The seeds of various garden poppies are used in Europe and Asia sprinkled on rice, cakes, etc.; and the seeds are now familiar, similarly used on pastries in this country. They are palatable and said to be important as a preventive of scurvy.

Passifloraceae PASSION-FLOWER FAMILY

Maypops
Passiflora incarnata L.

Use fruit.

The **Maypops** of the Southern States are familiar to the children of that region, the fruits, from midsummer to autumn, as large as a hen's egg and somewhat suggesting a lemon but with little nutriment. They are mildly sweet and acid, more eatable than edible.

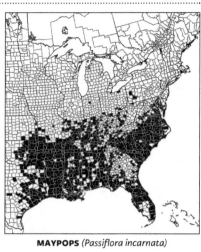

MAYPOPS *(Passiflora incarnata)*

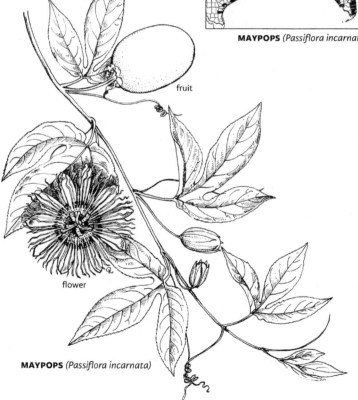

fruit

flower

MAYPOPS *(Passiflora incarnata)*

Phytolaccaceae POKEWEED FAMILY

Pokeweed, Pigeon-berry, Garget
Phytolacca americana L.

Synonym *Phytolacca decandra*
Key-characters tall, coarse herb, with large, alternate, entire, elliptic, pointed leaves, the principal ones often 6-10 inches long; the tall stems becoming purple and bearing opposite the leaves long-stalked, slender clusters of blackish-purple, 10-scalloped, flat berries.
Habitat rich, open soil of recent clearings, roadsides, and borders of cultivated fields.
Range common southward, extending north to the Great Lakes region and southern Maine.
Season of Availability young shoots, April (southward) to early June (and, when brought into the cellar, throughout the winter); berries, autumn.
Uses potherb, asparagus, pickle, coloring.

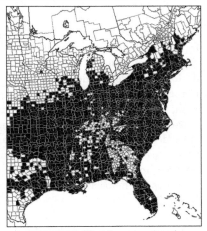

POKEWEED *(Phytolacca americana)*

Considering the availability of the **Pokeweed** and its popularity in southern Europe and in our own Southern States as a cultivated vegetable, it is remarkable how few people in the North are familiar with the plant. The new shoots when about six inches high are a desirable substitute for asparagus or spinach. Nearly all the earlier writers, as Manasseh Cutler, Jacob Bigelow, and the recorders of Indian food-plants, speak with enthusiasm of the Pokeweed. The peoples of southern Europe long ago imported the plant from America and have cultivated it as a garden vegetable; while in our own southern cities and in Philadelphia or in Chester County, Pennsylvania, the shoots are regularly displayed in the spring market. The only precautions necessary in using Pokeweed shoots are due to the facts that the large root (often as large as the fore-arm or shin) is poisonous, being highly purgative and sometimes used in medicine as a substitute for ipecac, and that the handsome, purple bark or rind of the mature stem, late in the season, is also poisonous. The young shoots do not have this purple coloring and are a perfectly wholesome and palatable vegetable. In cooking, however, it is a wise precaution to boil in two waters, throwing off the first water in order to dispose of any possible extract from the developing bark. One boiling is sufficient if only young sprouts are used. In the South the young shoots are made into pickles, very highly recommmended.

One of the most practical uses of Pokeweed is as a winter vegetable or substitute for asparagus, since large roots of the plant supply a phenomenally continuous crop of sprouts. In our experience we have found that twenty medium-sized roots (3 or 4 inches across) dug after the first heavy freezes of the autumn and chopped off to a length of 5 or 6 inches, then planted in a deep box of earth in a dark cellar, supply a family of six for three months with a weekly mess of "asparagus." The crowns bear a circle of almost innumerable incipient buds, and after the first shoots have been cut they are quickly replaced y a continuous series of new and equally strong shoots. By frequently watering the plants a succession of shoots is assured and these may be allowed to grow a foot or two high without developing the purple coloring. Peeled of their tough rind, cut into lengths and cooked and served as asparagus, these shoots are a decidedly welcome addition to the mid-winter diet. It is noteworthy that in France, where our species is cultivated, and in China, where a related species is used, the shoots are blanched before using.

The juice of the handsome 10-scalloped berries is a concentrated purple and is used for coloring frostings and candies; and some writers state that the berries are used in making pies and tarts. Others, however, state that the seeds are poisonous. The berries should, therefore, be used with caution. The purple juice has in the past been guilty of coloring other things than frosting and candy. Thus in 1783 Bryant wrote: "The Portugueze had formerly a trick of mixing the juice of the berries with their red wines, in order to give them a deeper colour; but as it was found to debase the flavour, the matter was represented to his Portugueze Majesty, who ordered all the stems to be cut down yearly before they produced flowers, thereby to prevent any further adulteration."

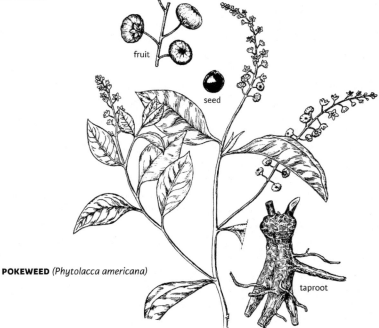

fruit

seed

POKEWEED *(Phytolacca americana)*

taproot

Plantaginaceae PLANTAIN FAMILY

Common Plantain
Plantago major L.

Use potherb.

The common dooryard **Plantain**, with broad leaves having strong string-like fibers running from the footstalk to the tip of the leaf, may be eaten as a potherb. Only in emergency would most people use it, for the fibers are tough. Otherwise it would not be so common.

Seaside Plantain, Goose-tongue
Plantago maritima L.

Synonyms *Plantago oliganthos, Plantago juncoides.*
Key-characters Plants perennial in clumps on rocks or in marshes and along shore, with fleshy leaves suggesting succulent and brittle grass-blades, with slender-stalked elongate spikes of insignificant greenish to bronze or drab flowers, the corolla papery or like thin parchment and capping the capsule, the latter opening by a cap at the summit which lifts off like a lid.
Habitat and Range maritime rocks, gravel and marshes, Labrador, Hudson Bay and Alaska, south to coast of New Jersey, marshes of Manitoba, and coast of California.
Season of Availability June to September.
Uses salad, green vegetable.

Seaside Plantain is not very generally known as one of the most available summer vegetables, but on the New England coast, especially by the fishermen of eastern Maine, and in Nova Scotia, where the plant is regularly gathered under the name of **Goose-tongue**, it is extensively used. The fresh leaves, freed from any shriveled or tough portions and washed, then cut and cooked like string beans, make a palatable vegetable. The more tender leaves dressed as a salad with oil and vinegar make a tasty dish, the natural sea-salts contained in the plant giving a pleasant flavor.

Brooklime, Water-Speedwell
Veronica americana Schwein. Ex Benth.
Veronica beccabunga L.
Veronica anagallis-aquatica L.

Key-characters fleshy plants, creeping at base and rooting at the lower nodes, with opposite, short-stalked to sessile, oblong, lanceolate or ovate toothed leaves an inch or two long; flowers in axillary, elongating, loose simple clusters, with spreading to loosely ascending flower-stalks, the petals united into a shallowly lobed somewhat spreading lilac to rosy or bluish or white corolla; stamens only 2; fruit a flattened and

rounded capsule, notched at apex.
Habitat Springy places, brooksides, ditches, etc.
Range one species or another from Newfoundland to Alaska, southward to North Carolina, Tennessee, Missouri, Oklahoma, Texas, etc.
Season of Availability spring and summer.
Uses salad and potherb.

Numerous European writers commend the **Brooklimes** as very desirable additions to the diet, especially as a preventive of scurvy and other malnutritional diseases. Bryant, in 1783, wrote: "The leaves are very pungent and bitterish, yet are eaten by many with bread and butter. The plant is in the highest esteem as an antiscorbutic, and is said even to surpass the Watercress; this may not be conceit only, by reason it has the pungency of the latter, and is much more astringent."

Other writers, including Chestnut, writing of western Indians, commend the plants as potherbs.

Speedwell
Veronica officinalis L.
Veronica chamaedrys L.

Use tea.

The common creeping **Speedwell**, with hairy stems and hairy, elliptical leaves, is said by Withering to be a possible substitute for tea, although he states that the **Bird's-eye Speedwell**, *Veronica chamaedrys*, which is becoming naturalized in America, makes a better tea.

SPEEDWELL *(Veronica officinalis)*

Platanaceae PLANE-TREE FAMILY

Plane-tree, Cottonwood, Sycamore, Buttonwood

Platanus occidentalis L.

Uses sugar, syrup.

Waugh stated that the Abenaki used the sweet sap for preparing syrup and sugar.

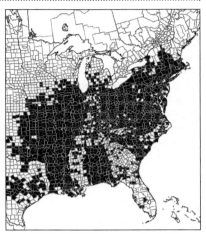

PLANE-TREE *(Platanus occidentalis)*

bark

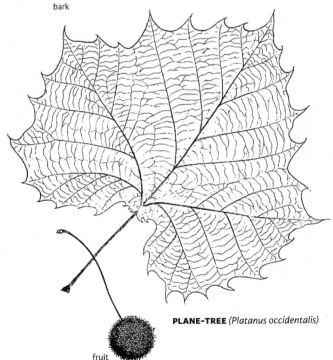

PLANE-TREE *(Platanus occidentalis)*

fruit

Plumbaginaceae LEADWORT FAMILY

Thrift, Foxflower
Armeria maritima (P. Mill.) Willd.

Synonym *Statice labradorica*
Key-characters a densely tufted plant, with soft and rather fleshy, linear leaves 2-6 inches long, the bases of the tufts covered with persistent, old, browned leaves; flowering stems somewhat wiry, erect, 2 inches to a foot or more high, terminated by a papery head of flowers 1/2-1 inch in diameter, and with a slender, reflexed, papery, tubular bract (like a closed umbrella) below the head; flowers with silvery-white or brownish papery calyx and delicately flesh-colored corollas.
Habitat and Range dry, rocky or mossy barrens and mountain-tops from Greenland south to northern and western Newfoundland and Mt. Albert, Gaspé Co., Quebec.
Season of Availability late spring and summer.
Use cooked vegetable.

Botanical travellers in Iceland have stated that there the **Thrift** (so closely related to our species as to be only doubtfully another species) is eaten; the bases cleaned and boiled in milk and then seasoned and dressed with butter. We have not tried our plant but its abundance, especially in northwestern Newfoundland and on the Labrador, should make the experiment an easy one.

THRIFT, FOXFLOWER *(Armeria maritima)*

Poaceae GRASS FAMILY

The Grass Family is the source of most of the important cereals as well as of sugar-cane and sorghum; and several of our wild grasses can be used as a source of grain-substitutes and sugar. Most of them, however, have too small grains or are too scattered to be of great practical value, especially since the separation of the husk from the grain is difficult without parching or soaking in lye. In recent years the use of fresh or dried grasses, finely ground, has been advocated for human foods; and all country boys (and some older ones) know the delight of nibbling the tender bases of the joints, freshly pulled off, of some grasses, or of nibbling the hard bulbous bases of Timothy. Before attempting to eat grasses on a large scale great care must be exercised to know the poisonous ones. For instance, one of the species of **Darnel**, *Lolium temulentum* L., has long been famous for its intoxicating grains (the specific name indicating this tendency); it is now believed that the intoxicating quality comes from infection of the grain by a parasitic fungus. The common **Velvet-grass** of fields, *Holcus lanatus* L., either fresh or wilted, often contains enough hydrocyanic acid to make the foliage seriously poisonous. Similarly, fresh foliage of **Sorghum**, so much cultivated for fodder, has poisoned stock, again through the hydrocyanic acid contained in the fresh leaves, although, when thoroughly dry, it is harmless and highly nutritious. Most people who pick the common weedy **Stink-grass**, *Eragrostis cilianensis* (All.) Vign. Ex Janchen, will not be tempted to eat it; they should not yield to morbid curiosity to taste so foul-smelling a grass, for either fresh or dry it is toxic to browsing animals. Furthermore, if there is any virtue in names, the cautious eater of grass will think twice before introducing to the family a pudding of ground *Bromus catharticus* Vahl. or its native relative, *B. kalmii* Gray.

In the present work we have not evaluated as human food the fresh leaves or the dried hay from our many hundreds of different species of nonpoisonous grasses.

··

Sand-reed or Beach-grass
Ammophila breviligulata Fern.
··

Synonym formerly confused with the European *Ammophila arenaria* (L.) Link
Key-characters the rigid or wiry grass of sand dunes, with long and arching, firm leaves which with their tips mark semicircles on the sand; the dense flowering spike whitish-brown, 3-10 inches long; the rootstocks rigid, very elongate and freely penetrating the sand.
Habitat and Range sand dunes, sand hills and other dry sandy areas along the coast from southern Labrador southward; and inland about the Great Lakes.
Uses emergency-food, nibble.

The wiry rootstocks of the **Sand-reed** are not likely to be sought for food; yet they would presumably serve in emergency. At least, Unger, after discussing the tropical Bread-fruit, said: "How far removed from those happy lands, where each Bread fruit tree constantly represents a ripening field of grain, are those regions of the earth where the hungering man is obliged to resort to the scanty nutriment of the root-stocks of the ferns, or, as in Iceland, to the root-stock of the sand-reed."

The leafy shoots of the Sand-reed are, when mature, so wiry and tough as to be uninviting; but note the following, from the account of Sable Island, far off the coast of Nova Scotia, by its botanical explorer, Dr. Harold St. John:

"Another equally important use of the Beach Grass is that of providing the fodder that supports the 'gang' of wild and semi-domesticated ponies, as well as the cattle. To one familiar with it in other places the Beach Grass would seem like very poor fodder. On the sheltered slopes of many of the dunes it grows . . . juicy and succulent, so much so that I used to pull young shoots and chew them as I plodded over the sand."

Sweet Vernal-grass
Anthoxanthum odoratum L.

Use tea.

The familiar **Sweet Vernal-grass** of fields and pastures, flowering in spring and early summer and giving off a delicious aroma when drying, is said to furnish a "decoction which is said to bear a considerable resemblance to tea."

SWEET VERNAL-GRASS (*A. odoratum*)

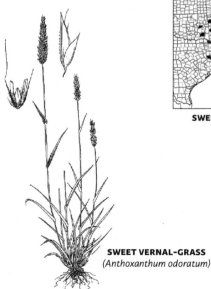

SWEET VERNAL-GRASS
(*Anthoxanthum odoratum*)

Cane

Arundinaria tecta (Walt.) Muhl. (Switch-Cane) and *Arundinaria gigantea* (Walt.) Muhl. (Large Cane)

Uses cereal and flour; cooked green vegetable.

Everyone in the flatter lands of the Southern States, northward on and near the coastal plain into Maryland, and up the Mississippi Valley to southern Ohio, southern Indiana and Missouri, knows canebrakes, impenetrable jungles of closely crowded coarse grass, the **Switch-Cane** growing 2 to 15 feet high, the **Large Cane** more tree-like and commonly 6 to 20 feet or, farther south, up to 30 feet high. Switch-Cane fruits in the spring from low and fertile stems arising directly from the strong rootstock. Individual colonies usually fruit only every three or four years. The grains are abundant and large; they have been recommended as good food. Large Cane is much more fickle about fruiting, but when, at long intervals of years, a colony does fruit, the crop of grains is tremendous. The following extract, based upon the life-long experience of the late Carl Mohr, distinguished student of the Alabama flora, are illuminating:

    "*Arundinaria macrosperma* [i.e. *A. gigantea*] . . . produces the panicles of its flowers in the axils of the branches at long and indefinite intervals of time. It is evident, therefore, that generations may pass by before the spectacle of such a canebrake in bloom is ever witnessed. For example, in the beginning of the summer of 1896 the inhabitants of Russell County were astonished suddenly to find the large canebrakes bending under the burden of their heavy, nutritious grains, which attracted large numbers of birds and beasts. The farmers regarded this as an entirely new plant, and, finding their stock grew fat upon the seed, stored away

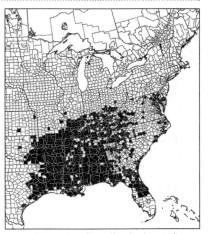

LARGE CANE *(Arundinaria gigantea)*

LARGE CANE *(Arundinaria gigantea)*

quantities of it, not only for future feeding, but under the delusion that if sown it would constitute a crop of small grain equal in value to any previously grown. But in the light of experience it is to be presumed that a period of not less than forty to fifty years has to pass before the propagation of this plant by sexual reproduction takes place. With the maturity of the seed the vitality of the plant is exhausted and the cane decays. In the succeeding season, from the spontaneous stocking of the ground with an abundance of seed, a new crop springs up. The seedlings produce no branches during the first year. These simple sprouts which are known as 'mutton cane', are tender and sweet and afford the best of pasturage."

The tender young shoots have been praised as human food, just as are young shoots of the closely related Bamboos of other regions; and, when the heavy fruiting comes in any particular colony, the harvest of grain should not be despised.

Slough-grass
Beckmannia syzigachne (Steud.) Fern.

Use grain.

The well known **Slough-grass** of low grounds from western Quebec to Alaska, southward to Illinois, Iowa, Kansas, New Mexico, etc., has abundant small grains free from the husks. Coville and others enumerate it among the various pinoles or parched seeds used by northwestern Indians.

Sandbur or Bur-grass
Cenchrus, 4 species.

Uses breadstuff, cool drink.

The universally despised **Sandburs**, grasses of warm and temperate regions (especially in sand), with a finger-like spike of very prickly burs from a quarter of an inch to nearly an inch in diameter, are familiar to all who have got the burs stuck in their clothes or working into flesh or fiercely clinging to the fingers. They are the last thing one would think of as human food, and with us are considered very dangerous for grazing animals. It is, therefore, at least startling to read in Dalziel's account of Nigeria and Senegal, that *Cenchrus biflorus*, with "Inflorescence with hard bristles, forming burs, which stick to clothing and to animals" and which in West Africa, like its allies everywhere else, "is classed as a pest," can be eaten: "An excellent fodder grass, eaten by all stock at all stages, even when seeding, in spite of the prickly involucres, and when dry. The seeds are edible and are collected by the Tuaregs, etc., for use as food; a cooling drink is also made of them. Elsewhere in scarcity, they are pounded and eaten raw, made into porridge . . . or mixed and cooked with other foods."

Dalziel does not tell how to handle the burs; the enthusiast might try singeing them in hot ashes before grinding. As compared with most of our species the burs of the African *C. biflorus* are not very fierce. It would surely be surprising if the insinuating ways of Bur-grass were its innocent method of inviting us to eat it!

Job's-tears
Coix lacryma-jobi L.

Use breadstuff.

The old fashioned garden plant, **Job's-tears**, a broadleaved annual grass with long inflorescences consisting of long-stalked, globose to ovoid, whitish bead-like fruits, with tufts of sterile scales, spreads to waste ground southward. In 1783 Bryant wrote of it: "This plant is cultivated in Spain and Portugal, for the use of the poor inhabitants in the time of scarcity, the seeds being then ground, and made into a sort of bread."

Crowfoot-grass
Dactyloctenium aegyptium (L). Willd.

Key-characters a weedy grass, with stems creeping at base and rooting at the lower joints, and terminated by a cluster of 2-6 finger-like 1-sided spikes 1-2 inches long with little scaly sharp-pointed florets crowded in 2 rows; grain, when ripe, reddish brown, covered by a loose, wrinkled coat.
Habitat door-yards, cultivated land and roadsides.
Range common in the Southern States, extending north, rather locally, to Massachusetts and Illinois.
Season of Availability late summer and autumn.
Use flour.

Various writers tell of the use of this diminutive grain by the Arabs, who gather the spikes or small "ears", dry them thoroughly, beat out the grains and grind them for bread or porridge; and Dalziel, writing of the *Useful Plants of West Tropical Africa*, says: "The seeds are collected by nomads, and by others in scarcity, and ground up to make porridge."

Crab-grass, Finger-grass, Twitch-grass
Digitaria sanguinalis (L.) Scop.

Use grain or cereal.

The common and very troublesome weed of sandy garden soil throughout the southern and often in the northern states, known variously as **Finger-grass, Crab-grass, Twitch-grass**, etc., is cultivated, according to Loudon, "in the cottage gardens in Poland," the seeds being used as a substitute for rice. Unger states that these "Manna Grits" furnish a wholesome and palatable nutriment and that the plant "is cultivated here and there on poor, sandy soils." Surely, if the ubiquitous Crab-grass, which is so unwelcome on "poor, sandy soil," can be made to yield a novel breakfast-food, many a discouraged farmer will become happy.

CRAB-GRASS *(Digitaria sanguinalis)*

Barnyard-grass, Cockspur-grass
Echinochloa [about 6 species including *E. crus-galli* (L.) Beauv., *E. muricata* (Beauv.) Fern., and *E. walteri* (Pursh) Heller].

Key-characters coarse annual grasses, with the leaf broad and ribbon-like and having a prominent pale midrib; cluster of fruits rather dense, made up of finger-like spikes and usually bearing long bristles (awns) from the tips of the husks (glumes).
Habitat *Echinochloa crus-galli* in barnyards and manured soils, a weed in cultivated fields; *E. pungens* chiefly on shores and in sloughs; *E. walteri* on the upper borders of salt marshes or in brackish ditches or sloughs.
Range *E. crus-galli*, a cosmopolitan weed; *E. muricata*, Maine to Minnesota and southward; *E. walteri*, Atlantic coast north to Massachusetts and locally inland; other species westward to the Great Plains and southward into Mexico.
Season of Availability mid-summer to autumn, the seeds falling promptly, so that care must be taken to catch the crop before it is overripe.
Use meal.

BARNYARD-GRASS *(E. crus-galli)*

The seeds of the **Cockspur-grasses** are half as large as Canary-seed, of a similar flattened egg-shape and lustre, readily separating from the husk by battering or winnowing. According to Kephart the western Indians use these seeds in quantities, parching them and grinding them to meal which has a good flavor. The plants are so abundant and the seeds so easily obtained that they are worth attention. A closely related species, **Japanese Millet**, *E. frumentacea* Link, is cultivated for food in the East Indies.

Goose-grass, Yard-grass
Eleusine indica (L.) Gaertn.

Use flour.

The low tufted (not creeping) annual of door-yards and waste ground, from Massachusetts to South Dakota and south into the Tropics, with 1-sided finger-like spikes crowded at the summit of the culm and resembling those of the preceding but with blunt florets, is also said by Dalziel to furnish good seeds for a porridge in times of scarcity.

Quack-grass, Couch-grass, Witch-grass, Dog-grass, Quick-grass
Elymus repens (L.) Gould

Synonym *Agropyron repens*
Key-characters an extensively creeping grass, with slender, wiry, white rootstocks tenaciously rooting at the joints; leaves flat, dark green; the slender, erect stalks terminated by an erect, finger-like spike made up of smaller spikes (spikelets) about 1/2 inch long and set in alternate notches of the axis.
Habitat fields, seashores and open ground, especially troublesome and vigorous as a weed in cultivated ground.
Range too common in the Northern States, Canada and Newfoundland.
Season of Availability whenever it can be dug.
Use flour.

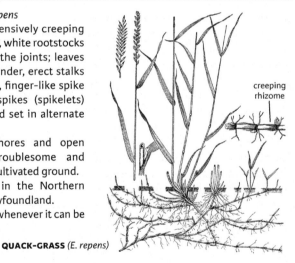

creeping rhizome

QUACK-GRASS (*E. repens*)

The ubiquitous **Quack-grass or Witch-grass** (with scores of other colloquial names) is usually known merely as a persistent and obnoxious weed, most difficult to eradicate and completely eating up the good of the land; but it was shown in the 18th century that it might be eaten if one cared to utilize it. Thus the British botanist, Withering, wrote: "The roots dried and ground to meal, have been used to make bread in years of scarcity."

Floating Manna-grass, Floating Meadow-grass
Glyceria, several species.

Key-characters leaves very narrow and elongate, often floating on the surface of shallow water; flower-cluster (inflorescence) long, with the many slender, flattened, finger-like spikes silvery green, 1/2-1 in. long, and closely ascending on the branches.
Habitat margins of ponds, streams and pools, or in inundated swamps.
Range several species [*Glyceria fluitans* (L.) R. Br., *G. borealis* (Nash) Batchelder, *G. septentrionalis* A.S. Hitchc., etc.] throughout temperate America, from Newfoundland to British Columbia and southward.
Season of Availability summer, when the seeds are ripening, taking care to harvest them promptly since they fall quickly.
Uses flour, thickening for soup.

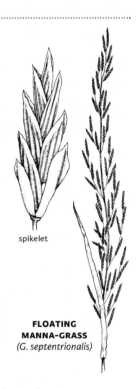

spikelet

FLOATING MANNA-GRASS
(*G. septentrionalis*)

In various parts of Europe the seeds of the **Manna-grass** have been considered a delicacy as a thickening for soups and gruels; and, according to Mrs. Lankester, the flour from these seeds makes a bread little inferior to wheaten bread. Our American representatives of the European species are very abundant, fruiting freely from June to August. Those who wish to gather the seeds will do well to profit by the Indians' experience in gathering the seeds of wild rice, paddling among the plants and beating off the seeds.

The following account by Bryant, in the 18th century, indicates the esteem in which Manna-grass has been held:

"These seeds are not regarded here [in England] as esculent grain, but in Poland they are yearly collected, and sent into Germany and Sweden, where they are sold by the name of Manna Seeds, for the use of the table of people of the first rank, and are much esteemed for their agreeable and nourishing quality. Linnaeus affirms, that... 'the grain itself will fatten Geese sooner than any yet known.' The poorer sort of people too might collect the seeds for sale as they do in Poland, for if they are so pleasant and agreeable at the tables of the German and Swedish gentlemen, why should they not be so at those of the English? The plant grows prodigiously plentiful... and in the middle of a hot day, I have seen the spikes quite covered with a brown substance, as sweet as sugar.'"

Strand-Wheat, Sea-Lyme-grass
Leymus mollis (Trin.) Pilger

Synonym *Elymus arenarius*
Key-characters coarse, whitish grass of sea-beaches and lake-shores, with flat, whitish, stiff leaves becoming strongly inrolled at tip, and dense finger-like, coarse spikes 3-8 inches long; the husks (glumes) of the spike 1/2-1 inch long; grain resembling an oat, 1/3-1/2 inch long.
Habitat and Range sea-beaches and strands of northern regions, from Arctic America southward in abundance to the Gulf of St. Lawrence, thence locally to Penobscot Bay, Maine, and very locally to Cape Cod; on the Pacific coast to California; also about Lake Superior.
Season of Availability grain ripe in August and early September.
Use flour.

Ever since the eleventh century the **Strand-Wheat** has formed a staple cereal of the Icelanders, one of their earliest sagas describing how they gathered the spikes (or ears) and loosened the grains by parching over a fire; and botanical travellers in Iceland a century ago described how the older inhabitants refused the imported wheat flour, preferring their own native *Melr*. About the shores of the Gulf of St. Lawrence and the Straits of Belle Isle the plant often occurs in such profusion that is might easily be gathered for use.

The Strand-Wheat should not be confused with the superficially similar **Sand-reed** or **Psamma-grass**, *Ammophila*, which abounds on sand dunes, but rarely on beaches, of the Atlantic coast. The Sand-reed has more slender leaves, the summit of its flowering stem is perfectly smooth, the summit of the stem in the Strand-Wheat being velvety; and the glumes and seeds of the Sand-Reed are much smaller.

Other species of Lyme-grass have been noted as used for bread-making by the Indians. They have the grain so hidden in long bristly glumes as to be not wholly available except in emergency.

Mountain-Rice
Oryzopsis asperifolia Michx.

Key-characters a tufted grass with many stiff, broad, evergreen, basal leaves about 1/3 inch wide and a foot or two long, usually dead and dry toward the tip; fruiting culms ½ to 1-1/2 feet high, rather stiff, terminated by a contracted cluster consisting of a few fruits, each 1/3-1/2 inch long; one of the husks terminated by a long, deciduous bristle.
Habitat dry woods and thickets.
Range western Newfoundland westward across Canada and south into the northern states.
Season of Availability late May to July.
Use flour.

More than a century ago the botanical explorer, Pursh, was so impressed by the **Mountain-Rice** that he wrote: "I . . . consider it worth the attention of farmers, as the considerable large seeds contain the finest flour of any grain I know!" The grains fall very quickly and the plants are rarely abundant.

Millet
Panicum miliaceum L.

Use grain or cereal.

The oriental **Millet** is so unimportant an element in our flora as to be almost negligible. The grains, often sold as "Canary-seed," are frequently swept up and carried to town dumps where a few plants can generally be found. The Millet has not been an important food of Europeans in recent times; but it supports vast populations of India and southern China, especially when the rice crop fails, and in ancient times it was an important cereal of the Mediterranean region.

Canary- or Bird-seed-grass
Phalaris canariensis L.

Uses flour, green vegetable.

Canary-grass, an erect annual, with a whitish-green to -drab, close ovoid head of flowers an inch or two long with grains nearly a quarter of an inch long, is familiar to all who have canaries. It was stated by Bryant that "In its native country the inhabitants grind it into meal, and make a coarse sort of bread with it". Canary-grass is common in waste places and about dumps, derived from sweepings. It should be easy to try it. Ochse states that in Java "the young tender plants . . . are very often gathered and eaten, raw or steamed, as lalab [mixed leaves, fruits, flowers or roots to be eaten] with rice."

Reed
Phragmites australis (Cav.) Trin ex Steud.

Key-characters a very coarse grass, commonly growing 6-10 feet high, with strong, cylindric, conspicuously jointed stem (reeds) about 1/2 inch in diameter; leaves about 1 in. broad, suggesting leaves of Indian-corn; flowers in a terminal, plume-like cluster, made up of innumerable small, bronzy flowering tufts (spikelets) which bear white hairs within. **Habitat** shallow water, ditches and wet bogs, either in fresh or brackish situations,

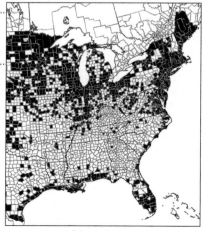

REED (*Phragmites australis*)

or often at the borders of salt marshes; in the interior oftenest in limy regions.

Range   Prince Edward Island and eastern Quebec, westward across the continent, and south to the Gulf of Mexico; rather local.

Season of Availability early spring, for the young shoots for pickling; late spring and early summer, before blooming, for the sweet flour.

Uses pickle, meal, confection, root-vegetable, potherb.

REED
(Phragmites australis)

The English botanist, Mrs. Phoebe Lankester, stated that the young shoots cut from the roots, especially where not exposed to light, make an excellent pickle.

Palmer, Coville and other students of Indian foods describe the preparation of the Reed for a confection. The stems are gathered early in the summer, before the blooms appear, and at that time are succulent and rich in starch and sugar. They are dried in the sun and when brittle are ground or beaten into flour; the finer part sifted out, and moistened slightly to make a gummy mass, which is roasted before the fire until it swells and browns slightly, and then eaten like taffy or marshmallows. Early explorers in our Southwest also told of the Indians eating the strong rootstocks of the Reed just as they dug them from the ground, preferably roasted or boiled like potatoes. As Mr. and Mrs. "Wittrock point out, an area of Reed, like the vast one seen from the trains in crossing northern New Jersey, could be "a source of food throughout the year. During the winter the rhizomes can be dug and boiled as potatoes; in the early spring the shoots that push up from the marshland can be prepared as we cook asparagus; the partly unfolded leaves can be cooked as a pot herb; finally, the large panicle of grain can be harvested for seed. The kernel is small and is coated with a dull red hull which is most difficult to remove, but the seed contains nutritious food materials rated between wheat and rice. The Indians did not remove the hull, but cooked the whole grain into a reddish gruel which was wholesome as a food, though not too appetizing in appearance."

Fox-tail Grasses

Setaria [including *S. italica* (L.) Beauv., *S. pumila* (Poir.) Roemer & J.A. Schultes, and *S. viridis* (L.) Beauv.]

Key-characters fruits in dense, finger-like, "fox-tail" spikes, with long, stiff bristles projecting beyond the seeds.

Habitat the commonest species are weeds of barnyards, roadsides and cultivated fields (*Setaria pumila, S. viridis,* etc.), one of the species (*S. italica*) being the common fodder

plant known as Hungarian Grass, German Millet, etc.; some native species along borders of salt marshes from Massachusetts southward and inland in low ground.
Range the common species cosmopolitan weeds.
Season of Availability late summer and early autumn, the seeds falling easily so that care must be taken to gather them promptly.
Uses meal, conserver of other foods.

The abundance of these grasses and the ease with which their fruit is gathered make them available for food, although the seeds are rather small and need to be parched to separate the husk. According to Bryant, in 1783, *Setaria italica* "is much cultivated in Italy, and some parts of Germany, where they make puddings of the seeds, and also boil them in most of their soups and sauces."

The spikes of **Fox-tail Grasses** have long and persistant bristles which, on drying, become somewhat stiff and scratchy. The following item from the Kew Bulletin of 1928 indicates a novel use for them:

FOX-TAIL GRASS (*S. viridis*)

"*Setaria verticillata* as a preventative of rats.—The following interesting note, on the method adapted by the Wasakuma tribe of the Shinyanga District to protect their corn-stores from rats has been communicated to us by the Director of Agriculture, Tanganyika Territory, who received it from the District Agricultural Officer, Shinyanga.

'The native food stuffs such as millet and maize are stored in large Lindos or circular grain stores made from mtama stalks or long grass, plastered with cow-dung, and built either inside the houses or under a separate roof. The Lindos are raised 2 to 3 ft. from the ground on stones and vary in size according to the wealth in grain of the owner.

'Over the top of the grain in the open mouths of the Lindos, the Wasakuma place the dried spikes of a grass called by them Makalamatta, or in Swahili, Marramatta. The bristly spikes wrap themselves around the fur of the rats and make themselves so unpleasant to the rats that they do not attempt to get at the grain below.'

"Specimens of this grass accompanying the above note have been determined as *Setaria verticillata* P. Beauv. It is the reversedly barbed bristles which become rigid at maturity that serve to fix the spikes to the fur of the rats."

Drop-seed Grass
Sporobolus cryptandrus (Torr.) Gray, and other species.

Use flour.

The **Drop-seed Grasses** are nearly unique in having their tiny grains free from the adherent husks which make most wild grasses unattractive as sources of grain. According to Vestal and Schultes, the Kiowa Indians beat out the easily removed but tiny grains and, after parching them, grind them into flour. The grains are so small that ordinarily the return from a colony of the grass must be relatively scanty.

Wild Rice, Water-Rice, Indian Rice, Water-Oats
Zizania aquatica L. and *Zizania palustris* L.

Key-characters broad-leaved grass of pond-, lake-, or river-margins, with long, broom-like flower-cluster, bearing staminate (pollen-bearing) flowers below, and pistillate (seed-bearing) flowers toward the summit of the cluster; fruits awl-shaped, nearly cylindric, about half an inch long, with the loosely rolled husk bearing a long bristle at tip.
Range at low altitudes, New Brunswick to Manitoba and southward; especially abundant in the Great Lakes and upper Mississippi region.
Season of Availability mid-summer and early autumn; the fruits dropping very quickly so that the crop must be gathered without delay, the Indian method being to paddle among the plants, beating the

WILD RICE (*Zizania*)

seeds out into their canoe-bottoms. In Radisson's account in 1668 occurs the following picturesque description:
"Our songs being finished we began our teeth to worke. We had there a kinde of rice, much like oats. It growes in the watter in 3 or 4 foote deepe. There is a God that shews himselfe in every countrey, almighty, full of goodnesse and ye preservation of those poore people who knoweth him not. They have a particular way to gather up that graine. Two takes a boat and two sticks, by which they gett ye eare downe and gett the corne out of it. Their boat being full, they bring it to a fitt place to dry it; and that is their food for the most part of the winter, and doe dresse it thus: ffor each man a handfull of that they putt in the pott, that swells so much that it can suffice a man."
Uses cereal, flour, soup.

Few American plants (except, of course, those which, like the potato and maize, have become staple crops) have attracted more attention from the explorer and historian than **Wild Rice**, because of its conspicuous habit, its abundance, its peculiar use by the Indians, and its present use as a cereal. Some of the tribes of the Middle States and Canada depended through a great part of the year almost entirely on Wild Rice for food. More than once has extended effort been made to introduce this food into modern civilization, but owing to the great expense of harvesting the crop, as compared with the ordinary field-cereals, and because of the practical impossibility of any form of cultivation, the attempts have been futile. For a detailed discussion of the history, cultivation, and many other details concerning Wild Rice see the papers by Stickney, by Brown & Scofield, and, more recently the extended paper by Chambers.

The grain now has considerable sale in the markets of the Great Lakes cities and occasionally, at an almost forbidding price, in the more eastern cities. The Indian method of preparation was to dry the seed for a time and then to parch for half an hour or an hour (some authors say for days) in a basket or other receptacle over a slow fire, stirring constantly to keep the grain from burning; then cool, beat to remove the husks and winnow. Unless thoroughly washed before cooking, the grain carries a disagreeably smoky taste. The Indians used the grain for thickening soup, for bread-flour, and to cook with game; it is used today as a breakfast-food and as an accompaniment of meat.

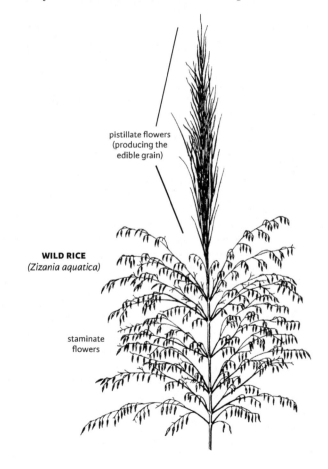

pistillate flowers
(producing the
edible grain)

WILD RICE
(*Zizania aquatica*)

staminate
flowers

Water-Millet
Zizaniopsis miliacea (Michx.) Doell & Aschers.

Key-characters tall subaquatic perennial grass, with stout creeping rootstock and long flat leaves ½ to 1-1/2 inches wide; stout culm bent or knee-like at the nodes; panicle lax, 1-2 feet long, with staminate and pistillate flowers separate but borne on the same branches, otherwise similar to Wild Rice (*Zizania*).
Habitat and Range swamps and margins of streams (often tidal), Texas to Florida, northward to southeastern Missouri and in tidal marshes to Maryland.
Season of Availability late autumn to early spring.
Use cooked vegetable.

We have not found any record of the use of *Zizaniopsis* rhizomes in America, but this perennial plant is so similar to the species of *Zizania* of China and Japan with stout rhizome that the difference is a technical one. The distinguished English student of Chinese plants, Dr. Hance, calling attention of the English and American gardeners to the use of the Chinese plant and admitting what every travelled American (including Mrs. Roosevelt) knows, that "Our American cousins are, as a rule, fonder, and I think better connoisseurs of vegetables than we English, and habitually like a larger choice of them at their meals", wrote of the Asiatic plant:

"Amongst the vegetables in esteem amongst the natives here is one called by them Kau-sun, and known to those Europeans who do not reject it, as some do, for the simple reason that it is Chinese, under the name of 'Cane-shoots'. As brought to market, this occurs in cylindrical pieces, of a white colour, 2-1/2 to 3-1/2 inches long, and 1 to 1-1/2 inch in diameter, tapering upwards into a conical point, and surrounded and surmounted by the leaves and culm, from which they are readily detached. In taste the raw shoot is not unlike a half-ripe nut; but it is never eaten uncooked, but by the Chinese is stewed with meat, and by foreigners cut longitudinally into two or three pieces, well boiled and served with melted-butter. Prepared in this way, it is, to my taste, one of the most agreeable and nicest vegetables I am acquainted with. It is difficult to describe its exact flavour; but it is, per-haps, nearest to that of unripe maize, as boiled and eaten by Americans under the name of 'green corn,' though it pos-sesses a peculiar richness and delicacy, to which I know no parallel in any other vegetable."

It is certainly probable that the vig-orous new tips of the rhizomes of *Zizan-iopsis* will be worth trying.

WATER-MILLET *(Zizianopsis miliacea)*

Polygonaceae BUCKWHEAT FAMILY

The **Buckwheat** itself, *Fagopyrum esculentum* Moench, and the **India-Wheat**, *F. tataricum* (L.) Gaertn., are extensively cultivated in the northern states and Canada, and occasionally persist about old fields and rubbish-heaps. They are not especially available, however, as wild foods since their occurrence is entirely sporadic.

Alpine Bistort
Bistorta vivipara (L.) Delarbre

Synonym *Polygonum viviparum*
Uses nut-like vegetable.

A small perennial abundant in Arctic regions, and extending south to New-foundland and to the mountains of New England and Colorado, with a thick tuber-like rootstock, which is in great demand among northern peoples for the almond-flavored nibble it furnishes. Kjellman states that by the natives of northeastern Siberia these roots are eaten as we would eat nuts and raisins; and the women while at work will have at hand a bowl of the roots of which they partake at frequent intervals. The spike has flowers at the summit but at the base bears quantities of small bulbs. The latter become purplish or reddish and, when ripe, fall off and take root, eventually producing the tuber-like rootstocks. Stripped from the spike they make a very attractive nibble, sweet, nutty and wholesome. Mr. Erling Porsild, who has lived much in northern lands, states that the rootstocks are very starchy but slightly astringent; they are best when cooked.

ALPINE BISTORT *(Bistorta vivipara)*

Mountain-Sorrel, "Scurvy-Grass"
Oxyria digyna (L.) Hill

Key-characters a succulent herb with tufts of long-stalked, round or kidney-shaped, acid leaves rising from a deep perennial root; the succulent stem a few inches to a foot high, bearing spire-like clusters of insignificant, reddish and green flowers, followed by thin-winged, reddish, round fruits 1/8 inch broad.
Habitat crevices of damp ledges.

Range from the alpine districts of the White Mountains northward, descending in western Newfoundland and Labrador to lower altitudes, and widely distributed in Arctic regions; also on the Rocky Mountains.
Season of Availability summer, while the leaves and stems are still tender.
Uses salad, potherb, purée.

The **Mountain-Sorrel**, which resembles a miniature rhubarb, with small rounded leaves, has always been highly esteemed in the Arctic regions as a "scurvy-grass", the new growth up to flowering time being eaten raw, when it tastes like a mild rhubarb and is a valuable addition to the diet. Cooked as a green the plant, we have found, is quite as good as the French Sorrel, Rumex Acetosa, and, like the latter plant, is especially attractive for a thick soup or puree. It is especially desirable as an ingredient of mixed alpine or arctic salads or potherbs, giving a pungent flavor.

The northern peoples have used the plant in still other ways: the Alaskan Indians are said to chop it with peppery cresses, while other tribes allow it to ferment as a sauerkraut. Kjellman tells of the Siberian Eskimo storing the fermented Sorrel for winter use.

Knotgrass
Polygonum aviculare L. and many allies.

Use grain.

The common weedy annuals of dooryards, shores, waste-places, alkaline depressions, etc., with freely branching stems, small narrow leaves, knee-like joints bearing thin, membrane-like and soon disintegrating sheaths and insignificant axillary flowers with small triangular or biconvex little nuts or "seeds" surrounded by the green to rose-tinged calyx, have supplied pinole or parched grain to various tribes of Indians. Not only the loosely spreading or depressed carpet-like species yield possible grains. Those from the erect *Polygonum douglasii* and other such species have been used.

On account of its lowly habit, with tough stems and its ability to withstand abuse, Knotgrass in Merry England

KNOTGRASS *(Polygonum aviculare)*

was used as a starvation-diet. Thus, Dr. Prior says: "The 'hindering knotgrass' of Shakespeare, (M. N. D. iii. 2), was probably so called from the belief that it would stop the growth of children, as in Beaumont and Fletcher's Coxcomb: 'We want a boy Kept under for a year with milk and knotgrass." ' No one seeking food is likely to eat it.

Smartweeds
Polygonum (or *Persicaria*), many species.

Uses seasoning, flour.

The leaves of the common **Smartweeds** are usually very peppery and make a quickly available seasoning in camp cooking. They should be used, however, with caution since they are very pungent and are apt to draw tears as quickly as cayenne pepper. Some species (including the **Black Bindweed** and **Climbing False Buckwheat**) have mild leaves and seeds, and the seeds of these species have sometimes been used by primitive races for making meal, which has the qualities of buckwheat flour. The grains are hard-shelled and with only a small amount of starchy matter.

Japanese Knotweed
Reynoutria japonica Houtt.

Synonym *Polygonum cuspidatum*
Key-characters erect shrub-like perennial herb 4-8 feet high, usually spreading underground and forming thickets of coarse smooth stems with widely spreading branches; nodes enlarged, sheathed by a papery cuff-like membrane; leaves stalked, rounded-egg-shaped, squared at base but abruptly pointed; flowers greenish-white, very numerous in branching axillary clusters, the calyx 5-parted.
Habitat and Range door-yards, neglected gardens, waste places and roadsides, Newfoundland and southern Canada, south to North Carolina and Missouri.
Season of Availability autumn to spring.
Uses root-vegetable, cooked green vegetable, salad.

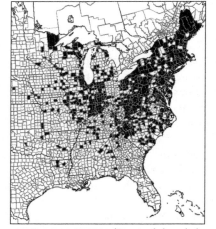

JAPANESE KNOTWEED (*Reynoutria japonica*)

When **Japanese Knotweed** first reached Europe from Japan a Belgian botanist in 1864, desiring to see if it had culinary value, dug some of the young rhizomes "two or three centimeters [an inch or two] under ground . . . we found them to have an agreeable flavor, not at all bitter; as to the young stems, at a height of only 10 or 12 cm., a flavor approaching that of sorrel but much less acid . . . cutting a quantity of the largest young stems, of a length of 15 to 20 cm. (half

underground, half above) we prepared
them in the ordinary way for vegetables
(boiled and dressed with butter, etc.)
and we are able to affirm de gusta: that
a plate of young stems of *Polygonum
cuspidatum* is a delicious article, as good
at least as asparagus, preferable to
chicory, and, above all, than sorrel."
Since we read this passage the young
stems (up to a foot or more high) have
been freely used. Steamed or boiled
for four minutes they became as soft
as cooked rhubarb and are delicious,
especially when chilled and dressed as
a salad.

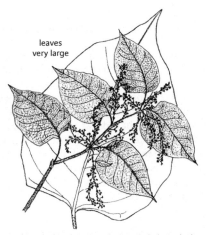

leaves
very large

JAPANESE KNOTWEED *(Reynoutria japonica)*

    Reynoutria japonica so rapidly mo-
nopolizes ground where it has got a
start that it should certainly be made
to recompense us by gracing the din-
ner-table.

    Another gigantic Asiatic species **Giant Knotweed** or **Sachaline** [*Reynoutria
sachalinensis* (F. Schmidt) Nakai (synonym: *Polygonum sachalinense*)], is superior
to the other. It is even taller and coarser than *R. japonica*, up to 12 feet high, the
stem angular-striate, the large heartshaped leaves up to a foot long, not abruptly
pointed, the flowers greenish. It was first cultivated in England about 1870 and
in America is rapidly spreading as does *R. japonica*. Sir Joseph Hooker, when
the plant was first cultivated in Europe, called it "by far the noblest species of
Polygonum known" but he added that "it has perhaps no rival for vigor of
growth and rapid multiplication by the root, which last quality has its drawbacks,
for it spreads widely, and obtrudes itself where not wanted, to the destruction
of its neighbours." In view of the present-day obtrusion and destruction of
neighbors by vigorous and rapidly reproducing types of man it is questionable
whether Sir Joseph's term "noblest" was well chosen!

    The leafy summits of young stems of Sachaline up to 2 feet high, cooked as a
potherb (boiled only a few minutes) are as good as or superior to French Sorrel.
As soon as the leaves become older they become unpalatable. "Rhubarb-sauce"
made from the peeled young stems, sweetened, is of superior quality, with a
suggestion of lemon-flavor. It should first be eaten in moderation until the
user is sure of its effect. Some people find it, like Rhubarb, slightly laxative.

Docks
Rumex (various species)

Key-characters stout plants; the leaves chiefly basal, commonly six inches to a foot or more in length and tapering or rounded to stoutish leafstalks; the point of attachment to the stem bearing a thin, papery and somewhat slimy, cuff-like membrane which, before becoming bruised, wraps around the stem; inflorescence a tall, wand-like cluster of tiny, insignificant green to purplish flowers, followed by fruits consisting of small seeds surrounded by thin, veiny wings.

These wand-like inflorescences, the sheathing membranous base of the leaf-stalk, and the smooth lower surfaces of the elongate leaves quickly distinguish the Docks from the common weed, Burdock, which has quite different uses. The Burdock has a large, heart-shaped leaf, which is downy beneath, a rank odor when bruised, and its inflorescence is a loose open mass of bur-like heads.

Habitats and Ranges several species both native in swamps and introduced into fields and roadsides, throughout temperate America, north to southern Labrador.

Season of Availability spring and summer until tough (see below).

Uses potherb, purée, breadstuff.

winged seed

The new leaves of all the **Docks** (about 15 species with us) are wholesome greens, cooking into a very soft mass and losing practically nothing in bulk, so that a small gathering makes a larger meal than most other greens. In order to take away the strong taste, the first one or two waters should be thrown off, and in order to prevent the greens being too watery, the final cooking should be done with as little water as possible. The common species with the leaves narrowed at base remain tender until the flowers are well formed, but the common roadside- and garden-weed, *R. obtusifolius* L., with the very veiny leaves round or heart-shaped at base, becomes very bitter after early summer.

The use of Docks as potherbs is very old among European peoples, and some tribes of American Indians used them. The Docks are gathered extensively by our Italian populace, but comparatively few of the other European stocks in America appreciate them. It is possible that they share the squeamishness of English women of the 17th century, described by Culpepper:

"Yet such is the nicety of our times

DOCK *(Rumex triangulivalvis)*

(forsooth) that Women will not put it in the Pot because it makes the Pottage black; Pride and Ignorance (a couple of Monsters in the Creation) preferring Nicety before Health."

The largest of our Docks, the **Patience-Dock or Patience**, *R. patientia* L., was long a popular garden vegetable in Europe and has been occasionally cultivated in this country as one of the "French Sorrels." The plant is thoroughly naturalized from eastern Maine to Newfoundland, but elsewhere it is less abundant than desirable. From its leaves a delicious puree is prepared.

The American Indians, especially in the West, used the seeds of various Docks in preparing meal; this would seem an eminently practical and sensible use, since the plant is very closely allied to buckwheat and it fruits in the greatest profusion. Meal prepared from Dock-seed should certainly be carefully tested.

Sorrels
Rumex (a few species).

Key-characters similar to the Docks but smaller; many of the basal leaves with blades like an arrow-head or spear-head, smaller than in the Docks, containing a sour juice. The Sorrels should not be confused with the Wood-Sorrels, *Oxalis*, which have clover-like leaves, with three leaflets.

Habitat and Range Sheep-Sorrel, *R. acetosella* L., with the basal lobes of the leaves usually wide-spreading and with slender, freely forking roots, common in dry, sterile fields and worn-out gardens; Garden Sorrel or French Sorrel, *R. acetosa* L., a stouter plant with stout rootstock and with the basal lobes of the leaves pointing back, thoroughly naturalized in fields, Newfoundland, Nova Scotia and eastern Quebec, locally elsewhere, especially northward.

Season of Availability spring and summer.

Uses salad, potherb, purée, seasoning, rennet, masticatory, acid drink.

The larger **Sorrel**, *Rumex acetosa* L., has long been in repute in Europe as a salad, potherb or seasoning, and as a rennet to curdle milk. In the French market the plant is abundant, although it is not now popular in England. Where abundant, the French Sorrel makes a desirable winter salad, the roots being boxed in the cellar, kept in a dark situation (the darker the better), watered and allowed to sprout. The self-bleached new growth of varying shades from white to pink makes a beautiful and delicious addition to salads. In his *Tour in Iceland*, Sir William Hooker says of this species: "A beverage is made by the common people, by steeping the plant in water till all the juice is extracted. This drink is kept some time; but soon becomes bad and putrid in warm weather."

The **Sheep-Sorrel**, *R. acetosella* L., is a popular nibble with children and is familiar to most trampers as a practical thirst-quencher. It is a readily available and attractive base for a purée, a small amount of the tender growth, after boiling, being mashed through a strainer, and added to a rice stock, milk or other stock, thickened with flour and butter, and seasoned to taste with salt and pepper. A small amount of the fresh leaves makes an unusual seasoning for fish, rice, or potatoes, or mixed with other salads.

The acidity is due to the presence of potassium oxalate, which, if eaten in excess, may be detrimental. Ordinary small nibblings of the fresh plant are quite safe and, as everyone knows, refreshing. When boiled the sorrels seem to be harmless. The recipe below has recently appeared in *The Herbarist* (no. 1, p. 29). It sounds attractive, and it is certainly easy to find the Sorrel.

"SORREL SOUP (for 6)

Wash Sorrel and put in saucepan with a little water {not covered). Cook slowly for about 1/2 hour. Put 4 cups of milk with small white onion {whole) in double boiler. Add 2 teaspoonfuls of butter and 2 tablespoonfuls of flour [thoroughly blended to avoid lumps] to the hot milk. Let stand, and add Sorrel and strain. Season. Use about a handful of the Sorrel."

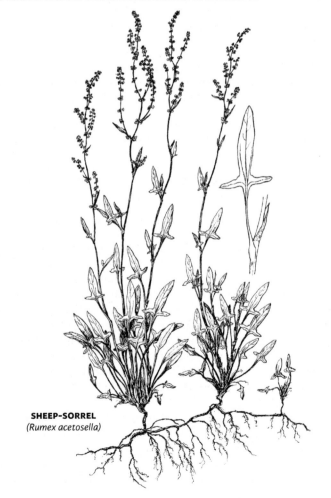

SHEEP-SORREL
(Rumex acetosella)

Pontederiaceae PICKEREL-WEED FAMILY

Water-Hyacinth
Eichornia crassipes (Mart.) Solms

Use potherb.

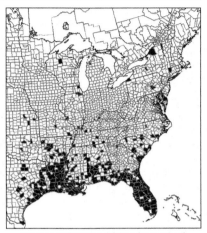

Water-Hyacinth, originally introduced from South America, has so multiplied in sluggish streams of the South, from Florida to Texas, north to North Carolina (rarely Virginia) and Missouri, that it often seriously clogs waterways. Everyone where it abounds knows it. Introduced into the Dutch East Indies it found a people who eat almost anything from beggar-ticks to castor-beans. They promptly welcomed Water-Hyacinth. Ochse tells us that "This beautiful plant, a native of Brazil, has . . . become a serious water-pest. In Java it was imported

WATER-HYACINTH *(Eichornia crassipes)*

in 1894; out of the Botanical Garden of Buitenzorg it has begun its victorious march through the East-Indian Archipelago." "The young leaves, petioles and inflorescences are eaten, steamed or cooked. . . When eaten raw this plant causes itching. This property disappears by cooking, though not entirely." Since the plant could well be called "victorious" Water-Hyacinth in the South, it will be a great advantage if it can be eaten.

Pickerel-weed
Pontederia cordata L.

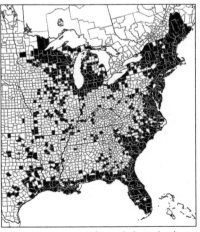

Key-characters a soft-stemmed herb of muddy or sandy margins of ponds and quiet streams, with a heart-shaped to arrow-shaped leaf borne near the summit of each of the thick flowering stems; flowers violet-blue, flecked with yellow, in a dense spike; fruits in a dense spike, each fruit wing-margined, about 1/3 inch long and consisting of a loose, baggy outer coat surrounding a solid starchy seed.
Habitat margins or shores of muddy or sandy streams or ponds.
Range throughout eastern America, northward into southern Canada.
Season of Availability late summer and

PICKEREL-WEED *(Pontederia cordata)*

early autumn, when the fruit is ripe.
Uses starchy nut-like seeds, potherb.

flowers and
fruit in spike

The fruits of **Pickerel-weed**, stripped
off the mature spikes are a pleasant
and hearty food. When tramping or
camping in the early autumn one can
secure much nutriment from them;
and it is wholly reasonable to suppose
that the dried fruits, stored for winter,
could be used as an acceptable and
novel cereal or bread-stuff.

The young, unrolling leaves of the
very similar *Monochoria* of southeastern
Asia are there a popular raw or cooked
vegetable. Everything but the root is
used. "On the markets there is a lively
trade in this vegetable." Certainly the
succulent stems and the young leaves
of Pickerel-weed should be tried.

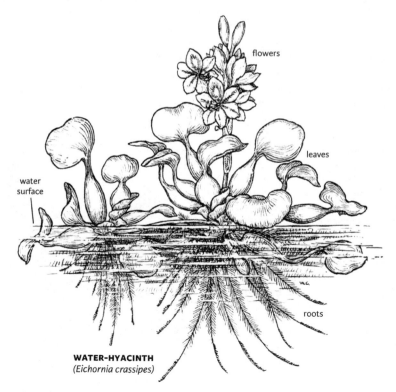

flowers

leaves

water
surface

roots

WATER-HYACINTH
(Eichornia crassipes)

Portulacaceae PURSLANE FAMILY

Purslane, "Pusley"
Portulaca oleracea L.

Key-characters and Habitat a depressed or matted, creeping annual herb of light soils, chiefly of gardens, with fleshy, jointed, freely forking, reddish-green or purplish stems; and very fleshy, narrowly wedge-shaped, reddish-green almost opposite leaves 1/2-2 inches in length; flowers sessile at the forkings of the stem, opening only in bright sunshine, with yellow petals; top of the seed-pod lifting off like a cap.
Range a common, though sometimes localized, weed throughout the United States and warmer parts of Canada.
Season of Availability summer and early autumn.
Uses potherb, salad, pickle, breadstuff.

The common **Purslane or "Pusley,"** made famous by Charles Dudley Warner, is so familiar that most people despise it as a mere weed. As a matter of fact, however, in many "victory-gardens" the crop of Purslane has more potential value for food than the ignorantly nursed or neglected planted crops. When cooked and seasoned like spinach, the tender young branches make one of the most palatable of potherbs, with little loss of bulk in cooking, so that a small patch of vigorous plants clipped of their new tips and allowed to sprout again is sufficient to supply a table throughout the summer. The fatty or slimy quality of Purslane is sometimes objectionable, but by chopping the cooked tips and then baking with bread-crumbs and a beaten egg this disagreeable quality in entirely disguised.

It is truly surprising how few sophisticated Americans appreciate the esculent qualities of Purslane, since our ancestors, both in America and in Europe, were fully cognizant of them. Thus we find the distinguished Manasseh Cutler, in the 18th century, stating that, as a potherb it is little inferior to asparagus, while in the 16th century John Gerarde wrote that "Rawe Purslane is much used in sallads with oile, salt, and vinegar." Others speak of it as a palatable and easily procured pickle. Thus the always delightfully concrete John Evelyn in 1706 gave these detailed directions:

"Lay the Stalks in an Earten-Pan; then cover them with Beer-Vinegar and Water, keeping them down with a competent Weight, to imbibe, three Days: Being taken out, put them into a Pot with as much White-wine Vinegar as will cover them again; and close the Lid with Paste, to keep in the Steam: Then set them on the Fire for three or four Hours, often shaking and stirring them: Then open the Cover, and turn and remove those Stalks which lie at the Bottom, to the Top, and boil them as before, till they are all of a Colour. When all is cold, Pot them with Fresh White-wine Vinegar, and so you may preserve them the whole Year round."

According to Dr. Edward Palmer, the seeds of this and related species are used by the southwestern Indians for making mush or bread, the plants being placed in large piles, dried, and then pounded to free the seeds. Be sure first to wash off all mud and sand.

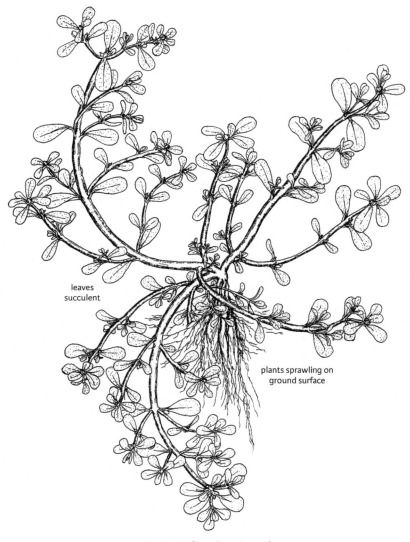

leaves
succulent

plants sprawling on
ground surface

PURSLANE *(Portulaca oleracea)*

Primulaceae PRIMROSE FAMILY

Pimpernel, Poor Man's Weatherglass
Lysimachia arvensis (L.) U. Manns & A. Anderb.

Synonym *Anagallis arvensis*
Uses potherb, salad.

Various European authors commend the **Pimpernel** as a potherb and they speak of it as a frequent ingredient in salads. Others, however, state that it is poisonous. We have not felt it worth experimenting with!

Sea-Milkwort
Lysimachia maritima (L.) Galasso, Banfi & Soldano

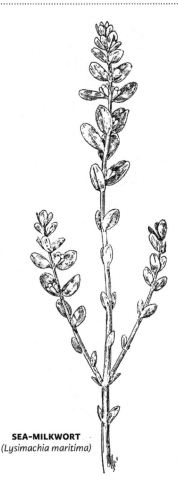

Synonym *Glaux maritima*
Key-characters a succulent plant of the sea-margin and of interior saline marshes, with simple to bushy-branched stems a few inches high; opposite, oblong, fleshy, dark green leaves about 1/2 inch long; pink-tinged, erect, axillary, bell-shaped flowers; and creeping rootstocks.
Habitat and Range saline shores south to New Jersey and to California and on alkaline areas of the interior.
Season of Availability early summer.
Use pickle.

Mrs. Lankester, writing in England, states that, "It is said that the leaves and stems of the plant make a good pickle after the manner of samphire." The great abundance of the plant along our northeastern seashores, especially from Cape Cod to southern Labrador, and the succulent leaves and stems of our large var. obtusifolia (commonly 5 inches, sometimes a foot, tall), invite experimentation.

SEA-MILKWORT
(Lysimachia maritima)

Potamogetonaceae PONDWEED FAMILY

Pondweeds
Potamogeton (various species, about 6 with fleshy rootstocks)

Use starchy vegetable.

It is stated by Johnson that the rootstocks of *Potamogeton natans* L. are farinaceous and edible. The farinaceous, new branches of the rootstocks of any of the larger species might prove edible (certainly the waterfowl are fond of them), but their habitat, at the bottoms of ponds and streams, makes them essentially inaccessible.

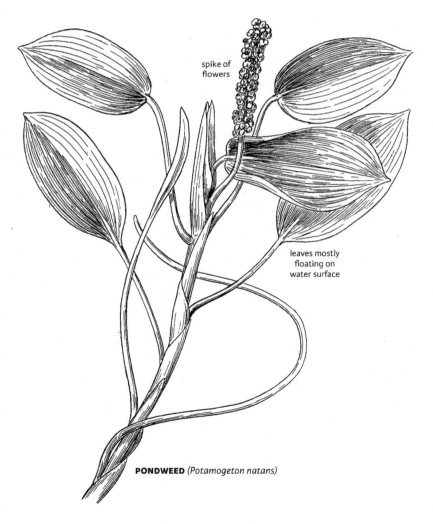

spike of
flowers

leaves mostly
floating on
water surface

PONDWEED *(Potamogeton natans)*

Ranunculaceae BUTTERCUP FAMILY

Marsh-Marigold, "Cowslip"
Caltha palustris L.

Key-characters a marsh plant of early spring, with round or kidney-shaped, succulent, green leaves closely scalloped around the margin, the leaf-stalk dilated at the base into a papery, sheathing portion (stipule); flowers orange-yellow, resembling buttercups, borne in leafy clusters on hollow stems which arise from among the leaves.
Habitat "They ioy in moist and marish groundes, and in watery medowes"— Gerarde. Especially in clay or limestone regions.
Range Newfoundland and southern Labrador to Alaska, south to South Carolina, Tennessee and Nebraska.
Season of Availability early spring (southward), summer (northward).
Uses potherb, pickle.

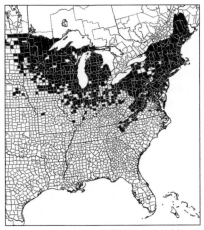

MARSH-MARIGOLD *(Caltha palustris)*

The **Marsh-Marigold**, or as it is more familiarly known in America, the "Cowslip" (not to be confused with the European Cowslip) has long been one of the most popular spring greens of New England. As early as 1784, the Massachusetts botanist, Manasseh Cutler, spoke of it as an esteemed potherb, and among New Englanders and in eastern Pennsylvania, at least, this verdict has been generally approved. In gathering the plant great care should be taken to include none of the poisonous species which occur in the same habitat, for the rich meadows where Marsh-Marigold abounds are the homes of the **White Hellebore**, *Veratrum viride* Ait. (see p. 57) and some of the deadly poisonous **Water-Hemlocks**, *Cicuta* (see p. 39), all of which, with ordinary care, are easily distinguished. The new leaves and stems of the Marsh-Marigold should be carefully picked over to exclude the stipules and mucilaginous bases, then boiled thoroughly for an hour or more, changing the water at least once and, if a mild potherb is desired, twice, since the first water extracts only part of the acrid principle which pervades the plant.

It is singular that the Europeans have so regularly looked upon the Marsh-Marigold as poisonous. Thus we find Johnson saying, "Turner, the old herbalist, recommends it for the toothache, but I would not advise anyone to apply it to that use who does not wish to blister his mouth, a result that would certainly follow"; and Henslow, writing on useful plants of Great Britain, states that several people have been poisoned by eating it. This dread of the European plant would naturally suggest that our American *Caltha* is distinct from the European species, but no distinctive characters between the two have been discovered. In order to test the question, Dr. Sidney F. Blake, while in England, secured a quantity of young Marsh-Marigold which was cooked at the house of the late Dr. Moss, the distinguished botanist of Cambridge, and subsequently Dr. Blake wrote home: "While visiting Dr. Moss at Easter I collected some *Caltha palustris* and had it cooked and then ate it. It certainly had no ill effects."

The only general use of the Marsh-Marigold in Europe is one that is also somewhat popular in America, the making of pickles from the flowerbuds. First soaked in salt water, then cooked in spiced vinegar, they are said to make a good substitute for capers.

Caution Do not eat Marsh-Marigold raw. The fresh plant contains the poisonous glucoside, helleborin, which is expelled in boiling.

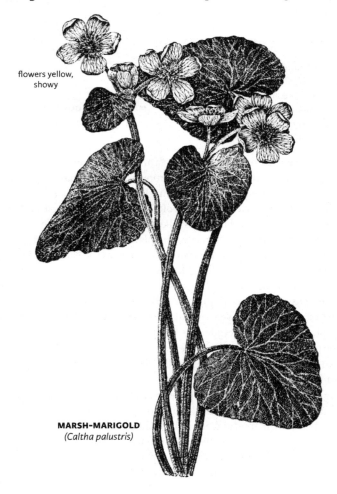

flowers yellow,
showy

MARSH-MARIGOLD
(Caltha palustris)

Bulbous Crowfoot or Buttercup
Ranunculus bulbosus L.

Uses starchy vegetable, relish.

Like other members of the genus, the **Bulbous Crowfoot** has a strongly acrid juice which is apt to cause blistering; but, as stated by Lightfoot, "not withstanding this corossive quality, the roots when boiled become so mild as to become eatable."

The round bulbs which have wintered over are in the spring surprisingly mild and sweet, with no more pungency than a somewhat strong radish, and when thoroughly dried they lose essentially all their acidity and become very sweet. As an emergency food they are worth remembering.

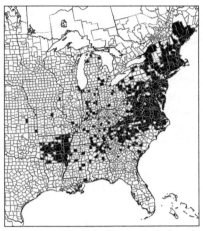

BULBOUS CROWFOOT *(Ranunculus bulbosus)*

Cursed Crowfoot
Ranunculus sceleratus L.

Use potherb.

In spite of its name and its strongly acrid fresh juice, the **Cursed Crowfoot** is said by European authors to have been used in emergency, the boiled plant being eaten as a spinach, care being taken to pour off the water by which the acrid principle, anemonol, has been extracted. Only in emergency would one try it.

BULBOUS CROWFOOT *(Ranunculus bulbosus)*

Resedaceae MIGNONETTE FAMILY

Wild or Yellow Mignonette
Reseda lutea L.

Use salad.

This rather rare weed, introduced from Europe and occurring occasionally on waste ground or by roadsides in the Eastern States, may be eaten when young as a salad, having the taste of cabbage.

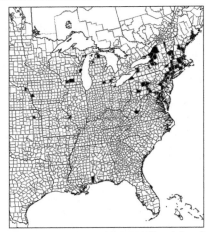

WILD OR YELLOW MIGNONETTE *(Reseda lutea)*

WILD OR YELLOW MIGNONETTE *(Reseda lutea)*

Rhamnaceae BUCKTHORN FAMILY

New Jersey Tea
Ceanothus americanus L. (and other species).

Key-characters low, straggling shrub, woody only at base, the branches dying back at the tips; leaves alternate, oval, on short stalks, very closely bordered with fine, bluntish teeth, pale below, dark-green above, having 3 strong ribs running from base nearly to apex; upper axils bearing long-stalked clusters of delicate, white flowers, the clusters in outline suggesting a bunch of grapes; fruit a 3-lobed pod inserted on a thin-edged disk.
Habitat and Range dry, open woods and rocky banks, central Maine to western Ontario, south to the Gulf.
Season of Availability summer.
Use tea.

NEW JERSEY TEA *(Ceanothus americanus)*

New Jersey Tea is probably one of our most famous of the native substitutes for oriental tea, and many writers speak of it as admirable, while others find it inferior. It contains no caffeine and is, therefore, not "bracing." According to a tradition at least, this tea was in great demand during the American Revolution. The learned Manasseh Cutler, writing in 1774, said:

"The leaves of this shrub have been much used by the common people, in some parts of the country, in the room of India tea; and is, perhaps, the best substitute the country affords. They immerse the fresh leaves in a boiling decoction of the leaves and branches of the same shrub, and then dry them with a gentle heat. The tea, when the leaves are cured in this way, has an agreeable taste, and leaves a roughness on the tongue somewhat resembling that of the bohea tea."

Porcher, writing from the South, speaks of this tea as "admirable" and says that the leaves must be dried in the shade.

The very similar *C. herbaceous* Raf., with leaves narrower and more elliptical, has presumably similar properties.

NEW JERSEY TEA
(Ceanothus americanus)

Rosaceae ROSE FAMILY

Service-berries, June-berries, Shad-bush, Sugar-Pear, Indian Pear
Amelanchier (about 20 species).

Key-characters trees or shrubs, with oblong or roundish, sharply' or coarsely toothed, slender-stalked, alternate leaves, and smooth grayish bark; flowers and fruits mostly in elongate, drooping clusters (racemes), solitary in a northern species; the berries on slender stalks, round to pear-shaped, red, becoming purplish or blue-black, with the conspicuous 5-toothed "blossom" (calyx-lobes) at the summit, the pulp juicy and sweetish, with 10 comparatively large seeds.
Habitat open situations or borders of woods, some species on rocks or gravels, others in swamps.
Range Newfoundland and southern Labrador across the continent, south to the Gulf of Mexico.
Season of Availability July, August, northward; May or June southward; the fruit in some areas not well developed or else blasted by a fungus, in others plump and juicy.
Uses fruit raw, cooked as sauce or in pies, or dried for winter use.

Few wild fruits of such excellent quality as the **Service-berries** are less known to the modern American, although by the Indians and the early European explorers of the continent the berries were among the most esteemed of our native fruits. In many localities the trees and shrubs do not fruit heavily or the fruits are distorted and spoiled by fungous diseases and insects; in other regions, however, the berries are abundant and should become well known. To the European taste the berries are best when made into puddings or pies, the thoroughly cooked seeds giving a flavor suggesting sweet cherry pie. The berries, especially if cooked first, are splendid for berry-muffins, yielding a rich almond flavor.

By the Indians the fruit was much used in the making of bread, being gathered in large quantities, beaten into a paste and then dried in cakes. This dried fruit was afterward mixed with the com-meal or the pemmican and, according to northern travellers, Sir John Richardson, Bourgeau, and others, the dried berries were used in puddings, for which use they "nearly equal Zante currants."

Chokeberries
Aronia, 3 species.

Key-characters slender, freely branching shrubs with alternate, oblanceolate leaves; the red, purple or blackish berries having the form of tiny apples about 1/3 inch in diameter, with the blossom (calyx-lobes) borne at the summit, the berries in flat-topped clusters, puckery.
Habitat sterile, dry or boggy places or in sterile thickets.
Range one species or another from Newfoundland to western Ontario and southward.
Season of Availability late summer and autumn.
Use jelly.

The raw berries have a good flavor but are very puckery, much as choke-cherries. It is stated, however, that the Indians used these fruits, destroying the puckery quality by cooking. They certainly yield a splendid, heavy and sweet jelly, dark-carmine and very solid. The berries are so very abundant and contain so much juice and such an abundance of pectin that it is pathetic to see the thousands of bushels of them go, every autumn, completely to waste. They could certainly be used to supply pectin which is often deficient in some fruits.

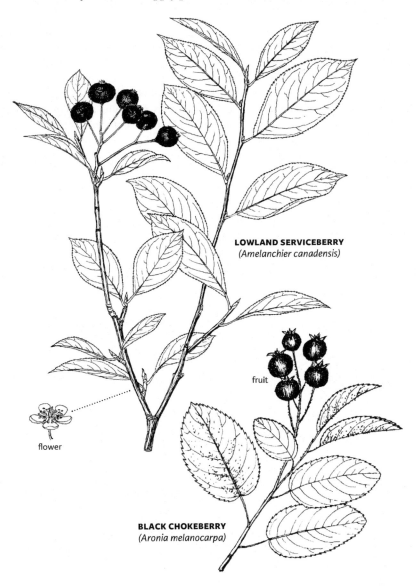

LOWLAND SERVICEBERRY
(*Amelanchier canadensis*)

fruit

flower

BLACK CHOKEBERRY
(*Aronia melanocarpa*)

Haw, Thorn, Thorn-Plum, Hawthorn
Crataegus (many species)

Uses jelly, marmalade.

(The species of **Haw** are very numerous—perhaps 100-300—and, because of our present very inadequate understanding of them, it is not yet possible so to define them as to make the distinctions clear to the amateur —certainly no professional understands them.)

The fruits of several species have a juicy pulp from which a delicious marmalade or jelly can be made. The quality of the fruit of the different species can, however, be determined only by experimentation, for all the fruits have large stones and only a minimum of pulp. The planted English Hawthorn has an inferior fruit, and the superior quality of some of the native American Haws was early recognized by Europeans, John Josselyn, as early as 1672, writing of "The Haws . . . very good to eat, and not so astringent as the Haws in England"; and Wood in his New England's Prospect going so far as to state that "the white thorne affords hawes as bigge as an English Cherrie, which is esteemed above a Cherrie for his goodnesse and pleasantnesse to the taste." The jelly from the better species of Haw requires comparatively little sugar.

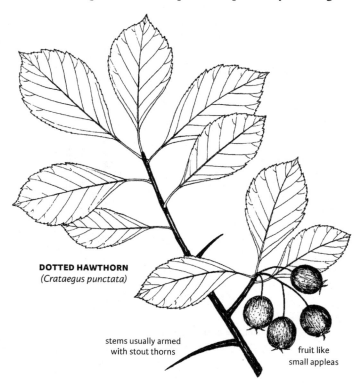

DOTTED HAWTHORN
(Crataegus punctata)

stems usually armed
with stout thorns

fruit like
small appleas

Shrubby Cinquefoil, "Widdy"
Dasiphora fruticosa (L.) Rydb.

Synonym *Potentilla fruticosa*
Use tea.

It is stated that the leaves of **Shrubby Cinquefoil** may be used as a substitute for tea. Those of some other species are brewed in country districts as a cure for diarrhea.

Strawberry
Fragaria virginiana Duchesne
Fragaria vesca L. (less desirable).

Uses fruit, tea, short-cake.

The wild **Strawberries** and their uses are so well known that they need no special discussion. The wild berries of *Fragaria virginiana* are vastly superior in flavor and richness to the cultivated berries. When people were not so much in a hurry the wild fruit was gathered in tremendous quantities for the table and for preserving. When the mother of the family was ready for the latter delicate process, the whole family took to the fields and clearings. The berries being small and readily crushed, great care was necessary not to include sticks, straws, leaves and buttercup-petals, for "picking over" was too difficult. The berries had to be picked free from the "hull" (calyx), and if the children all faithfully followed instructions, few "hulls" would get into the pails. Encouraged by pay of 3 cents a quart and the joy of a picnic-dinner out-of-doors, the picking went merrily, and it was a pretty poor family of pickers (at least in central or northern Maine) who could not return in late June or early July with half a bushel to a bushel

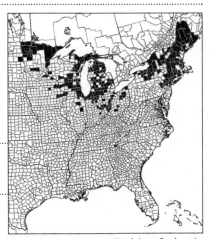

SHRUBBY CINQUEFOIL *(Dasiphora fruticosa)*

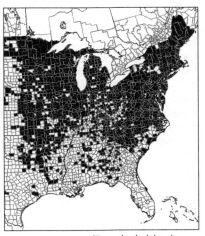

STRAWBERRY *(Fragaria virginiana)*
leaf, below

3-parted leaf

of luscious berries ready for the kettle. The few vagrant "hulls," leaves and straws quickly floated to the top of the kettle, and the family, after two days of such outing and the mother's long vigils in the kitchen, had a year's supply of the most delicious preserve and jam ever put up. Such picking and preserving of wild Strawberries still prevails in less sophisticated regions. It is wise, however, to be a little cautious about eating, unwashed, the berries so often urged upon the tourist by little French-Canadian children when, for example, one is driving around the Gaspé Peninsula. On one occasion, tempted by the dish of freshly picked berries offered by a little bronzed girl, the tourist protested the price, to receive the prompt explanation: "It's hard work. You see the little berry in the grass, you stoop down, pick the little berry, then bite off his tail, then put him in the cup. Then you see another, stoop down, pick the little berry, bite off his tail," etc. Cooking is a great purifier. Mother did not always know the intimate history of each small berry which went into the kettle. To her it was a "fine picking," the preserve and jam were perfect, and she was proud of the children.

Purple Avens, Water-Avens, Chocolate-root
Geum rivale L.

Key-characters erect herb, with slender but stiffish, purplish stems 1 or 2 feet high; the basal leaves coarsely divided, pinnate; the stem terminated by nodding flowers, with purple, triangular sepals 1/2 inch long, and buff to cream-colored veiny, wedge-shaped petals a little longer; the fruit a bristly head 3/4 inch in diameter.
Habitat and Range meadows and boggy spots throughout Canada and the northern states.
Season of Availability throughout the year, but probably best in autumn or early spring.
Use chocolate-substitute.

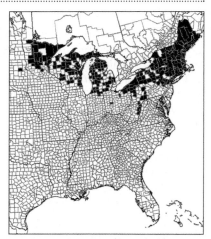

PURPLE AVENS (*Geum rivale*)

Mrs. H. K. Morrell, writing upon edible wild plants of Maine, states that the "root when boiled makes a drink like chocolate" and Prest, writing from Nova Scotia, makes a similar statement, adding that, although the drink has a choco-late- taste, it is astringent, with a slight addition of acid. The root should be well boiled and sugar added. In our own experiments we have as yet found no reason to be enthusiastic about this drink. If, however, the root were used in the fashion of the 16th century, there might be enthusiasm about it; for Parkinson tells us that

"Some use in the Spring time to put the roote to steepe for a time in wine, which giveth unto it a delicate flavour and taste, which they drinke fasting every morning, to comfort the heart, and to preserve it from noysome and infectious vapours of the plague, or any poison that may annoy it."

Crab-Apples
Malus, about 8 species.

Uses marmalade, jelly.

The native **Crabs**, of which there are a number of species occurring from New York westward and southward, have a quality quite distinct from the European Crab-Apples and the true apples, the fruit being somewhat gummy and with a distinctive odor and flavor. Although intensely sour when raw, the fruit of *Malus coronaria* (L.) P. Mill., at least, makes a delicious marmalade or jelly, the juice being more tart than that of the cultivated Crab-Apple and the skin containing an abundance of pectin.

PURPLE AVENS
(Geum rivale)

Silverweed, Argentine
Potentilla anserina L.

Uses sweet root-vegetable, emergency-food.

The **Silverweed**, or **Argentine** as it is called in French Canada, is characteristic of cool regions, extending south on gravelly or sandy shores to the northern States and the Rocky Mountain region. It is conspicuous on account of its long, feather-like leaves with many oblanceolate, toothed leaflets, green above and silvery-white beneath. Its long-stalked flowers resemble small yellow, single roses and are followed by fruits suggesting dry strawberries. Many of the root-fibres are thickened and fleshy, and northern peoples as

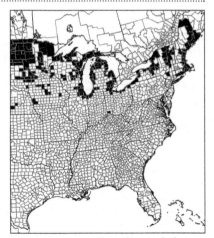

SILVERWEED *(Potentilla anserina)*

well as the American Indians are very fond of them, raw or cooked. They are said to taste in the early spring like sweet potatoes or parsnips. The northwestern Indians make regular pilgrimages to gather the Potentilla roots, and many European authors (Lightfoot, Mrs. Lankester and others) state that in the Hebrides and other Scotch islands the population has been often supported for weeks or months together by these roots!

"The roots of this plant taste like parsneps, and are frequently eaten in Scotland either roasted or boiled. In the islands of Jura and Col they are much esteemed, as answering in some measure the purposes of bread, they having been known to support the inhabitants for months together during a scarcity of other provisions."

Plums
Prunus (various species)

Uses fresh fruit, sauce, pies, preserves, jams, jellies.

The plums are somewhat arbitrarily separated from the cherries, but in general they have fleshier fruit and more flattened stones. There are several (about a dozen) wild species in eastern America, some of which have long been in repute. Such species as the **Beach Plum**, *P. maritima* Marsh., of coastal sands and rocks from southern Maine to Virginia, the **Wild Red or Yellow Plums**, *P. americana* Marsh. and *P. nigra* Ait., of rich thickets and borders of woods from New Brunswick westward, the **Chickasaw Plum**, *P. angustifolia* Marsh. of the South, and the **Wild-Goose Plum**, *P. hortulana* Bailey of Illinois and Missouri, are usually well known where they grow and are used for sauces, pies, preserves, jams and jellies. Each has its enthusiastic booster. We refrain from umpiring. They are all most desirable and when our country people become sufficiently interested they will spray the shrubs and trees to prevent the fungus-infections and to keep off the tent-caterpillars which so greatly reduce the wild crops. For directions for drying plums see p. 23.

Bird-, Fire- or Pin-Cherry
Prunus pensylvanica L. f.

Key-characters fruits borne in loose tufts along the branchlets, the bright red cherries on elongate stalks, very sour and with only a thin pulp.
Habitat and Range Dry borders of woods and especially in recently burned areas, Newfoundland to British Columbia, south through the Northern States and in the uplands to North Carolina, Tennessee and Colorado.
Season of Availability early summer.
Uses jelly, gum, masticatory.

The familiar **Bird-Cherry**, the only wild

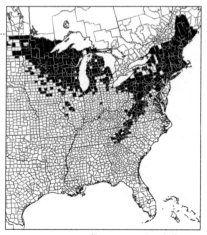

BIRD-CHERRY (*Prunus pensylvanica*)

light-red and early cherry in the northern states and Canada, is known to every country-bred person for its pleasantly sour fruit, which may be eaten raw, although the pulp is thin compared with the large stone. Mixed with currants or apple to make it jell it furnishes a delicious jelly.

The gum exuded from the trunk of the Bird-Cherry is similar to that produced from the trunks of cultivated species and is sought by some people as a chewing-gum.

Sand-Cherry
Prunus pumila L.

Key-characters a low or prostrate shrub of river-gravels and sandbars, with willowy branches and elongate foliage; bearing axillary, claret-red cherries half an inch in diameter, usually somewhat hidden in the gravel.
Habitat river-gravels and sands and lake-shores.
Range eastern Quebec to Manitoba, south to Pennsylvania and the Great Lakes States.
Season of Availability midsummer.
Uses fresh fruit, jelly.

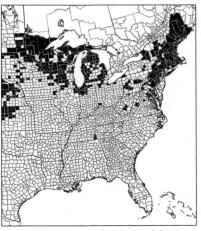

SAND-CHERRY *(Prunus pumila)*

The **Sand-Cherry** has the largest fruit of any of our native cherries. The ripe fruit is of a rich, slightly bitter flavor, palatable to many people, and the juice, mixed with sour apple-juice, makes a rich jelly. A large proportion of apple-juice must be used or the jelly will be nearly liquid.

A few other native Cherries, more local than the above, have similar uses.

Black or Rum-Cherry
Prunus serotina Ehrh.

Key-characters fruit in long or grape-like clusters, purplish-black; leaves with blunt or rounded marginal teeth.
Habitat and Range borders of dry woods, Nova Scotia and southern New Brunswick to the Dakotas and southward.
Season of Availability late summer and early autumn.
Use jelly.

Rum-Cherries have a slightly bitter, but rich, winey flavor and in early days of New England were in high repute for "Cherry Bounce," the recipe for which is not within the scope of this book. Jelly prepared from Rum-Cherries, with the addition of sour apple-juice (approximately half-and-half), is rich in flavor and dark in color and by many people is considered one of the best of jellies, in quality somewhat suggesting guava-jelly.

Choke-Cherry
Prunus virginiana L.

Key-characters similar to the Rum-Cherry, but usually with shorter clusters of cherries, with a strong acid and puckering quality and without the winey flavor; the leaves with fine, bristle-like teeth.
Habitat and Range banks of streams, rich thickets and fence-rows, Newfoundland to Manitoba and southward, abundantly through the northern states, becoming local southward to Georgia and Texas.
Season of Availability late summer and autumn.
Uses jelly, pemmican, drink.

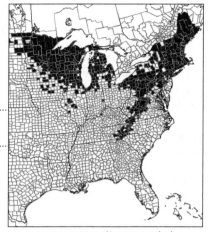

BLACK CHERRY (*Prunus serotina*)

The **Choke-Cherry** naturally attracted the attention of the early colonists, in 1634 William Wood reported that "they so furre the mouth that the tongue will cleave to the roofe, and the throate wax horse with swallowing those red Bullies (as I may call them,) being little better in taste. English ordering may bring them to be an English Cherrie, but yet they are as wilde as the Indians."

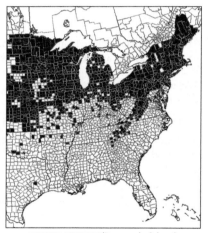

CHOKE-CHERRY (*Prunus virginiana*)

"With Wood's account practically all Americans have agreed, so much so that most people look upon the Choke-Cherry as a negligible fruit, occasionally to be tasted or to be tried upon the unwary. A delicious jelly, however, is prepared from the juice, mixed with apple-juice; an,d the northern Indians gathered the fruits and after thorough drying pounded them (stones and all), leached out the harmful hydrocyanic acid from the kernels of the stones and used the dried paste as an addition to pemmican or soaked out and, sweetened in the winter.

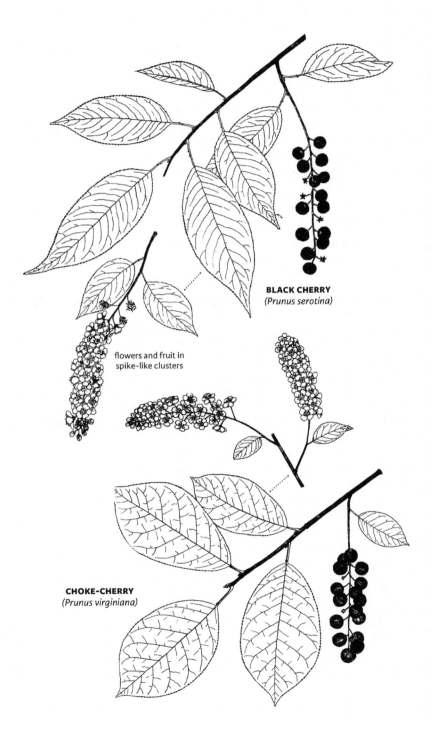

BLACK CHERRY
(Prunus serotina)

flowers and fruit in
spike-like clusters

CHOKE-CHERRY
(Prunus virginiana)

Wild Rose
Rosa (various species).

Uses salad, nibble, jelly, confection.

The petals of **Roses** are pleasant to nibble and are sometimes prepared as a salad, or candied. A few species have pulpy fruits which can be made into jelly. The best of these in our eastern flora is the Japanese Rose, Rosa rugosa Thunb., the large-flowered, very prickly species now so generally planted as a hedge-shrub and rapidly becoming naturalized along the sandy coast.

Raspberries, Blackberries, Dewberries, Cloudberry, etc.,
Rubus (many species).

Uses fruit, fresh, cooked or preserved, jelly, drinks, tea, nibble.

The genus *Rubus* furnishes many of the most familiar wild berries, all of them with pulpy fruits consisting of many small, mostly juicy drupelets, each containing a hard seed. The plants and their fruits are so familiar that for the most part they need no special discussion.

Besides the **Raspberries** (several species), **Blackberries** (100-200 or more species), **Dewberries** (two dozen or more), etc., the most famous of the genus is the **Cloudberry or Baked-Apple Berry**, *Rubus chamaemorus* L. This species abounds in boreal regions, in acid peats, extending south to Nova Scotia and eastern Maine and, locally, to alpine regions of New England. Southward it rarely fruits, but northward its berries are among the staple articles of food. Its erect stems are rarely a foot high, bearing a few simple and rounded, scalloped leaves, and terminated by a beautiful white flower (resembling a solitary blackberry-flower), followed by a large raspberry, pink when immature, then amber, and finally yellow and very juicy and soft. The berries have a flavor strongly suggestive of insipid baked apples; but their juice is rather mucilaginous, so that the taste for them usually has to be acquired by southern peoples, who at first incline disrespectfully to call them "rotten-apple berries." After the taste for them is once acquired, however, Baked-Apples or Bake-apples become one of the delights of northern travel.

The ripe, fresh berries of Baked-Apple eaten without sugar or cream are delicious, but with the addition of these dressings are positively luscious; the cooked berries are a poor article, mostly hard seeds and insipid juice. Sir John Richardson, travelling in the Arctic, well describes the fresh berry, saying: "It is perhaps the most delicious of the arctic berries, when in perfection, but cloys if eaten in quantity." The ripe berries are so soft and juicy that it is difficult to transport them, but in the North they are kept in snow which renders them firm. They can also be preserved whole in jars of cold water; and, of course, preserved after cooking.

Another species, the **Plumboy or Arctic Raspberry**, *Rubus acaulis* (now treated

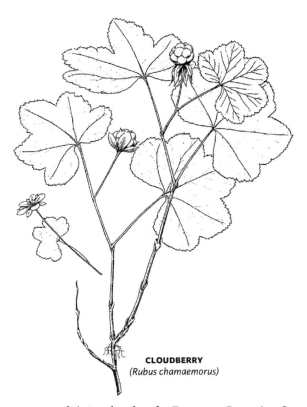

CLOUDBERRY
(Rubus chamaemorus)

as *R. arcticus* ssp. *acaulis*), is related to the European *R. arcticus* L., which was ranked by Linnaeus as the choicest of all European berries "both for smell and taste; its odour is of the most grateful kind, and as to its flavour, it has such a delicate mixture of the sweet and acid, as is not equalled by the best of our cultivated Strawberries." *R. acaulis*, as its name implies, is a very low species, coming south in peaty soils to Newfoundland, the Gaspé Peninsula and northern Minnesota. The fruiting stems, with glossy 3-divided leaves, rise only an inch or two above the moss and bear relatively large red berries. We have had the satisfaction of eating our fill only in Labrador and Newfoundland and there the berry justifies the enthusiasm of Linnaeus over its European cousin.

The native Raspberries are familiar to all in the regions where they abound and have always been picked by those who are fortunate enough to be near them and preserved in quantity for winter use. The Dewberries or Trailing Blackberries, growing close to the ground, are often overlooked or neglected, but many of them have superior fruit. In fact, in all the series of Blackberries (the High-bush, Low-bush and Dewberries) some species stand out as having rich, juicy and large berries, while in others the berries are inferior. In a group of species in which the distinguishing characters are very technical, experience is the best teacher.

The name Thimbleberry is variously used, sometimes for an elongate Blackberry, sometimes for the Black Raspberry, but the famous **Thimbleberry** of the upper Great Lakes region, from Lake Huron in Ontario and Michigan to the Lake Superior region of Minnesota, is a very different plant, *Rubus parviflorus* Nutt., a handsome shrub, with large leaves resembling glorified maple-leaves, large flowers like single white roses and big juicy and luscious berries.

The leaves of Blackberries and Raspberries are sometimes used as substitutes for tea; and the young, tender sprouts, when peeled, make a pleasant nibble. Cheney states, however, that the tea from leaves of **Black Raspberry**, *Rubus occidentalis* L., may be physiologically harmful.

THIMBLEBERRY *(Rubus parviflorus)*

Burnet
Sanguisorba (various species).

Use salad.

The Old World *Sanguisorba minor* Scop. (now classified as *Poterium sanguisorba* L.) once had a period of popularity as a salad, the young leaves said to taste like cucumber. This species is casually introduced into America but is not common. We have a coarser, native species, *S. canadensis* L., locally abundant in boggy meadows and shores from Labrador to Alaska, extending south to Georgia.

This plant apparently has no special repute but it should be tested as a possible salad.

Mountain-Ash
Sorbus, 3 species.

Uses breadstuff, acid drink.

The species of **Mountain-Ash** are so closely related that by some authors they have been considered to be one circumpolar species with geographic varieties [eastern species are the native *Sorbus americana* Marsh. and *S. decora* (Sarg.) Schneid., and the introduced *S. aucuparia* L.]. It is probable, at any rate, that they have similar qualities. The unripe fruit is very austere and has an unpleasant flavor, but when thoroughly ripe and mellowed by frost it becomes palatable. In some European countries the berries have been dried and ground into flour, and Kephart states that an infusion from the berries is sometimes used for a drink.

leaves
compound

AMERICAN MOUNTAIN-ASH
(Sorbus americana)

Rubiaceae MADDER FAMILY

··

Cleavers, Goose-grass

Galium aparine L.

··

Key-characters sprawling plant; the weak stems covered with backwardly curving, short bristles, the swollen joints bearing a circle of about 8 slender leaves; inflorescences small, consisting of 1-3 flowered clusters in the leaf-axils; fruit bristly, 2-lobed or twin, seed-like, about 1/8 inch in diameter.
Habitat rocky woods, rich thickets and gravelly sea-shores.
Range Newfoundland to Alaska, south to Virginia, Tennessee, northern Louisiana, Texas and Mexico.
Season of Availability seeds, June and July; young sprouts March to July.
Uses coffee-substitute, reducing diet, milk-strainer, potherb.

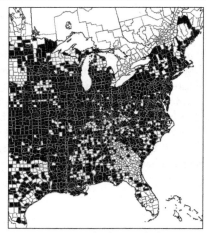

CLEAVER *(Galium aparine)*

European writers are agreed that the seeds of **Cleavers** make the best substitute for coffee in our northern flora. When dried and slightly roasted the seeds have the flavor or aroma of coffee. This fact is of special interest since the genus *Galium* belongs to the same natural family as true coffee. It is probable that the seeds of other species of the genus have, when roasted, a similar quality, but most species have smaller seeds than *G. aparine*.

In these times when the buxom form is so often looked upon askance Cleavers or Goosegrass might be utilized, for in the 16th century Gerarde wrote: "Women do usually make pottage of Cleuers with a little mutton and otemeale, to cause lanknesse, and keepe them from fatnes"; while Parkinson stated a full three centuries ago that "Clevers . . . is of subtill parts: it is familiarly taken in broth to keepe them leane and lanke, that are apt to grow fat." Furthermore, the same authority recorded another use, doubtless due to the matting of the stems on account of the retrorse hooks on branches and leaves: "the herbe serveth well the Country people in stead of a strainer, to cleare their milke from strawes, haires, or any other thing that falleth into it." This custom, according to Henslow, can be traced back to Dioscorides and these sieves are still used in Sweden.

Evelyn adds of "Clavers, Goose-grass, Aparine . . . the tender Winders, with young Nettle-tops, are us'd in Lenten Pottages." In the North, with us, the "tender Winders" are rarely available during Lent.

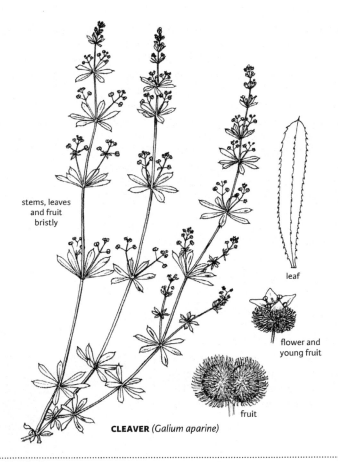

stems, leaves and fruit bristly

leaf

flower and young fruit

fruit

CLEAVER *(Galium aparine)*

Yellow Bedstraw, Cheese-rennet
Galium verum L.

Key-characters tufted perennial with smooth, ascending, slender, square stems; leaves very narrow, 8 (or sometimes 6) in circles or whorls, soon reflexed; flowers tiny, very numerous, yellow, 4-rayed, in a dense panicle.

Habitat dry fields and roadsides.

Range Newfoundland to Ontario and North Dakota, south to Virginia, West Virginia, Indiana, Iowa and Kansas, rather local, but often abundant.

Season of Availability summer.

Uses rennet, beverage.

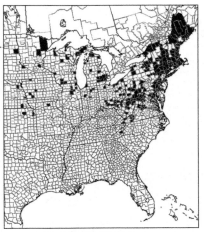

YELLOW BEDSTRAW *(Galium verum)*

Yellow Bedstraw or Our Lady's Bedstraw, *Galium verum*, is fragrant upon drying and was very early designated as the plant which filled the manger at Bethlehem, with the result that, being thus blessed and having a pleasing aroma when dry, it was for many centuries used in mattresses. Of more certain foundation is its use, mixed with calf-rennet, in the preparation of cheese. Gerarde, in the 16th century, quoting from the slightly earlier Matthiolus, told us that "The herbe thereof is used for Rennet to make cheese, as Mathiolus reporteth, saying, that the people of Thuscane or Hetruria, do vse it to turne their milke, that the Cheese which they make of sheepes and Goates milke might be the sweeter and more pleasant in taste, and also more holsome. . . .

"The people in Cheshire, especially about Namptwich where the best Cheese is made, do use it in their Rennet, esteeming greatly of that Cheese aboue other made without it."

A century later John Ray stated that a refreshing beverage is made by distilling the flowering tops.

Partridge-berry, Twin-berry, Snake-vine
Mitchella repens L.

Use berries.

The well-known **Partridge-berry**, with soft, trailing stems and rounded, evergreen leaves and with axillary 2-eyed red berries, has barely edible fruit. The berries are dry and very seedy, but without disagreeable flavor.

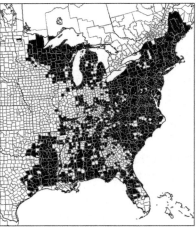

PARTRIDGE-BERRY (*Mitchella repens*)

plants trailing

Rutaceae RUE FAMILY

Hop-tree, Wafer-Ash
Ptelea trifoliata L.

Use substitute for Hops in making yeast or in brewing.

The small tree or large shrub, known as **Hop-tree** and found in alluvial thickets and on shores from New York to Minnesota, south to our southernmost states, was once in great repute as a substitute for hops. The circular and flattened fruits used like hops (i.e. a decoction of them added to yeast) produced a rapid increase of the latter indispensable concoction so much used in raising bread. They were also, like the hops, used in making beer.

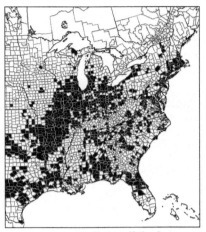

HOP-TREE *(Ptelea trifoliata)*

HOP-TREE *(Ptelea trifoliata)*

winged seed

Salicaceae WILLOW FAMILY

Willow
Salix (many species)

Use emergency-food.

The bast (inner bark) of **Willows** has sometimes been used dried and ground into flour as an emergency food. It is bitter and no one is apt to try it except in dire emergency.

Poplar, Cottonwood
Populus (many species)

Use emergency-food.

The bast can be used in emergency.

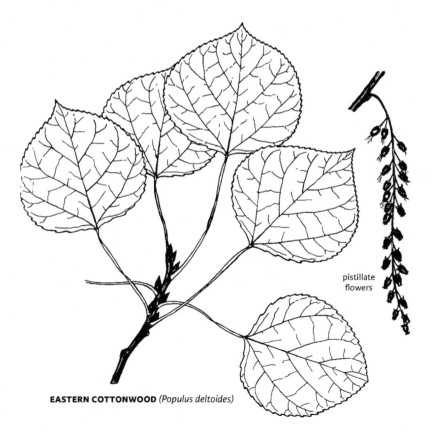

pistillate
flowers

EASTERN COTTONWOOD *(Populus deltoides)*

Santalaceae SANDALWOOD FAMILY

Bastard Toadflax
Comandra umbellata (L.) Nutt.

Key-characters plants with slender, creeping, slightly woody stems from which arise the leafy branches, a few inches high, bearing many alternate, thin, dry, pale, oblong leaves about an inch long; flowers greenish and white, erect, bell-shaped, with 5 lobes, borne in terminal clusters; the fruit an urn-shaped green, finally drab-brown nut about ¼ inch long crowned by the 5-lobed calyx.
Habitat dry, open woods, clearings and barrens.
Range Newfoundland to Manitoba and southward; other species west to the Pacific.
Season of Availability June (southward)–August (northward), as the nuts become fully grown but scarcely ripe.
Use nuts as nibbles.

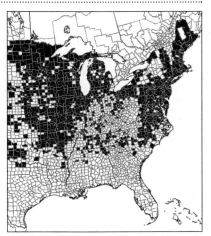

BASTARD TOADFLAX *(Comandra umbellata)*

The little urn-shaped nuts of western species of **Bastard Toadflax** have been popular with the Indians on account of their sweet taste. It is, therefore, gratifying to find that in our eastern species the fully grown but hardly ripe nuts are sweet and oily, a delicious nibble, but rarely found in sufficient quantity for more than a pleasant tid-bit.

fruit

BASTARD TOADFLAX
(Comandra umbellata)

Sapindaceae SOAPBERRY FAMILY

Maple
Acer (various species, formerly included in the Aceraceae)

Uses drink, syrup, sugar, breadstuff, cooked vegetable.

From the earliest times the Indians of the northern United States and southeastern Canada depended upon the sap of the **Maples** as a source of drink, syrup and sugar, and to some extent as a source of bread. Naturally enough, the **Sugar-Maple**, *Acer saccharum* L., has won most distinction, because by the whites it is the tree most depended upon for syrup and sugar; but many other species have sap from which good sugar may be made. In fact, Michaux considered the sap of the **River- or Silver Maple**, *A. saccharinum* L., sweeter and whiter, although the yield of sugar from a tree was only about one-half that of the Sugar-Maple. Other explorers too, for instance Sir John Richardson, were emphatic in their praises of the sugar made from sap of the River-Maple; and in the South the pale-barked **Sugartree**, *A. floridanum* (Chapman) Pax, was a regular source of sugar until sugarcane and sorghum were extensively grown.

The **Red Maple**, too, *A. rubrum* L., furnishes a good sap and sugar, although the sugar is inferior to that of Sugar-Maple and the yield is comparatively small; and the **Box-Elder** or **Ash-leaved Maple**, *A. negundo* L. has been highly valued as a source of sugar. Michaux stated that Box-Elder will not furnish good sugar; but many competent botanists, exploring in central Canada, have been very definite in their references to Box-Elder as a sugar-tree. Thus Richardson, who for years had no equal in his knowledge of our northern regions, writing from the Saskatchewan in 1840, said, under date of April 26: "The sugar harvest, which is collected in this district from the *Negundo fraxinifolium* (an old name for *Acer negundo*), commenced in 1820, on the 20th of this month, and lasted till the 10th of May. The flow of the sap is greatly influenced by the direct action of the sun, and is greatest when a smart night's frost is succeeded by a warm, sun-shining day."

Similarly, in the report of Palliser's Exploring Expedition along the boundary between Canada and the United States, we find the following memorandum, under date of April 10, 1857: "Everything is commencing to wear a spring aspect; the women of the fort are scattered along the banks of the river, busy gleaning their annual harvest of maple sugar. The tree from which they obtain sugar is not the true maple. It is the *Negundo fraxinifolium*." (the box-elder, *Acer negundo* L.)

The sugar, according to Richardson, is generally of a darker color than that from the Sugar-Maple.

During the past two generations the arts of tapping the Maples and of preparing syrup and sugar have been largely forgotten, except by the few who follow syrup- and sugar-making as a trade. Earlier generations of Americans, when our ways were healthily simple, annually looked forward to the early spring days when the sap would begin to flow and when they and their neighbors would gather for the sugaring. New England and Canadian literature is replete with references to these happy days, which, unfortunately, the majority of the present generation little comprehend, preferring, even when they have plenty of Maple-trees on their own land, to rely upon imported cane-sugar or, now and then as a special treat, to pay an enormous price for a bit of Maple-sugar. But who can read this passage from long-forgotten Sylvester Judd without a wish to take part himself in a real "sugaring"!

"It is spring; Hash is about beginning his annual labor of making maple sugar and burning coal; Margaret has promised him her aid, and then she is to have her own time. She carries the alder spouts to the Maples, rights the troughs that have been lying overturned under the trees, and kindles a fire beneath the large iron kettle that hangs from a pole supported between two rocks. Wreathing the trailing arbutus in her hair and making a baldric of the ground-laurel, with a wooden yoke stretched across her shoulders she carries two pails full of sap from the trees to the boiler. With a stick having a bit of pork on the end, she graduates the walloping sirup when it is likely to overflow, while her brother brings more sap from the remote and less accessible part of the camp. The neighbors, boys and girls, come in at the 'sugaring off'; the 'wax' is freely distributed to be cooled on lumps of snow or the axe-head; some toss it about in long, flexible, fantastic lines, some get their mouths burnt, all are merry. Her mother 'stirs it off', and a due quantity of the 'quick' and 'alive' crystal sweet is the result."

The Indian methods of preparing the sugar were unique: drawing the sap into bark or wooden vessels and boiling it down by throwing into it hot stones from the fire or allowing the sap to freeze over night, in the morning throwing off the ice and leaving the thickened syrup at the bottom of the vessel.

Nowadays we meekly pay the price (60 cents to $1.25 a pound) for maple-sugar as a confection; but note the following, from a description of the Gaspé Peninsula before it was "discovered" by the tourist:

"Supper, lodging, and breakfast for three and bedding and feed for the horse came to $2.56. Handing our host $2.75, with an effort to say politely in French, 'Keep the change, please,' I was met by firm refusal. But the necessary change could not be found. So our host, climbing on a chair, took down from the pantry-shelf one of those enormous French Canadian bread-pans, turned out its contents and, with an axe, chopped off five pounds of maple-sugar, for change. I wish I had handed him a five-dollar bill. That was before the new automobile road was finished and American tourists had changed the point of view."—M.L.F. in Harvard Alumni Bulletin, xxxiv. 422 (Jan. 8, 1932).

The sap from all the Maples as well as from other trees (hickory, birch, ash, etc.) is secured by "tapping" the tree, i.e., by boring a shallow hole into the sapwood with an augur and inserting a wooden or metal spigot perforated at the base and cut or moulded at the outlet into a channel. Pails or troughs are hung or set under the spigot and the sap, which usually flows best after a frosty night, secured and carried to larger receptacles for boiling. On a camping trip in early spring it is not only a pleasure but a decidedly practical matter to know how to tap a tree, for the sap is quickly evaporated over the fire and a good supply of syrup may be readily obtained.

For making maple-beer, Michaux gave the following directions: "Upon 4 gallons of boiling water, pour 1 quart of Maple molasses [syrup]; add a little yeast or leaven to excite the fermentation, and a spoonful of the essence of spruce: a very pleasant and salutary drink is thus obtained."

Other uses of the Maples are less inviting, for instance the sap-wood or inner bark gathered in the spring and dried has been used by various Indian tribes as a source of bread, the dried bark being pounded in a mortar and sifted before cooking; and the Calmucks, we are told, remove the wings and then boil the large seeds of the maples, afterward dressing them with butter and milk as a food.

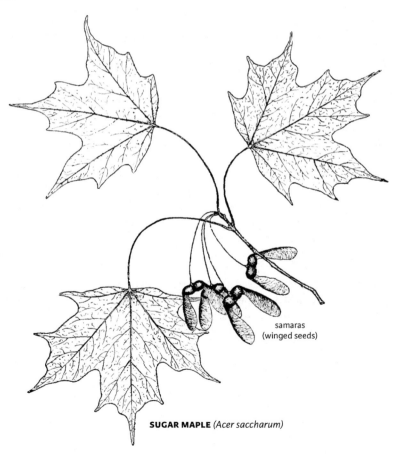

samaras (winged seeds)

SUGAR MAPLE *(Acer saccharum)*

Horse-Chestnut, Buckeye
Aesculus (5 or 6 species)

Use breadstuff.

The large nuts of the **Horse-Chestnut** and **Buckeyes** contain a bitter, poisonous principle, the glucoside aesculin, so that the raw nuts, although usually abundant and full of starch, are dangerous to eat. It has been stated by some European writers, as well as by students of the American Indians, that this bitter principle is readily removed by leaching, and that after its removal a wholesome and highly nutritious meal is left. The Indians roasted the nuts among hot stones, thus loosening the shells, peeled and mashed them, and then leached the meal with water for several days. According to the pharmaceutical authority, Dr. Heber W. Youngken, in a note in The Herbarist for 1939, "This glucoside, called 'aesculin'. . . is very sparingly soluble in water, forming a faintly blue fluorescing solution."

If the old statements in the South of the properties of powdered Buckeye-seeds are sustained, it is evident that not even fish can "drink like a fish," if they are given aesculin. The scholarly and very acute botanist, Rev. M. A. Curtis, wrote in 1860 of Red Buckeye, Aesculus pavia L.: "The powdered seeds and bruised branches, if thrown into small ponds and stirred a while, will so intoxicate fish that they rise to the surface and may be taken by hand."

The Indians were wise in leaching the meal for several days.

Balloon-vine
Cardiospermum halicacabum L.

Use potherb.

The tropical **Balloon-vine**, a climber with numerous leaflets and with tendrils, and large bladdery fruits, is sometimes cultivated and is inclined to become spontaneous in our warmer states. In tropical countries its young foliage is frequently cooked as a spinach.

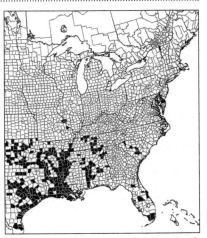

BALLOON-VINE *(Cardiospermum halicacabum) fruit, left*

Saxifragaceae SAXIFRAGE FAMILY

Golden Saxifrage
Chrysosplenium americanum Schwein. ex Hook.

Key-characters succulent matted or creeping plant of brooks, rills and springs, with crisp, roundish, mostly opposite leaves about 1/2 inch across; the forking tips of the branches bearing at the forks tiny green saucer-shaped flowers flecked above with red or orange.
Habitat and Range brooks, rills and wet moss, Quebec to Minnesota and southward through the northern states, and along the mountains to Georgia.
Season of Availability throughout the year.
Use salad.

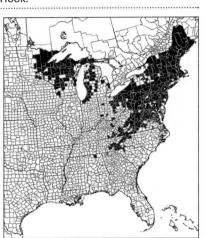

GOLDEN SAXIFRAGE *(C. americanum)*

We have not tried our American species, but European authors are so generally agreed that their species makes a good salad, that it will be quite safe to use our own, which often abounds and makes rapid growth in early spring. One should be certain, of course, that it is growing in uncontaminated water. Use disinfectant in washing it (see p. 11).

Lettuce-Saxifrage
Micranthes micranthidifolia (Haw.) Small

Synonym *Saxifraga micranthidifolia*
Key-characters a tall herb, with a rosette of large, thin, narrowly obovate, coarsely toothed basal leaves 4-10 inches long, and a tall, nearly naked flowering stem, bearing a loose, open cluster of small, white flowers on long, slender flower-stalks, followed by a 2-pronged capsule.
Habitat wet rocks and banks of streams.
Season of Availability spring.
Use salad.

According to Asa Gray, "Under the name of Lettuce, the leaves are eaten by the inhabitants [of the Carolina mountains] as salad."

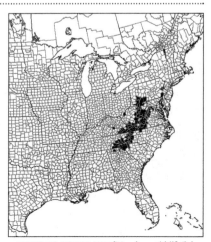

LETTUCE-SAXIFRAGE *(M. micranthidifolia)*

Swamp-Saxifrage
Micranthes pensylvanica (L.) Haw.

Synonym *Saxifraga pensylvanica,* and related species.
Key-characters similar to Lettuce-Saxifrage but with the leaves entire or only obscurely toothed.
Habitat and Range swampy meadows and thickets of the eastern United States, northeastward to southern Maine, northwestward to Minnesota.
Season of Availability spring.
Use salad.

The young leaves, just unrolling, are tender and not unattractive as a salad. Doubtless other species of the genus, with tender unrolling rosette-leaves could be eaten.

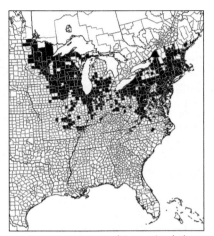

SWAMP-SAXIFRAGE *(M. pensylvanica)*

EARLY SAXIFRAGE *(M. virginiensis)*

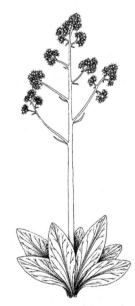

SWAMP-SAXIFRAGE *(M. pensylvanica)*

Smilacaceae GREENBRIER FAMILY

Carrion-flower, Jacob's-ladder
Smilax herbacea L.

Key-characters high-climbing vine with long curling tendrils; Stems comparatively soft and without prickles; the leaves thin; oval or roundish, pale beneath, with conspicuous parallel-arching veins; the flower-stalks 3-10 inches long, bearing nearly globular, loose clusters of slender-stalked, greenish, foul-smelling flowers and blue-black berries.
Habitat   alluvial thickets and rich clearings.
Range   western New Brunswick to Manitoba and southward. Other closely related species in the Central and Southern States.
Season of Availability spring, before the new shoots have hardened.
Use as asparagus.

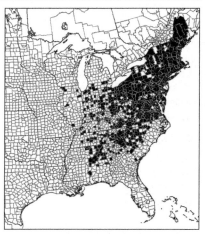

CARRION-FLOWER *(Smilax herbacea)*

The name **Carrion-flower** is applied to this plant on account of the very disagreeable odor of the flowers, which are pollinated by carrion-flies, but the carrion-odor is present only in the flowers. The young shoots, which are readily recognized in rich thickets by their asparagus-like appearance and their curling tendrils, are gathered and used like asparagus by nature-lovers in central Connecticut, and are reported to be a delicate and palatable vegetable. The shoots grow very rapidly and should be watched that they may be gathered while they are still tender.

The roots are tuberous, resembling the rootstock of Solomon's-seal, and presumably have the properties of the Green-briers discussed below.

Bryony-leaved Jacob's-ladder
Smilax pseudochina L.

Key-characters   In habit like *Smilax herbacea*, climbing by tendrils, but with the leaves more elongate and slightly fiddle-shaped at base; clusters of berries nearly globular, on long axillary foot-

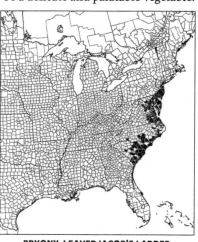

BRYONY-LEAVED JACOB'S LADDER
(Smilax pseudochina)

stalks; the blue-black berries on individual slender stalks, holding on all winter and with a sweet pulp containing 2 or 3 seeds.

Habitat low thickets and swamps.

Range on and near the coastal plain from Mississippi to southern New York.

Season of Availability late autumn to spring.

Use berry, as a pleasant nibble.

Whereas the conspicuous over-wintering long-stalked globes of blue-black berries of the wide-ranging **Carrion-flower** are disagreeable in taste and very rubbery, the very similar ones of **Bryony-leaved Jacob's-ladder** are delicious—sweet and date-like. On a winter tramp in pine barrens and other flat areas of the coastal plain they are a worth-while nibble, and, when found in abundance, really help out on lunch.

Cat-brier, Bull-brier, Green-brier, Saw-brier
Smilax rotundifolia L., *S. glauca* Walt., *S. bona-nox* L.
Bamboo-vine or Blaspheme-vine
Smilax laurifolia L.

Key-characters stems woody and green but slender and freely branching, usually bearing stiff prickles, climbing by tendrils; leaves becoming leathery, round, oval or fiddle-shaped or oblong; main flower-stalk rarely equaling the leaves; berries blackish, in small, umbrella-like clusters.

The commoner species may be recognized by the following key:

1 Leaves white or whitish beneath; stems prickly .... **S. glauca**
1 Leaves green on both sides 2
2 Stems and branches unarmed or rarely with a few weak prickles at base ....
.... **S. pseudochina**
2 Stems and branches armed with strong prickles 3
3 Leaves oval to round; main flower-stalk barely as long as the leafstalk ....
.... **S. rotundifolia**
3 Leaves mostly fiddle-shaped; main flower-stalk distinctly longer than the leaf stalk
.... **S. bona-nox**
3 Leaves oblong or nearly so, very thick and hard; main flower-stalk very short ......
.... **S. laurifolia**

Habitat and Range damp or sometimes dry thickets and open woods, rather generally through the southeastern United States; *S. rotundifolia* extending north to Minnesota and Nova Scotia, *S. bona-nox* to Illinois and New Jersey, *S. pseudochina* to Indiana and New Jersey, and *S. glauca* to Massachusetts.

Season of Availability roots, spring and autumn (or winter) when well filled; new shoots May to August.

Uses breadstuff, soup, cooling drink, jelly, as asparagus, salad.

The chief fame of the **Green-briers** is due to the use of the tuberous rootstocks of *Smilax pseudochina* by the southern Indians and after them by the whites. Early travellers in the South describe the reddish flour prepared from the rootstocks and the cooling drink and attractive jelly derived from them. The dried roots are chopped, pounded and strained, the powdery sediment dried in the open air when it forms a fine reddish flour. This is mixed with hot water and sweetened with honey or sugar, and when it cools becomes a delicious and nourishing jelly. One of the first accounts of this jelly was Captain John Smith's in 1626:

"Groundnuts, *Tiswaw* we call *China* roots; they grow in clusters, and bring forth a bryer stalke, but the leafe is far unlike, which will climbe up to the top of the highest tree: the use knowne is to cut it in small peeces, then stampe & straine it with water, and boyled makes a gelly good to eate."

But the famous traveller, William Bartram, who voyaged through the Southern States in the 18th century, seems to have been the chief source of information from whom others have drawn, and he states that the flour was also used in the preparation of bread or soup.

Porcher stated that, in the Confederate States and by the Confederate soldiers it was much used in the preparation of a drink resembling sarsaparilla (true Sarsaparilla is a tropical species of *Smilax*):

"The root is mixed with molasses and water in an open tub, a few seeds of parched corn or rice are added, and after a slight fermentation it is seasoned with sassafras." Porcher also states that the young shoots are used as asparagus and "impart the same odor to the urine."

The other species apparently were used somewhat indiscriminately with *S. pseudochina*, and in Catesby's *Natural History of Carolina, Florida, and the Bahama Islands*, one of the rarest and most famous books on the birds and plants of North America, there is a good illustration of *S. bona-nox*, while the accompanying text is essentially like those of Bartram's and of Porcher's accounts of the use of the roots and of the new shoots of *S. pseudochina*. It is obvious that, owing to its essential lack of prickles, the latter species is more inviting to the digger than the excessively prickly species, but the prickly species have perfectly good rootstocks, easily dug.

The widely distributed Cat-briers, *S. rotundifolia* and *S. glauca*, have long, whitish, cord-like rootstocks becoming several feet in length and on open sandy pond-shores they are readily secured. Soon after exposure to the air they become by oxidation a reddish color, like the flour described by Bartram. It is not absolutely necessary to powder the roots in order to make jelly from them. In our own experiments we simply cut the rootstocks into fine pieces, covered them with cold water and boiled for an hour, the water becoming dark-colored. This colored water was strained off, boiled again for a few minutes with sugar, when the syrup jelled. With an equal bulk of sugar the jelly on cooling became a firm sugary paste resembling gumdrops, while half the bulk of sugar gave a soft jelly. The jelly is of good flavor, somewhat flat but slightly bitter-aromatic and intensely sweet, that from *S. rotundifolia* tea-colored, from *S. glauca* honey-colored. Mixed with water the jelly makes a palatable, sweet drink.

The tender young shoots and unrolling leaves of the Cat-briers are slightly acid and the young leaves of *S. rotundifolia* are a familiar nibble among children under the name "Bread-and-butter." The vigorous, leading shoots, which abound in spring and early summer and may be gathered in decreasing quantity throughout the summer, make a delicious vegetable. Care should be taken to pick only the stronger shoots, which are tender for a length of 3 to 6 inches. These eaten raw, taking care to use only the very tender tips, or boiled in salted water, drained and allowed to cool and then dressed with a French dressing make a tempting salad. The salad prepared from the shoots of *S. rotundifolia* strongly suggests in flavor **Alligator Pear**; that from *S. glauca* is less attractive, having a mild bitter-aromatic flavor. The new shoots of other species are worth trying.

    Smilax laurifolia, **Bamboo-vine**, often in the South most appropriately called **Blaspheme-vine**, forms impenetrable and fiercely prickly tangles. Porcher says that the new shoots are eaten by Indians and African-Americans. We have not tried them; but if, by eating every new shoot we could discourage this obstructing and fierce species, we would gladly do our share.

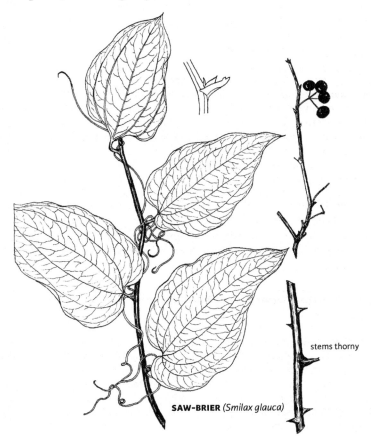

stems thorny

SAW-BRIER *(Smilax glauca)*

Solanaceae NIGHTSHADE FAMILY

The Nightshade family furnishes some of the most important garden vegetables: the potato, tomato and eggplant. It is likewise the source of such narcotic poisons as belladonna, tobacco and stramonium. The following, although not important as food-plants, have their advocates.

Matrimony-vine
Lycium barbarum L.
Lycium chinense P. Mill.

Use cooked vegetable.

The old-fashioned garden shrubs, the **Matrimony-vines**, with arching spiny branches, narrow, elongate leaves, greenish-purple flowers and orange-red to scarlet berries, have escaped and become naturalized along roadsides and in waste ground. In Europe and Asia the young leaves are sometimes cooked and eaten.

Husk-Tomato, Ground-Cherry
Physalis (various species)

Key-characters stems simple or forking, with alternate, usually toothed or angled leaves, nodding fruits with slender stalks and inflated papery husks 1-2 inches long, which cover the yellow, nearly globular, tomato-like berry.
Habitat and Range open soil, chiefly in the Central and Southern States, but extending locally into southern Canada and New England.
Season of Availability late summer and autumn.
Uses berries, raw, or preferably cooked or preserved.

The **Husk-Tomatoes**, unless perfectly ripe, have a strong flavor, but the ripe berries taste somewhat like tomatoes and when cooked make a very palatable preserve. The species are numerous and it is probable that the quality of the fruit is variable. A few species have been taken into cultivation and to a limited extent appear in city-markets.

Black-berried Nightshade, Morella
Solanum nigrum L.

Key-characters bushy-branched herb, with long-stalked, alternate, coarsely toothed or angulate, ovate leaves; berries black, 1/4-1/2 inch in diameter, many-seeded, on stalked clusters borne chiefly from the sides of the stem (not from the axils of the leaves). (Not to be confused with the so-called **Poisonous or Deadly Nightshade**, *S. dulcamara* L., a woody, climbing vine, bearing berries which are bright red when ripe.)
Habitat dry, open soil, borders of woods, roadsides, gravelly beaches or cultivated land.
Range throughout temperate or tropical America northward to southern Canada.

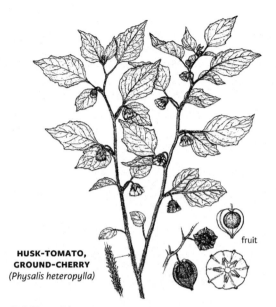

**HUSK-TOMATO,
GROUND-CHERRY**
(Physalis heteropylla)

fruit

Season of Availability midsummer to autumn.
Uses berries, raw, cooked or in pies and preserves; potherb.

The berries of the **Black-berried Nightshade** have a varying reputation, sometimes with seemingly good reason reputed to be poisonous, again treated as a harmless, edible fruit. In one of its very many forms and derivatives, it is sometimes cultivated under the absurd name "Garden Huckleberry," the thoroughly ripe berries being used as a cooked fruit or in preserves and pies. In flavor the berries have no suggestion of a huckleberry (unless it be the "mawkish" Squaw-Huckleberry); on the other hand they suggest a mildly bitter tomato.

Although there are few well authenticated cases of poisoning by eating the cooked berries, generally harmless, the green berries contain the toxic glucoside, solanine, but those who have especially looked into the question state that this disappears in ripening. The late Professor Charles E. Bessey published in the *American Botanist* for 1905 the following account of his education on this point.

"The note on page 75 of the October number of the Botanist reminds me of an incident which occurred in my class in Botany nearly thirty five years ago. I was lecturing on the properties of the plants constituting the Solanaceae, and, as a matter of course, said that the berries of the black nightshade (*Solanum nigrum* L.) were poisonous. A young fellow from Fort Dodge, Iowa, spoke up and said that the people in his neighborhood made them into pies, preserves, etc. and ate freely of them. I answered him, as became a professor of botany, by saying that as it was well known that black nightshade berries are poisonous, the student must have been mistaken. That was the young professor's way of settling things, and this particular thing remained settled for him for some years. After a while, however, I learned that the people in central and western

Iowa actually did eat black nightshade berries, and they were not poisoned either. Later, I learned the same thing in Nebraska for this species, and still more for the spreading nightshade (*Solanum triflorum* Nutt.), whose larger berries were freely used by the pioneers in the early days when other berries were scarce upon the Great Plains."

Furthermore, Sampson and other writers regularly state that the young leaves and stems are a good potherb (cooked of course).

BLACK-BERRIED NIGHTSHADE
(*Solanum nigrum*)

Staphyleaceae BLADDER-NUT FAMILY

Bladder-nut
Staphylea trifolia L.

Key-characters small tree or large shrub, with opposite, stalked leaves having 3 ovate, pointed leaflets; flowers in grape-like clusters, whitish, with 5 erect, narrow petals; fruit a large, inflated or bladdery pouch, with 3 lobes, each lobe containing 1-4 bony seeds.

Habitat and Range rich thickets, borders of woods and banks of streams, western New England to Minnesota and southward.

Season of Availability late summer and autumn.

Use nut-like seed.

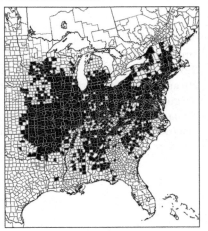

BLADDER-NUT *(Staphylea trifolia)*

It is often stated that the seeds of Old World species are in quality similar to pistachios; and the comparison has been transferred by some authors to the seeds of our species. We have not tried them.

BLADDER-NUT
(Staphylea trifolia)

Styracaceae STORAX FAMILY

Wild Olive, Opossum-wood or Silver-bell-tree
Halesia carolina L.

Use fruit as masticatory.

The nut-like fruits of the **Wild Olive**, a small tree occurring from Florida to Texas, and north to rich woods or stream-banks of western Virginia, West Virginia, southern Ohio, southern Indiana, southern Illinois and southeastern Missouri, are rolled in the mouth for their acidity.

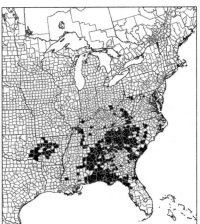

WILD OLIVE *(Halesia carolina)*

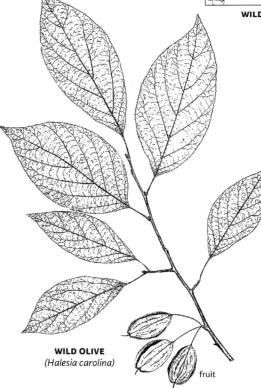

WILD OLIVE
(Halesia carolina)

fruit

Symplocaceae SWEET-LEAF FAMILY

Sweet-leaf, Horse-sugar
Symplocos tinctoria (L.) L'Hér.

Use masticatory.

The familiar **Sweet-leaf**, a shrub or small tree of rich woods in the South (Florida to Texas, north to Delaware and Arkansas) is familiar to most people on account of its pleasantly sweet and slightly acid, thickish and somewhat persistent oblong leaves. On a hot day in summer they are, when chewed, a most refreshing tid-bit, starting the flow of saliva and encouraging the chewer to forget the heat.

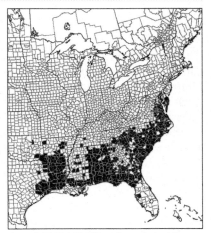

SWEET-LEAF *(Symplocos tinctoria)*

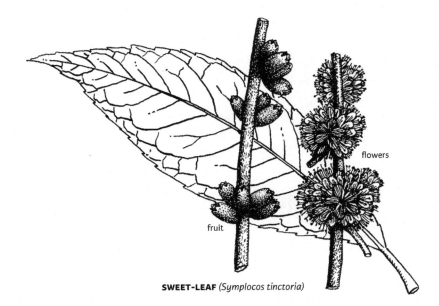

flowers

fruit

SWEET-LEAF *(Symplocos tinctoria)*

Trapaceae WATER-CHESTNUT FAMILY

Water-Chestnut, Water-Caltrop
Trapa natans L.

Uses nut, flour, cooked vegetable, confection.

The **Water-Chestnut**, which has been introduced at a few points in the eastern United States and which is now somewhat naturalized, often crowding out other plants, in ponds and slow streams, has the submersed leaves divided into thread-like segments but the floating leaves forming a rosette on the surface of the water, with coarsely toothed, rounded blades and inflated leaf-stalks. The nuts are an inch or two broad and usually armed with four strong spines. The seed inside has sometimes been used in Europe and Asia to make a coarse flour or as a coarse, roasted vegetable. It is said by Paillieux, however, to be very indigestible. In some European communities the nuts are candied much as are true chestnuts.

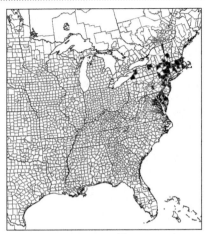

WATER-CHESTNUT *(Trapa natans)*

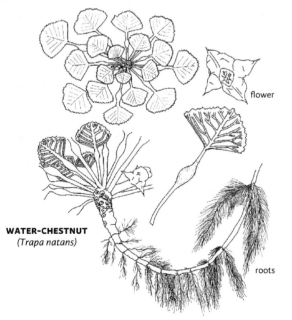

WATER-CHESTNUT
(Trapa natans)

flower

roots

Typhaceae CAT-TAIL FAMILY

Cat-tail, Cat-'o-nine-tail, Flag, "Bulrush," "Cossack Asparagus"
Typha latifolia L., *Typha angustifolia* L.

Key-characters tall plants with erect, stiff, tape-like pale-green leaves 1/4-1 inch broad, with a strongly developed rounded flange at the junction of the blade and the sheathing base; rootstock creeping and branching, ½-1 inch thick; flowers in dense terminal spikes, the lower part of the spike at first green, finally brown and producing "cotton" the upper part yellow and, after shedding the pollen, shriveling.
Habitat fresh or brackish water of marshes and borders of ponds and quiet streams, the last two species often in brackish marshes.
Range one or another throughout temperate North America, northward to southern Canada and western Newfoundland.
Season of Availability rootstocks, late autumn to spring; new shoots, spring and early summer; pollen and young flowering spikes, May (southward) to early August (northward).
Uses salad, starchy vegetable, bread, asparagus, cooked vegetable soup, pickle, jelly.

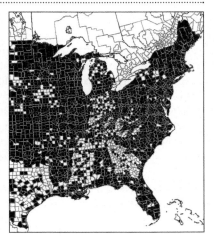

CAT-TAIL *(Typha)*

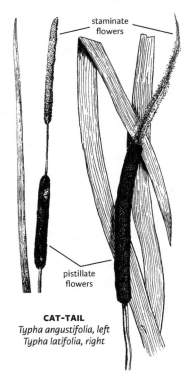

staminate flowers

pistillate flowers

CAT-TAIL
Typha angustifolia, left
Typha latifolia, right

In different regions the **Cat-tail** has won considerable attention as a food-plant, although it is noteworthy that its reputation varies in different areas.

The short, thickened leading shoots of the rootstock, when well filled with starchy material late in the autumn and through the winter to early spring, are said by Coville and other students of western Indians to be an important food, either as a salad or as a cooked vegetable; and in the 18th century Forster stated that the poorer whites of Virginia were very fond of the young rootstocks which have a sweetish taste. Prest, writing from Nova Scotia, states that, in order to secure the most nourishment, the roots should be grated, boiled, and then the starchy material strained off for use. The pithy core at the junction of the rootstock and the sprouting new stem is said by many writers to be edible, "tasting like tapioca," and eaten either roasted or boiled. Some years ago the magazines contained somewhat detailed accounts, by the late Professor P. W. Claassen of Cornell University, of the preparation of a highly nutritious flour from the central core of the rootstocks. Those who are specially interested will find much detail in Professor Claassen's account. In an analysis of the flour from Cat-tail roots, made during the first World War at the Sheffield Laboratory of Physiological Chemistry at Yale University, Jencks found that it "corresponds with starch. The 'flour' indicated a carbohydrate content of 56.8 per cent. Mice were fed for a week on otherwise adequate diets containing 30 per cent of the 'flour' without evident untoward results. The animals gained in weight upon the ration." Then, as a check, Yale students substituted for the mice.)

Porcher states that a jelly is extracted from the root, while by Waugh we are told that the Abenaki Indians used the juice from the root.

It has often been stated by European writers that the Don Cossacks use the young stems starting in spring as a vegetable, but Cossack officers who have travelled extensively state that "It is only fit for food when it grows in the marshes of the Don." The fondness of the people of the Don for this readily obtained vegetable is indicated by Sturtevant's extract from *Clarke's Travels in Russia*: "He found the people devouring it raw; 'with a degree of avidity as though it had been a religious observance.' It was to be seen in all the streets and in every house, bound into faggots. 'They peel off the outer rind and find a tender, white part of the stem, which, for about the length of 18 inches, affords a crisp, cooling, and very pleasant article of food.' Cameron states, also, that the young shoots may be used for pickles.

Dr. Edward Palmer, who for more than a quarter of a century explored the arid Southwest and adjacent Mexico, states that by the Pah-utes the young flowering spikes, before the pollen is developed, are considered a great delicacy, eaten either raw or boiled, steamed or made into a soup. It is also stated that the people of Bombay and other portions of India, harvest the abundant pollen and make a bread from it. This, if palatable, as it should be, may prove to to a welcome new breadstuff. The pollen should, obviously, be beaten into a nearly closed container.

From the above compilations it would seem that the Cat-tail is a worthy subject for careful investigations. We have personally investigated the young flowering spikes mentioned by Dr. Palmer and can say that the Pah-ute Indians had the satisfaction of discovering a remarkably palatable vegetable. The green flower-spikes should be gathered before the yellow pollen shows and boiled a few minutes in salted water and served. It will be found that the granular, cooked flower-buds have a flavor and consistency somewhat suggestive of both olives and French artichokes. The central axis of the spike is tough; consequently the pencil-like, green vegetable, if kept intact, must be nibbled by eating "end-on," as one would eat stick-candy; only the wiry core is left. This may seem an undignified procedure at table, but certainly all children who have been introduced to cooked Cat-tails have found it no obstacle, and it is quite as becoming a table-procedure as our eating of olives, sweet corn on the cob, or lollypops. A better way is to scrape off the boiled or steamed flowers from the hard axis, then mix them with oiled or buttered crumbs, seasoning, beaten egg and a little milk, and then bake. As in all such dishes, cream, if available, gives the finishing touch.)

Bur-reed
Sparganium L. (about 10 species)

Use starchy vegetable.

Late in the autumn tubers are produced from the creeping rootstocks of these plants and, according to Coville, they have been used as food by the Klamath Indians. The tubers are small and far apart in marshy ground, and the difficulty of securing them in quantity is too great to make them an important wild food.

AMERICAN BUR-REED
(Sparganium americanum)
cluster of fruit

NARROW-LEAF BUR-REED
(Sparganium angustifolium)

Ulmaceae ELM FAMILY

Hackberry, Sugarberry, Nettle-tree
Celtis occidentalis L. and several other species.

Key-characters trees or shrubs with a gray bark covered with prominent slender ridges and knobs of cork; branches forming a fine and wide-spreading spray; leaves alternate, somewhat suggesting elm leaves, narrowed to base, with unequal sides and 3 main veins; fruit scattered, reddish-purple or yellowish-brown berries (drupes) with a large stone and thin sweet pulp.
Habitat rocky woods and riverbanks.
Range western Quebec to Manitoba and southward; related species southward and southwestward.
Season of Availability late autumn, after several frosts, to spring.
Uses a sweet nibble or masticatory, condiment.

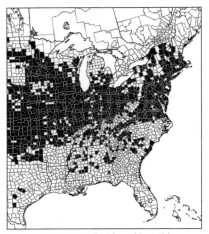

HACKBERRY *(Celtis occidentalis)*

The drupes, the size of bird-cherries, hang on the trees all winter, and have an extremely thin pulp and dry skin, both in taste and texture strongly suggestive of dates, especially after hard frost has sweetened the pulp. According to Gilmore, the Dakota Indians use the dried pits, pounded fine, as a seasoning in cooking meats. The white kernel inside the hard shell is soft and sweetish, resembling in taste the outer pulp.

The Ancients were amazingly fond of the thin pulp of the Mediterranean species, *Celtis australis* L., which, according to students of the Mediterranean flora, was the Lotus, "the food of the Lotophagi, which Heroditus, Dioscorides, and Theophrastus describe as sweet, pleasant and wholesome, and which Homer says was so delicious as to make those who ate it forget their native country" (Johns in *Treas. of Bot.*).

Elm
Ulmus (various species)

Uses emergency-food, masticatory, tea, cooked vegetable.

The chief food-value of the Elm lies in the mucilaginous inner bark of the **Slippery Elm**, *Ulmus rubra* Muhl., a tree characteristic of rich soils from the Great Lakes region southward and locally eastward to New England and the other coastal states. The inner bark was used by the Indians both as a masticatory and as a food, cooked with fat; and by many authors it is spoken of as a good emergency-food. According to Seton the half-grown seeds are edible, but we find no other authority for this statement. Kephart states that the inner bark of the common **American Elm** (*Ulmus americana* L.) is also available as emergency-food; and Vestal and Schultes state that by the Kiowa Indians it is brewed as a tea.

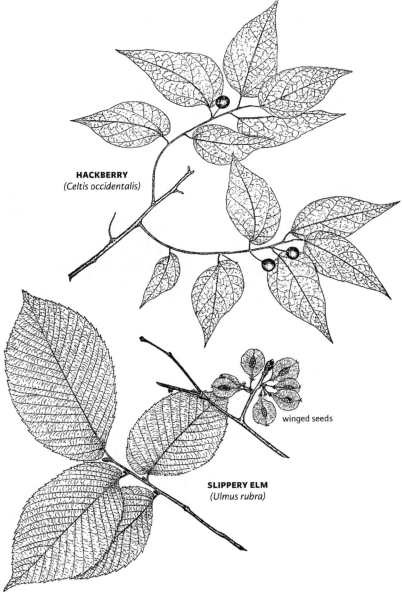

HACKBERRY
(*Celtis occidentalis*)

winged seeds

SLIPPERY ELM
(*Ulmus rubra*)

Urticaceae NETTLE FAMILY

Richweed, Clearweed
Pilea pumila (L.) Gray

Use potherb?

It has been suggested that the common **Richweed** may be an available potherb, this suggestion evidently based on the use of tropical species in this way. The plant is an easy one to try: a watery-stemmed and very smooth annual resembling nettles 3 inches to 2 feet high, with the minute green flowers in branching axillary clusters, growing in cool or moist and shaded places from Prince Edward Island to southern Ontario and southward, well developed in summer.

Nettles
Urtica (about 6 species)

Key-characters mostly erect herbs with opposite, coarsely toothed, oblong to egg-shaped, strongly ribbed leaves; the stems, leaf-stalks and lower surfaces of the leaves more or less covered with fine stinging bristles; flower-clusters slender and forking, borne in the upper axils in summer, bearing minute, greenish flowers. **Habitat** rich thickets, roadsides, rubbish-heaps, etc. **Range** several species, both native and introduced, throughout temperate America. **Season of Availability** late April and May, before the leaves become tough. **Uses** potherb, rennet.

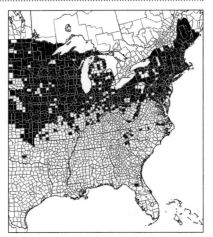

STINGING NETTLE *(Urtica dioica)*

The young leaves of **Nettles** have a fine reputation as a substitute for spinach, especially among the Scotch and Irish and on the continent of Europe; although, perhaps through prejudice, they have not become popular with the English stocks. The poet, Campbell, wrote:

"In Scotland I have eaten nettles, I have slept in nettle-sheets, and I have dined off a nettle-tablecloth. The young and tender nettle is an excellent potherb. The stalks of the old nettle are as good as flax for making cloth. I have heard my mother say, that she thought nettle-cloth more durable than any other species of linen."

The roots of most species are perennial and produce many shoots, so that the plant has been advocated in Scotland as desirable for winter use, the roots brought into the cellar promptly sending up shoots which are blanched as they come up through the earth or rubbish. The stinging propensities of the Nettle, the result of which Threlkeld naively said "may be felt everywhere," will deter all but the enthusiast from attempting to gather the greens.

Lightfoot, one of the earliest writers on Scotch natural history, says:

"In Arran, and other islands, a rennet is made of a strong decoction of nettles: a quart of salt is put to three pints of the decoction and bottled up for use. A common spoonfull of this liquor will coagulate a large bowl of milk very readily and agreeably, as we saw and experienced."

Holding plants over a fire for a few seconds will remove the stinging hairs.

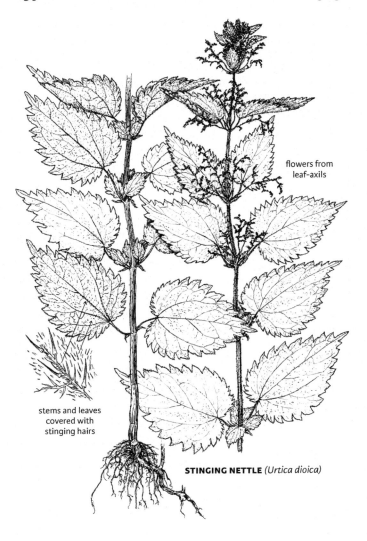

flowers from
leaf-axils

stems and leaves
covered with
stinging hairs

STINGING NETTLE (*Urtica dioica*)

Valerianaceae VALERIAN FAMILY

Tobacco-root, Edible Valerian
Valeriana edulis (ours var. *ciliata* (Torr. & Gray) Cronq. of the Upper Midwest).

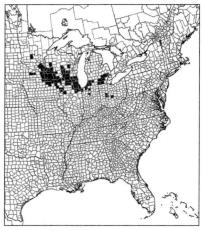

Key-characters herb with a very stout, brown, parsnip-like root which often forks deep in the ground, the whole fresh plant with a disgusting odor which has given the colloquial name Tobacco-root; leaves chiefly in a basal rosette, some of them simple and elongate, slightly broadened upward, others with a few lateral prongs and thus resembling antlers; flowering stem 1-3 feet high, bearing a very elongate cluster of small, whitish flowers, which are followed by rather large and hard seeds bearing a crown of curving hairs.
Habitat and Range rich prairies and low plains, from southern Ontario to Minnesota, south into Ohio, Indiana, Illinois and northeastern Iowa.

TOBACCO-ROOT *(Valeriana edulis)*

Season of Availability autumn and early spring, while the roots are well filled.
Uses root-vegetable, breadstuff, soup.

Although the fresh plant of **Tobacco-root** has a peculiar, strong odor which makes it repulsive to the whites, every one who has eaten the cooked root of the more western *Valeriana edulis* Nutt., properly prepared, has been enthusiastic over its palatable and nutritious qualities. To the Indians of the Great Basin those roots were an important source of food and they prepared them by baking for two days underground. According to Dr. Palmer the roots were also used as a source of bread and for soup. It is probable that the more eastern species, separated from the western one only on technical points, is similarly available as food. The offensive odor of the fresh plants of this genus apparently gave to a species of Europe and the Caucasus the quite expressive Latin name *Valeriana Phu!*

Corn-salad, Lamb's Lettuce
Valerianella locusta (L.) Lat. and several native species.

Synonym *Valerianella olitoria*
Use salad.

Corn-salad, occasionally raised in this country, is a frequent weed of roadsides from North Carolina and Tennessee northward to the Northern States, shooting up from the basal rosette in earliest spring and quickly ripening; the young plants springing up in late autumn. Though relatively unknown as a salad with us, doubtless because it is small and superseded by more vigorous salad-plants, especially those forced in winter, it was long a favorite from late autumn to early spring. Gerarde in 1597 explained the use and the English name Lamb's Lettuce as follows: "This herbe is colde and somthing moist, and not unlike in facultie and temperature to the garden Lettuce, in steede whereof in winter and in the first months of the springe it serues for a sallade herbe, and is with pleasure eaten with vineger, salt, and oile, as other sallades be, among which it is none of the woorst"; and further: "The plant which is commonly called . . . the white pot-herbe (which of some hath been set out for a kinde of Valerian, but vnproperly, for that it doth very notablie resemble the Lettuce as well in forme as in meate to be eaten, which property is not to bee founde in Valerin, and therefore by reason and authoritie I place it as a kinde of Lettuce with this name, Lambes Lettuce)."

Several quickly developing native species should be tested.

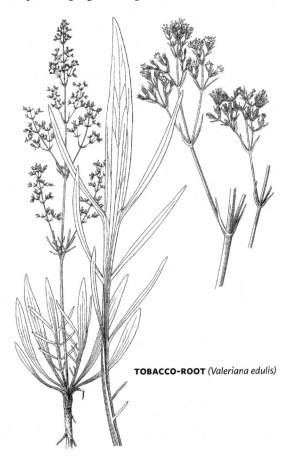

TOBACCO-ROOT *(Valeriana edulis)*

Verbenaceae VERVAIN FAMILY

Blue Vervain
Verbena hastata L.

Use breadstuff.

The common **Blue Vervain** of lowlands has slender spikes of flowers and of fruits borne in dense spire-like clusters; and, according to Chestnut, the seeds are gathered by the California Indians and after roasting used for meal. The seeds, which can be gathered in considerable abundance, have a mildly bitter taste, but it should be comparatively easy to test their quality with a view to determining how to obtain a palatable flour.

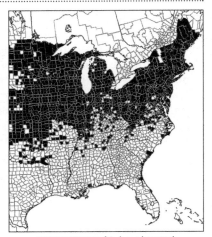

BLUE VERVAIN *(Verbena hastata)*

BLUE VERVAIN
(Verbena hastata)

Violaceae VIOLET FAMILY

Violets
Viola (various species)

Uses confection, thickening for soup.

The fragrant **English Violet** is, of course, familiar with us only as a cultivated plant which occasionally escapes to grassland; its flowers, candied, have long been popular, chiefly on account of their delicate fragrance.

The great botanist of South Carolina, Stephen Elliott, treating the violets with palmately dissected leaves as one variable species, but incidentally calling one of them *Viola esculenta* (now *V. palmata* var. *esculenta*), said "This Violet is very mucilaginous and much used by negroes in their soup." Porcher, somewhat later, called it Wild Okra and said of the species of "blue" violets with uncleft leaves (his inclusive *V. cucullata*): "This plant has been used in making soup during war times. To it may be added the wild okra, the dock and the lamb's quarter." Since the roots of violets are sometimes emetic, only the herbage and flowers should be used. Probably any of the "blue" violets might be used.

DOWNY YELLOW VIOLET
(Viola pubescens)

Vitaceae GRAPE FAMILY

Grapes

Vitis (a dozen species)

Uses jelly, marmalade, preserves, cold drink, the smaller and more acid fruits as masticatories.

The various **Wild Grapes** which occur from New Brunswick westward and southward are too well known to need special definition, and their fruits are in large demand for the making of jellies, marmalades and preserves. The best species northward is undoubtedly the **Fox Grape**, *Vitis labrusca* L., with large fruits, but some of the other northern species have fruits which, though small, are highly valued in the making of jelly. Of some of the sweeter-fruited species the Indians formerly gathered a great store, drying the fruit for winter use. Southward a different series of species has its enthusiastic gatherers, the **Muscadine**, *V. rotundifolia* Michx., being everywhere sought for its big, aromatic, sweet fruit which, as soon as fully ripe, drops to the ground and becomes hidden among fallen leaves. The form with amber-colored to cream-colored fruit, the **Scuppernong**, is generally grown in back-yards of the South. Not only is the Muscadine everywhere sought for its fresh fruit and for preserves and jellies, but Dr. Carver enthusiastically recommended the preparation of Muscadine "leather" ("delicious"):

"Gather when ripe, wash, put in a porcelain or granite preserving kettle, cover with boiling water, let simmer until the berries are hot through and the hulls have turned a reddish color, now stir in a scant tablespoon of baking soda to the gallon of fruit, stir well for three minutes, but do not mash the fruit; drain off this water, wash in three more waters, being careful each time not to mash the berries. They may now be dried whole or made into a leather the same as recommended for strawberries [see directions on p. 24]. I much prefer the leather, the hulls will be very tender and the fruit of a fine flavor. The seeds may be removed by passing through a colander. I wish every housewife would try this."

FOX GRAPE
(Vitis labrusca)

Zosteraceae EEL-GRASS FAMILY

Eel-Grass, Grass-Wrack, Sea-Wrack

Zostera marina L.

Habitat sandy or muddy sea-margin; once commonly cast up by storms, but in recent years largely destroyed by some epidemic.
Range shores of the northern Atlantic and northern Pacific.
Season of Availability throughout the year.
Use nibble.

Masters, in the *Treasury of Botany*, states that in the Hebrides the sweetish rootstocks and bases of the shoots are chewed for their palatable juice.

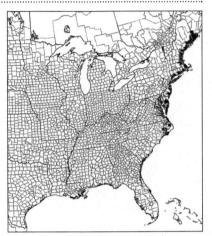

EEL-GRASS *(Zostera marina)*

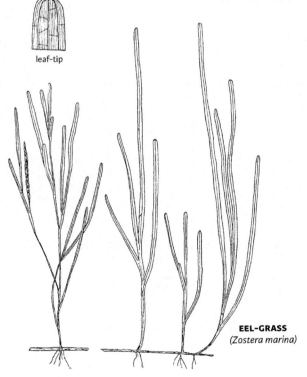

leaf-tip

EEL-GRASS
(Zostera marina)

CHANTERELLE *(Cantharellus cibarius)*, a highly prized edible mushroom.

CHAPTER FOUR

Mushrooms, Seaweeds, Lichens

1. *Mushrooms*

For many years in America, particularly from the late 19th into the early decades of the present century, the fashion of gathering and eating mushrooms so rapidly developed that there grew up in several communities a little group of people who knew and regularly gathered the edible mushrooms—the devotees of these peculiar growths who have been jocosely dubbed "the mycophagic cult." Those who are or were members of the cult in regular standing will find nothing in the present chapter to merit their attention, for they already know its contents and have access to one or more of the many volumes devoted exclusively to mushrooms and their recognition; and for those who wish to pursue the study of mushrooms with thoroughness these books are naturally the best sources of information, whether they use Atkinson's extremely conservative volume, the gigantic "mushroom bible" (McIlvaine's sumptuous book), or one of the other works indicated in the bibliography, or others of later vintage. By far the most authoritative treatment, simple, safe and with marvelous illustrations is "Icones Farlowianae." Much less expensive and with illustrations reproduced from paintings by the late L. C. C. Krieger, is "A Popular Guide to the Higher Fungi (Mushrooms)," published by the New York State Museum, from which, through the kindness of the director, Dr. C. C. Adams, we have been allowed to photograph several species. (**Note:** newer books are, of course, available and well-illustrated in color; see **Bibliography**, p. 416). We are greatly indebted to Dr. David H. Linder, Curator of the Farlow Library and Herbarium, who has freely advised us.

Unfortunately, there is no simple magic, as many uninformed persons suppose, by which edible species can be distinguished from poisonous species; and the popular notion, that the former are mushrooms, the latter toadstools is, of course, erroneous. The words mushroom and toadstool are synonymous, but the former is the better one to use. In many genera, as Amanita, Boletus, etc., actively poisonous and even deadly species superficially resemble others which the thoroughly trained enthusiast does not hesitate to eat. It is obvious, then, that the beginner must be extremely cautious about eating wild mushrooms and should never allow himself to be tempted into eating any mushroom unless he is absolutely certain of its identity.

As already stated, the student who wishes to follow up the mushrooms with any thoroughness must consult the books or papers enumerated in the bibliography. A few mushrooms, however, are so very distinct in form, color and texture as to be unmistakable, provided, of course, that the collector exercises reasonable care in observation. Some of the more marked and palatable of these are discussed and several of them illustrated below, and, as a safeguard, some of the most common of the violently poisonous or even deadly species are also shown.

POISONOUS SPECIES

For the beginner certain rules are absolutely necessary, lest the attractive but dangerous species should be eaten.

1. Never gather to eat mushrooms in the button of unexpanded stage. One is then too apt to confuse poisonous and edible species.

2. Never gather to eat nor mix with species to be eaten any mushroom with a membrane-like cup, bowl or bag or a scaly bulb at the base of the stem. Our deadliest species, the **Death-Cup or Deadly Amanita**, *Amanita phalloides*, has such a cup (volva) at base when young and at least ruptured portions of it may usually be found on old specimens. Another virulent species, the **Fly-Amanita**, *Amanita muscaria* (because poisonous to flies), has a scaly bulb at base. Above all things, avoid any mushroom with the cup (volva) at base (often half buried in the earth and consequently to be watched for with utmost care), a ring at or near the summit of the stem, and white gills on the under side of the cap. These are most likely to be members of the very dangerous genus Amanita, and if the spores (the fine dust-like particles which fall from the gills) are white no question is left as to the identity, for the combination of characters (volva or scaly bulb, ring, white gills and white spores) clearly indicates Amanita.

Our two most common poisonous *Amanitas* are, as stated, the **Death-cup**, with the top of the cap bright white, or pale yellow to brownish, and smooth, and the **Fly-Amanita**, with the top of the cap varying from bright yellow to red, its surface flecked with loosely whitish scales or shreddy white spots. Both species occur in woods, where the Fly-Amanita is one of the handsomest of mushrooms; and the Death-cup also occurs in rich, open ground.

3. Avoid all earth-growing mushrooms with the under side of the cap full of minute pores. These are mostly members of the great genus *Boletus*. Some species are famous for their edible qualities, but many others are well known to be violently poisonous. The species are extremely difficult to distinguish and, until one becomes an expert, it is the part of wisdom to let them alone.

4. Avoid all mushrooms with milky juice, unless the juice is red or deep orange. These mushrooms with milky juice constitute the genus *Lactarius* (which also contains some with watery juice) and, although the species with red or deep-orange juice is one of the most delicious of mushrooms, some of those with white or pale juice are very peppery or bitter and should be avoided.

5. Avoid the common woodland mushroom with the flattish-topped smooth cap bright red or rosy above, with the white gills radiating regularly like crowded spokes of a wheel, i.e. without any or at least many short, intermediate gills. This is *Russula emetica*, the name of which is sufficiently suggestive. Other species of *Russula* are found in woods and some are considered edible, but the beginner will be wisest if he lets them alone.

6. Avoid the beautiful saffron-yellow or yellowish- orange large mushroom, often occurring in late summer and autumn about the bases of stumps and old trees, with many crowded, solid stems and the convex caps overlapping, the broad gills extending irregularly down the stem, the surfaces phosphorescent in the dark. This very handsome species is **Jack-o'-Lantern**, *Omphalotus olearius* (formerly *Clitocybe illudens*), a tempting mushroom, said by those who have eaten it to be of excellent flavor but, most unfortunately, a violent emetic which produces discomfort and long-continued vomiting.

7. Until well trained in the careful study and identification of mushrooms, avoid any species not positively known to be harmless—and many harmless species are scarcely edible.

8. Avoid any mushroom which is beginning to decay.

To summarize, if the beginner carefully follows these eight rules, he will be avoiding the truly dangerous mushrooms and the somewhat poisonous kinds which are large enough or abundant enough to be specially inviting.

1. Avoid all mushrooms in the button stage.

2. Avoid all mushrooms with a membrane-like cup or scaly bulb at base.

3. Avoid all earth-growing mushrooms with the under side of the cap full of minute pores.

4. Avoid all mushrooms with white or pale milky juice.

5. Avoid all woodland mushrooms with flattish-topped, smooth cap bright red or rosy above, and with the white gills radiating like crowded spokes of a wheel.

6. Avoid the saffron-colored or yellowish-orange mushroom of old stumps, etc., with crowded solid stems, convex overlapping caps, broad gills extending irregularly down the stem, and surfaces phosphorescent in the dark.

7. Avoid any species not known to be edible.

8. Avoid any mushroom which is beginning to decay.

ABOVE
DEATH-CUP
(Amanita phalloides)

LEFT
FLY-AMANITA
(Amanita muscaria)

THE SICKENER *(Russula emetica)*

JACK-O'-LANTERN *(Omphalotus olearius)*

EDIBLE SPECIES
The following mushrooms are so characteristic that there is little danger of their being confused with poisonous species.

Meadow or Pasture Mushroom
Agaricus arvensis and *Agaricus campestris*

Key-characters *Agaricus arvensis:* stem short and stout, solid, with a small and thin ring at summit (at least when young) ; cap 2-10 inches broad, at first hemispherical, then becoming expanded-convex, thick and firm, whitish to whitish-brown, smooth and dryish on top, or tinged near the center of the top with yellow-ochre which becomes intensified when rubbed; veil (at first stretched across the gills on the lower side) of two layers, the outer peeling off and exposing the inner, which soon ruptures; gills in the button-stage white, soon becoming pinkish and finally purplish- brown; spores purplish-brown; the bruised mushroom slightly aromatic. *Agaricus campestris:* smaller, the cap usually 2-3 inches broad, flattened at first, then becoming convex, smooth or finally minutely silky in little flocks, the center of the top without the yellow tinge, the margin extended beyond the gills; the veil single; odor simply that of most mushrooms, not aromatic.
Habitat and Range open ground of pastures, fields, lawns and roadsides, often abundant, *A. campestris* oftenest where cow-manure has gathered, through temperate regions.
Season of Availability August to October.

Agaricus arvensis (sometimes called *Psalliota*) is the mushroom, i.e. the species, which is generally cultivated and sold in the market. *A. campestris*, although technically different in many details, is the commoner of the two in old pastures and manured areas. Though not so firm and solid it is a delicious species and is prepared like the mushroom of the market.

MEADOW OR PASTURE MUSHROOM

Shaggy Mane, Horsetail-Mushroom
Coprinus comatus

Key-characters usually tufted, the clumps often with numerous stems, but sometimes solitary; stem slender and hollow, bearing a narrow, loose ring about half-way up; cap not expanding until over-ripe, resembling a closed but very baggy umbrella or a slender barrel, 1-3 or -4 inches long, rounded at summit, densely shaggy over the surface with whitish or brownish locks, spreading open in maturity and turning to black or inky fluid; gills white, then pinkish, but in age black and changing to ink; spores black.
Habitat and Range fields, meadows, lawns, manured land, ash-heaps, etc., in temperate regions.
Season of Availability after rainy weather, early summer to autumn.

The **Shaggy Mane** is one of the most easily recognized of mushrooms, not only on account of the shaggy barrel-shaped cap, but on account of the mature plant rapidly deliquescing or changing to a blackish fluid, in which stage it is inedible. The firm caps washed and drained are excellent baked (seasoned and flecked with butter) or simmered in butter. They lose much water in cooking and, if all the flavor is wanted in eating, this black juice may be thickened with flour and the whole served on toast.

SHAGGY-MANE, HORSETAIL-MUSHROOM

Ink-cap, Inky Mushroom
Coprinus atramentarius

Key-characters growing in clusters or scattered; stem rather short and stoutish, frail and hollow, elongating in age; cap egg-shaped, grayish or smoky in color, smooth or slightly roughened, 1-3 inches high, expanding only when overripe and then becoming an inky wet mass; gills at first pale, changing gradually to blackish and becoming wet and inky; spores black.

Habitat and Range about manure-heaps, rubbish, rich fields and lawns (especially if recently manured), in temperate regions.

Season of Availability spring, late summer and autumn.

The **Ink-cap** is one of the most familiar of mushrooms and by many is considered good eating. It is not generally so highly esteemed as the Shaggy Mane but may be cooked in the same ways.

INKY-CAP, INKY MUSHROOM

Small or Early Inky Mushroom, Glistening Coprinus
Coprinellus micaceus

Synonym *Coprinus micaceus*

Key-characters densely tufted; the brittle, hollow stems slender; cap small, rarely more than 1% inches high, somewhat thimble-shaped, thin, yellowish-brown or drab, with fine stripes near the margin; gills pale, becoming pinkish-drab and finally black; spores black; whole plant quickly changing to a black inky mass.

Habitat and Range about the bases of dead or weakened trees, old stumps, lawns, etc., temperate regions, often on old bases of elms.

Season of Availability after rains of first warm days of spring through summer and frequently in autumn (often until killing frost).

The **Early Inky Mushroom** is highly appreciated by lovers of mushrooms because, although small, it comes during the first warm days when there are few other species available. The small caps usually occur in such abundance that a good mess is quickly gathered, great care being necessary to pull off the caps without getting the dirty and gritty bases of the stems, which are too easily pulled up. The caps (with all old and very black ones rejected) are simply cooked, by washing in two or three waters, draining through a colander, throwing into a sauce-pan with a little butter and seasoning, bringing to a boil and allowing to simmer for a few minutes. There is a superabundance of black, watery juice which may be thickened with flour to make a rich, creamy sauce. Some prefer to bake the caps about half-an-hour in a slow oven.

The little mushroom is so abundant that it may be canned (cold pack). On account of the excessive quantity of well flavored watery black juice the full value is best retained by mixing with dry bread-crumbs, beaten egg, milk and seasonings; then baking. The baked Inkys are delicious.

SMALL OR EARLY INKY MUSHROOM

Fairy-ring
Marasmius oreades

Key-characters forming regular or interrupted (often entirely obscure) broad rings in the grass; stem tough and solid, slender, white, an inch or two high; cap dull creamy-white, creamy-pink, buff or cracker- brown, convex or widely expanded (often with a bump in the middle), 1-2 inches broad, somewhat leathery in texture, not quickly decaying but drying in the bright weather and freshening again when wet; gills somewhat remote or with obvious intervals; spores white.
Habitat and Range open grassy places, lawns, fields, pastures, etc., in temperate regions.

Season of Availability early summer to autumn, especially after rains.

The **Fairy-ring** is pretty generally known and is most quickly discovered through the fact that where it occurs the grass grows ranker and greener than in the neighboring sections of the field. However, we can give no guarantee that the mushroom will always be found under such conditions! The leathery texture of this species is objectionable to some, but the flavor is delicate and when simmered for about half an hour, in butter and seasoning, with a little water added, it is usually thought delicious. When found in profusion, they may be strung on strong thread and dried for winter use.

FAIRY-RING

Oyster-Mushroom
Pleurotus ostreatus

Key-characters forming clumps on the trunks of trees; the very short and thick (or almost obsolete) whitish stem attached at the margin (not near the center) of the cap; the large white, gray or buff, leathery caps of a fan-shaped or oyster-shell outline, crowded and overlapping, 3-9 inches broad; gills broad, white, running irregularly down the stem as prominent but gradually disappearing veins; spores white. The very similar P. sapidus, scarcely distinguishable except for its pink spores, is by many considered superior to P. ostreatus.

Habitat and Range on dead branches, knot-holes, decaying tree trunks, etc., in temperate regions.

Season of Availability summer and early autumn (rarely after frosty weather).

Although by some considered not one of the best, the **Oyster-Mushroom** is quite safe to eat and, if gathered when young and before it has toughened, is palatable, either stewed in fragments or fried in butter or bacon- fat. McIlvaine is enthusiastic about it, saying: "When the tender parts are dipped in egg, rolled in bread crumbs, and fried as an oyster, they are not excelled by any vegetable, and are worthy of a place in the daintiest menu."

Elm-Mushroom
Hypsizygus ulmarius

Synonym *Pleurotus ulmarius*
Key-characters Clustered on tree-trunks; the long, thick, often curved, white stem attached somewhat to one side of the center of the cap; caps convex, becoming flat, with somewhat inrolled margin, whitish or shaded toward the summit with brown or yellow, 2-6 inches broad, many and overlapping, of rather tough texture; gills white, slightly wavy, abruptly notched at base; spores white.
Habitat and Range on dead or wounded trees, often elms, but by no means confined to them, temperate regions.
Season of Availability summer and especially autumn.

ELM-MUSHROOM

The **Elm-Mushroom** is often abundant, especially after heavy autumn rains, on dead trees and about injured branches or knot-holes. It is of better quality than the oyster-mushroom and by many people is highly valued. If the older caps are used only the tender parts should be cooked as the middle of the cap soon becomes tough.

Orange-milk Mushroom
Lactarius deliciosus

Key-characters growing solitary or scattered; stem stout, an inch or two high, orange or yellowish, commonly spotted, becoming hollow; cap 2-5 inches broad, orange, yellowish, or these colors suffused or blotched with drab or greenish tones, commonly with concentric bands or zones of color, somewhat slimy or viscid on top and with a central depression; gills very soft and brittle, crowded, running down to the stem; spores white; the bruised plant exuding a thick, milky, pleasantly aromatic, orange or saffron- red juice, which an exposure to the air gradually turns greenish.
Habitat and Range in damp woods, Newfoundland and Canada and the northern States, south in cool or upland regions; in northern New England and Canada oftenest under spruces and firs or in open bushy, spruce and fir thickets.
Season of Availability summer and autumn.

Lactarius deliciosus, as its specific name implies, has long been famous as one of the choicest of mushrooms, and it is often found in great abundance though sometimes tantalizingly scattered. It requires long cooking, forty minutes to an hour or more, either stewed or baked. The tendency of the red or orange juice to turn green is likely to frighten the novice but, if thoroughly cooked, the species is apparently quite safe to use.

ORANGE-MILK MUSHROOM

Lobster Mushroom
Hypomyces lactifluorum

Key-characters solitary or often clustered orange-red or in age darker red, funnel-shaped or irregularly vase-shaped, solid but fleshy mushrooms often 3-6 inches high and as broad or broader, depressed at summit, with no gills or only with obscure furrows and ridges on the outside. (This description applies to the highly characteristic and greatly modified mushroom, the *Hypomyces* itself of course being the filmy orange-red coat.)
Habitat and Range dry mixed or deciduous woods, throughout the eastern States and southern Canada.
Season of Availability summer and early autumn.

This is a most singular and delicious mushroom. Technically the *Hypomyces* is the orange-red surface of the mushroom, a minute parasitic species which grows over the surface of a true mushroom, completely or almost completely obliterating the gills and adding vastly to the weight and edibility of the host. It is now demonstrated that the host is commonly the very peppery white-juiced *Lactarius piperatus*. If so, then indeed is *Hypomyces* an unusually good parasite.

The brilliant orange-red funnels or vases may be found in dry, old woods, often hardly showing above ground, but lifting slightly the dead pine needles and other leaves. In pastured regions the cattle are likely to destroy the crop; at

LOBSTER MUSHROOM

least in one rich habitat in Maine we have found it difficult to get ahead of the cows and have often discovered the hidden treasures by noticing where cattle had previously been nosing them out.

The red parasitized *Lactarius* when fresh, furnishes one of the most substantial and satisfying of vegetables. Cut into thin pieces crosswise and stewed, in a little water, for an hour or more, then seasoned and the juice thickened, it is very rich and suggestive of young shell beans.

Perplexing Hypholoma
Hypholoma sublateritium

Synonym *Hypholoma perplexa*
Key-characters forming tufts; the tough and rather fibrous hollow stems 2-4 inches long and about ⅜ inch thick, reddish-brown to yellowish at base; the cap 1 to 2½ or 3 inches across, convex to flattish, smooth, brownish or reddish, with yellowish margin and whitish flesh; the thin and approximate gills at first yellowish, changing to greenish, then brown or purplish.
Habitat and Range on decaying bases of stumps or fallen logs of hardwood, through much of our range.
Season of Availability September to November, often appearing after early frosts or with the caps frosted but uninjured.

Although not one of the choicest, this *Hypholoma* is often so abundant in the autumn that great quantities can be gathered. It is solid, nutty and very acceptable, browned in butter, oil or bacon-fat, or escalloped with crumbs, eggs, milk and seasoning. It is too flavorless to be wholly attractive when stewed.

PERPLEXING HYPHOLOMA

Chanterelle
Cantharellus cibarius

Key-characters a fleshy and thickish, rather firm, egg-yellow or chrome-yellow mushroom of funnel-shape, 2-5 inches high, with the border of the funnel often wavy or irregular, sometimes decidedly one-sided, the surfaces opaque or dull, not shining; gills with blunt edges, rather stout and with numerous parallel forkings which are often connected by little cross-veins; spores whitish-yellow. The similar *C. aurantiacus* has a dull-orange or brownish cap, with yellow gills.

Habitat and Range old woods, on the ground or on decaying logs and fallen branches, often abundant, in southern Canada and generally through the northern and eastern States.

Season of Availability summer and early autumn.

The **Chanterelle**, especially *Cantharellus cibarius*, is one of the famous mushrooms, highly valued both in Europe and America, and in Europe sold in the markets. It is often found in dry pine, fir or spruce woods in such quantities that it would be easy quickly to fill a bushel- basket. Cut into thin shreds across the gills and stewed for half-an-hour or more and well seasoned it is always an inviting dish. It may also be fried in butter. When found in quantity, Chanterelle may be strung, suspended at the top of the kitchen and dried for winter use.

The similar *C. aurantiacus* (now classified as *Hygrophoropsis aurantiaca*) is sometimes as good as *C. cibarius* but sometimes a little bitter; and other species, with elongate, trumpet- or cornucopia-forms, are edible, though not always of the best flavor.

CHANTERELLE

Caution If you find a bright yellow mushroom growing in large clusters around stumps, leave it alone. It may be the poisonous **Jack-o'-Lantem** (see p. 387), sometimes called the **False Chantarelle**. It has sometimes been confused with the true Chantarelle, but they are not difficult to distinguish. The habit of growing in great clusters, and the thin, close to crowded gills of the Jack-o'-Lantem are quite distinctive. Fresh specimens of the Jack-o'-Lantern give off a pale, phosphorescent light when placed in a dark room, and this is a good test for it. However, if the specimens are old or a little dried out, they may not give off the light, so its absence should not be taken as proof that your specimen is not the Jack-o'-Lantern.

Graylings
Cantharellula umbonata

Synonym *Cantharellus umbonatus*
Key-characters a leathery, gray or fawn-colored, top-shaped or vaseshaped mushroom growing in and attached to the common Hair-cap Moss, *Polytrichum*; the cap regular or irregular and puckered at edge, of rather thin texture but tough, 1-3 inches broad, usually depressed and with a hump (umbo) at the center; gills whitish, thin and remote, running down to the leathery stem.
Habitat and Range occurring, as said, in carpets of Hair-cap Moss, *Polytrichum,* and not easily gathered without pulling some of the moss with the mushroom. Common in southern Canada and the northern States, on cool slopes or in damp thickets and open woods, wherever the *Polytrichum* abounds.
Season of Availability summer and especially autumn and even, in open winters, to January.

The little *Cantharellula*, which the late Ralph Hoffmann, the writer on ornithology, appropriately named "Grayling," is one of the best of mushrooms for stewing. It has the characteristic, so well known in the Fairyring, of drying in bright weather, softening in wet weather, and only very slowly or very tardily showing any tendency to decay. It may, consequently, be gathered through a long period; and we have often found it in excellent condition in warm days of December or during the "January thaw." We annually dry many quarts of Graylings for winter use.

GRAYLINGS

Beef-steak Mushroom
Fistulina hepatica

Key-characters forming short-stalked to closely sessile brackets on trees and stumps; the brackets or shelves mostly solitary or scattered, shaped like a broad opened fan, or, when scalloped on the margin, suggesting a liver; the fleshy and juicy shelf about half an inch thick, dark-red and when wet sticky or slimy above, usually with distinct lines of color radiating from the base and middle; under surface yellowish or buff, full of fine pores.

Habitat and Range dead trunks and stumps of hard-wood trees, especially the nut-trees, locally abundant in the eastern states, commonest southward, too rare northward.

Season of Availability after rains, midsummer to early autumn.

Caution Do not confuse the **Beef-steak Mushroom** with the hard and woody *Ganoderma lucidum* (formerly *Fomes lucidus*), which forms large, very shiny, red or chestnut-purple shelves and brackets on trees. The hard bracket-mushrooms are inedible and if mistaken for Fistulina hepatica will cause disappointment.

The Beef-steak Mushroom is said by enthusiasts to be as good when broiled as a tenderloin steak. The juice is acid and some people find it offensive. Others, however, enjoy it. The acid and much of the slime may be removed by soaking in salt water. Slice, season and broil, or slice and fry in butter, or cut into thin slices crosswise (the slices streaked with red like a steak) and stew in water and butter for half-an-hour.

BEEF-STEAK MUSHROOM

Sulphur Mushroom
Laetiporus sulphureus

Synonym *Polyporus sulphureus*
Key-characters forming large overlapping sulphur-yellow (or orange- shaded) brackets on the trunks or bases of dead or injured deciduous trees or on logs and stumps; the masses of brackets a foot or more across, the individual brackets attached separately to the host or more commonly fused at base; caps fan-shaped, flattish above or convex, the under surface full of minute pores; texture of the brackets rather firm and tough.
Habitat and Range on old trunks, logs and stumps of decaying hardwood trees, through the eastern states.
Season of Availability midsummer to frost.

Caution The **Sulphur Mushroom** is scarcely to be confused with anything else, but the beginner should make sure that he finds the abundant fine pores, not broad gills, on the under surface, and that the shelves are not long-stalked. The highly emetic **Jack-o'-Lantern**, *Omphalotus olearius*, with overlapping saffron-yellow, stalked caps and with broad gills running down the stem, grows on trees and stumps and must be clearly distinguished.

SULPHUR MUSHROOM

The Sulphur Mushroom, on account of its rather tough quality must be cut into very thin slices crosswise and simmered or slowly stewed for half-an-hour or more, when it is excellent. It is particularly delicious if, after parboiling, it is finely chopped, mixed with crumbs and a white sauce, and made into croquettes.

Hedgehog-Mushroom
Hydnum and *Hericium*

Key-characters forming irregular shelves, tufts or festoons, with long processes or elongate fingers or teeth hanging down in a dense fringe or shaggy mass, usually white or yellowish.
Habitat and Range on dead trees, old logs, etc., in woods, cool and temperate regions.
Season of Availability summer and autumn.

There are several types of **Hedgehog-Mushrooms**, some too difficult for the beginner to distinguish, some tough and inedible. The edible species with slender fingers or soft spines stewed or mixed with crumbs, beaten egg and scalded milk, seasoned and then baked, are by some considered delicious, by others not specially inviting.

HEDGEHOG-MUSHROOM

Coral-Mushrooms
Clavaria, Clavulinopsis (various species)

Key-characters erect or ascending plants, either bushy in habit, with many upright, simple or forking and often fused branches, suggesting some types of coral, or with simple club-shaped bodies; texture soft and brittle; colors various, creamy white, yellow, pale-brown and drab or reddish.

Habitat and Range on leaf-mold in the woods or on dead wood, old logs, decaying branches, etc., one or another species in most parts of the United States and Canada.
Season of Availability summer and autumn.

The **Coral-Mushrooms** are all considered safe to eat. Some are of superior quality, some slightly bitter, but their distinctions are too technical for this book. The larger freely forking kinds often occur in great quantity and it is then easy to fill a large basket; but it should be remembered that immediately after heavy rain the plants are apt to be very watery and tasteless. We like them best stewed or broken into fragments, mixed with crumbs and beaten egg and scalded milk, well seasoned and baked.

The little, simple **Yellow Clubs** (*Clavaria pulchra*, now classified as *Clavulinopsis laeticolor*) are common in spruce and fir woods northward and are excellent raw, delicate and nutty. They also make a delicious dish if prepared like an oyster stew.

YELLOW CLUBS

Puffballs
Lycoperdon and *Calvatia* (various species)

The **Puffballs** which when young have white flesh are all harmless and several of them are of excellent quality. When the flesh is at all dark-colored the Puffball should not be eaten and at least one kind with dark flesh is held in suspicion. The Puffballs vary from tiny rounded or balloon-shaped species, which are too small to be useful, to the Giant Puffball, *Calvatia gigantea*, which varies from a few inches to a foot or more in diameter and which occurs in grassy fields, disturbed soil and rich thickets. The Giant Puffball may be peeled, sliced and fried, or it, as well as the smaller species, after peeling may be cut into bits and stewed or mixed with crumbs, beaten egg, scalded milk and seasoning and baked.

Caution Always reject Puffballs in which the flesh is not white and firm.

Morel
Morchella (various species)

Key-characters stem stout and hollow, somewhat pebbled or granular on the surface; cap not separable from the stem, of various forms from cylindric or conical to globose or depressed, with a deeply corrugated surface consisting of fleshy interlacing ridges and deep pits, usually darker- colored than the stem, hollow inside.

Habitat and Range several species, one or another in rich woods, thickets, borders of woods, orchards and other half-shade, temperate regions.

Season of Availability May and June, in warm weather following rain.

The **Morels** are ranked among the very choicest of edible fungi, but unfortunately they are local and likely to occur as scattered individuals. Sometimes, especially where there has been a brush-fire, they come up in quantity and we have, in such a spot, been able to fill a large knap-sack. When found in such quantity they may be strung and dried over the kitchen range for winter use. Morels are cooked in various ways: stuffed and baked for half-an-hour; tossed in butter, etc.; always good if they are well cooked and the rich juice, boiled down and thickened, is served as a sauce.

2. Seaweeds

The Seaweeds are comparatively unimportant for food, but four species of our Atlantic coast have some value. They contain iodine and are often prescribed for those inclined to goiter and other conditions due to deficiency of iodine in the diet.

Irish Moss
Chondrus crispus

Key-characters fronds tough and elastic or leathery, when wet mucilaginous or slimy, when dry crisp and shrunken, flattened, 3-6 inches high, freely forking and subdividing several times, with the terminal lobes crowded, whitish, creamy, or greenish to purple or even black.
Habitat and Range at or just below high tide, chiefly upon rocks, but commonly cast up on different types of shore, from North Carolina northward.

IRISH MOSS *(Chondrus crispus)*

Irish Moss is extensively sold by the grocer for the making of blanc mange, and is of course familiar to all house-wives. The growing plants are usually of dark colors, from olive to purple or black, but the market commodity consists of sun-blanched creamy-white fronds which have been cast up on the beach. It is singular that green, purple or black Irish Moss is looked upon with suspicion, so used are we to cooking only the old, dead and pallid fragments!

Dulse
Palmaria palmata

Synonym *Rhodymenia palmata*
Key-characters plants with a very short stem which quickly broadens into a thin, tongue-shaped or fan-shaped, ribless and nerveless, dark-red or claret-colored expanse, the fans variously cleft into flat thumbs or fingers and these again sometimes with short round-tipped lobes; the whole plant a few inches to a foot or so long.
Habitat and Range on rocks or attached to coarser seaweeds and kelps, from low-water mark to considerable depths, Atlantic coast.

DULSE *(Palmeria palmata)*

Dulse is often seen in our markets, where in the dried condition it is unattractive in appearance. It is a popular food, either cooked or raw, in Europe but has never become a staple with us, though it is often nibbled as a relish.

Laver
Porphyra (various species)

Key-characters frond thin and with a satiny sheen, red, dark-purple or purple-brown, simple or variously lobed or cleft, with strongly ruffled margin, varying from a few inches to a foot long; easily distinguished by its red, purple or purple-brown color, filmy and elastic texture and satiny lustre.
Habitat and Range near low tide on rocks, boulders and other supports, general on the coast, and freely cast up on shores.

LAVER *(Porphyra)*

Laver is a pleasant relish, eaten raw or nibbled, and it may be cooked and used in making soup. The Chinese are specially fond of it and at various times the Chinese in America have imported Laver in quantity from China, not knowing that there is plenty on both our Atlantic and Pacific coasts. Dr. Berkeley, in *The Treasury of Botany*, supplies the following recipe: "A condiment prepared from the common Porphyra, which is greatly esteemed by some, while to others it is an object of unmitigated disgust. The taste for it, like that for olives, is only acquired by use. The best way of preparing it for table is to mix the quantity required for immediate use with a few tablespoonfuls of stock, and a little lemon-juice. It is then to be made quite hot in a well-tinned or silver saucepan, and poured upon toast."

Edible Kelp
Alaria esculenta

Key-characters a characteristic kelp, with short, cylindric stem and a ruffled or wavy olive-green or -brown, thinnish, unperforated frond a few inches wide and from one to many feet long, distinguished from our other kelps (except the Sea-Colander, *Agarum turneri*, which has very numerous round holes or perforations in the frond) by having a strong midrib running from base to apex and by bearing from near the base slender-stalked, tongue-shaped, ribless secondary fronds upon which the fruit is borne.
Habitat and Range rocky bottoms and submerged ledges, below high, tide, from Massachusetts northward.

EDIBLE KELP *(Alaria esculenta)*

The thick midribs, divested of the broad wing-like, olive membrane, have had some use in Europe as food, as have the heavily fruiting lateral fronds, both of which are said to have a sweet taste.

3. *Lichens*

About the last sources of food we should ordinarily think of are the dry, juiceless, gray, drab or brown lichens, often mistakenly called "mosses," which carpet sterile ground or expand their flat or crisped surfaces on rocks, fences or trees. But several of the lichens have been important food and in a number of cases man has fought off starvation by their use. The famous lichen-manna of North Africa and western Asia would certainly seem as unpromising a source of food as could be imagined, being mere small lumps, often no larger than a pinhead or a pea. Yet the following extract from Lindsay's most helpful *Popular History of British Lichens*, from which we have drawn much of our information regarding the edible species, certainly indicates its importance in emergency.

"Two foreign species of this genus, *Lecanora esculenta* and *L. affinis*, are of great interest, from having repeatedly, under extraordinary circumstances, served as the food of large numbers of men and cattle, in various countries lying between Algeria and Tartary. They are said at various times and in divers places to have appeared suddenly, covering with a layer, sometimes from three to six inches thick, large tracts of country; and the inhabitants, believing their origin to have been from heaven, have designated them a species of manna, and have imitated their flocks, in times of scarcity of food, by eating them. . . . Several 'rains of manna'. . . have been described by travellers. . . . The manna is usually found in the form of small lumps, from the size of a pin's head to that of a pea or small nut, which are greyish or whitish, hard, irregular in form, inodorous, and insipid. . . . As an illustration of the circumstances under which manna-rain is said to fall, Anchercloi states that in 1829, during a war between Russia and Persia, a large tract of country round a town on the south-west shore of the Caspian, whose inhabitants were in a state of famine, was suddenly covered by a Lichen which fell from heaven. The sheep were noticed to eat it with avidity; the idea immediately occurred to the famishing inhabitants that this substance might prove equally agreeable or nutritious to themselves, and accordingly it was converted into bread."

The explanation of the "rains of manna" is, of course, that the lichen grows attached on the ground elsewhere and the fragments, being light, are transported by wind.

Probably the most famous instance of use of a Lichen as emergency-food in American annals was the long period when Sir John Franklin, Dr. (later Sir John) Richardson, George Back (all famous names in American botany) and their Canadian voyageurs staved off starvation for many weeks in the region northwest of Hudson Bay by living on **Tripe de Roche**, black, tough and dry blister-like lichens of the genus *Umbilicaria*, growing on rocks. These uninteresting-looking lichens contain abundant starch and when boiled yield a jelly similar to blanc mange; but they also contain a bitter and purgative principle. This substance, it is stated, can be removed by steeping the **Rock-Tripe** in dilute soda-water, after which the nutritious lichen is wholesome. But Franklin and his party were not situated to remove the purgative principle. From Franklin's intensely dramatic journal we extract a few pertinent records of a starving party of dauntless scientists, written on different days during a period of nearly two months.

"Some tripe de roche was collected, which we boiled for supper . . . they refused to pick tripe de roche, choosing rather to go entirely without eating, than to make any exertion. . . . Having persuaded the people to gather some tripe de roche, I partook of a meal with them. . . . My associates were all in the same debilitated state, and poor Hood was reduced to a perfect shadow, from the severe bowel complaints which the tripe de roche never failed to give him. . . . The want of tripe de roche caused us to go supperless to bed. . . . The tripe de roche disagreed with this man and with Vaillant, in consequence of which, they were the first whose strength totally failed. We had a small quantity of this weed in the evening, and the rest of our supper was made of scraps of leather ... the weather not permitting the gathering of tripe de roche, we had nothing to cook. . . . Next morning the breeze was light and the weather mild, which enabled us to collect some tripe de roche, and to enjoy the only meal we had for four days. We derived great benefit from it, and walked with considerably more ease. . . . The tripe de roche had hitherto afforded us our chief support, and we naturally felt great uneasiness at the prospect of being deprived of it, by its being so frozen as to render it impossible for us to gather it.... We endeavoured to pick some tripe de roche, but in vain, as it was entirely frozen."

Several other lichens have been used in emergency and a few species have considerable fame as sources of palatable blanc mange and even bread. Some of our most important edible species are illustrated and discussed below, but most lichens are too difficult of distinction for the beginner.

Tripe de Roche, Rock-Tripe
Umbilicaria (various species)

Key-characters commonly forming circular or nearly circular cartilaginous or leathery (when dry brittle and with curling edges) dark blisters, attached to rocks at the center; color gray, olive, dark brown or black.

TRIPE DE ROCHE *(Umbilicaria)*

Habitat and Range on rocks, one or another species throughout our range and extending to the Arctic.

Sufficiently discussed in the preceding paragraphs.

Iceland Moss
Cetraria islandica (L.) Ach.

ICELAND MOSS *(Cetraria islandica)*

Key-characters a tufted lichen, making broad somewhat foliaceous (leaf-like) olive or brown mats, often with blood-red blotches, from which arise very numerous erect, somewhat cartilaginous, freely forking, olivaceous, tubular or slenderly funnel-form tufts which divide at summit into many finely dissected divisions.
Habitat and Range on the ground, from the Arctic regions to the bare mountains and hills of the northern States, the coast of New England, and the higher mountains of North Carolina.

The **Iceland Moss** is said to contain 80 per cent starch, also gummy matter, fat, a bitter principle and various mineral salts. The bitter principle is purgative, as in Tripe de Roche, but can be removed by parboiling in water and soda. The jelly derived from Iceland Moss (after the bitter has been removed) is like blanc mange and is considered highly nutritious and digestible. It is stated that one pound of the plant, boiled in water, yields eight pounds of the jelly. The Icelanders and other northern peoples not only use the plant in the preparation of puddings but in the making of soups and, powdered, in making bread. Cows, horses and other domestic animals are fattened by being fed upon it; and, in fact, the Iceland Moss is so highly esteemed in the North that it has been affirmed of the Icelanders that "a bountiful Providence sends them bread out of the very stones."

Tree-Lungwort
Lobaria pulmonaria (L.) Hoffm.

Synonym *Sticta pulmonaria*
Key-characters forming very large, coarsely but deeply lobed, thin but leathery, loosely overlapping expanses, greenish or olive above and with abundant oblong or squarish depressions bordered by interlacing ridges, pale-brown on the under surface.
Habitat and Range on trees or damp rocks, Newfoundland, Canada and the Northern States, south in the uplands to South Carolina.

The **Tree-Lungwort** is one of the most familiar large lichens of the cool forests and it early got its name from the supposed resemblance of its pitted and reticulated thallus to the structure of the lungs. It was supposed, on account of this resemblance, that jelly prepared from it was valuable food for consumptives. Although the Tree-Lungwort contains comparatively little starch, the jelly is slightly nutritious and is worth remembering in case of emergency. The moose is reputed to feast extensively on this plant.

TREE-LUNGWORT *(Lobaria pulmonaria)*

Reindeer-Moss
Cladonia rangiferina (L.) Weber ex F.H. Wigg., and allied species

Synonyms *Cladina rangiferina, Lichen rangiferinus*

The **Reindeer-Moss** is so very common on open ground and slightly shaded situations of northern and cool regions and is so familiar as forming the deep elastic carpets of wet weather (crisply brittle in dry weather), that it scarcely needs description. The plant, which northward forms tremendous carpets to a depth of six inches or a foot, received its name because it is the favorite winter food of reindeer (similarly of our American caribou). It is, therefore, collected in northern countries as fodder for domestic animals and it has more than once been asserted that the milk of cattle fed upon it "becomes wholly cream" and that their flesh is peculiarly fat and sweet.

Reindeer-Moss is also eaten by humans, either powdered and mixed with other flour for making bread or boiled to make a blanc mange or mucilaginous soup.

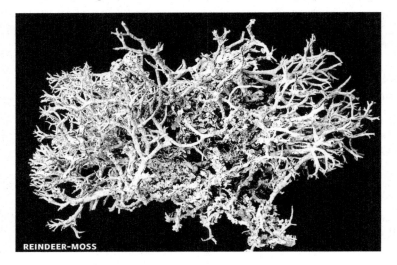

REINDEER-MOSS

Bibliography

The following list of books and papers, although by no means a complete bibliography of the subject covered in the preceding chapters, covers the chief sources from which we have drawn. Additional references can be found via online searches, such as at *www.amazon.com*. **Part I** lists popular books on the identification, harvest, and use of wild food plants. **Part II** is an edited version of the bibliography contained in the 1943 edition of this book.

Part I

EDIBLE WILD PLANTS

Angier, Bradford. *Field Guide to Edible Wild Plants*. Stackpole Books, 1974.

Brill, Steve. *Identifying and Harvesting Edible and Medicinal Plants in Wild (and Not So Wild) Places*. William Morrow, 1994.

Brown, Tom Jr. *Tom Brown's Field Guide to Wild Edible and Medicinal Plants*. Berkley, 1985.

Coon, Nelson. *Using Wayside Plants*. Hearthside, 1957.

Couplan, Francois. *The Encyclopedia of Edible Plants of North America*. Keats Publishing, 1998.

Derby, Blanche Cybele. *My Wild Friends: Free Food From Field and Forest*. White Star Press, 1997.

Elias, Thomas S., and Peter A. Dykeman. *Field Guide to North American Edible Wild Plants*. Outdoor Life Books, 1982.

Erichsen-Brown, Charlotte. *Medicinal and Other Uses of North American Plants*. Dover, 1979.

Fernald, Merritt Lyndon and Kinsey, Alfred Charles. *Edible Wild Plants of Eastern North America*. Harper and Row, 1943.

Foster, Steven, and James A. Duke. *A Field Guide to Medicinal Plants*. Houghton Mifflin Co., 1990.

Gibbons, Euell and Tucker, Gordon. *Euell Gibbons' Handbook of Edible Wild Plants*. Donning, 1979.

Gibbons, Euell. *Stalking the Blue-Eyed Scallop*. David McKay, 1964.

Gibbons, Euell. *Stalking the Faraway Places*. David McKay, 1973.

Gibbons, Euell. *Stalking the Good Life*. David McKay, 1971.

Gibbons, Euell. *Stalking the Healthful Herbs*. David McKay, 1966.

Gibbons, Euell. *Stalking the Wild Asparagus*. David McKay Co. Inc., 1962.

Gilmore, Melvin R. *Uses of Plants by the Indians of the Missouri River Region*. University of Nebraska Press, 1977. (Reprint; first publication 1919)

Grieve, M. *A Modem Herbal*. Dover Publications, Inc., 1931.

Hall, Alan. *The Wild Food Trailguide*. Holt, Rhinehart, and Winston, 1973.

Hamerstrom, Frances. *The Wild Food Cookbook, From the Fields and Forests of the Great Lakes States*. Amherst Press, 1989.

Harrington, H.D. *Edible Native Plants of the Rocky Mountains*. University of New Mexico Press, 1967.

Harris, Ben Charles. *Eat the Weeds*. Barre, MA: Barre, 1961.

Henderson, Robert K. *The Neighborhood Forager: A Guide for the Wild Food Gourmet*. Chelsea Green, 2000.

Hutchens, Alma R. *Indian Herbology of North America*. Merco, 1969.

Kindscher, Kelly. *Edible Wild Plants of the Prairie*. University Press of Kansas, 1987.

Marrone, Teresa. *Abundantly Wild: Collecting and Cooking Wild Edibles in the Upper Midwest*. Adventure Publications, 2004.

Martin, Laura C. *Wildflower Folklore*. CThe Globe Pcquot Press, 1984.

Mcpherson, Alan. *Wild Food Plants of Indiana and Adjacent States*. AuthorHouse, 2007.

Medsger, Oliver Perry. *Edible Wild Plants*. New York: Macmillan, 1939.

Meuninck, Jim. *Basic Essentials: Edible Wild Plants and Useful Herbs*. Globe Pequot, 1988.

Nyerges, Christopher. *Guide to Wild Foods and Useful Plants*. Chicago Review Press, 1999.

Peterson, Lee. *A Field Guide to Edible Wild Plants*. Houghton Mifflin Harcourt, 1999.

Phillips, Roger. *Wild Food*. Little, Brown and Co., 1989.

Pond, Barbara. *A Sampler of Wayside Herbs*. Crown, 1974.

Richardson, Joan. *Wild Edible Plants of New England*. The Globe Pequot Press, 1981.

Saunders, Charles Francis. *Edible and Useful Wild Plants of the United States and Canada*. Dover Publications, 1920.

Spencer, Edwin Rollin, Ph.D. *All About Weeds*. Dover Publications, 1940.

Squier, Thomas K. *Living Off the Land*. Academy Books, 1989.

Tatum, Billy Jo. *Billy Jo Tatum's Wild Foods Field Guide and Cookbook*. Workman Publishing Company, 1976.

Taylor, Ronald J. *All About Weeds*. Mountain Press Publishing, 1990.

Thoreau, Henry David. *Wild Fruits*. (Ed. Bradley Dean.) W.W. Norton, 2000.

Tilford, Gregory L. *Edible and Medicinal Plants of the West*. Mountain Press, 1997.

Tull, Delena. *Edible and Useful Plants of Texas and the Southwest*. University of Texas Press, 1987.

Vennum, Thomas Jr. *Wild Rice and the Ojibway People*. Minnesota Historical Society Press, 1988.

Weatherbee, Ellen Elliot and Bruce, James Garnett. *Edible Wild Plants: A Guide to Collecting and Cooking*. Weatherbee and Bruce, 1979.

Young, Kay. *Wild Seasons: Gathering and Cooking Wild Plants of the Great Plains*. University of Nebraska Press, 1993.

PLANT IDENTIFICATION
GENERAL

Chadde, Steve W. *A Great Lakes Wetland Flora. A complete, illustrated guide to the Aquatic and Wetland Plants of the Upper Midwest*. 4th ed. 2012.

Chadde, Steve W. *Minnesota Flora: An illustrated guide to the Vascular Plants of Minnesota*. 2013.

Chadde, Steve W. *Wisconsin Flora: An illustrated guide to the Vascular Plants of Wisconsin*. 2013.

Crow, G., and C. Hellquist. *Aquatic and Wetland Plants of Northeastern North America* (2 vols.). University of Wisconsin Press, 2000.

Eastman, J. 1995. *The Book of Swamp and Bog: Trees, Shrubs, and Wildflowers of Eastern Freshwater Wetlands*. Stackpole Books.

Elpel, Thomas J. *Botany in a Day*. 4th ed. HOPS Press, 2000.

Fassett, N. *A Manual of Aquatic Plants*. The University of Wisconsin Press, 1957.

Flora of North America Editorial Committee. *Flora of North America North of Mexico*. Set, partially published. Oxford University Press, 1993.

Gleason, H., and A. Cronquist. *Manual of Vascular Plants of Northeastern United States and Adjacent Canada*. 2nd ed. The New York Botanical Garden, 1991.

Haines, Arthur. *New England Wild Flower Society's Flora Novae Angliae: A Manual for the Identification of Native and Naturalized Higher Vascular Plants of New*

England. Yale University Press, 2011.

Holmgren, N. (editor). *Illustrated Companion to Gleason and Cronquist's Manual.* New York Botanical Garden, 1998.

Kartesz, J.T. *Floristic Synthesis of North America, Version 1.0.* Biota of North America Program (BONAP), 2010.

Magee, Dennis, Harry E. Ahles, Abigail Rorer. *Flora of the Northeast: A Manual of the Vascular Flora of New England and Adjacent New York.* 2nd ed. University of Massachusetts Press, 2007.

Mohlenbrock, Robert H. *Vascular Flora of Illinois: A Field Guide.* 4th ed. Southern Illinois University Press, 2013.

Swink, F., and G. Wilhelm. Plants of the Chicago Region. 4th ed. Indiana Academy of Science, 1994.

Voss, E.G. *Michigan Flora, Part I Gymnosperms and Monocots.* Cranbrook Institute of Science Bulletin 55 and University of Michigan Herbarium, 1972.

Voss, E.G. *Michigan Flora, Part II Dicots (Saururaceae–Cornaceae).* Cranbrook Institute of Science Bulletin 59 and University of Michigan Herbarium, 1985.

Voss, E.G. *Michigan Flora, Part III Dicots (Pyrolaceae–Compositae).* Cranbrook Institute of Science Bulletin 61 and University of Michigan Herbarium, 1996.

Voss, E.G. and A. A. Reznicek. *Field Manual of Michigan Flora.* University of Michigan Press, 2011.

Weakley, Alan S. *Flora of Virginia.* Botanical Research Inst of Texas. 2012.

TREES AND SHRUBS

Barnes, Burton V. and Wagner, Warren H. Jr. *Michigan Trees.* University of Michigan Press, 1981.

Elias, Thomas S. *Trees of North America.* Times Mirror, 1980.

National Audubon Society. *Field Guide to North American Trees: Eastern Region.* 1980.

Petrides, George A. *A Field Guide to Trees and Shrubs.* Houghton Mifflin Harcourt, 1998.

Phillips, Roger. *Trees of North America and Europe.* Random House, 1978.

Smith, W. *Trees and Shrubs of Minnesota.* The University of Minnesota Press, 2008.

Soper, J., and M. Heimburger. *Shrubs of Ontario.* The Royal Ontario Museum, 1982.

Stokes, Donald W. *The Natural History of Wild Shrubs and Vines.* The Globe Pequot Press, 1989.

Symonds, George W. D. *The Shrub Identification Book.* William Morrow & Co., 1963.

WILDFLOWERS

Black, M., and E. Judziewicz. *Wildflowers of Wisconsin and the Great Lakes Region: A Comprehensive Field Guide.* The University of Wisconsin Press, 2009.

Case, F., Jr. *Orchids of the Western Great Lakes Region.* Cranbrook Institute of Science Bulletin No. 48. 1987.

McKenny, Margaret and Roger Tory Peterson. *A Field Guide to Wildflowers: Northeastern and North-central North America* (Peterson Field Guides) 1998.

Neiring, William A. *The Audubon Society Field Guide to North American Wildflowers.* Alfred A. Knopf, 1979.

Newcomb, Lawrence. *Newcomb's Wildflower Guide.* Little, Brown and Company, 1977.

Peterson, Lee. *A Field Guide to Edible Wild Plants of Eastern and Central North America.* Houghton Mifflin, 1999.

Smith, W. *Orchids of Minnesota.* The University of Minnesota Press, 1993.

FERNS

Billington, C. *Ferns of Michigan.* Cranbrook Institute of Science Bulletin No. 32. 1952.

Chadde, Steve W. *Midwest Ferns: A Field Guide to the Ferns and Fern Relatives of the North Central United States.* 2013.

Chadde, Steve W. *Northeast Ferns: A Field Guide to the Ferns and Fern Relatives of the Northeastern United States.* 2013.

Cobb, Boughton. *A Field Guide to Ferns.* Boston: Houghton Mifflin, 1956.

Cody, W., and D. Britton. *Ferns and Fern Allies of Canada.* Publication 1829/E. Research Branch, Agriculture Canada, 1989.

Tryon, R. *Ferns of Minnesota.* 2nd ed. The University of Minnesota Press, 1980.

Tryon, R., N. Fassett, D. Dunlop, and M. Diemer. *The Ferns and Fern Allies of Wisconsin.* The University of Wisconsin Press, 1953.

MUSHROOMS

Arora, David. *Mushrooms Demystified.* 2nd ed. Ten Speed Press, 1986.

Barron, George. *Mushrooms of Northeast North America: Midwest to New England.* Lone Pine Field Guide, 1999.

Kauffman, C.H. *The Gilled Mushrooms (Agarieaceae) of Michigan and the Great Lakes Region.* Dover (1971 reprint), 1918.

Krieger, Louis C. *The Mushroom Handbook.* Dover (1967 reprint), 1936.

Lange, Morton and F.B. Hora. A Guide to Mushrooms and Toadstools. E.P. Dutton, 1963.

Lincoff, Gary. *The Audubon Society Field Guide to North American Mushrooms.* Alfred Knopf, 1981.

McKnight, Kent H. and Vera B. McKnight. *A Field Guide to Mushrooms: North America* (Peterson Field Guides), 1998.

McIlvaine, Charles and Robert Macadam. *One Thousand American Fungi.* Dover (1973 reprint), 1902.

McKenny, Margaret and Daniel Stuntz. *The Savory Wild Mushroom.* University of Washington Press, 1971.

Miller, Orson K. *Mushrooms of North America.* E.P. Dutton, 1972.

National Audobon Society. *Field Guide to North American Mushrooms.* 1981.

Rinaldi, Augusto and Vassili Tyndalo. *The Complete Book of Mushrooms.* Crown, 1974.

Smith, Alexander. *Mushrooms in Their Natural Habitats.* Hafner (1973 reprint), 1949.

Smith, Alexander. *A Field Guide to Western Mushrooms.* University of Michigan Press, 1975.

Smith, Alexander, Helen V. Smith, and Nancy Smith Weber. *How to Know the Gilled Mushrooms.* William Brown, 1979.

Smith, Alexander, Helen V. Smith, and Nancy Smith Weber. *How to Know the Non-Gilled Mushrooms,* 2nd edition. William Brown, 1981.

Smith, Alexander, and Nancy Smith Weber. *The Mushroom Hunter's Field Guide* (revised). University of Michigan Press, 1980.

Weber, Nancy Smith and Alexander Smith. *A Field Guide to Southern Mushrooms.* University of Michigan Press, 1985.

LICHENS AND MOSSES

Crum, H. *Mosses of the Great Lakes Forest.* University Herbarium, University of Michigan, 1976.

Crum, H., and L. Anderson. *Mosses of Eastern North America* (2 vols). Columbia Univ. Press, 1981.

Walewski, Joe. *Lichens of the North Woods* (North Woods Naturalist) Kollath-Stensaas, 2007.

McKnight, Karl B., Joseph R. Rohrer, Kirsten McKnight Ward, Warren J. Perdrizet. *Common Mosses of the Northeast and Appalachians* (Princeton Field Guides). Princeton University Press, 2013.

Brodo, Irwin M., Sylvia D. Sharnoff, and Stephen Sharnoff. *Lichens of North America.* Yale University Press, 2001.

POISONOUS PLANTS

Blackwell, Will H. *Poisonous and Medicinal Plants*. Prentice Hall, 1990.

Hardin, James W., and Jay M. Arena, M.D. *Human Poisoning from Native and Cultivated Plants*. Duke University Press, 1969.

Turner, Nancy J. and Szczawinski, Adam F. *Common Poisonous Plants and Mushrooms of North America*. Timber Press, 1991.

Part II

The American Botanist ed. by Willard N. Clute. Vol. I (1901)–XLVIII (1942).

Anonymous. *Lily Flowers and Bulbs used as Food*. Kew Bull. Misc. Inf. 1889. pp. 116-118.

Anonymous. [On the Chinese Yam, *Dioscorea Batatas*], Gard. Chron. For 1854: pp. 467-468.

Anonymous. *Le Polygonum cuspidatum, son histoire, sa description sommaire, sa culture, ses usages economiques et culinaire*. Ill. Hort. Vol. X. Misc. 45-47. 1863.

Arnold, A. F. *The Sea-beach at Ebb-tide*. New York, The Century Co. 1903.

Ash, Thomas. *Carolina; or A description of the present state of that country*. London. 1682.

Atkinson, G. F. *Studies in American Fungi. Mushrooms*. Ithaca, Andrus & Church. 1900 and later eds.

Barrows, D. P. *The Ethno-Botany of the Coahuila Indians of Southern California*. Chicago, Univ. of Chicago Press. 1900.

Barton, Benjamin H. and Castle, Thomas. *The British Flora Medica*. Revised by Jackson, John R. London. 1877.

Bartram, Wm. *Travels through North and South Carolina*. Philadelphia. 1791.

Berry, R. M. F. *Fruit Recipes*. New York, Doubleday Page and Co. 1907.

Bigelow, Jacob. *American Medical Botany*. 3 Vols. Boston. 1817.

Blankinship, J. W. *Native Economic Plants of Montana*. Mont. Agric. Coll. Experiment Station, Bull. 56. 1905.

Blake, S. F. *The Ostrich Fern as an Edible Plant*. Am. Fern. Journ. Vol. XXXII. pp. 61-68. 1942.

Blasdale, W. C. *A Description of some Chinese Vegetable Food Materials*. U.S. Dept. Agric., Office of Experiment Stations, Bull. 68. 1899.

Brown, Edgar, and Scofield, C. S. *Wild Rice: Its Uses and Propagation*. U.S. Dept. Agric., Bureau of Plant Industry, Bull. 50. 1903.

Bryant, Charles. *Flora Diaetetica: or History of Esculent Plants*. London. 1783.

Burr, Fearing. *Field and Garden Vegetables of America*. Boston, 1865.

Cameron, L. C. R. *The Wild Foods of Great Britain*. London, Geo. Routledge and Sons, Ltd. 1917.

Carr, Lucien. *The Food of Certain American Indians and Their Methods of Preparing It*. Proc. Am. Antiq. Soc., n. s. Vol. X, pp. 155-190. 1895.

Carver, George W. *Nature's Garden for Victory and Peace*, revised and reprinted. Agric. Research and Expt. Sta. Tuskegee Institute, Bull. no. 43. Tuskegee Institute, Alabama, October, 1942.

Carver, Jonathan. *Travels Through The Interior Parts of North America*. London. 1778. Chap. 19 [Reprinted in Bull. Lloyd Library, Reprod. Ser., Bull. 5. 1907].

Catesby, Mark. *The Natural History of Carolina, Florida, and the Bahama Islands*. 2 vols. London. Ed. of 1754.

Chamberlain, A. F. *The Maple amongst the Algonkian Tribes*. Amer. Anthropologist, Vol. IV, pp. 39-43. 1891.

Chamberlain, A. F. *Maple Sugar and the Indians*, ibid., pp. 381-384. 1891.

Chamberlain, L. S. *Plants Used by the Indians of Eastern North America*. Amer. Naturalist, Vol. XXXV, pp. 1-10. 1901.

Chambers, Charles E. *The Botany and History of Zizania aquatica L. ("Wild Rice")*. Ann. Bep. Smithsonian Inst, for 1940, pp. 369-382, with illustr. 1941.

Charlevoix, P. F. X. *Histoire et Description Générale de la Nouvelle France*. 3 vols. Paris. 1744.

Cheney, Ralph H. *Tea Substitutes in the United States*. Journ. N.Y. Bot. Gard. Vol. XLIII. pp. 117-124. 1942.

Chestnut, V. K. *Plants Used by the Indians of Mendocino County, California*. Contrib. U. S. Nat. Herbarium, Vol. VII. no. 3, pp. 295-408. 1902.

Chouard, Pierre. *Plantes alimentaires méconnues pour le début de printemps*. Bev. Hort. Vol. CXIII. 308-310. 1941.

Claassen, P. W. *A Possible New Source of Food Supply. [Cat-tail flour]*. Scientific Mo. August, 1919.

Correa de Serra, Joseph. *Notice respecting several Vegetables used as Esculents in North America*. Trans. Hort. Soc. London, Vol. IV. no. lxvii. pp. 443-446. 1822.

Coville, F. V. *The Panamint Indians of California*. Amer. Anthropologist, Vol. V. pp. 351-361. 1892.

Coville, F. V. *The Wild Rice of Minnesota*. Bot. Gaz. Vol. XIX. pp. 504-506. 1894.

Coville, F. V. *Some Additions to our Vegetable Dietary*. Yearbook, U. S. Dept. of Agriculture, 1895, pp. 205-214.

Coville, F. V. *Notes on the Plants Used by the Klamath Indians of Oregon*. Contrib. U. S. Nat. Herbarium, Vol. V. no. 2, pp. 87-108. 1897.

Coville, F. V. *Observations on recent Cases of Mushroom Poisoning in the District of Columbia*. U.S. Dept. Agriculture, Div. Botany, Circular No. 13. 1898.

Coville, F. V. *Wokas, A Primitive Food of the Klamath Indians*. U. S. Nat. Museum, Bep. 1902, pp. 725-739.

Croom, H. B. *A Catalogue of Plants ... of Newbern, North Carolina*. New York. 1837.

Culpepper, Nicholas. *The English Physician, Enlarged*. London. 1653.

Cushing, F. H. *Zuni Breadstuffs*. The Millstone (Indianapolis), Vol. IX. pp. 1-62 [in part]. 1884.

Cutler, Manasseh. *An Account of Some of the Vegetable Productions, Naturally Growing in this Part of America, Botanically Arranged*. Memoir Amer. Acad. Vol. I. pp. 396-493. 1785.

Dalziel, J. M. *The Useful Plants of West Tropical Africa*. Appendix to Hutchinson, J. and J. M. Dalziel, *Flora of West Tropical Africa*. The Crown Agents for the Colonies, London. 1937.

Darlington, William. *American Weeds and useful Plants*, revised by Thurber, George. New York. 1859.

Delabarre, E. B. *The Flora [of Labrador]*. Chap. XVI in Grenfell, W. T., Labrador, pp. 391-425. New York, Macmillan Co. 1913.

Dorsey, J. O. *Omaha Sociology*. 3d Ann. Rep. Bureau Amer. Ethnology, pp. 303-310. 1884.

Dunbar, J. B. *The Pawnee Indians*. Mag. Amer. History, Vol. V. pp. 323324. 1880.

Dyer, T. E. Thiselton. *The Folk-lore of Plants*. London. 1889.

Evelyn, John. *Acetaria: or, a Discourse on Sallets*, ed. 2. Appended to Terra, ed. 3, as pp. 131-213. London. 1706.

Farlow, W. G. *Marine Algae of New England and adjacent Coast*. Washington. 1881. Reprinted from Report, U. S. Fish Comm, for 1879.

Icones Farlowianae. *Illustrations of the larger Fungi of eastern North America*. William Gilson Farlow, with descriptive text by Edward Angus Burt. pp. i-x, 1-120, 103 colored plates. The Farlow Library and Herbarium of Harvard University. 1929.

Fernald, M. L. Note in: Rhodora, Vol. XIII pp. 124-125. 1911.

Fernald, M. L. and Wiegand, K. M. Note in: . Rhodora, Vol. XII. p. 109. 1910.

Fewkes, J. W. *A Contribution to Ethnobotany.* Amer. Anthropologist, Vol. IX. pp. 14-21. 1896.

Georgeson, C. C. *The Economic Plants of Japan.* Am. Gard. Vols. XII and XIIL 1891 and 1892. Vol. XII, Vol. XIIL.

Gerarde, John. *The Herball or Generali Historic of Plantes.* London. 1597.

Gilmore, M. R. *A Study in the Ethnology of the Omaha Indian.* Coll. Nebraska State Hist. Soc. Vol. XVIL pp. 314-357. 1913.

Gilmore, M. R. *Some Native Nebraska Plants with Their Uses by the Dakota.* pp. 358-370. 1913.

Gilmore, M. R. *Uses of Plants by the Indians of the Missouri River Region.* Bureau of Amer. Ethnology, Ann. Rep. Vol. XXXIII. pp. 43-154. 1919.

Halsted, B. D. *The Poisonous Plants of New Jersey.* N.J. Agricultural Experiment Station, Bull. 135. 1899.

Hance, H. F. *On a Chinese culinary Vegetable [Hydropyrum=Zizania].* Journ. Bot. Brit, and Foreign, Vol. X. pp. 146-149. 1872.

Hardy, G. A. *Fifty Edible Plants of British Columbia.* Brit. Col. Prov. Mus., Handbook, No. 1. 1942.

Havard, Valery. *Food Plants of the North American Indians.* Bull. Tor- rey Bot. Club, Vol. XXII. pp. 98-123. 1895.

Drink Plants of the North American Indians, ibid. Vol. XXIII. pp. 36-46. 1896.

Hawkes, E. W. *The Labrador Eskimo.* Canada, Dept, of Mines, Geol. Survey, Memoir 91. 1916.

Hedrick, U. P. See Sturtevant.

Hedrick, U. P. *The Herbarist,* a Publication of the Herb Society of America. 1935-date. Hervey, A. B. Sea Mosses. Boston. 1882.

Higginson, Francis. *New England's Plantation.* 1630. Edit.: A. Young. Boston, 1846. pp. 238-268.

Hooker, W. J. *Journal of A Tour in Iceland.* 2 vols. London. 1813.

Hopkins, Milton. *Wild Plants used in Cookery.* Journ. N. Y. Bot. Gard. Vol. XLIII. pp. 71-76. 1942.

Hough, Walter. *The Hopi in Relation to their Plant Environment.* Amer. Anthropologist, Vol. X. pp. 33-44. 1897.

Hough, Walter. *Environmental Interrelations in Arizona.* Vol. XI. pp. 133-155. 1898.

Jackson, J. B. *New Food Products.* Annual for 1895, Cooper, Wholesale Societies Ltd. Engl, and Scotland. 1894.

Jencks, Zalia. *A note on the Carbohydrates of the root of the Cat-tail (Typha latifolia).* Proc. Soc. for Experimental Biology and Medicine. Vol. XVII. pp. 45-46. 1919.

Jenks, A. E. *The Wild Rice Gatherers of the Upper Lakes.* 19th Ann. Rep. Bureau Amer. Ethnology, pt. 2, pp. 1013-1137. 1898.

Johnson, Charles. *The Useful Plants of Great Britain.* London. 1862.

Josselyn, John. *New England's Rarities Discovered.* London. 1672.

Kalm, Pehr or Peter. *Beschreibung der Beise nach dem Nordlichen Amerika.* 3 vols. Gottingen. 1754.

Kautfman, C. H. *The Agaricaceae of Michigan.* Mich. Geol. and Biol. Surv. Publ. no. 26 (Biological Series, no. 5). Lansing. 1918. (Very fine photographs and authoritative text, applicable throughout the Northern States and Southern Canada).

Kephart, Horace. *The Book of Camping and Woodcraft.* Chap. XVTI. Edible Plants of the Wilderness, pp. 232-255. New York, The Century Co. 1909, and later eds.

Krieger, L. C. C. *Common Mushrooms of the United States.* National Geographic Magazine, Vol. XXXVII, pp. 387-439. May, 1920. (Authoritative, carefully written and wonderfully illustrated.)

Krieger, L. C. C. *A Popular Guide to the Higher Fungi (Mushrooms) of New York State.* New York State Museum, Handbook 11: 538 pp., 32 plates, 126 figures. Albany. 1935.

Lankester, Edwin [anonymous]. *Vegetable Substances Used for the Food of Man*. London and Boston, Library of Entertaining Knowledge, vol. XXIV. 1832.

Lankester, Mrs. [Phoebe]. *The Popular Portion of Syme, J. T. B., English Botany*, ed. 3. 12 vols. and Supplement. London. 1873-1892.

Lawson, John. *The History of Carolina*. London. 1714.

Lighttoot, John. *Flora Scotica*. 2 vols. London. 1777.

Lindley, John. *The Vegetable Kingdom*, ed. 3. 1853.

Lindley, John, and Moore, Thomas. *The Treasury of Botany*, ed. 2. 2 vols. London. 1884.

Lindsay, W. L. *A Popular History of British Lichens*. London. 1856. Linnaeus, Carolus. Flora Lapponica. Amsterdam. 1737.

Low, A. P. *Report on Explorations in the Labrador Peninsula. Canada*, Geol. Surv. Rep. n.s. Vol. VIII. 1896.

McIlvaine, Charles. *One Thousand American Fungi*. Indianapolis, Bowen-Merrill. 1900.

McNair, James B. *Spices and Condiments*. Field Mus. Nat. Hist. Bot. Leaflet 15. 1930.

Medsger, Oliver Perry. *Edible Wild Plants*, with Introduction by Seton, Ernest Thompson. New York, Macmillan Co. 1939.

Michaux, F. A. *The North American Sylva*, edit. Smith, J. J. 3 vols. Philadelphia. 1853.

Muenscher, Walter Conrad. *Poisonous Plants*. The Rural Science Series, New York, Macmillan Co. 1939.

Newberry, J. S. *Food and Fiber Plants of the North American Indians*. Pop. Sci. Mo. Vol. XXXII. pp. 31-46. 1887.

Northcote, Lady Rosalind. *The Book of Herbs*. London, John Lane. 1903.

Ochse, J. J. in collaboration with R. C.

Bakhuizen van den Brink. *Vegetables of the Dutch East Indies*. English edition of "Indische Groenten." Dept. of Agric., Industry and Commerce of the Netherlands East Indies. 1931.

Paillieux, A. et Bois, D. *Les Plantes Aquatiques Alimentaires*. Bull. Soc. d'Acclimation de France. 1888.

Palmer, Edward. *Food Products of the North American Indians*. Report U. S. Commiss. Agriculture for 1870. pp. 404-428. 1871. [Anonymous. Also ascribed to J. R. Dodge].

Pammel, L. H. *A Manual of Poisonous Plants*. Cedar Rapids, Iowa, The Torch Press. 1911.

Parker, A. C. *Iroquois Uses of Maize and Other Food Plants*. N. Y. State Museum, Bull. 144. 1910.

Parkinson, John. *Theatrum Botanicum*. London. 1640.

Parkinson, John. *Paradisi in Sole Paradisus Terrestris*. London. 1656.

Patterson, F. W. and Charles, Y. X. *Some common Edible and Poisonous Mushrooms*, U.S. Dept. Agriculture, Farmer's Bull. no. 796. 1917.

Penhallow, D. P. *Note on a few of the Useful Plants of Northern Japan*. Am. Nat. Vol. XVI. pp. 119-121. 1882.

Porcher, F. P. *Resources of the Southern Fields and Forests*. Richmond. 1863. Also: Charleston, 1869.

Porsild, A. E. Edible *Roots and Berries of Northern Canada*. National Museum of Canada, Ottawa. 1937.

Powers, Stephen. *Aboriginal Botany*. Proceed. Calif. Acad. Sci. Vol. V. pp. 373-379. 1874.

Prior, B. C. A. *On the Popular Names of British Plants*. London, ed. 2, 1870; ed. 3, 1879.

Rafinesque, C. S. *Medical Flora*. 2 vols. Philadelphia. 1828 and 1830.

Richardson, Sir John. *Arctic Searching Expedition*. New York. 1852.

Roberts, Kenneth et al. *Letters and Editorials on Edibility of Skunk- Cabbage* and its Confusion with White Hellebore. Boston Herald, May 10-15, 1943.

St. John, Harold. Sable Island, with a Catalogue of its Vascular Plants. Proc. Bost. Soc. Nat. Hist. Vol. XXXVI. No. 1 (Contrib. Gray Herb. Harvard Univ. no. lxii.). 1921.

Safford, W. E. The Useful Plants of the Island of Guam. Contrib. U. S. Nat. Herbarium, Vol. IX. 1905.

Sanford, S. N. F. New England Herbs. New England Museum of Natural History. Boston. 1937.

Sargent, C. S. The Silva of North America. 14 vols. Boston and New York, Houghton, Mifflin and Co. 1891-1902.

Saunders, Charles Francis. Useful Wild Plants of the United States and Canada. New York, Bobert M. McBride & Co. 1920.

Scott, A. B. Foods that Cost Us Nothing. Ladies Home Journal, June, 1917, p. 41.

Seton, E. T. Emergency Foods in the Northern Forest. Country Life in America, Vol. VI. pp. 438-440. 1904.

Seton, E. T. The Woodcraft Manual for Boys. New York, Doubleday Page & Co. 1917.

Smith, Huron H. Ethnobotany of the Menomini Indians. Bull. Public Mus. Milwaukee, Vol. IV. no. 1. 1923.

Smith, Huron H. Ethnobotany of the Meskwaki Indians. Bull. Public Mus. Milwaukee, Vol. IV, no. 2, 1928.

Smith, Huron H. Ethnobotany of the Ojibwe Indians. Bull. Public Mus. Milwaukee, Vol. IV. no. 3. 1932.

Smith, Huron H. Ethnobotany of the Forest Potawatomi Indians. Bull. Public Mus. Milwaukee, Vol. VII. no. 1. 1933.

Stickney, G. P. Indian Use of Wild Rice. Amer. Anthropologist, Vol. IX. pp. 115-121. 1896.

Stone, G. E. Edible Weeds and Pot Herbs. Mass. State Board Agric. Nature Leaflet, no. 19. 1907.

Stout, A. B. Gum-jum or Gum-tsoy: a Food from the Flowers of Day-lilies. Journ. N. Y. Bot. Gard. Vol. XXXIV. pp. 97-100. 1933.

Sturtevant, E. L. Kitchen Garden Esculents of American Origin. American Naturalist, Vol. XIX. pp. 444-457, 542-553, 658-669. 1885.

Sturtevant, E. L. History of Garden Vegetables. Amer. Naturalist, Vols. XXI, XXII, XXIII. 1889.

Sturtevant, E. L. Notes on Edible Plants, edited by Hedrick, U. P. New York Dept. Agric. Ann. Rep. XXVII. Albany, 1919.

Syme, J. T. B. English Botany; or Coloured Figures of British Plants, ed. 3. 12 vols. and Supplement. London. 1873-1892.

Torrey, John. A Flora of the State of New York. 2 vols. Albany. 1843.

Trumbull, J. H. and Gray, Asa. Notes on the History of Helianthus tuberosus, the so-called Jerusalem Artichoke. Amer. Journ. of Science and Arts, ser. 3, Vol. XIII. pp. 347-352. 1877.

Unger, F. On the Principal Plants used as Food by Man. U.S. Comm. of Patents, Rep. for 1859, pp. 299-362. 1860.

Van Brunt, Elizabeth Remsen. Culinary Herbs: Their Culture, Traditions, and Use. Brooklyn Bot. Gard. Record, Vol. XXXII. No. 1. 1943.

Vestal, Paul A. and Schultes Richard Evans. The Economic Botany of the Kiowa Indians. Botanical Museum, Cambridge, Mass. 1939.

Waghorne, A. C. Berries and Fruits of Newfoundland. Daily Colonist, July 10, 1888.

Waghorne, A. C. A Summary Account of the Wild Berries and other Edible Fruits of Newfoundland and Labrador. St. John's. 1888.

Waghorne, A. C. The Flora of Newfoundland, Labrador and St. Pierre et Miquelon. Trans. Nova Scotia Inst. Sci. ser. 2, Vol. I. pp. 359-375; Vol II. pp. 83-100, 361-401. 1893-1898.

Waugh, F. A. *Salad Plants and Plant Salads*. Vermont Agric. Experiment Station, Bull. 54. 1896.

Waugh, E. W. *Iroquois Foods and Food Preparation*. Geol. Surv. Canada, Dept. Mines, Mem. 86. 1916.

Wherry, Edgar T. *Go Slow on Eating Fern Fiddleheads*. Am. Fern. Journ. Vol. XXXII. pp. 108, 109. 1942.

Wittrock, Marion A. and G. L. *Food Plants of the Indians*. Journ. N. Y. Bot. Gard. Vol. XLIII. pp. 57-71. 1942.

COLTSFOOT *(Tussilago farfara)*; previously a popular remedy for sore-throats and coughs, but no longer recommended due to a potentially dangerous alkaloid; see page 152.

Glossary

abaxial On the side away from the axis, usually refers to the under-side of a leaf (compare with adaxial).

acaulescent Without an upright, leafy stem.

achene A one-seeded, dry, indehiscent fruit with the seed coat not attached to the mature wall of the ovary.

acid Having more hydrogen ions than hydroxyl (OH) ions; a pH less than 7.

acuminate Tapering to a narrow point, more tapering than acute, less than attenuate.

acute Gradually tapered to a tip.

adaxial On the side toward the axis, usually refers to the top side of a leaf (compare with *abaxial*).

adnate Fused with a structure different from itself, as when stamens are adnate to petals (compare with *connate*).

adventive Not native to and not fully established in a new habitat.

alkaline Having more hydroxyl ions than hydrogen ions; a pH greater than 7.

alluvial Deposits of rivers and streams.

alternate Borne singly at each node, as in leaves on a stem.

ament Spikelike inflorescence of same-sexed flowers (either male or female); same as catkin.

androgynous Spike with both staminate and pistillate flowers, the pistillate located at the base, below the staminate (compare with *gynaecandrous*).

angiosperm A plant producing flowers and bearing seeds in an ovary.

annual A plant that completes its life cycle in one growing season, then dies.

anther Pollen-bearing part of stamen, usually at the end of a stalk called a filament.

anthesis The period during which a flower is fully open and functional.

anthocyanic Pigmented with antho-cyanins, this usually manifested as a tinging or suffusion of pink, red, or purple.

aphyllopodic Having basal sheaths with-out blades; with new shoots arising laterally from parent shoot (compare with *phyllopodic*).

apiculate Having an apiculus.

apiculus An abrupt, very small, pro-jected tip.

appressed Lying flat to or parallel to a surface.

aquatic Living in water.

areole In leaves, the spaces between small veins.

aril A specialized appendage on a seed, often brightly colored, derived from the seed coat.

aristate Tipped with a slender bristle.

armed Bearing a sharp projection such as a prickle, spine, or thorn.

aromatic Strongly scented.

ascending Angled upward.

asymmetrical Not symmetrical.

attenuate Tapering gradually to a pro-longed tip.

auricle An ear-shaped appendage to a leaf or stipule.

awl-shaped Tapering gradually from a broad base to a sharp point.

awn A bristle-like organ.

axil Angle between a stem and the at-tached leaf.

barb Sharp, thorn-like projection.

basal From base of plant.

basic A pH greater than 7.

beak A slender, terminal appendage on a 3-dimensional organ.

beard Covering of long or stiff hairs.

berry Fruit with the seeds surrounded by fleshy material.

biennial A plant that completes its life cycle in two growing season, typically flowering and fruiting in the second year, then dying.

bifid Cleft into two more or less equal parts.

blade Expanded, usually flat part of a leaf or petiole.

bloom A whitish powdery or waxy coating that can be rubbed away.

bog A wet, acidic, nutrient-poor peatland characterized by sphagnum and other mosses, shrubs and sedges. Technically, a type of peatland raised above its surroundings by peat accumulation and receiving nutrients only from precipitation.

boreal Far northern latitudes.

brackish Salty.

bract An accessory structure at the base of some flowers, usually appearing leaflike.

bractlet A secondary bract (*Typha*).

branchlets A small branch.

bristle A stiff hair.

bud An undeveloped shoot, inflorescence, or flower, in woody plants often covered by scales and serving as the overwintering stage.

bulb A group of modified leaves serving as a food-storage organ, borne on a short, vertical, underground stem (compare with *corm*).

bulbil A bulb-like structure borne in the leaf axils or in place of flowers.

bulblet Small bulb borne above ground, as in a leaf axil.

ca. About, approximately (Latin *circa*).

caducous Falling off early, as stipules that leave behind a scar.

callosity A hardened thickening.

callus A firm, thickened portion of an organ; the firm base of the lemma in the Poaceae.

calcareous fen An uncommon wetland type associated with seepage areas, and which receive groundwater enriched with primarily calcium and magnesium bicarbonates.

calcium-rich Refers to wetlands underlain by limestone or receiving water enriched by calcium compounds.

calyx All the sepals of a flower.

campanulate Bell-shaped.

capillary Very fine, hair-like, not-flattened.

capitate Abruptly expanded at the apex, thereby forming a knob-like tip.

capsule A dry, dehiscent fruit splitting into 3 or more parts.

carpel Fertile leaf of an angiosperm, bearing the ovules. A pistil is made up of one or more carpels.

caruncle An appendage at or near the hilum of some seeds.

caryopsis The dry, indehiscent seed of grasses.

catkin Spikelike inflorescence of same-sexed flowers (either male or female); same as ament.

caudex Firm, hardened, summit of a root mass that functions as a perennating organ.

cauline Of or pertaining to the above-ground portion of the stem.

cespitose Growing in a compact cluster with closely spaced stems; tufted, clumped.

chaff Thin, dry scales; in the Asteraceae, sometimes found as chaffy bracts on the receptacle.

cilia Hairs found at the margin of an organ.

ciliate Provided with cilia.

circumboreal Refers to a species distribution pattern which circles the earth's boreal regions.

clasping Leaves that partially encircle the stem at the base.

clavate Widened in the distal portion, like a baseball bat.

claw The narrow, basal portion of perianth parts.

cleistogamous Type of flower that remains closed and is self-pollinated.

clumped Having the stems grouped closely together; tufted.

colony-forming A group of plants of the same species, produced either vegetatively or by seed.

column The joined style and filaments

in the Orchidaceae.

coma A tuft of fine hairs, especially at the tip of a seed.

composite An inflorescence that is made up of many tiny florets crowded together on a receptacle; members of the Aster Family (Asteraceae).

compound leaf A leaf with two or more leaflets.

concave Curved inward.

conduplicate Folded lengthwise into nearly equal parts.

cone The dry fruit of conifers composed of overlapping scales.

conifer Cone-bearing woody plants.

connate Two like parts that are fused (compare with *adnate*).

connivent Converging and touching but not actually fused, applies to like organs.

convex Curved outward.

convolute Arranged such that one edge is covered and the other is exposed, usually referring to petals in bud.

cordate With a rounded lobe on each side of a central sinus; heart-shaped.

coriaceous With a firm, leathery texture.

corm A short, vertical, enlarged, underground stem that serves as a food storage organ (compare with *bulb*).

corolla Collectively, all the petals of a flower.

corymb An indeterminate inflorescence, somewhat similar to a raceme, that has elongate lower branches that create a more or less flat-topped inflorescence.

costa (plural costae) A prominent midvein or midrib of a leaflet.

crenate With rounded teeth.

crenulate Finely crenate.

crisped An irregularly crinkled or curled leaf margin.

crown Persistent base of a plant, especially a grasses.

culm The stem of a grass or grasslike plant, especially a stem with the inflorescence.

cuneate Tapering to the base with relatively straight, non-parallel margins; wedge-shaped.

cyme A type of inflorescence in which the central flowers open first.

deciduous Not persistent.

decumbent A stem that is prostrate at the base and curves upward to have an erect or ascending, apical portion.

decurrent Possessing an adnate line or wing that extends down the axis below the node, usually referring to leaves on a stem.

dehiscent Splitting open at maturity.

deltate Triangle-shaped.

dentate Provided with outward oriented teeth.

depauperate Poorly developed due to unfavorable conditions.

dicots One of two main divisions of the Angiosperms (the other being the Monocots); plants having 2 seed leaves (cotyledons), net-venation, and flower parts in 4s or 5s (or multiples of these numbers).

dioecious Bearing only male or female flowers on a single plant.

dimorphic Having two forms.

disarticulation Spikelets breaking either above or below the glumes when mature, the glumes remaining in the head if disarticulation above the glumes, or the glumes falling with the florets if disarticulation is below the glumes.

discoid In composite flowers (Asteraceae), a head with only disk (tubular) flowers, the ray flowers absent.

disjunct A population of plants widely separated from its main range.

disk In the Asteraceae, the central part of the head, composed of tubular flowers.

dissected Leaves divided into many smaller segments.

disturbed Natural communities altered by human influences.

divided Leaves which are lobed nearly to the midrib.

dolomite A type of limestone consisting of calcium magnesium carbonate.

dorsal Underside, or back of an organ.

drupe A fleshy fruit with a single large seed such as a cherry.

echinate With spines.

eglandular Without glands.

elliptic Broadest at the middle, gradually tapering to both ends.

emergent Growing out of and above the water surface.

emersed leaf Growing above the water surface or out of water.

endangered A species in danger of extinction throughout all or most of its range if current trends continue.

endemic A species restricted to a particular region.

entire With a smooth margin.

erect Stiffly upright.

erose With a ragged edge.

escape A cultivated plant which establishes itself outside of cultivation.

evergreen Plant retaining its leaves throughout the year.

excurrent With the central rib or axis continuing or projecting beyond the organ.

exserted Extending beyond the mouth of a structure such as stamens extending out from the mouth of the corolla.

falcate Sickle-shaped

false indusium A modified tooth or reflexed margin of a fern leaf that covers the sorus.

fen An open wetland usually dominated by herbaceous plants, and fed by inflowing, often calcium- and/or magnesium-rich water; soils vary from peat to clays and silts.

fern Perennial plants with spore-bearing leaves similar to the vegetative leaves and bearing sporangia on their underside, or the spore-bearing leaves much modified.

fibrous A cluster of slender roots, all with the same diameter.

filament The stalk of a stamen which supports the anther.

filiform Thread-like.

flexuous An elongate axis that arches or bends in alternating directions in a zig-zag fashion.

floating mat A feature of some ponds where plant roots form a carpet over some or all of the water surface.

floodplain That part of a river valley that is occasionally covered by flood waters.

floret A small flower in a dense cluster of flowers; in grasses the flower with its attached lemma and palea.

follicle A dry, dehiscent fruit that splits along one side when mature.

floricane the second-year flowering stem of *Rubus* (compare with primocane).

genus The first part of the scientific name for a plant or animal (plural genera).

glabrate Nearly glabrous or becoming so.

glabrous Lacking hairs.

gland An appendage or depression which produces a sticky or greasy substance.

glandular Bearing glands.

glaucous Having a bluish appearance.

glumes A pair of small bracts at base of each spikelet the lowermost (or first) glume usually smaller the upper (or second) glume usually longer.

grain The fruit of a grass; the swollen seedlike protuberance on the fruit of some *Rumex*.

gymnosperm Plants in which the seeds are not produced in an ovary, but usually in a cone.

gynaecandrous Having both staminate and pistillate flowers on the same spike, the staminate located at the base, below the pistillate (compare with *androgynous*).

gynophore The central stalk of some flowers, especially in cat-tails (*Typha*).

halophyte A plant adapted to growing in a salty substrate.

hastate More or less triangular in outline with outward-oriented basal lobes.

haustorium A specialized, root-like connection to a host plant that a parasite uses to extract nourishment.

hardwoods Loosely used to contrast most deciduous trees from conifers.

herb A herbaceous, non-woody plant.

herbaceous Like an herb; also, leaflike in appearance.

hilum The scar at the point of attachment of a seed.

hirsute Pubescent with coarse, somewhat stiff, usually curving hairs, coarser than villous but softer than hispid.

hispid Pubescent with coarse, stiff hairs that may be uncomfortable to the touch, coarser than hirsute but softer than bristly.

hummock A small, raised mound formed by certain species of sphagnum moss.

humus Dark, well-decayed organic matter in soil.

hybrid A cross-breed between two species.

hydric Wet (compare with *mesic, xeric*).

hypanthium A ring, cup, or tube around the ovary; the sepals, petals and stamens are attached to the rim of the hypanthium.

imbricate Overlapping, as shingles on a roof.

indehiscent Not splitting open at maturity.

indusium In ferns, a membranous covering over the sorus (plural *indusia*).

inferior The position of the ovary when it is below the point of attachment of the sepals and petals.

inflorescence A cluster of flowers.

insectivorous Refers to the insect trapping and digestion habit of some plants as a nutrition supplement.

interdunal swale Low-lying areas between sand dune ridges.

internode Portion of a stem between two nodes.

introduced A non-native species.

invasive Non-native species causing significant ecological or economic problems.

involucral bract A single member of the involucre; sometimes called phyllary in composite flowers (Asteraceae).

involucre A whorl of bracts, subtending a flower or inflorescence.

irregular flower Not radially symmetric; with similar parts unequal.

joint A node or section of a stem where the branch and leaf meet.

keel A central rib like the keel of a boat.

lance-shaped Broadest near the base, gradually tapering to a narrower tip.

lateral Borne on the sides of a stem or branch.

lax Loose or drooping.

leaf axil The point of the angle between a stem and a leaf.

leaflet One of the leaflike segments of a compound leaf.

lemma In grasses, the lower bract enclosing the flower (the upper, smaller bract is the palea).

lens-shaped Biconvex in shape (like a lentil).

lenticel Blisterlike openings in the epidermis of woody stems, admitting gases to and from the plant, and often appearing as small oval dots on bark.

ligulate Having a ligule; in the Asteraceae, the strap-shaped corolla of a ray floret.

ligule In grasses and grasslike plants,

the membranous or hairy ring at top of sheath between the blade and stem.

linear Narrow and flat with parallel sides.

lip Upper or lower part of a 2-lipped corolla; also the lower petal in most orchid flowers.

lobed With lobes; in leaves divisions usually not over halfway to the midrib.

local Occurring sporadically in an area.

low prairie Wet and moist herbaceous plant community, typically dominated by grasses.

margin The outer edge of a leaf.

marl A calcium-rich clay.

marsh Wetland dominated by herbaceous plants, with standing water for part or all the growing season, then often drying at the surface.

megaspore Large, female spores.

mesic Moist, neither dry nor wet (compare with hydric, xeric).

microspore Small, male spores.

midrib The prominent vein along the main axis of a leaf.

mixed forest A type of forest composed of both deciduous and conifer trees.

moat The open water area ringing the outer edge of a peatland or floating mat.

monecious Having male and female reproductive parts in separate flowers on the same plant.

monocots One of two main divisions of the Angiosperms (the other being the Dicots); plants with a single seed leaf (cotyledon); typically having narrow leaves with parallel veins, and flower parts in 3s or multiples of 3.

muck An organic soil where the plant remains are decomposed to the point where the type of plants forming the soil cannot be determined.

mucro A sharp point at termination of an organ or other structure.

naked Without a covering; a stalk or stem without leaves.

native An indigenous species.

naturalized An introduced species that is established and persistent in an ecosystem.

needle A slender leaf, as in the Pinaceae.

nerve A leaf vein.

neutral A pH of 7.

node The spot on a stem or branch where leaves originate.

nutlet A small dry fruit that does not split open along a seam.

oblanceolate Reverse lance-shaped; broadest at the apex, gradually tapering to the narrower base.

oblique Emerging or joining at an angle other than parallel or perpendicular.

oblong Broadest at the middle, and tapering to both ends, but broader than elliptic.

obovate Broadly rounded at the apex, becoming narrowed below.

ocrea A tube-shaped stipule or pair of stipules around the stem; characteristic of the Smartweed Family (Polygonaceae).

opposite Leaves or branches which are paired opposite one another on the stem.

organic Soils composed of decaying plant remains.

oval Elliptical.

ovary The lower part of the pistil that produces the seeds.

ovate Broadly rounded at the base, becoming narrowed above; broader than lanceolate.

palea The uppermost of the two inner bracts subtending a grass flower (the lower bract is the lemma).

palmate Divided in a radial fashion, like the fingers of a hand.

panicle An arrangement of flowers consisting of several racemes.

papilla (plural: *papillae*) A short, rounded or cylindrical projections.

pappus The modified sepals of a composite flower which persist atop the ovary as bristles, scales or awns.

parallel-veined With several veins running from base of leaf to leaf tip, characteristic of most monocots.

peat An organic soil formed of partially decomposed plant remains.

peatland A wetland whose soil is composed primarily of organic matter (mosses, sedges, etc.); a general term for bogs and fens.

peltate More or less circular, with the stalk attached at a point on the underside.

pepo A fleshy, many-seeded fruit with a tough rind, as a melon.

perennial Living for 3 or more years.

perfect A flower having both male (stamens) and female (pistils) parts.

perianth Collectively, all the sepals and petals of a flower.

perigynium A sac-like structure enclosing the pistil in *Carex* (plural *perigynia*).

petal An individual part of the corolla, often white or colored.

petiole The stalk of a leaf.

phyllary An involucral bract subtending the flower head in composite flowers (Asteraceae).

phyllode An expanded petiole.

phyllopodic Having the basal sheaths blade-bearing; with new shoots arising from the center of parent shoot (compare with *aphyllopodic*).

pinna The primary or first division in a fern frond or leaf (plural *pinnae*).

pinnate Divided once along an elongated axis into distinct segments.

pinnule The pinnate segment of a pinna.

pistil The seed-producing part of the flower, consisting of an ovary and one or more styles and stigmas.

pith A spongy central part of stems and branches.

pollen The male spores in an anther.

prairie An open plant community dominated by herbaceous species, especially grasses.

primocane The first-year, vegetative stem in *Rubus* (compare with *floricane*).

pro sp. When a taxon is transferred from the non-hybrid category to the hybrid category, the author citation remains unchanged, but may be followed by an indication in parentheses of the original category.

prostrate Lying flat on the ground.

raceme A grouping of flowers along an elongated axis where each flower has its own stalk.

rachilla A small stem or axis.

rachis The central axis or stem of a leaf or inflorescence.

radiate heads In composite flowers, heads with both ray and disk flowers.

ray flower A ligulate or strap-shaped flower in the Asteraceae, where often the outermost series of flowers in the head.

receptacle In the Asteraceae, the enlarged summit of the flower stalk to which the sepals, petals, stamens, and pistils are usually attached.

recurved Curved backward.

regular Flowers with all the similar parts of the same form; radially symmetric.

rhizome An underground, horizontal stem.

rib A pronounced vein or nerve.

rootstock Similar to rhizome but referring to any underground part that spreads the plant.

rosette A crowded, circular clump of leaves.

samara A dry, indehiscent fruit with a well-developed wing.

saprophyte A plant that lives off of dead organic matter.

scale A tiny, leaflike structure; the structure that subtends each flower in a sedge (Cyperaceae).

scape A naked stem (without leaves) bearing the flowers.

section Cross-section.

secund Flowers mostly on 1 side of a stalk or branch.

sedge meadow A community dominated by sedges (Cyperaceae) and occurring on wet, saturated soils.

seep A spot where water oozes from the ground.

sepal A segment of the calyx; usually green in color.

sheath Tube-shaped membrane around a stem, especially for part of the leaf in grasses and sedges.

shrub A woody plant with multiple stems.

silicle Short fruit of the Mustard Family (Brassicaceae), normally less than 2× longer as wide.

silique Dry, dehiscent, 2-chambered fruit of the Mustard Family (Brassicaceae), longer than a silicle.

simple An undivided leaf.

sinus The depression between two lobes.

smooth Without teeth or hairs.

sorus Clusters of spore containers (plural *sori*).

spadix A fleshy axis in which flowers are embedded.

spathe A large bract subtending or enclosing a cluster of flowers.

spatula-shaped Broadest at tip and tapering to the base.

sphagnum moss A type of moss common in peatlands and sometimes forming a continuous carpet across the surface; sometimes forming layers several meters thick; also loosely called peat moss.

spike A group of unstalked flowers along an unbranched stalk.

spikelet A small spike; the flower cluster (inflorescence) of grasses (Poaceae) and sedges (Cyperaceae).

sporangium The spore-producing structure (plural sporangia).

spore a one-celled reproductive structure that gives rise to the gamete-bearing plant.

sporophyll A modified, spore-bearing leaf.

spreading Widely angled outward.

spring A place where water flows naturally from the ground.

spur A hollow, pointed projection of a flower.

stamen The male or pollen-producing organ of a flower.

staminode An infertile stamen.

stem The main axis of a plant.

stigma The terminal part of a pistil which receives pollen.

stipe A stalk.

stipule A leaflike outgrowth at the base of a leaf stalk.

stolon A horizontal stem lying on the soil surface.

style The stalklike part of the pistil between the ovary and the stigma.

subspecies A subdivision of the species forming a group with shared traits which differ from other members of the species (subsp.).

subtend Attached below and extending upward.

succulent Thick, fleshy and juicy.

superior Referring to the position of the ovary when it is above the point of attachment of sepals, petals, stamens, and pistils.

swale A slight depression.

swamp Wooded wetland dominated by trees or shrubs; soils are typically wet for much of year or sometimes inundated.

talus Fallen rock at the base of a slope or cliff.

taproot A main, downward-pointing root.

tendril A threadlike appendage from a stem or leaf that coils around other objects for support (as in *Vitis*).

tepal Sepals or petals not differentiated from one another.

terete Circular in cross-section.

terminal Located at the end of a stem or stalk.

thallus A small, flattened plant structure, without distinct stem or leaves.

thicket A dense growth of woody plants.

threatened A species likely to become endangered throughout all or most of its range if current trends continue.

translucent Nearly transparent.

tree A large, single-stemmed woody plant.

tuber An enlarged portion of a root or rhizome.

truncate Abruptly cut-off.

tubercle Base of style persistent as a swelling atop the achene different in color and texture from achene body.

tundra Treeless plain in arctic regions, having permanently frozen subsoil.

turion A specialized type of shoot or bud that overwinters and resumes growth the following year.

umbel A cluster of flowers in which the flower stalks arise from the same level.

umbelet A small, secondary umbel in an umbel, as in the Apiaceae.

upright Erect or nearly so.

urceolate Constricted at a point just before an opening; urn-shaped.

utricle A small, one-seeded fruit with a dry, papery outer covering.

valve A segment of a dehiscent fruit; the wing of the fruit in *Rumex*.

variety Taxon below subspecies and differing from other varieties within the same subspecies (var.).

vein A vascular bundle, as in a leaf.

venation The pattern of veins on an organ.

ventral Front side.

ventricose Inflated or distended.

verrucose Covered with small, wartlike projections.

verticil One whorled cycle of organs.

verticillate Arranged in whorls.

villous Pubescent with long, soft, bent hairs, the hairs not crimped or tangled.

vine A trailing or climbing plant, dependent on other objects for support.

viscid Sticky, glutinous.

whorl A group of 3 or more parts from one point on a stem.

wing A thin tissue bordering or surrounding an organ.

woody Xylem tissue (the vascular tissue which conducts water and nutrients).

xeric Dry (compare with hydric, mesic).

STINGING NETTLE *(Urtica dioica)*; despite the plant's stinging hairs, the young shoots and leaves are a delicious green when cooked like for spinach. The plant has also been used as a rennet to curdle milk in cheese-making; see page 376.

Index

CLOUDBERRY *(Rubus chamaemorus);* a delectable berry of Arctic regions and a few locations in New England and northeastern Minnesota in the United States; see page 344.

CPSIA information can be obtained
at www.ICGtesting.com
Printed in the USA
LVOW04s1611190716
496926LV00021B/636/P

CH Ref   8 -16